THE GLOBALIZATION OF CORPORATE MEDIA HEGEMONY

SUNY series in Global Media Studies

Yahya R. Kamalipour
and Kuldip R. Rampal, editors

THE GLOBALIZATION OF CORPORATE MEDIA HEGEMONY

EDITED BY

Lee Artz
and
Yahya R. Kamalipour

State University of New York Press

Published by
State University of New York Press, Albany

© 2003 State University of New York

For information, address State University of New York Press,
90 State Street, Suite 700, Albany, NY 12207

Production by Diane Ganeles
Marketing by Anne M. Valentine

Library of Congress Cataloging-in-Publication Data

The globalization of corporate media hegemony / edited by Lee Artz and Yahya R. Kamalipour.
    p. cm. — (SUNY series in global media studies)
  Includes bibliographical references and index.
  ISBN 0-7914-5821-0 (alk. paper) — ISBN 0-7914-5822-9 (pbk. : alk. paper)
    1. Mass media—Social aspects. 2. Social classes. 3. Globalization. I. Artz, Lee. II. Kamalipour, Yahya R. III. Series.

  HM1206 .G586 2003
  302.23—dc21

                                                                2002036482

10 9 8 7 6 5 4 3 2 1

Contents

III. LEADING THE PERIPHERY
TO MEDIA HEGEMONY

IV. CULTURAL VARIATIONS
IN GLOBAL MEDIA HEGEMONY

V. POPULAR RESISTANCE TO
GLOBAL MEDIA HEGEMONY

Acknowledgments

In completing this book project, we have benefited from the kind support and cooperation of many people throughout the world, including colleagues who have participated in panels and symposia at the two Global Fusion conferences hosted by Southern Illinois University. We especially would like to offer our deepest gratitude to the contributing authors of this book, for without their genuine interest, hard work, and support, this project could not have materialized. Also, we would like to thank the authors' colleges/universities and organizations for providing financial, research, administrative, and secretarial support to them during the course of this project.

Furthermore, we are indebted to the following individuals for their valuable support and encouragement throughout this project. We thank Danielle Glassmeyer and Alicia Denny at Loyola University Chicago for their insightful reviews and professional copyediting of many of the essays. We are also grateful to Sandra Singer, Vice Chancellor for Academic Affairs, and Dan Dunn, Dean of the School of Liberal Arts and Social Sciences at Purdue University Calumet, and to the Office of Faculty Research at Loyola University Chicago.

At the State University of New York Press, we are appreciative of the interest and support of editorial, production, marketing, and everyone else involved in the various stages of this project.

Of course, we are indebted to our respective families for their unconditional love, emotional support, and understanding.

PART I

Leading Media Hegemony
in a Transnational World

CHAPTER 1

Globalization, Media Hegemony, and Social Class

Lee Artz

Three concepts—globalization, media hegemony, and social class—provide the necessary framework for understanding contemporary international communication. Yet, these terms and the conditions they purport to represent are so contested that each writer must begin by either summarizing the historical debates or providing singular definitions. The disagreements over globalization, hegemony, and class will not be resolved in texts, of course, but only in the course of ongoing social struggles. Consequently, researchers, scholars, and commentators—including those featured in this volume—can at best offer journalistic descriptions and theoretical observations that are differentiated primarily by the quality of their research, analytical expertise, and conscious or unconscious political preferences. Specifically, this text invites the conversation on media globalization to consider the dynamics of class conflict and negotiation as an analytical perspective having prescriptive potential.

Globalization

Despite the lack of consensus on either its definition or significance, globalization is the concept of the day, invariably invoked in debates over the dramatic and often contradictory economic, political, cultural, and technological developments affecting contemporary international relations. *The Economist* and *Business Week* have devoted entire issues to "borderless capital" and the "new economy" (e.g., October and November 1997), while progressive journals such as *The Nation*, *Race & Class*, and *Monthly Review* feature ongoing exchanges over whether globalization is simply a ruse by capitalist pundits (Sweezy, 1997) or the dawn of a new capitalist era. Globalization has been understood as the worldwide triumph of capitalist democracy (Fukayama, 1992) and the internationalization of civilization that no longer needs nation-states (Ohmae, 1995) or the final epoch of finance capitalism (Burbach, Nunez, & Kagarlitsky, 1997) and the rise of a "culture of entertainment

3

incompatible with the democratic order" (Herman & McChesney, 1997, p. 9). Giddens nondescriptively suggests that globalization is simply modernity intensified as "world-wide social relations . . . link distant localities" (1991, p. 63), while Mohammadi finds that globalization of technology stretches the "relations of power and communication" across the globe (1997, p. 3), and Pieterse recognizes a "uniform, standardized" world society based on "techno-logical, commercial, and cultural synchronization" by and for the global North (1995, p. 45). And there are many, many more definitions and perspectives. Yet, whatever the meaning ascribed, globalization has become the elusive catchword for defining and critiquing the new world order, indicating that however we may define or understand the condition, we are now at least aware that we are all subject to its existence.

We undoubtedly live in a world that has grown smaller, while national boundaries remain, and nation-states continue to structure life for their citi-zens, as governments energetically advance the tenets of the market, while leading corporations use partnerships, joint ventures, and mergers to recruit regional capitalists who direct their respective governments to make struc-tural adjustments favorable to "free trade." Consequently, as individual state regulations remove obstacles to international production, distribution, and consumption, transnational corporations have expanded operations. Infor-mational, instructional, symbolic, and ideological changes within each coun-try (and internationally) have facilitated and justified the political and eco-nomic structural changes necessary for the globalization of free market capitalism. Institutional policies by the International Monetary Fund (IMF), the World Bank, the United Nations, the International Telecommunications Union, and various regional agreements, such as the North America Free Trade Agreement (NAFTA) and the Free Trade Agreement of the Americas (FTAA), depend on government approval and enforcement. The state-approved policies presume and promote deregulation, privatization, and commercialization of national industries and public services, including media and telecommunications.

In other words, contrary to claims that capitalist globalization has superseded the nation-state (e.g., Hardt & Negri, 2000), in each case govern-ments have promoted global capitalism and legalized its activity within state boundaries. Obviously, governments are subject to the political contradictions within the nation-state, including the prevailing social struggles over resource distribution and political power among social classes and groups, as well as whatever cooperation or contestation exists among elites. Throughout the global South, military governments have continually assured elite control through force, as in South Korea, Indonesia, Paraguay, Colombia, and else-where. Even in those nation-states averred to be newly democratic (e.g., Brazil, Nigeria, Indonesia), civilian regimes function as instruments of elite rule with little concern for the working poor—albeit always facing the possibility of popular mass protest or revolt. It should be no surprise to find governments adopting regulations that continue to favor national elites who have hopes of entering the global free market, including in media, the culture industry, and telecommunications. Mosco and Mazepa's analysis of Silicon North in Ottawa, Canada, included here gives a clear example.

In Brazil, Robert Marinho's media monopoly Rede Globo, a recipient of Time-Life and CIA contributions in the 1960s, a defender of the Brazilian dictatorship, and now a "quasi-monopoly of sound, image, and textual media" (Amaral & Guimaraes, 1994, p. 26) has teamed with AT&T to capitalize on the privatization of the nation's telecom services. As deregulation overcame the region, Globo also formed a joint venture with News Corporation and TCI for cable and satellite services to Latin America.

In Mexico, following NAFTA and the privatization of public industry and increased foreign direct investment, some two dozen Mexican capitalists became billionaires. Carlos Helu, who now controls the formerly public telephone company, bought the Internet provider Prodigy, CompUSA, and stock in Apple Computers (Marichal, 1997). The Azcárraga family expanded the reach of its Televisa empire by purchasing Univisión in the U.S., establishing a subsidiary in Chile, and entering into joint ventures with News Corp, TCI, and Globo, among others. Meanwhile, the Mexican government awarded two newly privatized television stations to Ricardo Salinas—a chain store owner partnered with a government-favored importer and NBC—establishing the Azteca network (Fromson, 1996). In short, Helu, Azcárraga, Salinas, and other elites have not circumvented the nation-state, but instead have prospered because the government—whether PRI or Fox—licenses, protects, and promotes their interests nationally and globally.

In Italy the media are the government—at least in the person of Silvio Berlusconi. Adopting the U.S. advertising/programming model, Berlusconi parlayed an advertising agency into three television networks. He joined with Germany's conservative media mogul Leo Kirch in several European joint ventures. Berlusconi withstood a semipopulist challenge to limit his broadcasting empire, coordinated in part by an Italian government that not only rescued him from "various judicial enquiries and legal proceedings" in the 1980s but also streamlined the process of media monopolization and commercialization (Tunstall & Palmer, 1991, p. 73). Berlusconi's further global aspirations depend in part on whether the suprastate European Union Parliament drops its limits on media concentration and a requirement for 50% domestic content on television broadcasting (Stille, 2000).

Similar accounts of national governments servicing corporate elites, in media and other industries, occur on every continent, both in industrialized and developing countries. States are not withering in the face of unfettered freedom, rather the new hegemonic imperative directs them to obey the logic of the market. As Herman and McChesney (1997) note, "centralizing and globalizing firms need and seek political support for their advances" (p. 172). When national governments adopt market-driven policies of deregulation, privatization, and commercialization, they become complicit in the dismantling of public enterprises, including the media and culture, or at the very least regulating away viable public media and cultural independence. In other words, the nation-state has not been passed over, but has become "an accomplice to its own dispossession" as it undergoes "redefinition according to the demands and pressures of supra-national actors" (Mattelart & Mattelart, 1992, p. 133). In short, governments have become facilitators for transnationals and their globalization policies.

The logic of global capitalist production and distribution recruits national, regional, and local participants according to the pragmatics of profits, efficiency, and corporate use. Transnational capital plays a pivotal role in the globalization process—representatives of the transnational corporations (TNCs) provide the political leadership that spearheads the deregulation and privatization of public transnational services, including telecommunications and the media (Burbach, 2001, p. 31). Globalization of the market includes the globalization of a particular model of government, one that is market friendly. Thus, governments serving the elites of developing capitalist nation-states function less to protect national independence and cultural sovereignty and more to adjust regulations and practices that might favor participation by their own domestic elites in the global marketplace. In this volume, Kundnani's assessment of the British government's passion for the Internet and communication technology highlights a dramatic Western example.

Communication Studies and Globalization

Whether one applauds or resists this new global impulse to privatization, all seem to agree that media and communications technology have been instrumental in the process. In the field of communication, the study of globalization follows at least three fairly disconnected approaches, mirroring in part the larger political and social debate over globalization and the public good and in part some disciplinary traditions. One models the administrative research of past decades in its appraisal of the comparative advantage of transnational media corporations (Gershon, 1997) and uncritical focus on the "convergence of technological innovation" in a pluralist world (Stevenson, 1994, pp. 17, 277–310) with little regard for the social consequences of vertically integrated and deregulated transnational media monopolies. In contrast, critical stances arise from investigations of the political economy of global media, their holdings, operations, and influences (Bagdikian, 1997, Herman & McChesney, 1997)—albeit often without many details regarding the social and cultural consequences of a concentrated global media. Meanwhile, ethnographic and cultural studies are more sanguine about the reach of global media (often accepted as if "there is no alternative"), as they discover cultural responses— from homogeneity to hybridity and "glocalization"—indicating that cultures, communities, and other regional entities continue to contribute to a global culture (Lull, 1995; Robertson, 1992, Straubhaar, 1997). This text is filled with case studies and commentaries about the contradictions and complexities of intercultural exchange in the era of globalization: Eko surveys commercialized African radio, Algan assesses the privatization of Turkish radio, Sowards analyzes the cultural reach of MTV Asia, Min measures the independence and cultural resistance of Korean cinema, and Straubhaar and La Pastina provide an overview of Brazilian media's cooperation with successive elite governments.

As in the debates over economic and political globalization, disagreements over the significance of media globalization seem to accept the existence, if not the meaning, of certain conditions. Disputes may rage, but most recognize that communication technology has made possible dramatically increased information and data flow, streamlining capitalist production and distribution on a global scale and allowing a more rapid dispersal of news and entertainment. Although the terminology may be disputed, most also accept that transnational media corporations (TNMCs) are profit-driven, capitalist enterprises that produce and distribute commodified communication content globally and expand and benefit from the deregulation and privatization of the media, nationally and internationally. At this point, the struggle for meaning ensues: Negroponte (1995) and colleagues cheer on the rise of the information superhighway and the new "knowledge economy," stressing the democratic potential of new technologies and how they might circumvent or overcome the power of the state (Castells, 1998); Hamelink (1997) and others (e.g., Mattelart, 1994; Tomlinson, 1999) want an accounting of the TNMC's commercialization of culture that undermines public communication, human rights, and social solidarity, while some still question the cultural power of global media activity, contending that local actors can appropriate almost any media content for their own resistive purposes (e.g., Fiske, 1987).

The theoretical tension between the perspectives of political economy and the cultural studies approach might be assuaged if either followed their quest to conclusion. A study in political economy that stops short of ascertaining concrete social relations and cultural practices is incomplete. Political economy is nothing if it is not an explanation of actual social activity in the context of power, production, and use (Garnham, 1990; Mosco, 1998). Likewise, a cultural studies approach that dismisses [or brackets] the conditions of power and production to focus exclusively on local uses of communication content is naïve at best and duplicitous if intentional (Budd & Entmann, 1990). Cultural studies would benefit immeasurably from concretizing the social conditions of reception and use (Artz, 1997; Condit, 1989). In either case, Antonio Gramsci's (1988) conception of hegemony helps resolve the static academic standoff by placing cultural activity in its socioeconomic and political context, recognizing both the structural constraints of power and the creative agency of conscious political activity. Given that perspective, this text disputes any reductive claim that global media simply dominate without regard to cultural resistance and social negotiation, and yet focuses on the social and cultural consequences of the corporate media influences rather than any particular audience response or semiotic interpretation. Here, hegemony (understood as leadership by consent) does not "move beyond" political economy or cultural studies, but incorporates and enhances their perspectives to better understand the globalization of the free market and the parallel globalization of commercial media models.

The Globalization of Inequality

Before considering the role of media and media hegemony in winning popular consent for globalization, however, some appreciation of the social contradictions confronting the world and its cultures is needed. A cursory look finds that consent is wide, but paper-thin, resting primarily on a narrow strata of elites and their service and political professionals who have benefited from concentrated foreign direct investment, even as the internationalization of production systems has pushed the majority of the world further from security and comfort. Indeed, class inequalities have crossed borders as resolutely and clearly as the satellite signals that announce the new global order, as particular norms of production and distribution have been universalized (e.g., low wages, efficient flexibility, English language dominant, centralized control, decentralized production, etc.) (Mattelart & Mattelart, 1992). Globalization has redistributed resources within nations to the domestic elite and internationally to the TNCs. The concepts of core and periphery, North and South, developed and developing are increasingly not national or geographic markers, but indicators of social class. Certainly there are "rich" countries and "poor" countries, but the "trend is one of ever-growing poverty and marginalization in the first world, while the third world has a large number of nouveau riche who are able to buy and sell in the global economy, creating vast fortunes that match or rival many in the first world" (Burbach, 2001, p. 39).

As for Eastern Europe and Russia—the formerly second world—shock-therapy privatization directed by Harvard-educated economists has brought a "total economic collapse, as a self-serving and carnivorous capi-talist" elite rises astride the survival poverty of millions (Kagarlitsky, 1997, p. 119). The European Children's Trust reports that "at least 50 million children in Eastern Europe and the former Soviet Union live in poverty" that "has increased more than tenfold in the past decade because of reduc-tions in government spending on health, education, and social programs" ("Poverty," 2000, p. 14). The Western media has been silent, but since the breakup of the planned economy, "conditions have become much worse—in some cases catastrophically so. . . . [While] the old system provided most people with a reasonable standard of living and a certain security" ("Poverty," 2000, p. 14), capitalist globalization has "freed" millions from those expectations.

Worldwide, the free market system has treated humanity no better. One-third of the world is unemployed or underemployed. And, "despite three decades of rapidly expanding global food supplies, there are still an estimated 786 million hungry people in the world" according to the Institute for Food and Development Policy (Cook, 2001, p. 24). Surely, the new millionaires can avoid such realities in their gated-communities, sky-boxes, and travels to Rio, Fiji, the Virgin Islands, where "careful, or colorful landscaping, sweeping white beaches, rooms with breathtaking views, and fine Caribbean dining envelope visitors with a strategically planned opulence" (Farrant, 2001, p. 7E). Like most of globalization's accomplishments, vacation paradise is nearby if you can afford it, "if you choose to ignore the dire circumstances lurking just around the corner. . . . [But] poverty smacks your senses the moment you ven-ture outside. Ramschackle houses with boarded up windows, dilapidated cars on blocks out front, threadbare yards, and weary-looking inhabitants, their long faces gnarled by lives long on economic misery" (Farrant, 2001, p. 7E). Inequalities in education, housing, health care, and quality of life accompany such impoverished human conditions. The disparities in access to communi-cation technology, delineated here by Sussman, may lack the graphic purchase attending other social inequalities, but perhaps highlight the incredible gap between rich and poor in the capitalist world system: 85% of the world's pop-ulation have no access to telephone, while 97% of Internet host domains are located in the global North.

There is more to the balance sheet of worldwide wealth: crushing poverty, child labor, malnutrition, illiteracy, and slavery. Twenty-seven million slaves (greater than the Atlantic slave trade, greater than the population of Canada) work daily for transnationals and their subcontractors, making char-coal for the Brazilian steel industry, casting bricks in Pakistan, and working in agriculture in India. Nor is slavery confined to South East Asia, Africa, or South America. It exists in the United States and Britain, where women and farm workers are locked in factories with armed guards (Bales, 1999).

By almost any measurement, poverty in the twenty-first century is unprecedented, rather it is the result of an international free market system that speculates in currency and investment, seeks to minimize labor costs, and repeatedly leads to overproduction resulting in massive unemployment and social instability (Chossudovsky, 1997). Naïve belief in U.S. exceptionalism provides no protection, as the current recession gives evidence of market speculation, overproduction, and sudden unemployment. In short, with or without the globalization terminology, the world—core and periphery—faces an unprecedented decline in the quality of life for millions, while a handful (like the 400 U.S. trillionaires) increase their incredible wealth.

Hegemony

If we understand hegemony in the classic Gramscian sense as the "process of moral, philosophical, and political leadership that a social group attains only with the active consent of other important social groups" (Artz & Murphy, 2000, p.1), it would seem unlikely that any political or cultural leadership could maintain support under such bleak conditions. In fact, capitalist hegemony should not be overstated. Western leadership is everywhere unstable, increasingly U.S. unipolar, and in constant need of threat and coercion. Lacking organized alternatives, millions tolerate and accommodate IMF and market dictates. Still, millions more resist. Santiago-Valles' essay in this volume describes the media activity of two movements of resistance in the Carribean, while Downing closes the book with examples of radical media that indicate further expressions of resistance. Even localized or diffuse resistance movements pose challenges to hegemonic leaderships with demands, resistive practices, and independent communication. In Chiapas, Mexico, the Philippines, Indonesia, Haiti, Brazil, Ecuador, and throughout many countries of the North (e.g., Italy, France, and Britain), well-organized social and political movements have hobbled transnational policies and their national manifestations—although the political potential of social movements is frequently obscured by commercial media, as Goeddertz and Kraidy reveal here in their case study of media accounts of antiglobalization protests in Seattle. Partly delusion, partly propaganda, global corporate media imagine only the benefits and stability of globalization, but the majority of the world does not join in the accolades and fanfare that resound mostly among the TNCs, their junior class partners, and the global corporate media.

Elites everywhere have adopted the mantra of deregulation, privatization, and commercialization as the world order of capitalist hegemony proceeds with declining social liberalism and rising economic conservatism

(Tehranian & Tehranian, 1997). National elites have internalized free market values and modeled their domestic social and cultural policies on "successes" in the North. Numerous revealing catch phrases—dollarization, McDonaldization, Disneyfication—indicate that capitalist elites of the second- and third-tier almost universally employ format modeling in national planning, television programming, and other economic, social, and cultural policies. Despite the callousness of the IMF, World Bank, and other trade and development institutions, transnational capitalism seldom needs coercion to armor the consent of elites. In every country, the dirty work of enforcement against subordinate classes falls to domestic free market zealots and their state power enforcers. From Argentina to South Africa, national governments confirm their commitment to IMF packages and the global free market system with social austerity and political repression against the working poor.

Much like TNCs merging with local entities to circumvent regulations or disfavor, to whatever extent materially possible, domestic capitalist leaders seek to recruit allies from other classes and social groups. Indeed, hegemony is more solid and more efficient than coercion because resulting social institutions educate, recreate, and extend leadership policies as normal, common sense practices—a point well argued by Murphy in his contribution to this text. To varying degrees, elites provide favor outside their circles through appeals to nationality, national patriotism, ethnicity, race, religion, or any other available cultural marker as a means for constructing a social bloc around hegemonic policies. Resulting policies advance elite interests, but more importantly, when practices and policies significantly represent the cooperating nonelite allies, cross-class participation in hegemony increases. Propaganda becomes ideology becomes common sense.

This analytical deployment of hegemony relies on Gramsci's rendering (Artz & Murphy, 2000; Buci-Glucksmann, 1980; Gramsci, 1988; Sassoon, 1987). Other interpretations of hegemony appear throughout a multitude of social critiques. Indeed, the term—if not the Gramscian concept—has become almost standard in contemporary scholarship, ranging from cultural analyses (e.g., Cloud, 1996; Fiske, 1987; Hall, 1986), to treatises in political science (Scott, 1990), history (e.g., Brow, 1990; Lears, 1985) and sociology (Gitlin, 1987). Unfortunately, Gramsci's crisp class-rendering of hegemony as a process of cultural and political leadership attained only with the conscious consent of others has been whittled to a process of negotiation between various discursive communities (e. g., Bennett, 1992; Condit, 1994; Laclau & Mouffe, 1985) or more commonly passed off as coterminous with domination (e.g., Lull, 1995). Perhaps the most significant distinction between other applications and a clearly Gramscian approach is the presence or absence of class as a determinant.

Social Class

In contrast to widespread use of the terms globalization and hegemony, social class barely registers in most analyses of contemporary social practices, including media and cultural production. Moreover, although class politics are central to globalization and hegemony, discussing class in a text on media and globalization is a risky business. The concepts and relations are complex and unfamiliar to many.

Some communication scholars (e.g., King, 1987) accept the prevalent academic belief that power in the United States is overwhelming democratic and pluralist—the result of some combination of merit, skill, and persuasion. By extrapolation, globalization of American politics and culture—especially privatization of media and individual consumerism—would extend democratic vistas to currently underdeveloped societies (e.g., Gershon, 1997; Hachten, 1992; Stevenson, 1994). Accordingly, class and caste divisions that exist outside the industrial North and developing South will presumably disappear as free market production and individual consumption progresses (Fukayama, 1992). Otherwise, references to social class are summarily dismissed as being too simplistic for the postmodern world (Nelson & Grossberg, 1988) or they are thoroughly contested as outmoded (Hardt & Negri, 2000; Laclau & Mouffe, 1985).

The debate is further obscured, because "there is little agreement among social scientists . . . on the exact meaning of class or the explanatory power of the word itself" (McNall, Levine, & Fantasia, 1991, p.1). Ironically, many contemporary media studies (e.g., Carey, 1989; Lull, 1995) accept the inherent social dimensions of communication practices, but—reflecting the ideological hegemony of "capitalist democracy"—the concept of socioeconomic class is regularly avoided, ignored, or rejected. Yet, if one reads closely, it is obvious that the specter of social class haunts contemporary writings on media and culture, albeit usually as euphemism: elite, subordinate, minority, rich, poor, marginalized.

Because social class as a concept emerges most fully from both social structure and human agency, it pulls together the seemingly antagonistic approaches of political economy and cultural studies. More importantly, recognizing social class helps identify the impetus for and contradictions in globalization and helps clarify the workings of media hegemony.

Every society can be characterized by how the necessities of life are produced from nature—by the social relations that organize production, distribution, and consumption of necessities among groups and individuals in society. Capitalist society in its globalized condition has highly industrialized productive forces producing goods collectively with highly stratified social relations—domestically and internationally—that also distribute benefits, rights, and responsibilities hierarchically. Now a globalized economic system of production and trade, capitalism is privately owned and operated for individual corporate profit. International capitalism employs communications technology to organize the immense productive power of collective wage labor in geographically decentralized locations, centralizing the diffusion of production of commodities for corporate sale. In contradiction to the highly collective production process—with hundreds of thousands involved in the creation, production, and distribution—neither the producers of goods nor society as a whole direct, control, or decide the goals of social production. Instead, the means of production—from natural resources to factories, railroads, and buildings—are privately owned and operated for narrow corporate profit. Mineral deposits, forests, water, and even the airwaves have been ostensibly "owned" by the public, as millions of citizens participate in transforming nature's bounty into items for human consumption, but the international move to privatization turns legal exploitation over to deregulated, commercialized corporate interests. In short, globalized production is increasingly socialized, but corporate decisions are narrowly bureaucratic and authoritarian. Moreover, the benefits and profits from such social production are unevenly distributed among social groups and individuals.

The primary social contradiction of contemporary capitalism is structurally expressed as an antagonism within these productive relations, relations that are not simply between individuals but social relations between classes. Individuals are everywhere and always crystallized from social experience, and all such experiences occur within historically-contingent, structured human relations, including social classes. Social class can be defined as a group of people who relate to production in similar ways and share a common location in the social relations of production (Therborn, 1983, p. 39). Thus, for example, the capitalist class comprises those who own the means of production but rarely work there. The working class does not own the means of production but sets them in motion by physically using tools, machinery, and labor power on raw materials and their products. In terms of production, the working class owns only its labor power, which must be sold to the capitalist for a wage, whereas the capitalist depends on the worker to create goods, which must be sold for a profit. Other classes can be similarly defined according to their relationship to the means of production. For example, the managerial middle class is excluded from ownership of the means of production and also generally does not work with the means of production. Instead, the manager's position is administrative and supervisory, organizing the labor process and commanding much of the knowledge about the overall productive process (Poulanzas,

1978). Administrative control of cultural production also gives those middle classes political legitimacy and power (Mattelart & Mattelart, 1992, p. 130).

These broad class categories are very rough sketches. In each case, we could delineate class groupings within a class and in relation to the overarching social structure (Wright, 1985). Finance capitalists have a different relationship to the means of production than do industrial capitalists or small business entrepreneurs. Likewise, industrial workers have a different relationship to the means of production than do teachers, retail clerks, or service workers. A much longer explanation and argument can be found elsewhere (e.g., Wright, 1985, 1991), but for the upcoming discussion on class and culture, we do not need to empirically identify all the relational nuances between social class positions in the United States. It should suffice to say that classes can be generally defined in terms of their relationship to the means of production, which lends analytical sense to the social structure.

Of course, structures don't act, people do. Moreover, by recognizing that the production of things occurs simultaneously with the production of social relations—including ideological practices, symbolic representations, and public discourses necessary to hegemony (Artz & Murphy, 2000; Bourdieu, 1991, 1987; Garnham, 1990)—we see that social class has a "subjective component, is a process, is defined in relation to other classes and is historically contingent" (McNall et al., 1991, p. 4). In other words, the importance of any class depends on its relation to the means of production *and* on its relationship to other classes and society as a whole. These social relations are framed (but not predetermined) by the structural conditions of production, including the size and strategic social position of each class and the political power of each class as determined by battles, alliances, and interactions with the rest of society.

The conditions and relations of class may be abstractly characterized, but their efficacy is imminently concrete. As Bourdieu (1987) argues, class structures only set the probabilities for social formations: "one cannot group anyone with anyone while ignoring fundamental differences, particularly economic and cultural ones. But this never entirely excludes the possibility of organizing agents in accordance with other principles of division" (p. 8). Other conditions, identities, and experiences, such as gender, race, ideology, culture, and institutional action shape the actual political formation of classes. Class structure only provides the context for other social processes—including hegemony, because material and political resources available for winning allies and building consent depend on the structure and practices organizing each society. Similar class structures allow for different class formations and representations (Cohen, 1990; Levine, 1988; Poulanzas, 1978). As individuals and groups become aware of their lived experience, they choose strategies drawn in large part from their class position and activity. Such human action expresses and supports or challenges the structures and norms in political, ideological, and symbolic terms (Wacquant, 1991, p. 56).

Within countries of the global North, certain class formations are likely, easy, and stable: managers are convenient and willing allies of corporate owners; skilled workers, engineers, and planners are likely hegemonic allies of supervisors; and given sufficient incentive, skilled workers, small business owners, and farmers will be supportive of capitalist norms. Other formations are not likely: corporate owners joining union organizing drives or supporting worker demands for shorter hours and higher wages. Of course, race, gender, nationality, and religion influence class formations, as well, but the social structure sets some limits. It is more likely that black professionals or even employed black workers would join hegemonic institutions on dominant terms than it is that white CEOs would challenge corporate hiring practices on behalf of black workers. Why? Because structural parameters subject individual class members to a set of mechanisms that impinge on their lives as they think, choose, and act in the world (Wright, 1991, p. 23). Stuart Hall's (1984) rebuttal to postmodern dismissals of class analysis pinches reality too much. It is not that certain connections between class position and class action are necessary or non-necessary. More accurately, specific class actions are more or less possible, more or less probable, while some actions may be beyond imagination because they are beyond our actual experience, outside our vocabulary and sensibility.

The production of goods and relations has social and cultural manifestations, meaning that social class is not solely an economic condition, but has a symbolic, social range. In every working-class community, which can be readily identified in most every country of the world, groups are at least loosely affiliated through the site of production, whether it is oil, steel, auto, or agriculture, for example. Within these communities, recreation, entertainment, and social practices such as music, religion, education, and conversation occur with particular shared vocabularies, meanings, and codes. In other words, cultural practices reflect representations of shared class positions and experiences (Bourdieu, 1978, 1984). The prevalence of beer, football, video rental, and television in certain communities has some material basis in available disposable income and leisure time. In contrast, opera, polo, and yachting require different economic resources and create different vocabularies and meanings as well.

Cross-border renderings of U.S.-born rap music, for instance, invariably occur among urban poor, most frequently among the racially oppressed youth in urban centers, whether in Britain, Ghana, or Brazil—where samba, accordion folk, and rap cross-pollinate in the *favelas* as "ghetto music" (Billon, 1998). Cultural codes may not be determined by the class position of the artist or the audience, but nonetheless, identifiable codes parallel and give voice to distinct class experiences that occur under very specific, concrete social and cultural conditions. In beat and lyric, the strident resistance of rap (sometimes politically conscious, sometimes antisocial) represents part of the experience of black working-class youth in the United States and logically and aesthetically appeals to urban minority youth frustrated in similar social positions. Rap is not so much appropriated as it is shared for similar communicative purposes.

Similarly, as Sowards reveals here in her discussion of MTV Asia, elite youth with considerable disposable income comprise the primary audience for American and Americanized pop music in South East Asia because across the region domestic capitalists and the administrators and professionals for domestic and multinational firms have access to comparable resources, share similar social and political positions in government and corporations, and support and benefit from similar political and economic policies—above all privatization. It seems almost natural that the offspring of this fairly homogenous corporate-dependent elite would find their cultural preferences from the same source that their parents find their economic leadership—the Western core. In the case of MTV Asia, Asian "spokesmodel" VJs host the party for Western consumerist culture and music. By and large, working-class youth are on the periphery of MTV Asia culture, pocket CDs, cell-phones, concerts, and all. At most, urban working-class youth aspire to that Asianized American culture through the purchase of knock-offs or by listening to mass market radio, while the overwhelming majority of the urban and rural poor remain in the margins of consumption with unmet rising expectations. In short, as in economics and politics, the cultural agenda in most countries is constrained but not dictated by the socioeconomic elite pursuing their own interests and identities.

Media Hegemony

Hegemony is not mechanical, not simply coercive, nor deceitfully manipulative. Rather, hegemony is the political outcome of a leadership's ability to intellectually and morally move society towards a reluctantly or enthusiastically agreed-upon set of cultural and economic practices. In other words, although hegemony is not a communication process per se, cultural and political discourses must reflect, organize, and interact with other social practices. Hegemony must be constructed using some of the ideas and concerns of all groups.

Leaderships only become hegemonic because they convince others to become allies through persuasive political and cultural practices, which necessarily require normalized interpretations best communicated to the masses via the media. Hence, capitalist hegemony needs parallel media hegemony as an institutionalized, systematic means of educating, persuading, and representing subordinate classes to particular cultural practices within the context of capitalist norms. If culture is the ideological cement of society, then, to secure corporate interests, capitalist globalization needs media hegemony to recruit, tame, and popularize interpretations, information, and cultural behavior complementary to deregulation, privatization, and commercialization.

Internationally, media hegemony is obvious. Numerous scholars have documented well the stampede to privatization (Thussu, 2000; Herman & McChesney, 1997) and the universal predominance of mass entertainment and consumerism. The amateurish propaganda of formerly state-run media systems has been shoved aside by the more ideologically sophisticated commercial media systems. In the process, public media have been dismissed as tantamount to government media, as if private broadcasters better represent the public good. Privatized media systems appropriate global and domestic cultural offerings into "glocalized" commodities for sale to culturally distinct regional audiences, from "Who Wants to Be a Millionaire" and rap to "Betty La Fea" and Islamic pop. As the global capitalist media marches behind the same market band that leads other corporations, the upbeat drumroll for expansion sends the global players rushing for consuming audiences everywhere, from Eastern Europe to East Asia and Latin America.

The current global class structure with all of its contradictions and complexity provides more material and political resources to the leading global corporations and their regional allies (who have collaborated in creating international regulatory institutions) than it does to the working class (which remains poorly organized even on the national level). Consequently, representatives and supporters of capitalist hegemony can offer tangible rewards to subordinate individuals and groups, including working and middle classes, who sign on to the globalization of consumerism. Transnationals and their regional allies also dominate international and national public discourse with their control of global mass communication. In contrast, appeals by the subordinate majority for human solidarity and democratic communication currently lack both political organization and a conscious global media expression.

The social and political strength of capitalism is its ability to satisfy other classes with individual material rewards that undermine the intrinsic working-class strength of solidarity and collectivity (Therborn, 1983). It has been decades since the working class in the United States has politically organized its ranks. Under its current leadership, it has little to offer materially or culturally to the broad middle classes. In Latin America, Asia, and to a lesser extent in Europe, the rewards of capitalism have been more elusive, prompting new leaderships to champion working-class-inspired social programs featuring considerable political action. For example, the Workers Party in Brazil, the labor union movement in South Korea, Lavalas in Haiti, and even Hugo Chavez's "Bolivarian Revolution" in Venezuela advance populist programs hegemonically appealing to the working-class majority, the urban poor, and the peasantry.

Globalization of the free market also means that periodic contractions of production will further damage the developing world, especially because public and social services have been privatized and commercialized in the recent period. Meanwhile in the United States, a new recession (415,000 lay-offs in October 2001) has slapped awake investors and speculators, and potentially could affect the consciousness of American workers, whose appreciation of the benefits of consumerism depends on continued employment and affordable credit. In short, the seemingly unstoppable spread of capitalist hegemony will most likely stumble in the not-too-distant future, as recession, unemployment, and reductions in the quality of life tarnish the gloss of globalization.

Two responses to this scenario continue to push globalization forward, even as its ability to recruit allies dwindles. First, the United States and its junior partner Britain defend "enduring capitalism" at all costs, including military action, verifying Gramsci's declaration that hegemony is consent armored with coercion. Anticipating international dissatisfaction with an economic downturn and its class-biased assault on the world's majority, political leaders in the global North are prepared to protect what Gramsci called the kernel of capitalism—its economic power—its control over resource, production, and distribution. The U.S. wars in Afghanistan and Iraq are only the most recent visible sign of the global North's willingness to enforce its dominance, preferably with (at least tacit) consent of significant national and class allies. Restrictions on domestic civil liberties and militarily targeting social movements abroad further clarify the conscious intent of the strongest capitalist states, warning all, in the words of White House press secretary, Ari Fleischer, to "watch what they say, watch what they do" (Hart & Ackerman, 2001, p. 6).

Secondly, partnered with coercion dances partly complicit, partly oblivious consumerist entertainment, seducing thought to pleasure, reflection to escape. Herein lies the goal of capitalist cultural hegemony: to create a world culture—homogenized or hybridized—that ingratiates itself via individual satisfactions or ideologically induced national identities. This class deployment of coercion and consent simultaneously pummels the working class and pampers it with cultural confection and political pablum, thereby retarding its independent political growth and highlighting capitalist cultural hegemony (Halle, 2001; Freedman, 2001).

The ever-present question facing commercial media is how to deliver audiences to advertisers. Past practices have relied on direct export of the

Western product (e.g., Hollywood and network offerings dubbed into the language of the "foreign" audience with little regard for cultural variation). Consequently, after decades of intervention, cultural imperialism, and the "comparable advantage" of Western media, a homogenous middle-class culture has grown up internationally around pop music, fast food, action movies, animated features, and other McDonaldized, Disneyfied, Hollywood fare. However, global corporate media lead in many ways—subsidiaries through direct investment, joint ventures, the purchase of local operations, and even the promotion of alternative cultures. More importantly than the particular form, at issue for the globalization of cultural hegemony is the social use of media.

The most recent adjustment by the hegemonic leaders of global corporate media has been the export of the "model." Game show formats, soap opera genre, reality television, and other models are now sold by corporate owners to national and regional media operators, who culturally "dress-up" the Western media guest. ABC's "Who Wants to Be a Millionaire" has some two dozen variations around the world (White, 2001); O Globo has perfected the U.S. soap opera for export; and commercial radio advertising/music formats predominate in Africa, Latin America, and elsewhere.

Above all, media hegemony indicates leadership and dominance, not control and domination. Indeed, the power of media hegemony is in its participatory effectiveness—second-tier capitalist media owners, protected and bolstered by their own nation-state politicos, advance the policies and practices of capitalist globalization through culturally familiar representations. Whatever the specific variant or hybridization, the dominance of the hegemonic model and values are apparent: atomized, individualized, and consumerist entertainment rules. Crabtree and Malhotra describe media practices in India as a case in point, in their essay included here.

While, cultural imperialism has not ended (too many examples of forced takeovers and media monopoly belie as much), leading global media have found hegemonic persuasion more cost-efficient and politically effective. Throughout the world, deregulating reform of the media has accompanied the parallel political reform of governments, reflecting the intimate connections between civil society and the state. Of course, liberalization of the media does not guarantee an open, democratic society: Guatemala, El Salvador, and Qatar have private media but few civil liberties. In fact, many governments continue to mete out punishment and repression, but they do so with more legitimacy when they have the cover of two-candidate elections and privatized media. In most cases, private media defend the newly reformed states, if not the particular governing party. In all cases, privatized media legalized by the newly reformed states promote cultural forms (entertainment, escapism) and practices (individualism, consumerism) that advance and reinforce market relations at the expense of public interests.

Occasionally, resistance by sections of the working class and other politically disenfranchised groups—or conflicts between factions of the capitalist class—spill over into public discourse and media coverage, opening the door to some limited working-class and indigenous participation, as in Mexico following Chiapas, or in Ecuador, the Philippines, and Indonesia over the last several years. Yet, no matter how deep the social crisis, private media seldom balk from staunch support of their national capitalist class (Fox, 1988)—with the possible brief exception of Joaquin Chamorro's *La Prensa* in Nicaragua during the 1970s. Corporate media may vary in size, stature, temperament, and format, but never in allegiance to their class. This allegiance to a class perspective is apparent in corporate media's global culture, a culture that has several identifiably remarkable characteristics:

1. Ownership of the production and distribution of the global culture continues to narrow, despite the modest rise of regional aspirants and the resistance of some governments, as in China and France.
2. Entertainment formats predominate. From Ghana to Brazil to Singapore and the West, broadcasting, music, and movies are entertainment.
3. Consumerism rules. Marked by individualism, immediate gratification, and unfettered acquisitiveness, consumerism is expressed in hierarchical fictional and nonfictional narratives in privatized mass communication.
4. Cultural variations draw from rich and diverse traditions, as in Brazilian telenovelas and rap, Nigerian juju videos, and Islamic and green pop in Turkey. Yet, when controlled and represented by corporate media, most advance and none challenge the basic individualist, consumerist tenets of the capitalist market.
5. The global culture of corporate media features two complementary yet distinct representations: homogeneity and hybridity.

Homogeneity reflects the intercultural dominance of the Western model; hybridity reflects the creative contributions and resistances to intercultural exchanges by cultural artists and audiences. Included in this text is Chew, Cramer, and Prieto's case study of Televisa's international hit program, "Sábado Gigante," that illustrates how homogenity can develop across nations, classes, and cultures through a pleasing pan-ethnic identity construction. Likewise, the international success of MTV, network game shows, pop music, and other homogenous cultural products indicate that subordinate, yet aspiring, classes around the world find pleasure, comfort, and assurance in a Westernized homogeneity of consumption.

In response to the globalization of homogeneity, audiences and artists in various locales have creatively appropriated the commodified cultural products to fit local cultural or political needs. "Glocalized" cultural practices often represent local interests and meanings, subverting global media messages with more politically conscious interpretations and uses (Kraidy, 1999; Robertson, 1992), but just as frequently power remains intact except for the local particulars. If the model is still a store, not a community hall, it provides no real alternative to the supermarket chain. At any rate, corporate media have adjusted quickly, realizing that hybrid alterations of Western products are largely nonthreatening, potentially very profitable, and politically valuable as evidence of corporate media's cultural diversity and sensitivity. In addition to the locally generated hybrid culture, TNMCs now produce their own commodified hybrids gleaned from cultures around the world. Homogenous or hybrid, the question of power remains.

Here, cultural studies remind us that the consumption of media commodities is a social practice, open to interpretations and use beyond the intent of the producer. The cultural meaning and consequence of any text have as much to do with the social and political context of reception as they do with the sender-receiver dynamic. In Managua, Nicaragua, Brazilian soap operas are viewed by entire neighborhoods at the homes of those few with televisions, permitting much more democratic communication and meaning construction than that done by the single viewer passively atomized in a North living room. Still, as Mattelart and Mattelart (1992) reply, interpretations by readers and viewers are neither autonomous nor necessarily superior to the meanings proposed by writers and producers. Without access to mass communication resources, audiences everywhere are handicapped if their constructions of meanings are creative reactions to the productions of others, primarily the corporate few.

What is progressive about cordoning off human subjects as active receivers who are relegated to meaning-construction of others' texts? Why not have a society and a media that allows subjects to be subjects by producing their own texts? The "reader-as-producer" perspective expresses little concern regarding globalization, despite the fact that most intercultural communication and dialogue pass through corporate media and advertising filters—simultaneously pasteurizing cultural activity and bolstering capitalist media hegemony.

Media hegemony thrives because (in very practical terms) it not only affordably presents the most popular versions of Western culture—the representative epitome of individual success—it also appears to be the best promoter of indigenous culture and cultural diversity. Perhaps the music world and the human condition in general benefit from the global distribution of corporate finds of independent, indigenous, or hybrid mixes. However, in hegemonic terms, any music, movie, art, or political discourse or social commentary that passes through corporate media filters must meet the hegemonic prerequisites of entertainment and profit, thereby weakening or undermining its political edge, class independence, and counterhegemonic potential.

Media and cultural hegemony speak for and lead the working class and other diverse subordinate groups because mass culture provides favorable and rewarding representations and images. From "Roseanne" and "Drew Carey" in the United States, to "Betty La Fea" in Brazil, and the popular radio show "Our New Home" on Afghan radio, life is good! We all can laugh, work, play, and shop in our own little worlds without regard, concern, or (hopefully) even awareness of any unpleasantness outside. Individually consumed mass pleasure makes for a solid consumerist hegemony, and the central tenet of capitalist media hegemony worldwide is to promote an interclass culture of pleasure based on continuous consumption. In image and narrative, this interclass culture is strictly American middle class in outlook: professional, managerial, or entrepreneurial and aspiring to move closer to corporate central.

To the extent that the global media set agendas and popularize models of entertainment, mass culture closes public discourse. To the extent that cultural practices resist commercialization, either by hybrid appropriations or by independent communication, they open public discourse to the possibility of a truly new world order. Cultural variations are not the issue, as corporate media will happily emphasize the cross-cultural character of the elite or moderate intercultural contributions that might jolt the U.S. middle-class palette into hybrid cross-overs (e.g., African music via Paul Simon, de-Latinizing Ricky Martin for a mass audience). More importantly, advertising and entertainment "undermines people's will to understand" their own social conditions and individual potential, as hegemonic middle-class lifestyles are emulated and even internalized (Mattelart & Mattelart, 1992, p. 153). Furthermore, a media focus on daily life undercuts access to history and the future, while a focus on individual consumption and desire denies access to collective, democratic, social possibilities for humanity.

The problem with the culture industry is not only in the stories they tell of hyper-individualism (Artz, 2000), but also in how they occupy the collective consciousness with celebrity, trivia, and self-aggrandizement. Pleasure is marketed as the goal, but it is always just beyond our reach, requiring another consumer purchase, then another. Of course, pleasure is not the same as happiness, satisfaction, or fulfillment—but the globalization of corporate media hegemony based on advertising thrives on individual desire, legitimizing mass consumption, mass production, and privatization—obstructing humanity's fulfillment as a by-product. Hybrid variations that do not challenge atomized pleasure, mass hedonism, or the commercial model may surely represent subordinate classes and cultures, but they do so as unwitting servants for capitalist cultural hegemony. For instance, by independently producing his own hybrid blend of Ghanian "highlife" music with American pop and reggae,

Kojo Antwi may have revived his country's classic "highlife" sound, but he cannot stem the multinational "flooding of sub-Saharan Africa with flimsy pop" (Zachary, 2001, p. 32), especially if pop impresario Quincy Jones takes over Antwi's productions and softens them for the world music market. In other words, the economic goals of global corporate media ultimately conflict with the social and cultural needs of communities, nations, and working classes worldwide. As the local media become commercialized, they are subjected to the laws of market more than the needs of the community. Privatized media subvert the local even if local, because they emulate the commercial global media and model its values.

Global capitalism will not willingly advance either democratic international institutions or democratic cultural exchanges. To paraphrase the abolitionist Frederick Douglass, capitalist globalization concedes nothing without demand. As noted already, lack is created, planned, and organized by a social production obeisant to corporate goals. Likewise, media and cultural adhering to privatization and commercialization are created, planned, and organized for similar corporate goals.

Global capitalism, in other words, creates a consumer market and cultivates a consumer ideology, but an increase in the quantity of goods does not systematically improve the well-being of people. TNCs, however, measure value in terms of sales of audiences to advertisers and sales of goods to audiences. Not surprisingly, advertising appears as the legitimate forebear of democratic freedom—free flow of information and free consumer choice indicate and define the ultimate free society. One would better break with the advertising/development model and measure the social use of the media in terms of the quality of human life.

Global Culture:
Privatization, Media Hegemony, and Class Power

The global corporate media harvest a global culture that can be packaged, advertised, and sold as neat, stylized, individual commodities: movies, videos, songs, CDs, magazines, and their synergistic cultural accessories from clothing to food and personal care items. The success of the entertainment and advertising model promoted by transnational media indicates the hegemonic leadership of global capital, as millions are attracted to the wafting, sweet smell of consumer pleasure. To continue to please the consumer palette, global media and their advertisers continually seek out new products and new markets, continually recruiting, appropriating, and stimulating—but always within a commodified frame. The diversity of cultural experiences, practices, and manifestations is off-limits to the corporate media unless it can be privatized. It isn't so much that corporate media want to restrict the textures and variations of the human experience, it is that in their rush to riches, the corporate media undermine the very creativity they seek, by uprooting cultural practices from their social ground and replacing them with an artificially sweetened facsimile. Paul Simon discovers South African rhythms, produces them as pop hits with colorful African background singers and dancers, then record giants market this world music to the world, including back to the creative communities of its origin. This is not an aesthetic critique, nor an appeal to limit cross-cultural exchange—some of the most interesting music, art, and cuisine develop from hybrid mixings. The problem is simply that future cross-cultural exchange may become sterile if world culture follows the corporate trail. When homogenized hybrids are subsidized by TNMC promotions, both mediocre and profound alternatives that don't fit the acclimatized world culture of the market are shoved aside, marginalized. Already, upscale music groups in every developing country mimic U.S. pop, forsaking their own cultural traditions and the potential to create new ones, by following the celebrity, commodity culture of the North. Meanwhile, talent scouts and corporate trend seekers sniff out local talent like pigs looking for truffles—without supervision the finds in both searches are trampled. Gems of culture aren't treasured or polished; instead, they are carefully cut to fit the individualized display style suited for maximizing corporate sales.

The privatizing of media and culture transforms social experience into measurable, marketable, individualized consumer products. The dominance of consumerist hegemony—popularized by a global media hegemony of privatization and advertising—also disorganizes the working class and other subordinate groups, because it breaks down communities into atomized consumers, rewarding each with self-centered, impersonal, escapist entertainment that distracts individuals from societal functions and possibilities. Ultimately, the attractive individual pleasures enjoyed are like all confections—fleeting, addictive, and unnourishing to body and soul.

Politically speaking, the hegemony of consumerism advances the capitalist system. In ideological discourse, consumerism delegitimizes collective concerns and working-class values. "In the 1930s working people had a positive image in national culture [in the U.S.] and working class values were generally treated with respect . . . ordinary people were portrayed as equal in intelligence to the ambitious and wealthy, and morally superior as well. In the 1950s, however, all this changed. On TV shows, leading men wore suits and came home from offices, not factories, while the occasional blue-collar protagonists who did appear were treated as buffoons" (Levison, 2001, p. 28). As Butsch (2002), Scharrer (Moran, 2000), and Zaniello (1996) have thoroughly demonstrated, working-class characters continue to be disparaged in media fiction, while news frames generally distort working-class political activity as ill-advised and threatening to consumers (e.g., Goldman & Rajagopal, 1991;

Parenti, 1986). "Overall, mainstream news reporting of labor obscures class relations because capitalist hegemony prefers [and attracts] working class audiences that are interested in private consumption and have no political interest in production relations. Because the media monopoly determines how news will be defined, produced, and consumed, issues in strikes can be framed in terms of consumption, not production" (Artz & Murphy, 2000, p. 278). In ideological practice, consumerism helps corporations escape the leverage of organized working-class and social movement action, because consumerism privileges individual concerns while ignoring, obscuring, or disparaging social or collective concerns as those dreaded "politically motivated" "special interests." Globalized capitalist hegemony dramatically expands the division of labor across geographic regions, further dividing the working class by national, ethnic, and cultural difference, at least temporarily.

Global media and its world culture offer a simulated democracy in the form of individual consumer choice. This world culture often appears as vibrant, eclectic, and open because the creative stimulus for corporate media product is drawn in large measure from diverse cultures and their representations. This *vox populi* artistic and democratic gloss lasts as long as the shine of a new plastic toy—short-lived and constantly in need of replacement—because a global culture of corporate media hegemony seeks consumers and profits first, not human needs.

On the other hand, the cultural and political impulses of the subordinate—the working classes, national minorities, and other oppressed groups around the world—have immense potential power. Collective solidarity in political action and cultural expression could knock down the commercial barriers to free cultural exchange, and millions could "write their own stories" without the guiding hand of the media market, as Dorfman (1983) so eloquently expresses in his narration of the rising consciousness of the oppressed during the Allende years in Chile. A globalization of democracy, participation, unmediated cultural expression is desirable and possible.

An international culture of human solidarity led by the working-class majority in all of its diversity would build on but surpass the resistance and subversion present in hybrid cultural practices and localized political activity. Of course, to be liberating, a noncorporate global culture must be part of a larger political project. It must become a social crusade that uses media and culture to articulate and organize a new hegemonic project with a new class leadership, new cultural identities, and new political activities (much like the Harlem Renaissance and the Garvey Movement in the 1920s, the U.S. labor movement in the 1930s, the Cuban revolution of the 1960s, the Nicaraguan revolution of the 1980s, or even Chiapas in Mexico today).

Alternative cultural practices are not inherently counter-hegemonic, especially if they are quiescent, nonchallenging. Resistance, either as negotiated hybridization of the dominant or as politically independent, can also camouflage power in working to improve the existing hegemony—seeking specific reform in an otherwise unchallenged structure. A successful hegemony, including media hegemony, invites such reforms because it leads by improving the participation and contribution of subordinates to the institutions and practices of hegemony. Indeed, one remains inside the logic of the dominant, including its hegemony, unless one participates in an organized alliance of the culturally active, politically conscious, and economically powerful (in social class position) that can construct a new hegemonic project.

Above all, hegemony means political and cultural leadership. Cultural hegemony means society in all of its divisions has internalized and normalized the relations and practices as common sense. Contemporary cultural hegemony is bundled in capitalist globalization, corporate media hegemony, and social class divisions, all ideologically tied together by consumerism. To break such a hold, assumptions and beliefs must be shaken by contradictory practices; recurring crises within capitalist hegemony must be countered with political programs that consciously offer and pragmatically deliver material, political, and cultural rewards from an alternative leadership. A new global culture for humanity must identify contradictions and breaks within capitalist hegemony and then consciously challenge its hierarchal relationships and cultural norms with calls for participatory social democracy.

As the essays in this text reveal, transnationals, their media, and national elites acting as junior partners respond to all challenges often with coercion but always with refined persuasive appeals that deliver representations favorable to capitalist hegemony. Around the world, radical media, social movements, and cultural and political expressions of working people and their allies are simultaneously resisting free market globalization and envisioning a globalization of human values and participation. In this confrontation, any new hegemony will necessarily need to project its political program to millions via an independent media that clearly speaks on behalf of working people and humanity for a new world order.

Tantum possumus, tantum scimus
(We do what we know)

References

Amaral, R., & Guimaraes, C. (1994). Media monopoly in Brazil. *Journal of Communication, 44* (4), 26–38.

Artz, L. (1997). Social power and the inflation of discourse: The failure of popular hegemony in Nicaragua. *Latin American Perspectives, 24,* 92–113.

Artz, L. (2000, June). Animating hierarchy: Disney and the globalization of capitalism. In M. Budd (Ed.), *Rethinking Disney.* (forthcoming).

Artz, L., & Murphy, B. O. (2000). *Cultural hegemony in the United States.* Thousand Oaks, CA: Sage.

Bagdikian, B. (1997). *The media monopoly* (5th ed.). Boston: Beacon.

Bales, K. (1999). Disposable people: New slavery in the global economy. Berkeley, CA: University of California Press.

Bennett, T. (1992). Useful culture. *Cultural Studies, 6,* 395–408.

Billon, Y. (Director). (1998). *Samba Opus IV. Sao Paulo* [Film]. Paris: RFO, M6, & Les Films du Village.

Bourdieu, P. (1978). Sport and social class. *Social Science Information, 17,* 819–840.

Bourdieu, P. (1984). *Distinction: A social critique of the judgment of taste* (R. Nice, Trans.). Cambridge, MA: Harvard University Press.

Bourdieu, P. (1987). What makes a social class? On the theoretical and practical existence of groups (L. J. D. Wacquant & D. Young, Trans.). *Berkeley Journal of Sociology, 32,* 1–16.

Bourdieu, P. (1991). *Language and symbolic power* (G. Raymond & M. Adamson, Trans.). Cambridge, MA: Harvard University Press.

Brow, J. (1990). Notes on community, hegemony, and the uses of the past. *Anthropological Quarterly, 63,* 1–6.

Buci-Glucksmann, C. (1980). *Gramsci and the state.* London: Lawrence & Wishart.

Budd, M., & Entmann, R. M. (1990). The affirmative character of U.S. cultural studies. *Critical Studies in Mass Communication, 7,* 169–184.

Burbach, R. (2001). *Globalization and postmodern politics: From Zapatistas to high-tech robber barons.* Sterling, VA: Pluto Press.

Burbach, R., Nunez, O., & Kagarlitsky, B. (1997). *Globalization and its discontents: The rise of postmodern socialisms.* Chicago: Pluto Press.

Butsch, R. (2002). Five decades of class and gender in domestic situation comedies. In L. Linder & M. Dalton (Eds.), *America viewed and skewed: Critical readings in television situation comedies.* (forthcoming).

Carey, J. (1989). *Communication and culture: Essays on media and society.* Boston: Unwin Hyman.

Castells, M. (1998). *The information age: Economy, society and culture vol. 3: End of millennium.* Oxford: Blackwell.

Chossudovsky, M. (1997). *The globalization of poverty: Impacts of IMF and World Bank reforms.* London: Zed Books.

Cloud, D. L. (1996). Hegemony or concordance? The rhetoric of tokenism in "Oprah" Winfrey's rag-to-riches biography. *Critical Studies in Mass Communication, 13,* 115–137.

Cohen, L. (1990). *Making a new deal: Industrial workers in Chicago*. New York: Cambridge University Press.

Condit, C. M. (1989). The rhetorical limits of polysemy. *Critical Studies in Mass Communication, 6*, 103–122.

Condit, C. M. (1994). Hegemony in a mass-mediated society: Concordance about reproductive technologies. *Critical Studies in Mass Communication, 11*, 205–230.

Cook, J. (2001, May 14). Conspiracy of theory. *In These Times*, pp. 24–25.

Dorfman, A. (1983). *The empire's old clothes, what the Lone Ranger, Babar and other innocent heroes do to our minds*. New York: Pantheon.

Farrant, R. (2001, April 22). Virgin Islands splendor tempered by squalor. *Ft. Wayne (IN) Journal Gazette*, pp. 7E, 10E.

Fiske, J. (1987). *Television culture: Popular pleasures and politics*. London: Methuen.

Fox, E. (Ed.). (1988). *Media and politics in Latin America*. Beverly Hills, CA: Sage.

Freedman, S. G. (2001). *How three families and the American political majority moved from left to right*. New York: Touchstone.

Fromson, M. (1996). Mexico's struggle for a free press. In R. R. Cole (Ed.), *Communication in Latin America: Journalism, mass media, and society* (pp. 115–138). Washington, DC: Scholarly Resources.

Fukayama, F. (1992). *The end of history and the last man*. London: Hamish Hamilton.

Garnham, N. (1990). *Capitalism and communication: Global culture and the economics of information*. Beverly Hills, CA: Sage.

Gershon, R. A. (1997). *The transnational media corporation: Global messages and free market competition*. Mahwah, NJ: Lawrence Erlbaum.

Giddens, A. (1991). *Modernity and self-identity: Self and society in the late modern age*. Cambridge: Polity Press.

Gitlin, T. (1987). Prime time ideology: The hegemonic process in television entertainment. In H. Newcomb (Ed.), *TV: The critical view* (pp. 426–454). New York: Oxford University Press.

Goldman, R., & Rajagopal, A. (1991). *Mapping hegemony*. Norwood, NJ: Ablex.

Gramsci, A. (1988). *Selected writings. 1916–1935* (D. Forgacs, Ed.). New York: Shocken.

Hachten, W. A. (1992). *The world news prism: Changing media, clashing ideologies* (3rd ed.). Ames, IA: Iowa State University Press.

Hall, S. (1984). Signification, representation, ideology: Althusser and the post-structuralist debates. *Critical Studies in Mass Communication, 2*, 91–114.

Hall, S. (1986). Gramsci's relevance for the study of race and ethnicity. *Journal of Communication Inquiry, 10*, 5–27.

Halle, D. (2001). *America's working man: Work, home, and politics among blue-collar property owners*. Chicago: University of Chicago Press.

Hamelink, C. (1997). International communication: Global market and morality. In A. Mohammadi (Ed.), *International communication and globalization* (pp. 92–118). Thousand Oaks, CA: Sage.

Hardt, M., & Negri, A. (2000). *Empire*. Cambridge: Harvard University Press.

Hart, P., & Ackerman, S. (2001, December). Patriotism & censorship. *Extra!* pp. 6–9.

Herman, E., & McChesney, R. (1997). *The global media: The new missionaries of corporate capitalism*. Washington, DC: Cassell.

Kagarlitsky, B. (1997). The post-communist world: From crisis to catastrophe. In R. Burbach, O. Nunez, & B. Kagarlitsky (Eds.), *Globalization and its discontents: The rise of postmodern socialisms* (pp. 153–169). Chicago: Pluto Press.

King, A. (1987). *Power and communication*. Prospect Heights, IL: Waveland.

Kraidy, M. (1999). The global, the local, and the hybrid: A native ethnography of glocalization. *Critical Studies in Mass Communication, 16*, 456–476.

Laclau, E., & Mouffe, C. (1985). *Hegemony and socialist strategy: Towards a radical democratic politics*. London: Verso.

Lears, T. J. (1985). The concept of cultural hegemony: Problems and possibilities. *American Historical Review, 90*, 567–593.

Levine, R. (1988). *Class struggle and the new deal*. Lawrence, KS: University of Kansas Press.

Levison, A. (2001, May 14). Who lost the working class? *The Nation*, pp. 25–32.

Lull, J. (1995). *Media, communication, culture: A global approach*. New York: Columbia University Press.

Marichal, C. (1997, May-June). Latin America in the age of billionaires. *NACLA Report on the Americas*, pp. 29–31.

Marin, R. (2001, December 12). TV sitcoms distinguish themselves with class. *Chicago Tribune*, p. E5.

Mattelart, A. (1994). *Mapping world communication: War, progress, culture* (S. Emanuel & J. Cohen, Trans.). Minneapolis: University of Minnesota Press.

Mattelart, A. & Mattelart, M. (1992). *Rethinking media theory: Signposts and new directions* (J. A. Cohen & M. Urquidi, Trans.). Minneapolis: University of Minnesota Press.

McNall, S. G., Levine, R. F., & Fantasia, R. (Eds.). (1991). *Bringing class back in: Contemporary and historical perspectives*. Boulder, CO: Westview.

Mohammadi, A. (1997). Communication and the globalization process in the developing world. In A. Mohammadi (Ed.), *International communication and globalization* (pp. 67–89). Thousand Oaks, CA: Sage.

Mosco, V. (1998). *The political economy of communication*. Thousand Oaks, CA: Sage.

Negroponte, N. (1995) *Being digital*. New York: Knopf.

Nelson, C., & Grossberg, L. (Eds.). (1988). *Marxism and the interpretation of culture.* Urbana, IL: University of Illinois Press.

Ohmae, K. (1995). *The end of the nation state: The rise and fall of regional economies.* New York: HarperCollins.

Parenti, M. (1986). *Inventing reality: The politics of the mass media.* New York: St. Martin's Press.

Pieterse, J. N. (1995). Globalization as hybridization. In M. Featherstone, S. Lash, & R. Robertson (Eds.), *Global modernities* (pp. 45–68). Thousand Oaks, CA: Sage.

Poulanzas, N. (1978). *Class in contemporary capitalism.* London: Verso.

Poverty and disease threaten millions of kids, report warns. (2000, October 12). *Chicago Tribune,* p. 14.

Robertson, R. (1992). *Globalization: social theory and global culture.* Thousand Oaks, CA: Sage.

Sassoon, A. S. (1987). *Gramsci's politics* (2nd Ed.). Minneapolis: University of Minnesota Press.

Scott, J. C. (1990). *Domination and the arts of resistance: Hidden transcripts.* New Haven, CT: Yale University Press.

Stevenson, R. L. (1994). *Global communication in the twenty-first century.* New York: Longman.

Stille, A. (2000, January 24). Emperor of the air: Berlusconi owns Italian politics, but he wants more. *The Nation,* pp. 17–20.

Straubhaar, J. (1997). Distinguishing the global, regional and national levels of world television. In A. Sreberny-Mohammadi, D. Winseck, J. McKenna, & O. Boyd-Barrett (Eds.), *Media in global context: A reader* (pp. 284–298). New York: St. Martin's.

Sweezy, P. (1997). More (or less) on globalization. *Monthly Review, 49,* 1–4.

Tehranian, M., & Tehranian K. K. (1997). Taming modernity: Towards a new paradigm. In A. Mohammadi (Ed.), *International communication and globalization* (119–167). Thousand Oaks, CA: Sage.

Therborn, G. (1983). Why some classes are more successful than others. *New Left Review, 138,* 37–55.

Thussu, D. K. (2000). *International communication: Continuity and change.* New York: Oxford University Press.

Tomlinson, J. (1999). *Globalization and culture.* Cambridge: Polity Press.

Tunstall, J., & Palmer, M. (1991). *Media moguls.* London: Routledge.

Wacquant, L. J. D. (1991). Making class: the middle class(es) in social theory and social structure. In S. G. McNall, R. F. Levine, & R. Fantasia (Eds.), *Bringing class back in: Contemporary and historical perspectives* (pp. 39–64). Boulder, CO: Westview.

White, L. A. (2001, October). Who wants to be a millionaire, a survivor, and be watched by big brother? An analysis of the internationalization of television show formats. Paper presented at meeting of Global Fusion 2001. St. Louis, MO.

Wright, E. O. (1985). *Classes*. London:Verso.

Wright, E. O. (1991). The conceptual status of class structure in class. In S. G. McNall, R. F. Levine, & R. Fantasia (Eds.), *Bringing class back in: Contemporary and historical perspectives* (pp. 17–38). Boulder, CO: Westview.

Zachary, G. P. (2001, April 16). Loving the highlife. *In These Times*, pp. 30–32.

Zaniello, T. (1996). *Working stiffs, union maids, rebs, and riffraff: An organized guide to films about labor*. Ithaca, NY: ILR/Cornell.

CHAPTER 2

Informational Technology and Transnational Networks: A World Systems Approach

Gerald Sussman

In a world economy now widely envisioned as a system of networked communicative, informational, and economic exchange, it should be sobering that massive poverty, limited social accessibility and mobility, and class domination remain stark and unrelenting features of all societies, including the leading "information societies." In this chapter, I critically examine the present conditions and relationships within the techno-economic regime that guides development in the Third World (or South), and the historical and political economic forces that helped to shape them. Reviewing technology and media infrastructure initiatives undertaken during the colonial and early postcolonial periods, which gave rise to a "development of underdevelopment" (Frank, 1966) and a Third World, I argue that the diffusion of mass media and communications technology continues to be driven primarily by transnational economic institutions and their political allies to increase concentrations of wealth and power and continue the project of world capitalist domination started about six hundred years ago. The uses of transnational mass media and communications technology have entrenched a regime of global accumulation and pursued the acquiescence of working classes. The decline of socialist and social democratic movements in the 1980s and 1990s, which had once offered some promise of reducing massive social inequality based on statist intervention and international cooperation, has allowed the rise of a neoliberal momentum in support of private transnational market regulation.

Communications and institutional and economic restructuring are at the center of this momentum. Despite a popular rhetoric about the democratizing potential of electronic communications systems, global informational networks on the whole have had profoundly negative effects on national and cultural sovereignty, economic distribution, and urban sprawl. I argue that progressive structural changes in the world economy cannot occur without a radical shift in the discourse about technology and social change. A reconstitution of political power and sovereignty is dialectically and reflexively joined to such a discourse and is the foundation of a more equitable relocation of authority and means for fostering socially and ecologically useful production, redistributing social surplus, and expanding democratic participatory processes.

The Condition of Unequal and Uneven Development

The conditions that led to the restructuring and informatization of the world economy in the past quarter-century are part of a rapid spatialization of capital in the postwar era. For the South, the export-oriented industrialization strategy adopted by selected countries in the 1960s and 1970s was a response to both a crisis in the world (and Third World) economy and the timely development of new technological and political economic capacities embedded in international telecommunications, informatics, high-speed commercial aircraft, containerization, and transnational corporate organizational structure. These forces of production enabled significantly reduced costs (superexploitation) in the means of producing and distributing commodities, information, and services, a worldwide economic management system, and a general reduction in the "friction of distance"—the "annihilation of space by time"—all the while externalizing the costs to workers, the environment, the household, and civil society.

This was also a period of rising technological and debt dependency in the Third World. Following nearly two decades of postwar industrial rehabilitation in western Europe and Japan, transnational corporations (TNCs) had made concerted efforts in the 1960s to relocate plants overseas, while flooding the Third World with commercial advertising to speed the circulation of commodities and stimulate the absorption of surplus production. Telecommunications investment in export processing zones, maquiladoras (plants along the United States-Mexico border), and industrial parks were a precondition for this new wave of TNC activity in the Third World, allowing more flexible, decentered production with centralized communications, command, and control in corporate headquarters. As a result of the Eurodollar crisis of the 1970s and stagflation in the OECD (Organization for Economic Cooperation and Development—the developed capitalist nations of Western Europe, Japan, and the United States) countries, the U.S. government and the TNCs pushed the World Bank and large private financial houses to focus lending on particular Third World countries, resulting in a $2 trillion Third World debt burden by the mid-1990s with the attendant net outflow of Third World wealth. Between 1984 and 1990 alone, the Third World suffered a net transfer of $178 billion in loan repayments to commercial banks (Bello & Cunningham, 1994, p. 11).

Private and public lending began to overtake government assistance programs as the main source of foreign currency in Third World economies, leading to a reverse flow of dollar investments—from the Third to the First World. The inspiration behind U.S. technology transfer programs was not humanitarian so much as a political economic calculus for laundering public funds into private capital and creating dependency relations. President Kennedy had made these motives explicit in the 1960s (Sussman & Lent, 1991). The Agency for International Development (AID), the main foreign economic assistance program of the United States, more recently reiterated the commercial and "national interest" behind aid: "The principal beneficiary of American foreign assistance programs has always been the United States. Close to 80% of USAID's contracts and grants flow back to American firms" (cited in Reynolds, 1997, p. 13).

In recent years, however, overall direct foreign investment (DFI), like government assistance, has been deserting the South: from half of worldwide DFI in 1960 to one-quarter in 1974 to 16.9% in 1988–1989 and is highly concentrated in 10 countries: China, Mexico, Malaysia, Argentina, Thailand, Indonesia, Brazil, Nigeria, Venezuela, and South Korea (Broad & Landi, 1996, p. 10). Just 14% of the South's population base received two-thirds of direct foreign investment targeted to the Third World as a whole, 28% of the world population getting 92% of DFI. And almost all of it is focused on the urban core areas (Hoogvelt, 1997, p. 77). The direction of these flows is suggestive of a general disinterest of corporate elites toward those regions most in need of economic assistance.

A persistent and worsening feature of Third World economies (and the world as a whole) is the gross misallocation of resources, ranging from access to basic health care, education, housing, and clean water to telephone, computers, and agricultural technology. The overwhelming majority of Third World citizens have no telephones (with access rates in rural areas averaging below 1 telephone per 1,000 population), have no full-time electrical power, and no constant source of adequate food supply or medical care, much less opportunities for advanced education or upward social mobility. Research and development capacity is a key to pulling the South out of the condition of long-term poverty and dependency, but this is a highly protected U.S./Western asset.

The extreme maldistribution of income is another feature that separates the First and Third Worlds. Belgium, with 10 million people, has as large a GDP as all of sub-Saharan Africa, with over 650 million people. Of the largest 100 economic entities in the world (a list including corporate assets and national GDPs), more than half are transnational corporations. The South as a whole has nearly 80% of the world population, but only 20% of world income, 10% of its patents, less than 15% of its telephone lines, and 30% of the world's newspaper output. As of 1999, fewer than 400 Americans had over $1 trillion in assets—more than the income of half the world's population.

There are certainly great differences among Third World countries: 39 countries (with well over half of the world's population) have a per capita income of less than $425, while a few class-stratified oil-rich Middle East countries and Singapore have mean incomes comparable to some of the core industrial countries. The "newly industrializing countries" (NICs) of Asia (Singapore, South Korea, Taiwan, and Hong Kong) have had impressive though unstable rates of economic expansion and trade, which has brought prosperity to many along with huge class disparities. China has had a remarkable rate of growth over the past decade, but the manner of its economic expansion also has brought the reappearance of a conspicuous class structure. Argentina and Chile, with important natural resources and older industrial bases, are now relatively stable, although development has included long periods of right-wing dictatorship, state violence, and class repression. In contrast, socialist Cuba, with a low per capita income, has been able to maintain a universal health care and education program—the best in Latin America—even after the collapse of its east European and Soviet allied regimes and throughout a 40 plus-year U.S. embargo.

For the South as a whole, however, the 30% drop in primary commodity prices and rise in indebtedness from an average of 32% to 61% of GDP from 1980–1990 was the more common reality (Schwartz, 1994, p. 260; Winseck, 1997, p. 230.

Media and Informational Bridgeheads

Mass media and information systems were critical aspects of regime maintenance in both the colonial and postcolonial periods. Throughout Latin America in the 1930s, U.S. commercial radio established broadcasting centers that, together with domestic private media interests, overwhelmed initiatives toward noncommercial, public, and state-owned stations. The Columbia Broadcasting System (CBS) and the National Broadcasting Company (NBC), both U.S. commercial broadcasting institutions, ran the Cadena (Chain) de las Americas and the Cadena Panamerica networks, respectively, with affiliates all over the continent (Fox, 1988, p. 13). This provided avenues for American goods to penetrate the region and for American advertising agencies (such as J. Walter Thompson and McCann-Erickson) to create markets for its northern corporate clients. The long-term strategy worked: Brazil, for example, which started with noncommercial radio, has a broadcasting system today that is saturated with advertising for both local products as well as for Coca-Cola, General Motors, Levi's jeans, Volkswagen, and many other foreign goods (Oliveira, 1993). Where radio did not directly serve commercial/advertising interests, as in colonial Indonesia, the ruling power introduced short wave transmission in the 1920s to help keep the Dutch-speaking community in touch with business, cultural, and political news from the homeland and help sustain it as a ruling stratum.

In the early postwar period, the Third World, especially Latin America, was seen by U.S. state and corporate planners as increasingly important consumer markets for the absorption of a revitalized U.S. export economy. The penetration of mass media was critical in this objective, as U.S. television interests began their first assault on Latin America. Soon all major U.S. networks, together with Time-Life, had investments in Latin American television. For example, by the 1960s, ABC International was part-owner of 54 Latin American and other Third World television stations in 24 countries (Bunce, 1976). The Department of Defense, a major broadcaster around the world (38 TV and 200 radio stations), also participated (Williams, 1975, pp. 40–41). Thus, U.S. programs and consumer values became prevalent, as "I Love Lucy," "The Flintstones," and "Batman" became part of the region's cultural lexicon at the same time that right-wing governments purged the media of socially progressive political content.

The United States overwhelmed Third World broadcasting and print media with a global commercial cultural presence that imprinted Procter & Gamble, Colgate, Coca Cola, and other brand names in millions of households, villages, and barrios (Herman & McChesney, 1997, p. 21). Even if Western Europe and Japan have since joined the ranks of global advertising firms, the style and values of the trade in culture were and remain essentially American (Thussu, 1998a). The advertising age can be seen as an American global rewrite of Macaulay's ignoble nineteenth century dictum on British education policy in India: to create "a class of persons, Indian in blood and colour, but English in taste, in opinion, in morals and in intellect" (Anderson, 1983, p. 86).

In sub-Saharan Africa, Indonesia, and elsewhere, the imperial powers set up radio stations "to provide information and entertainment to the colonial administrators and white settlers," providing Europeans political and cultural contacts with the metropolitan countries while transferring British and continental culture to the western-educated administrative class of Africans. Except for Nigeria, sub-Saharan Africa did not get television until after independence. The last to gain their political independence from the European powers and with little foreign assistance to this sector, Black Africa today has the most impoverished telecommunications and mass media facilities in the world (Boafo, 1991, pp. 105–107).

Colonialism distorted not only trade patterns, but also affected communication routes. And today, with few exceptions, the concentration of telephones and other electronic communications in the South has followed historic colonial and preferential trade and investment routes. The location of voice and text messaging, Internet services, and television and other mass media continues to be concentrated in the major trade and industrial centers, typically capital cities or in newly created, decentered industrial parks and free trade zones. Telephone traffic between east and west Africa is still routed through European capitals (Hamelink, 1995, p. 302). Moreover, whereas the leading OECD countries are characterized by wide access to telephone, some 50 Third World countries (including Ghana, India, Indonesia, Kenya, Myanmar, Nigeria, Pakistan, the Philippines, and Vietnam) are well below or barely reach the level of two telephones per 100 people. Some 85% of the world's people, 125 years after the Bell patent, still have no telephones, and two-thirds have never made a telephone call. The 29 OECD countries have 15% of the world's population, 71% of the world's telephones, 90% of the world's mobile telephone users, 95% of all computers, and 97% of Internet host domains (two-thirds in the United States and Canada).

All of Africa, about 14% of the world's population, has fewer than 1% of global Internet users—95% located in South Africa (United Nations Economic and Social Council, 2000, p. 18). The United States and Canada alone have more than 98% of global Internet protocol bandwidth, with the United States acting as the hub of global Internet traffic. According to a report of the United Nations Economic and Social Council: "Given the foreign exchange constraints of many developing countries, this arrangement merely exacerbates the differential access to information and knowledge as it leads to prohibitive connection costs in many developing countries" (United Nations Economic and Social Council, 2000, p.18). The United States and the former Soviet Union control more than half of the world's geostationary space orbits (the South uses less than 10%).

These inequities go unrecognized in the United States and most of the North, but are clearly understood in the Third World South. The nonaligned nations movement in the 1970s, led by Yugoslavia, India, and Algeria, with the support of the socialist states, declared that "a new international order in the fields of information and mass communications is as vital as a new international economic order" (cited in Frederick, 1993, p. 165). In 1980 UNESCO's MacBride commission called for a "new world information and communication order" (NWICO) to challenge unrestricted operations of foreign mass media and advertising in Third World countries, promote two-way flows of culture and information, and enable poorer countries to form news agencies and acquire technology and training from the West. In response, the Reagan and Thatcher governments withdrew from UNESCO. Under combined Anglo-American pressure, a new UNESCO leadership abandoned NWICO—as transnational corporations and cooperative state officials continued their exploitative operations.

World Systems Approach

The condition of political, economic, military, cultural, and technological domination over Third World regions by the Western powers during the colonial era never rested solely on the preponderance of external power, such as the way "dependency" analyses (including those of Keith Griffin, Paul Baran, Paul Sweezy, and an earlier Andre Gunder Frank) have usually argued. Rather, such domination was, and could only be, constituted as a collaborative project, albeit an inequitable and often coercive one, of endogenous and exogenous forces, classes, and actors. In varying degrees, the integration of the Third World into the world system created new class schisms on a global scale in both the dominated and dominating countries, the principal one being between capital on one side and workers and peasants on the other. As Brazilian political economists, Fernando Henrique Cardoso and Enzo Faletto (1979) argued, "We conceive the relationship between external and internal forces as forming a complex whole whose structural links are not based on mere external forms of exploitation and coercion but are rooted in the coincidence of interests between local dominant classes and international ones, and, on the other side, are challenged by local dominated groups and classes" (p. xvi). Tragically, Cardoso personally demonstrated his own observation; as president of Brazil after 1994 he inaugurated the selling off of public telecommunications to bidders from the United States, Canada, France, and Italy (Schiesel, 1998, p. C1).

Dependency and world systems analyses attempt to overcome an ahistorical and apolitical approach to development (modernization) that tended to reinforce postcolonial ideological hegemony based on the "rational choice" paradigm. However, the world systems approach moves beyond dependency theory, and presents a theory of class structure that transcends national borders and social boundaries and the limited prerogatives of nation-state actors and institutions. Since the 1980s, the ideological attacks on the welfare state have legitimated an increasing convergence of political and market interests operating from transnational production and financial platforms and a more technology-intensive international division of labor. Early postwar modernization theory, which was possessed of the notion that the logic of the market and limited intervention of the state represented the best hopes of reproducing material progress in the South, was revitalized with the collapse of the European socialist states and the unimpeded expansion of transnational capital into formerly Soviet-influenced areas.

Early modernization writers, such as Daniel Lerner, Ithiel de Sola Pool, and Wilbur Schramm, uncritically looked to mass media and information technology as the incubator of social, economic, and political development in Third World countries. Pool, a political science professor, believed that Western-style mass media would inculcate in the Third World modern (i.e., U.S.) aspirations of achievement (Pool, 1966). Lerner, his widely referenced colleague at MIT, shared similar political culturalist assumptions about poverty and how change occurs: "What is required to motivate the isolated and illiterate peasants and tribesmen who compose the bulk of the world's population is to provide them with clues as to what the better things of life might be" (Lerner, 1963, pp. 341–342). Lerner, Pool, and other defenders of a "free flow" of information doctrine ignored the self-serving and destabilizing effects of foreign media and information systems on Third World societies, especially as they impacted the poor. They paid little attention to the historical-colonial circumstances under which modern communications systems were introduced in the South and assumed that cultural choices were more matters of personal selection rather than historical responses within hegemonic contexts.

Implicit in their analyses was that the peoples of the South collectively lacked what Harvard psychologist David McClelland (1961) constructed as the "need for achievement" necessary for development. The antidote to the condition of "underdevelopment" was essentially motivational, a desire for material progress that could be inoculated through the transfer of American media and identification with "modern" (Western) social-psychological and cultural values (McClelland, 1961; Sussman & Lent, 1991). In short, the main function of commercial mass media is to dissuade the South from the path of cultural independence, nationalism, and socialism and lure their economies more deeply into the vortex of "civilization" and its world markets (Rothkopf, 1997).

Third World Urbanization, Globalization, and Informatization

Colonial resource extractions and labor exploitation, interpreted by modernization theorists as preparatory "stages" for "takeoff," were integral to the urbanization, industrialization, and informatization of the West. Third World cities, many of which long predated Europe's, served as regional transfer points funneling labor, raw materials, or the transshipment of goods to ports and vessels bound for Europe and the Americas. African men and women taken as slaves to coastal cities were plantation replacement labor for the Indians annihilated in the Caribbean and the Americas. Before telegraphy and submarine cables, written communication between Britain and India would take five to eight months and a reply could take two years. The new technologies, establishing an electrical informational web for the political administration and commercial exploitation of the colonial territories, were enthusiastically welcomed by all the European powers, including those that did not themselves control the submarine cables.

The Chinese had struggled unsuccessfully in the late nineteenth century to block British telegraphic cables and landlines from their country, much as Native Americans had attempted to prevent a similar incursion upon their lands (Headrick, 1988, pp. 97–99; Winston, 1998, p. 245). Such imperial impositions, as with earlier forced importations of opium, led to the discrediting of the emperorship, antiforeign Chinese rebellions, and the revolutions of 1911 and 1949. From the imperialist side, Cecil Rhodes, colonizer of Southern Africa and one of the most passionate advocates of British expansionism, captured the moment in unambiguous candor: "We must find new lands from which we can easily obtain raw materials and at the same time exploit the cheap slave labour that is available from the natives of the colonies. The colonies would also provide a dumping ground for the surplus goods produced in our factories" (cited in Ponting, 1991, p. 222).

One of the continuing legacies of colonial rule has been the distorted development of Third World cities, creating problems for the postcolonial South of seemingly unresolvable magnitude. Domestic compradors and their transnational allies made Third World cities into peripheral enclaves dependently integrated with foreign trade and investment, creating in the long term a pattern of urbanization without industrialization. Gavin Williams noted that, in contrast to Europe,

> the colonial city developed . . . as a centre of commerce and administration, rather than industrial production. It originated as a means whereby the metropolitan rulers established a base for the administration of the countryside, and the exploitation of its resources, and consequently the transfer of the surplus extracted from the countryside to the metropolis. At the same time, the city itself engaged in the parasitical extractions of a surplus from the countryside. (cited in Smith, 1996, p. 63)

The spatial location of communications and transportation nodes in the colonies strategically linked fractions of the South to counterparts in the West through class alignments within the world economy. Telecommunications, road planning, and port facilities were organized by the colonizing powers primarily to move raw materials from the hinterlands to the "mother" countries and for the overall coordination and administration of colonial rule. As Anthony Hopkins noted with respect to colonial west Africa, "Communications were designed mainly to evacuate exports. There were few lateral or inter-colonial links, and little attempt was made to use railways and roads as a stimulus to internal exchange" (cited in Smith, 1996, p. 85).

Core cities of the Third World (centers of business, finance, transportation, communications, education, media, entertainment, etc.) concentrate most of the domestic and international economic activity, making them natural lures for large numbers of displaced peasants and limited foreign capital migration, which intensifies the infrastructural difficulties of providing jobs and social services to the poor. Metropolitan Bangkok, for example, contains 10% of the population of Thailand but 86% of the country's GDP in banking, insurance, and real estate, and 74% of its manufacturing. Abidjan, Lagos, Sao Paulo, Manila, Dhaka, and other core cities of the South have similar patterns of concentration of economic activity (Kasarda & Parnell, 1993, p. xi). These population and economic distortions also impose themselves on rings of surrounding rural areas, where increasingly corporate-run, export-oriented, and technology-based agriculture instigates new class relations through wholesale dislocation of peasants, who are landless, and migrate to the ranks of the urban, largely unemployed working class.

Consequently, the economic development and information investment that does occur in Third World countries is generally concentrated in elite groups within urban business districts. Local managers of international and joint venture companies rely on complicit governments to promote and carry out political, economic, and cultural policies that exacerbate income and information inequalities and alienate privileged fractions from lower economic classes. This also has contributed to urban migration and severe overpopulation of Third World cities, which, following World Bank and IMF prescriptions, fail to provide services to the majority of new migrants—creating threats of epidemics, social conflicts, and other crises of overcrowding. Lagos, a city with 300,000 residents in the 1950s, had 8 million by 1990. Mexico City rose to 24 million inhabitants by 1995; Sao Paulo, almost 22 million; Seoul, 19 million; Bombay and Calcutta, 13 million; and Manila and Jakarta, 11 million. By the year 2000, these seven cities alone were estimated to have added 30 million people, a 30% urban population increase in just five years.

Brazil and Mexico, the two largest countries in Latin America, already have highly class-stratified urban concentrations (United Nations, 1993). Twenty of the world's 25 largest cities are in the South. Most of this growth is driven by migration of the poor—a result of desperate social and economic conditions in the rural areas, the appropriation of lands for export agriculture, and sometimes war. Some 100 million people in the South are being added to the poverty roles each year, the number severely malnourished already having reached one billion by the early 1990s. This is largely the result of uncritical "modernization" approaches that have distorted the allocation of development resources and urged upon Third World countries a strategy of urban-based growth, with heavy emphasis on the free import of foreign commercial mass media and habits of consumption.

With a few notable exceptions, the South suffers an economic dualism that is conspicuously seen in housing, health care, social mobility, education, labor rights, and communications access. Despite the initiatives taken by intergovernmental agencies such as the International Telecommunication Union, which in 1973 invoked the principle of "equitable access" for all member states, there has been little transfer communications technology to Third World countries (Hamelink, 1994, pp. 88–89). New telecommunications investments have been concentrated in core cities to enhance the interests of local businesses and TNC subsidiaries, reinforcing transnational alliances and creating pressures for privatization and commercialization. In the sell-off of the Bahamas Telecommunications Company to private interests, the prime minister conceded that the state was "unable to maintain the telecommunications infrastructure demanded by the business community" (Herman, 1997, p. 13).

Third World cities and industrial enclaves have become spatially integrated into a new international division of labor, based on the World Bank's open market, export-oriented industrialization model of development that features highly segmented, largely nonunionized, workforces in industrial parks and free trade zones engaged in the processing of electronics, automobiles, garments, sports equipment, and other commodities for transnational corporations and foreign markets. This has introduced a severely distorted type of economic development that is largely unrelated to the evolution of class forces, technical capacities, or basic needs of Third World countries. Remote towns and villages are linked to capitals or to port cities through a highly abstracted wage relationship and distant foreign management but not to one another. The digitally networked infrastructure of capital accumulation that binds the transnational economy is incompatible with the value that Third World cultures, including the business classes, usually assign to interpersonal and social communication and relationships. Thus, for cultural and other reasons, long-distance business transactions via telecommunications are less likely to instigate capital formation at the domestic level (Calhoun, 1986, pp. 333–334).

In order to maintain this transnational division of labor structure, information processing becomes particularly critical to such labor-intensive industries as tourism, insurance, finance, and banking. In the Philippines, back offices in data entry can generate 700 million keystrokes per month with 20% of the wage rate of the leading OECD countries with extremely low turnover rates (1% to 2% compared to 35% in North America) and tough managerial discipline of workers (Graham & Marvin, 1996, pp. 153–154). Jamaica built a teleport to facilitate links to the transnational business community and to subcontract back office work from the United States (Skinner, 1998). Transnational financial institutions can hire data entry workers and software writers and editors in the Caribbean, China, and south Asia to process and transmit information to the headquarter cities at one-tenth to one-twentieth the pay scale of their U.S. counterparts. The deepening new international division of labor has led to the recent employment in the United States of female prison inmates in North Carolina to process hotel bookings from "800" telephone numbers, effectively forcing international labor to compete with indentured servitude.

The declining cost and improved transmission capacities of telecommunications has made it very efficient for TNCs to operate "offshore back offices" in Third World countries, but this requires the latter to provide modern and expensive infrastructure for that purpose. Banks, insurance companies, airlines, and hotels use workers, primarily women, in Jamaica, China, and the Phillipines to punch keystrokes in monotonous repetition at rates as low as $1 per 1,000. This relocation of work enables TNCs to employ large numbers of temporary and part-time nonunionized workers and to segregate this labor section from its northern workforce. The major capital cost for the foreign employer is for the highly portable personal computers (Wilson, 1995, pp. 205, 211, 218).

TNCs were willing to move to remote locations such as Bataan in the Philippines, Penang in Malaysia, Kaohsiung in South Korea, and Tijuana in Mexico because satellite or microwave links kept them in touch with branch offices in the capital cities of those countries and from there to headquarters in New York, Tokyo, London, or elsewhere. They could, therefore, maintain centralized control of their "offshore" operations via advanced communication linkages and enjoy the benefits of lower production costs, especially labor. In Mexico and the Philippines, for example, television set components and assemblies are currently produced at about one-tenth to one-twentieth the labor cost in the United States. More than 90% of components for U.S.-produced color television sets are made in Mexico and East Asia (Bello, 1994, p. 89). With NAFTA and foreign investors such as Japan's Sony, Hitachi, and Matsushita and South Korea's Samsung moving to Tijuana, "the necessity of building TVs in the United States evaporated," and so did American jobs. TNC television set manufacturers substituted $9–an-hour American jobs with $50–a-week wages in Mexico (DePalma, 1996).

Questions of Sovereignty

There are substantial differences between media practices in the Third and First World. Unlike the BBC today, Nigerian television is an exclusive federal government monopoly. Television and other telecommunications equipment purchases during the oil boom of the late 1970s and early 1980s contributed substantially to Nigeria's $26 billion foreign debt by 1990, and unregulated commercial program imports would make hard currency deficits only worse. The introduction of FM radio stations in the country, according to one West

African scholar, "seem[s] to have been established primarily to transmit the latest sounds for the youth and the highly sophisticated urban elite" (Boafo, 1991, pp. 112, 115).

In Lagos, the most popular radio station, Radio Two, "devotes a high percentage of its transmission hours to foreign popular music. Out of a total of 154 records monitored on the station on a selected day in July 1983, 70% were foreign, 26% Nigerian, and 4% from other African countries" (Boafo, 1991, p. 115). The first African newspaper, *The East African Standard,* was published in English in Nairobi, and today two of Kenya's three daily newspapers are in English. U.S. TV programs such as "Baywatch" are seen throughout much of Africa, with reruns selling for $450, a price that compares favorably with the far higher costs of producing local programming (CPSR, 1998).

Apart from the unequal terms of commodity trade and the out-of-control debt dependency that holds many Third World countries hostage, there is the lingering legacy of "cultural, media, and informational imperialism." This phrase refers to the flooding of the Third World with the media content of the West, including international news coverage, films, television programs, music, advertising, public relations, as well as educational materials, books, magazines, theater, and other lifestyle symbol transfers that encourage wasteful consumption of foreign goods and services, divided cultural identity, and emigration. In Brazil, for example, almost all of the films shown on television come from Hollywood or other wealthy countries, even though Brazil is a substantial television program exporter in its own right. Most other Third World countries are similarly immersed in imported cultural products, dominated by "a handful of global conglomerates with something to sell" (George Gerbner, cited in Traber & Nordenstreng, 1992, p. 14). The problem of cultural invasion is not simply one of contact with foreigners, inasmuch as all societies have experienced some degree of assimilation of external cultural values, but rather the extremely unequal terms of exchange on which these contacts are organized and the weak financial and technological foundations for developing modern endogenous arts and media.

The often-celebrated "success story" of the Brazilian telenovela (TV soap opera) (Rogers & Antola, 1985) has not only created a large audience in Brazil, crowding out foreign programs on prime time, but also has been exported to other Latin American countries and to Portugal. As some would have it, this example refutes the thesis of U.S. "cultural imperialism." Yet, the Brazilian telenovela presents, in addition to an escapist, romantic, patriarchal storyline, a conspicuous merchandising of products displayed in each episode and raw marketing methods (including the pretesting of story endings on sample viewers to enlarge the audience). In short, the telenovela is a market manipulation of local culture, adopted from its mentor, the United States, with the purpose being not to represent reality, educate, or inculcate progressive Brazilian values, but to promote pacification and consumerist escapism. Rather than counteract the impact of homogenizing American material culture on the South, with few exceptions Brazilian television reinforces and helps internalize and globalize these values by creolizing them with a thin veneer of local color (Oliveira, 1993; Sklair, 1991).

Before the 1980s, India, a major producer of television and film, was well known for its dedication to self-reliance, both in technical fields and in indigenous popular culture. Since the 1980s, however, the government has moved toward more foreign investment and advertising and a more urban-centered, elitist, and Western-style entertainment-oriented approach in media development (Pendakur, 1991). India now has a glut of television and cable, including Rupert Murdoch's Star TV. The third largest cable market in the world, Indian cable television features dozens of small local operators, a top-rated local version of "Who Wants to Be a Millionaire," a French fashion channel, Hollywood reruns, American-style game shows, MTV, BBC, CNN, Disney, CNBC, Discovery, a Sony entertainment and movie channel, six music-video channels—but, as yet, no "Survivor" formats, which for most Indians who live a hand-to-mouth, dollar-a-day existence would add nothing new to their lives (Landler, 2001, pp. C1, C12).

The circuit of capital under the traditional international division of labor was such that workers and peasants in the South bought back commodities produced with their own labor and national resources. In the nineteenth century, Malayans provided the British with the *gutta percha* insulating material used in oceanic cables that enabled an informational infrastructure for empire. This has not changed much under the new international division of labor. Third World workers receive few benefits from the global production system that is founded on the "communications revolution," even though millions are directly involved in its creation. In India, for example, computer specialists, working at a fraction of their Western counterparts' salaries, provide all of British Telecommunications software programming and much of Texas Instruments, Dell, and Microsoft products (Hoogvelt, 1997, p. 126).

The removal of trade and investment barriers and the demand for intellectual property rights also threaten internal and independent development prerogatives of Third World countries. As one response, government officials from 19 nations, including Mexico and Brazil, met in Ottawa in the summer of 1998 at the invitation of the Canadian government to discuss the threat of free trade to the preservation of national cultures, particularly targeting what are seen as incursions by U.S. entertainment industries upon the independence of their broadcasting systems, book and magazine publishing, and film production. Intellectual property rights stand in the way of access to information in the more industrially developed countries as well, prioritizing property interests and classified information ahead of shared knowledge and social development values.

Development or Refeudalization?

The industrial character of the leading capitalist nations was developed on the strength of urbanization, proletarianization of farmers and peasants, state intervention, and rapid technological innovation, especially in production machinery, industrial organization, transport, and the means of communication. Third World states cannot expect to reproduce that process of historical change as long as they remain tethered to a world system of transnational class alliances, dependence on foreign direct investment, and the approval of the World Bank/IMF community—that continues to generate uneven development, including conspicuous divisions of wealth and privilege between classes, and spatial and economic segregation of urban and rural sectors and within.

Contrary to central tenets of neoliberal economics, the state has continually been a key actor in the development of the market economy, starting with the activities of government-funded colonial charter companies and state patronage to rail and telegraph companies. The Western state and its continuous sponsorship of military force and military-industrial contracting, was indispensable in bringing the Third World under foreign political control and in the creation of an international division of labor. China has demonstrated that a strong and relatively autonomous Third World state not only can bring about political independence and unification but can be a powerful advocate for the development of a national market structure.

In Asia, newly industrialized countries with strong interventionist states such as Singapore made critical differences by negotiating strategies of local economic development and through ownership of key growth industries. Forced early on into becoming an open market system with a weak state structure as a condition for its independence in 1946, the Philippines went from being the strongest postwar economy in Asia to one of the weakest and most unstable in the region. In Latin America, Mexico is another recent example of a country that has adopted free market neoliberalism and opened its telecommunications structure to foreign ownership. Mexican television programming, filled with advertising for Frito-Lay and other imported snack foods, induces children to consume useless calories (instead of more traditional and nutritious foods like tortillas and beans), as privatization appropriates the fields to grow asparagus and other crops for export to the United States and Canada (Barnet & Cavanagh, 1994, pp. 246, 253; Pursell, 1995, p. 313).

China's telecommunications policy will be a test case for the rest of Asia. Under state-guided market development, China has raised the level of telephone access by 73 million phone lines between 1990 and 1997, an increase greater than that of the rest of the Third World countries combined. As of 1997, China was involved in 16 joint ventures producing a variety of equipment ranging from integrated circuits to digital public exchanges. Dan Schiller found it "significant that no less than three-quarters of the capital required by China's telecommunications growth was sourced domestically" and that, "in sharp contrast to the position of WTO signatories, self-sufficiency in this strategic industry continued to comprise an acknowledged goal" (Schiller, 1999, p. 51). That could change, however, once China becomes part of the WTO. China has already struck a deal with Murdoch's Star TV to deliver cable to 40 million Chinese.

The more common response is found in states less able to resist the pressures of the international alliance of industrial and finance capital and First World states, which is reflected in the highly stratified information flows in the world economy. One example is seen in the way that the leading industrial countries, especially the United States, dominate the flows of Third World international telephone calling patterns, such that "the developing countries have little independent contact with each other and concentrate their international interaction with the dominant powers"(Louch, Hargittai, & Centeno, 1999, pp. 85, 92, 95). Communicative access for most workers and peasants of the world is probably going to remain closer to what Richard Ingersoll sees in the West as "a rearticulation of class structure within the metropoli of the fast world, with 'infocrats' at the top controlling production of electronic information." Beneath them are "various grades of 'cyberproletariats,'" whose work is tied to telematics, and a disconnected underclass of computer illiterates in the inner-city ghettos and declining industrial suburbs (cited in Knox, 1995, p. 15).

Communication workers of the world are people without citizenship in the "Global Village," yet they are the ones who make it possible (Sussman & Lent, 1998). The assembly workers in Hong Kong who manufacture the telecommunications, computer, and consumer electronics components and the telephone operators and repair workers who help traffic the action on stock, commodities, and currency exchanges get no commissions or royalty shares. The people who build film or television sets for Hollywood, European, and Canadian productions or international coproductions receive no "Oscars," not even credits or honorable mentions. In East Asia, where cartoon images for American animation studios are reproduced by the millions, there are no free trips to the premieres in the "City of Dreams." Data entry workers in the Caribbean who process the information for airlines, banks, and insurance companies do not get frequent flyer mileage, have no money market accounts, and probably do not even have health care coverage.

The Internet is often held up as an alternative to corporate-dominated global information structures. While the Internet represents one communication tool for those who seek social change, it is not adequate to bring about a significant alteration of the terms of social and economic exchange. Moreover, it remains available only to a small portion of the world's people, and there is no assurance that it will remain affordable or otherwise accessible for political ends even for those who currently use it.

Real change in the dominant mode of communications will require a more liberatory political discourse that emerges from a global alliance of labor, environmentalists, business owners, and other forces opposed to the globalization and homogenization of jobs, food and commodity production, popular culture, built forms, the genetic pool, and other resources that have prospered in diversity and are better left to the *vox populi* and as a legacy to the commonwealth.

References

Anderson, B. (1983). *Imagined Communities: Reflections on the Origin and Spread of Nationalism*. London: Verso.

Barnet, R., & Cavanagh, J. (1994). *Global dreams: Imperial corporations and the new world order*. New York: Simon and Schuster.

Bello, W. (1994). *Dark victory: The United States, structural adjustment, and global poverty*. London: Pluto.

Bello, W., and Cunningham, S. (1994, September/October). Reign of error: The World Bank's wrongs. *Dollars and Sense*, 10–13.

Bissio, R. R. (1990). Ten myths on democracy and communication. *Kasarinlan* [Manila], *5* (3), 83–86.

Boafo, S. T. K. (1991). Communication technology and dependent development in Sub-Saharan Africa. In Gerald Sussman and John A. Lent (Eds.), *Transnational communications: Wiring the Third World* (pp. 103–124). Newbury Park, CA: Sage.

Broad, R., & Landi, C. M. (1996). Whither the North-South gap. *Third World Quarterly*, *17* (1), 7–17.

Bunce, R. (1976). *Television in the corporate interest*. New York: Praeger.

Calhoun, C. (1986, December). Computer technology, large-scale social integration, and the local community. *Urban Affairs*, *22* (2), 329–349.

Canham-Clyne, J. (1995, July/August). Message to Congress: Cut corporate welfare, not Medicare. *Public Citizen*, *1*, 9–11.

Cardoso, F. H., & Faletto, E. (1979). *Dependency and development in Latin America.* Berkeley: University of California Press.

Castells, M. (1996). *The rise of the network society.* Oxford, UK: Blackwell.

CPSR-Global (Computer Professionals for Social Responsibility) Listserv (1998, April 21). Digest 796 *(cpsr-global@cpsr.org).*

DePalma, A. (1996, June 2). Tijuana booms as Asian companies build close to U.S. market. *San Jose Mercury News,* 1E, 4E.

Fox, E. (1988). Media policies in Latin America: An overview. In E. Fox (Ed.), *Media and politics in Latin America: The struggle for democracy* (pp. 6–35). Newbury Park, CA: Sage.

Frank, A. G. (1966, September). The development of underdevelopment. *Monthly Review, 18,* 17–31.

Frederick, H. H. (1993). *Global communication and international relations.* Belmont, CA: Wadsworth.

Frederick, H. H. (1994). Computer networks and the emergence of global civil society. In L. M. Harasim (Ed.), *Global networks: Computers and international communication* (pp. 283–295). Cambridge, MA: MIT Press.

Graham, S. and Marvin, S. (1996). *Telecommunications and the city: Electronic spaces, urban places.* London: Routledge.

Hamelink, C. J. (1994). *The politics of world communication: A human rights perspective.* Thousand Oaks, CA: Sage.

Hamelink, C. J. (1995). Information imbalance across the globe. In J. Downing, A. Mohammadi, & A. Sreberny-Mohammadi (Eds.), *Questioning the media: A critical introduction,* 2nd ed., (pp. 293–307). Thousand Oaks, CA: Sage.

Headrick, D. R. (1988). *The tentacles of progress: Technology transfer in the Age of Imperialism, 1850–1940.* New York: Oxford University Press.

Herman, E. S. (1997, September/October). The global attack on democracy, labor, & public values. *Dollars and Sense,* 10–16.

Herman, E. S., and McChesney, R. W. (1997). *The global media: The new missionaries of global capitalism.* London: Cassell.

Hoogvelt, A. (1997). *Globalization and the postcolonial world: The new political economy of development.* Baltimore, MD: Johns Hopkins University Press.

International Telecommunication Union (1998, March). *World telecommunication development report: Universal access executive summary.* Geneva: ITU (Online version).

International Telecommunication Union (1999, October). Challenges to the network: Internet for development executive summary. Online at: *http://www.itu.int/ti/publications/traffic/direct.html*

Kasarda, J. D., and Parnell, A. M. (1993). Introduction. In J. D. Kasarda, and A. M. Parnell (Eds.), *Third World cities: Problems, policies, and prospects* (pp. ix–xvii). Thousand Oaks, CA: Sage.

Knox, P. L. (1995). World Cities in a World-System. In P. L. Knox and P. J. Taylor (Eds.), *World cities in a world-system* (pp. 3–20). Cambridge: Cambridge University Press.

Landler, M. (2001, March 23). A glut of TV in India. *New York Times,* C1, C12.

Lerner, D. (1963). Toward a communication theory of modernization. In L. Pye (Ed.), *Communications and political development* (pp. 327–350). Princeton, NJ: Princeton University Press.

Louch, H., Hargittai, E., and Centeno, M. A. (1999). Phone calls and fax machines: The limits to globalization. *Washington Quarterly, 22* (2), 83–100.

MacBride, S. (1980). *Many voices, one world: Communication and society, today and tomorrow.* New York: Unipub.

McClelland, D. (1961). *The achieving society.* New York: Van Nostrand.

McDowell, S. D. (1994). International services, liberalisation, and Indian telecommunications policy. In Edward A. Comor (Ed.), *The global political economy of communication: Hegemony, telecommunication and the information economy* (pp. 103–124). New York: St. Martin's.

Oliveira, O. S. (1993). Brazilian soaps outshine Hollywood: Is cultural imperialism fading out? In K. Nordenstreng & H. I. Schiller (Eds.), *Beyond national sovereignty: International communication in the 1990s* (pp. 116–131). Norwood, NJ: Ablex.

Pendakur, M. (1991). A political economy of television: State, class, and corporate confluence in India. In G. Sussman & J. A. Lent (Eds.), *Transnational communications: Wiring the Third World* (pp. 234–262). Newbury Park, CA: Sage.

Ponting, C. (1991). *A green history of the world: The environment and the collapse of great civilizations.* New York: Penguin.

Pool, I. de S. (1966). Communication and development. In M. Weiner (Ed.), *Modernization: The dynamics of growth* (pp. 105–116). Washington, DC: Voice of America Forum Lecture Series.

Pursell, C. (1995). *The machine in America: A social history of technology.* Baltimore, MD: Johns Hopkins University Press.

Reuters (1999). In Congo, the Net precedes phone. Reproduced online by Wired News *(http://www.wired.com/news/news/business/story/17507. html),* February 19, 1999.

Reynolds, P. K. (1997). Ethics in the global community: The case of international development and implications for communication scholarship. Paper presented at the International Communication Association Conference, May 22–26, Montreal.

Rogers, E., & Antola, L. (1985). Telenovelas: A Latin American success story. *Journal of Communication, 35,* 24–35.

Rothkopf, D. (1997, Summer). In praise of cultural imperialism? *Foreign Policy,* 38–53.

Schiesel, S. (1998, July 30). Brazil sells most of state phone utility. *New York Times,* C1, C4.

Schiller, D. (1999). *Digitial capitalism: Networking the global market system.* Cambridge, MA: MIT Press.

Schwartz, H. M. (1994). *State versus markets: History, geography, and the development of the international political economy.* New York: St. Martin's.

Skinner, E. (1998). The Caribbean data processors. In G. Sussman and J. A. Lent, (Eds)., *Global productions: Labor in the making of the "Information Society"* (pp. 57–90). Cresskill, NJ: Hampton Press.

Sklair, L. (1991). *Sociology of the global system.* Baltimore, MD: The Johns Hopkins University Press.

Smith, D. A. (1996). *Third World cities in global perspective: The political economy of uneven urbanization.* Boulder: Westview.

Sussman, G. (1997). *Communication, technology and politics in the Information Age.* Thousand Oaks, CA: Sage.

Sussman, G., & Lent, J. A. (Eds.). (1991). *Transnational communications: Wiring the Third World.* Newbury Park, CA: Sage.

Sussman, G., & Lent, J. A. (Eds.). (1998). *Global productions: Labor in the making of the "Information Society."* Cresskill, NJ: Hampton Press.

Sutter, Mary (1997, March). Telmex holding its own in phone customer wars. *Journal of Commerce and Commercial,* 1A, 5A.

Thussu, D. K. (1998a). Infotainment international: A view from the South. In D. K. Thussu (Ed.), *Electronic empires: Global media and local resistance* (pp. 63–82). London: Arnold.

Traber, M., & Nordenstreng, K. (1992). *Few voices, many worlds: Toward a media reform movement.* London: World Association for Christian Communication.

United Nations. (1993). *World urbanisation prospects 1992.* New York: U.N.

UNESCO. (1997). *Statistical Yearbook, 1997.* Paris: UNESCO.

United Nations Economic and Social Council (2000). *Development and international cooperation in the twenty-first century: The role of information technology in the context of a knowledge-based global economy. Report of the Secretary-General.* (E/2000/52). New York: UNESCO.

Williams, R. (1975). *Television: Technology and cultural form.* New York: Schocken Books.

Wilson, M. (1995). The office farther back: Business services, productivity, and the offshore back office. In P. Harker (Ed.), *The service quality and productivity challenge* (pp. 203–224). Boston: Kluwer.

Winseck, D. (1997). Contradictions in the democratization of international communication. *Media, Culture & Society, 19*, 219–246.

Winston, B. (1998). *Media technology and society: A history: From the telegraph to the Internet*. London: Routledge.

CHAPTER 3

Without Ideology?
Rethinking Hegemony in the
Age of Transnational Media

Patrick D. Murphy

The first line in Emile G. McAnany and Kenton T. Wilkinson's edited volume *Mass Media and Free Trade* (1996) reads, "(s)ince the end of the cold war, trade has taken over from ideology as the focus of global attention." (p. 4). Such a declaration by critical communication scholars registers a shift away from questions of ideological hegemony and toward a preoccupation with market forces, intangible assets (concepts and brand names), virtual companies, borderlessness, franchising, et cetera; in short, the power and presence of an emerging global commercial sphere. Oddly, it is also indicative of a discourse advanced by new-age, "invisible hand" libertarians (e.g., Friedman, 1999) that many mass communication scholars now seem to share; namely that free markets disperse ideological control as economic exchange and power repel each other. But ironically it is within this global commercial sphere that mass communication has assumed a role that extends well beyond the commercial. Through a mixture of marketing, telecommunications and art, cultural norms, practices and activities are transformed into commodity forms. This social marketing dynamic draws on a human economy embedded and enmeshed in institutions, economic and noneconomic, to cultivate an ideological base for consumer culture in countries rich and poor throughout the world. And while the market place's cosmological reordering may not be materializing with uniformity from country to country or region to region, it is nevertheless pervasive enough even in its diversity to indicate that the notion of hegemonic ideology still warrants critical attention.

In this essay I argue that despite the discursive shift from ideology to market forces, globalization cannot be approached first and foremost as a trade issue by critical communication scholars. Rather, it must be seen as a phenomenon, a process, and a predicament of social organization and cultural life that articulates hegemonic power by transgressing boundaries and fragmenting audiences. These characteristics imply a certain openness in the relationship between power and experience, but as a cultural dynamic I argue that

55

globalization is fundamentally tied to ideological processes that are at work everywhere at once; that is, globally across various contexts that are quite culturally distinct. Political scientists and economists are of course correct to argue that globalization involves the integration of nation-states, markets and technologies; the internationalization and interconnection of political organization, and information systems. It is a mistake, however, to dismiss the power of global capitalism—and its chief ideological tool, corporate media conglomerates—to ideologically condition a moral order, to transform the way people conceptualize their lives, shape common sense, or even to limit the boundaries of imagination.

I am not arguing that the elaboration of this power is either automatic or final. As Gramsci and others have asserted, hegemony is never fixed once and for all (Gramsci, 1971; Artz & Ortega Murphy, 2000; Hall, 1985; Laclau & Mouffe, 1985; Mouffe 1979). However, the normative orientations and ideological bearing from which it stems are simply too provocative and ubiquitous for critical scholars, in the name of a politics of specificity, to postmodernize hegemonic theory and watch globalization from one small corner in hopes that its project will simply implode under the weight of regional cultural diversity or deconstruct via the antagonism of popular class resistance. Indeed, doesn't such a disengaged position ultimately relieve academics from any responsibility for action? Moreover, doesn't it support the charge that Western intellectual production is compliant with Western international interests (see Miyoshi, 1996; Tetzlaff, 1991; Tuhiwai Smith, 1999)? Ziauddin Sardar (1998), for one, provides a convincing argument for why we should view postmodern theory as the perfect edifice for "new" cultural imperialism and Western absorption of the Other.

It is within the current theoretical wrestling match over the modern or postmodern and micro- or macrocultural processes that I find myself in agreement with Willis (2000) in that there is a need to move away from the "dominant individualistic view" of cultural negotiation, and instead reengage the notion that cultural creativity is usually collective and socially originated, and meaning-making intrinsically framed, enabled, and constrained by powerful external structural determinants. For communication researchers such a return to structural concerns need involve a combined commitment to macro and micro questions of power and identity that move beyond singular text- or place-focused resistance and accommodation studies. In a time when many media scholars seem satisfied celebrating difference via micro assessments of postcolonism and the plurality of cultures, it is noteworthy that these calls for cultural studies connected to structural determinants are coming from anthropologists.

And if these calls are not enough, there are other, more fundamental reasons to revisit hegemonic theory in the age of globalization, such as consumer capitalism's appeal to base human instincts, and hegemonic culture's ability to appropriate subaltern expression, discard its political voice and/or commodify social issues. Consider, for instance, that the fruits of the North American market upon which globalization rests promise its participants economic security, material bounty, and personal well-being—much more than just novel ideas for much of the world's disenfranchised population, an estimated three billion of whom live on just $2 a day (Naím, 2000, p.11). Or that the culture industries both benefit from transgressive politics and devalue social experience, as they transform the cultural capital of even the most defiant, marginalized, and socially stressed communities into capitalist currency (Curtin, 1999; Frank, 1997; Stephens, 1998; Tinic, 1997).

Such facts and trends demand that we engage in a theoretical adjustment, one that involves rethinking how the postmodern processes (fragmentation, borderlessness, pastiche, textual openness, etc.) charted by so many theorists over the last couple of decades are in fact extensions of a refined and increasingly nuanced ideological hegemony. To make this adjustment politically and socially relevant, it should be framed by a careful assessment of multisited, regional processes of democratization, social repression, and exploitative agendas, the adoption of neoliberal policies, the emergence of new alliances of power, new social actors, new cultural identities, and ethnic recovery at the crossroads of accelerated underdevelopment and compulsive modernization. Research along these lines could provide a grounded understanding of:

- the interplay between structural determinism (media conglomeration, ownership, information flow, marketing, access, etc.) and everyday life (e.g., how media influence the way people see, feel, and dream about things like success, status, prestige, love, freedom, opportunity, beauty, recreation, ownership, and even struggle);
- media role in transformations in social norms and institutions (class relations, politics, sexuality, gender roles, race relations, family, religion, space, etc.);
- the relationship between media, consumption desires, and democracy;
- and the emergence of new forms of cultural expression and social interaction that reflect media use.

The study of these points of analysis are necessary because they can reveal the complex relationship between structural reorganization and cultural responses that are taking place globally. Such a project requires that critical communication scholars interrogate how the culture industries function to invite a broad range of social participation and public communication along with oppression and marginalization.

Within this context of global-local, economic-cultural, and hege-monic-subaltern reside at least five interrelated reasons to rethink hegemony and consider a reinvestment in the concept for the study of media and glob-alization. Through these five points I assert that there are two underlying themes intimately tied to the evolution of global hegemonic ideology. First, globalization does not mark a break from the exploitative relationships the West has established with the Third World; rather it reveals that current eco-nomic initiatives such as privatization and neoliberalism (increasingly artic-ulated as natural and normative) are intimately connected with colonialism and imperialism. Second, transnational media cultivates a utopian impulse, one that posits that consuming products necessarily makes life "better" and that individual identities can be enhanced (indeed, even reinvented) via the products one selects and lifestyles one adopts. This cultivation is achieved through a flexibility and creativity that can accommodate a wide range of cul-tural patterns. The key is that this flexibility and creativity are devoid of any real critical edge, and so ultimately may serve to weaken participatory democracy and naturalize the ideology of consumer capitalism even when it appears as "countercultural." I conclude the article by arguing for a renewed interest by critical scholars in questions of power and experience by resur-recting a general concern for hegemonic culture and its relation to "common sense" within global contexts.

Global Capitalism and Media Conglomeration

From a structural and historical vantage, colonialism signifies a physical occu-pation of the territory of non-Western nations. Later, cold war politics insti-tutionalized "modernization" in the Third World, signaling an occupation both political and mental in nature that has been referred to as "dependency" and "cultural imperialism" (Rodríguez & Murphy, 1997). Under the auspices of economic reforms such as privatization, and with the aid of nongovern-mental organizations (NGOs), globalization is now said to be moving in to take total possession (Barber, 1996; Chomsky, 1998; Escobar, 1995; Sardar, 1998). This possession can be linked to the ideological power of mass culture and its association with an ongoing refeudalization of politics by large organi-zations and interest groups, which continually situate the commercial logic of public relations, entertainment, and advertising in the place of more tradi-tional public communication (Dahlgren, 1995). Certainly, these converging forces do not dictate consensus, as the December 1999 WTO protests in Seattle and the Zapatista movement in Mexico have dramatically demon-strated, and oppositional groups have frequently used communication tech-nologies for their own purposes (Downing, 2001). Still, the backlash against free market reform has manifested itself more in rhetorical flourishes than in policy reform or sustained political action. For instance, protectionist threats are now commonplace around the globe, but tariffs on industrial goods continue to decline (Naím, 2000).

In the United States, commercialization of information began to take shape during the age of the press barons, but exploded during the post-World War II economic boom, when leisure time increased, and television slowly colonized living rooms, forever transforming everyday life rituals. The ensuing commercialization of leisure took form in the newly media-saturated society, eventually permitting broadcasting to harmonize, extend, and organize the "free time" of persons through interchangeable units within the industrialization of time (school time, prime time, summer vacation, etc.) (Gitlin, 2000, p. 578). By the 1960s this atmosphere was colored by a quest for authentic experience, packaged and represented as hip, bohemian, and countercultural (Frank, 1997). This initiative was marked by a cross-fertilization of various discourses (political, social, and "underground"), providing the perfect forum for the formation of consumer democracy, and facilitating a rupture of boundaries between what were previously seen as three distinct but interactive spheres: the economy, the polity, and culture. And as the political and cultural spheres were drawn into and commodified by the economic sphere, "the notion of democratic participation and individual rights found their way to the marketplace, where they were reborn in the guise of consumer sovereignty and consumer rights" (Rifkin, 2000, p. 141). Gitlin (2000) summarizes media's place in this process, arguing that through format and formula, commercial media gradually convinced us to think of ourselves and behave

> as a market rather than a public, as consumers rather than citizens. Public problems (like air pollution) are propounded as susceptible to private commodity solutions (like eyedrops). In the process, commercials acculturate us to interruption through the rest of our lives. Time and attention are not one's own: the established social powers have the capacity to colonize consciousness, and unconsciousness, as they see fit. By watching, the audience one by one consents. Regardless of the commercial's "effect" on our behavior, we are consenting to its domination of the public space. (p. 579)

Through the elaboration of this consent, a slow but powerful ideological process began to shape both a moral order and common sense, aligning the cultural practice of consumption with freedom, individuality, civil liberties, etc. In its current form, the trend described by Gitlin and others has been steered by some very significant developments in the past few years, not the least of which are media enterprise convergence, privatization and/or exploitation of public domains (as happened with the 1996 Telecommunications Act), and technological innovation that sometimes appears supported for its own sake—such as "taking classrooms into the twenty-first century" with the Internet, while student test scores fall in math, science, and English or the rise of corporate "sponsored educational materials" (SEM) freely distributed to schools and teachers. Within this environment democratic participation has come to look more and more like consumer choice, as media conglomerates claim to be just "giving people what they want" (McChesney, 1999). This trend in consumer democracy continues to gain momentum despite the fact that with the growth of mega-media corporations and thus fewer sources of information, it is becoming less possible to think of it as a real market.

Cold war politics and deficit financing assured that a "spin-off" of the metropolis' trend would find its way to the "periphery" at an early stage as both product (programming, films, music, merchandise, etc.) and infrastructure (technology, training, and personnel) (Mattelart, 1983). Not surprisingly, patterns consistent with those of the West are now characteristic in developing countries, due in no small part to the development of a global media market and related commercialization of national media systems. In the name of democracy and opening markets, "global media's news and entertainment provide an informational and ideological environment that helps sustain political, economic and moral basis for marketing good and for having a profit-driven social order" (Herman & McChesney, 1997 p. 10). Media's cultivation of this atmosphere encourages the perspective that social status is concomitant with the consumption of goods; a perspective that supports neoliberal notions that market forces rather than participatory democracy or distributive justice can bring progress.

But it is important to acknowledge that the groundwork for this apparent ideological-economic shift is not just a product of corporate strategies and neoliberalism. As Chomsky (1998) shows, contrary to dominant neoliberal doctrine, which predicts the demise of the state in the wake of economic globalization, corporate power is actually indebted to and reliant on government assistance, not fair play in the free market—a trend that has been established through political and economic initiatives applied by the West to "domesticate" societies, particularly the "service areas" (the South). The role of the state in such ventures has been essentially to socialize risk and cost, privatize power and profit, and to secure human and material resources. Ironically, the political economy of what Chomsky describes has actually benefited from the cultural absorption fears of smaller, less industrialized/developed polities. Historically, rather than being overly concerned with Americanization or Westernization, many smaller nations have been more fearful of those threats that are closer and more overtly problematic (e.g., Belize of Guatemala, Korea of Japan, Sri Lanka of India, the Baltics of Russia) (Appadurai, 1990).

Trends of conglomeration and privatization in the 1990s capitalized on the residues of this history. In terms of mass media, the result has been the emergence of a handful of transnational culture industries, particularly though not exclusively those anchored in the United States, with unprecedented control over the global flow and content of information (Albarran & Chan-Olmstead, 1998; Gershon, 1997; McAnany & Wilkinson, 1996; McChesney, 1999).

Diversification and Control

To locate ideological control or economic *hegemons* in transparent or absolute forms within this environment is no easy task, because the very collapsing of economic, cultural, and political spheres casts more than just a few shadows on the picture. For instance there is what Curtin (1999) has described as the rise of the "neo-network era" in broadcasting caused in large part by deregulation, new technologies, and relentless competition determining the power and stability of national frameworks. By decentralizing production and distribution, networks have established a dual strategy to reorganize and exploit markets. First is the elaboration of mass cultural forms aimed at broad national and global markets "that demand low involvement and are relatively apolitical (e.g., Hollywood films or broadcast television)" (p.60). The second strategy is generally comprised of much more intense and edgy fare aimed at specific niche markets with high investment in a given subculture with defined boundaries. Curtin argues that this dual strategy marks the interplay between Fordist and neo-Fordist principles, as diversification invites opportunities for the micromarket phenomenon to crossover "into a mainstream phenomenon, making it potentially exploitable through a greater number of circuits within the media conglomerate" (p. 61).

These observations become manifest internationally as indigenous (national) culture industries around the globe become linked to transnational media conglomerates through foreign direct investment, horizontal and vertical integration, joint ventures, and neoliberal reforms (Herman & McChesney, 1997). Strover, Burkart and Hernández (1999) identify specific initiatives that have fostered global-local success for media industries, such as language and content adaptations in film and television programming and working with government sponsored programs designed to promote national cultural identity or local media industries. Unauthorized initiatives such as pirate reproduction could be added to this list, as they serve to extend the ideological domain of corporate interests. But regardless of the perceived origin, the important point here is that there is a tendency towards "glocalizing" consumption, as products are often strikingly global in form and convention, even as they are appropriated and applied by corporate strategists to reflect national, traditional, or local characteristics. For example, Maynard (2000) reports that in Japan, Coke is perceived as a Japanese product because images of its culture of origin are nonexistent—a desired outcome of a "multilocal" advertising strategy. In the case of media products the origins and cultural connections are many times even more oblique because the content seems to "act local."

The impact of such multilocal strategies are even more troubling in newly industrialized nations that are the home of many "second-tier media firms," such as Mexico's Televisa, Brazil's Globo, Argentina's Clarín, and Venezuela's Cisneros Group. According to McChesney (1999), these firms

> tend to dominate their own national and regional media markets, which have been experiencing rapid consolidation as well. They have extensive ties and joint ventures with the largest media TNCs, as well as with Wall Street investment banks. . . . As a result, they tend to have distinctly pro-business political agendas and support expansion of the global media market, which puts them at odds with large segments of the population in their own home countries. (pp. 12–13)

From an ideological perspective what is significant about the developing pattern of media ownership and production and its glocalized marketing initiatives are that they obfuscate some of the previously more visible markers of class power and global imbalances of media flow and representation (e.g., foreign vs. national, North vs. South, center and periphery, external vs. internal hegemony). Moreover, within this emergent mediascape, consumption and the freedom to choose are too often presented as social indices that mark the contours of modern democratic societies: in other words, what democracy should "look like" and how it should function. In many nations this problematic develops through the privileging of the accumulation of material goods, experiences, and up-scale lifestyles as inherently democratic aspirations. This dynamic, when coupled with the "leap frogging" effect of the media (the notion that electronic media allow societies to "leap" over important social conditions such as attaining literacy for the development of an informed citizenry and public sphere) suggests that the kinds of democracies evolving in various locations are oriented first and foremost toward consumerism—a problematic in need of close study in multisited contexts.

This is not the only aspect of media's connection to global "democratization." Interestingly, while the transnational effect of media conglomeration offers nations new status in the global flow of information and ideas, it also challenges state interest in cultural sovereignty. As Latin American cultural critic Néstor García Canclini points out, processes of democratization can open up spaces where existing problems become more visible, "facilitating a plurality of voices, opening up channels for debate" (Murphy, 1997, p. 82) on multiculturalism and human rights. Such "leaks" and "slippages" in the connection between free market reform and democratization reveal that the globalizing process is not just a location of determinism and control of the powerful, and can in fact encourage subversive responses (e.g., tactics of the subaltern, the implosion of meaning, the open character of textuality, and popular culture's propensity for resistance).

Nonetheless, structures of power and social injustice do not readily crumble by themselves, and social systems of domination, no matter how dispersed and fragmented, still seek to preserve themselves. To evoke questions and concerns implicated by the collusion of corporate media and its formation of a "public" sphere grounded in consumer democracy, however, is not to turn back to classic charges of cultural imperialism. Rather, as Tetzlaff (1991) astutely argues, the ruling forces of society actually serve their position through social and semiotic fragmentation. "The parallel movements of concentration and diversification are not contradictory. On the contrary, the latter provides the basis in which the former is constituted" (p. 16). Tetzlaff continues that control is obscured, naturalized, and articulated through a diversity of activities and contents that grant limited forms of autonomy and incorporate limited rewards. This camouflaged-control is theorized to do two things essential to hegemonic leadership: First, it can help reconstitute a shared ideological commitment that surfaces from within because it is tied to multiple discourses and underlying principles that people (whether constituted collectively as a public or a market) see as ultimately beneficial. Second, it can provide parameters for what could best be called limited opposition, whereby it is possible to be oppositional locally without being oppositional globally, and vice versa.

Cultural Hybridity and the Hegemonic Echo

Between these two points, but also in conjunction with the leaks of power, is the space where neotribalism, individualism, identity politics (racial, gender, diasporic, etc.), and so forth are shaped in opposition and relation to processes of globalization. As various authors have observed (Bhabha, 1994; García Canclini, 1990, 1999; Rowe & Schelling, 1991; Stoddard & Cornwell, 1999), the "hybrid cultures" produced bear the traces of particular traditions, languages, systems of belief, and texts that have altered them, and so are often paradoxically comprised (e.g., traditional myth and commercial iconography, spiritual and pragmatic practices, scientific and magical ontologies). Such formations retain a strong identification with local notions of authenticity and places of origin. Yet to celebrate hybridity for its vitality and resistant qualities or merely to cast it aside as a sign of compromised cultural authenticity is to miss its complexity and significance. Rather, the presence of hybrid cultures should be seen as formations that underscore ideological tensions, intrusions of power, and conflicting ways of life that emerge through dual investments in "legitimate" cultural frameworks and ethnic recovery.

　　Such cultural elaborations, played-out both materially and discursively, should be approached and analyzed by critical scholars as sites of what Colombian communication scholar Jesús Martín-Barbero (1993) has described as the echo of the hegemonic within popular culture. The "echo" is an important locus of analysis because it can tell us the most about how ideological power is legitimated and customized through local-contextual practices and frameworks of belief—such as common sense. For instance it can underscore how popular memory is given new currency in modern, capitalist society and how traditional forms of expression can coexist within larger, master discourses. But it can equally demonstrate how, via the discourse of consumer capitalism, ideology penetrates even those regions and communities not geographically connected to what Latin American scholars call the *metropolis* (meaning everything from the West and the North to the region's own modern urban centers). What we find is that memory and ideology coalesce in the forms of popular practice and common sense, a process that prolongs traditional knowledge as well as reveals how hybridity functions as cultural mitigation and surfaces as a "zone of symbolic ferment where power relations are surreptitiously re-inscribed" (Kraidy, 1999, p. 460). Whether read as postmodern pastiche or ideological accommodation, the "hegemonic echoes" within hybridity need to be made primary points of analysis for researchers concerned with globalization, power, and cultural change.

Defiance and Multiculturalism in the Global Market

Not to be outdone by popular practice, global capitalism has its own version of cultural hybridity. Corporate cultural hybridity, a main corollary in the transnational processes of acquisition, diversification and control, can be defined as how "raw" cultural products such as music, fashion, and art of marginal and deviant subcultures in both developing and developed regions are mined by the culture industries and globalized for mass consumption. Consider, for instance, the global commercial success of hip-hop culture and mass fandom of rap music despite the fact that rappers regularly use localized slang and profanity to demark individuality, social location and authenticity (e.g., "the street") (McLeod, 1999). That is, counter to what many rappers and their fans would like to think, "keepin' it real" has evolved into an intangible asset for marketers to reach alternative audiences around the world that hunger for the authentic. And this is not some sort of anomaly. Rather it is quite consistent with how cultural hegemony has come to function, and function well, within the confines of free market competition.

Historically, the cultural capital and locational properties of subaltern artists and styles (e.g., political voice, circumstances of creation, artistic trajectory) have been domesticated and channeled to re-present meaning in a way that makes it accessible to broader audiences (Curtin, 1999; Miller & McHoul, 1998; Stephens, 1998). One of the more fully developed examinations of this process is provided by Frank (1997), who shows that since the 1960s a host of self-designed corporate revolutionaries have positioned rebel youth culture as the cultural mode for the corporate moment:

> Commercial fantasies of rebellion, liberation, and outright "revolution" against the stultifying demands of mass society are common place almost to the point of invisibility in advertising, movies and television programming. . . . The music industry continues to rejuvenate itself with the periodic discovery of new and evermore subversive youth movements and our televisual marketplace is a 24–hour carnival, a showplace of transgression and inversion of values, of humiliated patriarchs and shocked puritans, of screaming guitars and concupiscent youth, of fashions that are uniformly defiant, of cars that violate convention and shoes that let us be us. (pp. 4–5)

For marketers such mining of sociocultural experience is a calculation to accommodate "the market"—be it mass or niche—but surfaces rather benignly as an organic byproduct of "the marketplace of ideas" and elaborated in effort to "give people what they want." Even an apparently counterhegemonic activity such as media piracy works to support this agenda because it is predicated on reproducing productions that have already gained popular appeal locally. But in its most bizarre yet perhaps telling manifestation, commodification actually appears as a popular class reappropriation of hegemonic representations of what it means to be, for example, "Mayan," "Rastafarian," "Maori," "Hawaiian," "Punjabi," and so on. Such ironic twists in culture and consumption are salient reminders that the culture industries can control, contain, and profit from culture in the name of multiculturalism and in multilocational contexts.

And make no mistake, global capitalism and multiculturalism are effective, albeit strange, bedfellows. It is a partnership, however, not without paradoxes—chief among these the tension between voice and representations on the one hand and the corporate colonization of culture on the other. In one instance, the global institutionalization of culture illuminates difference and opens pathways for marginal segments of society to be seen and heard. But by the same token it diffuses the threatening or challenging aspects of difference and voice by camouflaging preexisting social imbalances and marginalization under the participatory veneer of consumer democracy. In other words, hegemony appears: subordinate renderings follow the political economy of corporate production and the political leadership of corporate representatives. As an example Stephens (1998) shows how Jamaican reggae artist Bob Marley was transformed by the recording industry from being connected "locally" to cultural subversion, black resistance/memory and revolutionary voice with local currency to a "global" image of racial harmony, spiritual voice, and mysticism with commercial weight.

This duplicity is anchored in a long lineage of colonial engagements, and underscores both Said's (1993) and Tuhiwai Smith's (1999) assertions that the modern West depends on its colonies for self-definition. With the move from colonialism/imperialism to transnationalism/globalization, however, is the danger that the repackaging of culture as a commodity allows consumers in the global market to freely enjoy "global culture" with usually little more than the tourist's vision of its origins. Tuhiwai Smith calls this "trading the Other," arguing that it is a

> vast industry based on the positional authority and advantages gained under imperialism. It is concerned more with ideas, language, knowledge, images, beliefs and fantasies than any other industry. Trading the Other deeply, intimately, defines Western thinking and identity. As a trade, it has no concern for the peoples who originally produced ideas or images, or how and why they produced those ways of knowing. (p. 89)

And it is important to realize that the consumers of this trade are not just upper middle-class travelers of exotic locals or university students surfing the web in search of authentic native sounds, as a wide range of international cultural goods available in almost any Mexico City *tianguis,* Moroccan *kasbah,* or Hong Kong market attests.

Reception Studies

Some writers have charged that the transnational flow of ideas and images has been detrimental to local and national cultures (e.g., Ekachai & Thirakanont, 1999; Griffin, Viswanath, & Schwartz, 1994; Sardar, 1998; Tauxe, 1993). However, from U.S. serials and romance novels to Brazilian *telenovelas* and Indian films, most media reception work indicates that audiences around the world are able to maintain creative agency over meaning construction (e.g., Gillespie, 1995; Juluri, 1999; Orozco, 1991; Parameswaran, 1999; Tufte, 1999). Moreover, reception is thought to have a more politically transformative effect in that the increased flow of ideas and images across cultural boundaries can challenge old forms of marginalization and domination, and foster a heightened awareness of debates surrounding specific issues such as social class, race, gender, ethnicity, civil rights, etc. (Fuenzalida & Hermosilla, 1989).

But influence is double edged, for just as globalizing mediations may expose economic disparities, political inconsistencies and cultural distress, the menu of ideas and images served up also increases audiences' desire to know, to experience and to emulate. Therefore, by and large most reception work leaves one asking: How truly subversive is the activity of negotiating meaning? How much agency do media consumers actually exert over the "narrative transparency" of transnational mediated texts? Sinclair, Jacka, and Cunningham (1996) argue that even the seminal reception study by Liebes and Katz, *The Export of Meaning*, fails to tie its analysis of microsituational processes to structural factors (scheduling, program philosophy, political and economic environment) that might provide further insight into audiences' meaning-making. Add to these troublesome points Tetzlaff's (1991) provocation that the textual rewards of mediated messages may just be "the bribes that ensure the subordinate's adherence to the behavioral goals of the system by providing a small measure of subjective autonomy" (p. 20). Collectively such skeptical, if not fearful, queries are worthy of further pursuit, especially as media conglomerates grow ever larger and, as Marx long ago predicted, consumer capitalism roams the planet in search of profits.

One of the first steps should involve recognizing that cultural resistance, at least the kind theorized as "emancipatory" in cultural studies over the last 15 years or so, largely fails to manifest itself against power blocks in more progressive political action or fully engage its "insurrectionary potential" (Escobar, 1995). That is, while reception studies have found that corporately produced and controlled "global" media texts may be polysemic, these texts also support processes of power and ideology that privilege certain ways of conceptualizing the world (e.g., consumer capitalism). Drawing on the work of Ann Gray and others, Justin Lewis (1999) observes that this duality is present even in "resistance studies" that celebrate the instability of meaning, arguing that if "one looks at the *evidence* within cultural studies audience research literature, there is at least as much data suggesting consent . . ." (p. 252, his emphasis). In fact, using the United States as an example, an argument could be made that the current procorporate hegemony is sustained through a loose and open yet inevitable myth of democratic fairness, and thus is in large part actually indebted to popular resistance that is not engaged vigorously in political activity. Could this dynamic be one of the essential ingredients of the success of transnational, hegemonic discourses?

Self-definition in Transnational Hegemonic Culture

From the points provided above it is possible to get a sense of how hegemonic power is predicated on and articulated through complex kinds of interdeterminacy. That is, the reproduction and maintenance of hegemonic culture is determined by more than one underlying structure or dynamic. For media planning, production, and distribution, multiculturalism is tied to cultural frameworks of integrated and diversified economic initiatives that depend on political power to maintain unregulated, financially secure, and low-risk markets. Because these hegemonic relations are manifold, we could describe alternatively how the web of interdeterminacy is linked together and articulated, the more important point being that the series of complex interrelationships is what enables globalization to conquer, and conquer rather seamlessly, sociocultural obstacles. This is also what provides the fodder for cultural transformations around the world, and thus is responsible in part for their postmodern feel—a condition that has been described in terms of hybridity, hyperreality, deterritorialization, simulacra, intertextuality, and so on.

No matter how interlaced, manifold, or hyperreal they may seem, hegemonic processes are predicated on a structure of dominance in that they reflect certain tendencies, discourses, and institutional frames, and have certain identifiable configurations. In the age of globalization these points of dominance are anchored in free-market capitalism as master narrative. For such reasons, as Hall (1985) reminded us many years ago, "structure" remains an important area for critical inquiry. For critical theorists working through and concerned with contemporary questions of culture and power, the task then becomes a rather tricky one: how to maintain critical attention to questions of macro narratives of power and structure while also recognizing diversity, uncertainty, processes of disorder, and the play of local, pluralistic contexts that often inspire cultural creation—as various researchers from different global vantage points have recently observed (García Canclini, 1999; Juluri, 1999; Kraidy, 1999; Stoddard & Cornwell, 1999).

My reaction to such a critical task, dually marked by the residues of neo-Marxist thought and postmodern dilemmas, is to ask who or what do global media audiences rely on for self-definition? This is a deceivingly simple question, but suggests a number of research trajectories. For example, we could focus on the audience as a civil construct, which would turn our attention toward questions of how audience members align themselves and are aligned by public communication, and its ties to nationalism, social station, class condition, media policy, regulation, program funding, private institutions, freedom and constraints of information flow and access, alternative media, and the role of (or potential for elaborating) a public sphere. Or, as a means to gauge the ideological limits of transnational commercial culture, media audiences could be approached as markets. In this case we might analyze audiences' relationship with marketing strategies and the role of big company marketers as spiritual leaders and public myth tellers that ascribe cultural values to products, services, and experiences by playing on the interpretive schemes and dreams of audience members (e.g., personal autonomy, acceptance, love, self-esteem, good friendships, leisure time, and sex) (Applbaum, 1998; Jhally, 1995). Another inroad to the study of self-definition is that of the interpretive community. Here social place, space, and community relations are pivotal constructs, as they frame the negotiation of meaning (e.g., class identity, identification, para-social interaction, pleasure, resistance) in terms of presentation of self and the sharing and alteration of cultural codes. These kinds of study have contributed greatly to our understanding of audience activity, but are often either text-led or wholly focused on the sociology of reception. More integrated, long-term studies that collapse this gap have recently been produced (e.g., Gillespie, 1995; Mankekar, 1999; Tufte, 2000) and suggest positive directions in the study of media reception. However, there remains a need for critical communication researchers (other research traditions have been doing this "objectively" for years) to extend the notion of interpretive community to studies of production personnel; that is, who and what do production personnel *as a community* in TV, film, news, music video, or Web design align themselves with as part of their creative process? Ethnographic study of production communities could provide insights on what forces and constraints shape the creative process of production, the intricacies of program decision-making, the worldview of professional/managerial personnel and the creation, maintenance, and alteration of representations.

Finally we could fix our interpretive gaze on the relationship between the symbolic power of media institutions, cultural practice, and what some prominent theorists have called "common sense" (Geertz, 1983; Hall, 1995). Of the four investigative trajectories presented here—and these are by no means exhaustive—I believe that this particular focus has received the least amount of attention, yet it is the most critical area of analysis, if we are truly to get a grip on what is really going on when we talk about globalization. The dearth in research on common sense and globalization is not surprising because it is quite a slippery concept and difficult to operationalize. Where or how does one study common sense, for instance? Can we access common sense via a series of in-depth, phenomenological interviews of various members of interpretive communities? Do we emphasize the common sense nature of material life in terms of its performativity (e.g., street art, music, clothing, architecture, alternative media, film, and other forms of storytelling from the margins of society)? Or do we return to and apply the ethnographic notion of long-term participant observation—absent in the vast majority of reception work—to media consumption. And with all of these trajectories, how can we develop complex and rigorous multisited interpretations that reveal patterns and the depth of globalization?

Why Bother with Common Sense?

If our concern as critical scholars remains the connection between power and experience, such methodological dilemmas need to be worked out because there are some compelling arguments for considering the capacity of common sense to exhibit how hegemonic ideology is naturalized, challenged and/or transmuted in cultural life. First of all, there is Hall's (1995) view that ideology works by constructing for individual and collective subjects "positions of identification and knowledge which allow them to 'utter' ideological truths as if they were their authentic authors" (p. 19). He asserts that this is not because these utterances emanate from the subjects' innermost, authentic, and unified experience, but rather because people formulate intentions "within" and "speak through" ideology. And there is Geertz's (1983) assertion that as a cultural system common sense "rests on the same basis that any other such system rests: the convictions by those whose possession of it is its value and validity" (p. 76) and is "not what the mind cleared of can't spontaneously apprehend; it is what the mind filled with presuppositions concludes" (p. 84). In short, we are talking here about common sense's ontological status.

But focusing on common sense to locate the presence of a hegemonic echo is no simple task. It requires close, long-term study of research communities and collective ways of knowing, and thus requires an isolation and characterization of its stylistic features (what Geertz calls "tonalities"). This involves seeking out common-sense practices, and the elaboration and defense of truth claims of colloquial reason; a global research trajectory of self-definition that ultimately leads us to look for global colloquialisms. This notion may sound humorous, but what it implies is how hegemonic constructs are echoed in common sense as a form of cultural investment—a dynamic much more dense in form and practice than most postmodernists would lead us to believe, as ideology tends to "disappear from view into the taken-for-granted 'naturalized' world of common sense" (Hall, 1995, p. 19). The challenge for researchers thus becomes to ferret out how the worldview expressed reveals ideological fragments (e.g., value system and moral direction) from varying institutional sources, and how that view is maintained and customized through social relationships within various global contexts.

Questions that should be taken up in light of these conceptualizations of common sense involve discursive unity, cultural productivity, aesthetic preferences, the internalization and legitimization of social differences and class divisions, as well as the role of confrontational representations. For instance, how do interpretive communities come to know the interplay between power, agency, and experience as their own subjective, collective struggle complete with recognizable barriers and rewards? How are ideological elements fixed to and acquire class, regional, and/or community characteristics? How does media's circulation of ideas and images inscribe viewers into the global hegemony of consumer culture if it also provokes a critical consciousness of social disparities, ethnic hierarchies, and global imbalances? What role does popular memory play globally in confronting and/or altering hegemonic power? What patterns and emerging practices can link common sense to something that we can define as a lived global culture? These are some of the broader questions that could be approached. More specifically we could ask how do interpretive communities develop nostalgia for something never experienced, adopt notions of masculinity that break with cultural mores, exhibit novel sexuality in the face of traditional cultural norms, or learn to use aggression for problem solving?

And what of other dynamics? For instance what does it mean if the popular classes around the world do indeed invest in their own traditions in relation to media consumption (e.g., cultural reconversion)? Does it imply that they continue to live within the boundaries of localized sense of community yet at the same time begin to understand "cultural resistance" (and thus implicitly, political) as the re-invention of tradition? If so, what does it mean if and when that resistance surfaces in the form of corporate logos or mass produced hip-hop styles? Are such appropriations merely ways to express "rebellion," or do these investments instanciate more troubling connections, say an understanding of "freedom" and "democracy" in terms of the ability to choose consumer goods and services, or "pleasure" as a matter of material accumulation.

Does the introduction of Western ideals about "human rights" as concomitant with individual civil rights undermine non-Western notions of collectively? If so, what can the pervasiveness of such common sense trends suggest about the potential for political struggle, self determination, the elaboration of a public sphere, of community life, resource control and management, the funds through which artistic and aesthetic trends are developed and guided, or even the politics of imagination?

Remaining Critical

Can we continue to see these cultural battle grounds as little more than postmodern hybridity with human agency and consciousness safe within the interplay between globalization, cultural diversity and multiple, border crossing selves? It is hard to see how, as clearly consumer capitalism is the master discourse of globalization, secured, developed and administered through a complex web of corporate and political power. While maintaining a postmodern facade, this web is actually quite reminiscent of the historical-hegemonic blocs described by Gramsci (1971) in that they are in competition and dependent on popular culture to modify and renew their power and acquire support. Thus culture, in its most flexible, global sense, is both the medium and means through which this evolving global hegemony feeds.

If we accept that issues of power and experience are of utmost importance for the study of media and globalization, then the reason for rethinking the utility of hegemonic theory lies in its ability to remain engaged in the political and the cultural, the structural and the everyday. Moreover, maintaining a critical focus on hegemonic power is perhaps more important than ever because it interrogates the very bill of goods that free market capitalism is selling to the world, and how global communities are negotiating a transnational metropolitan-based master discourse of consumer democracy. And finally, a commitment to interrogate hegemonic culture invokes two long-standing concerns of critical scholars: first, how systems of domination are maintained and social order preserved; second, how the power and presence of hegemonic ideology does not rest on the passivity nor subjugation of the popular classes, but rather the active appropriation and negotiation of meaning. New investigations need to re-engage these concerns by examining how global hegemony is echoed in common sense patterns of socialization, canons of style, and self-representations, tastes, art, and language. Inquiries that explore these investments may not be as stimulating as analyzing populist movements or peasant insurrections (e.g., the Zapatista movement in Chiapas) or as entertaining as demonstrating the deconstructive potential of postmodern parody. However, they are perhaps more important, and in many respects more difficult to chart, because mechanisms of domination and subordination are often camouflaged in hybridity and can indicate shifts, even ruptures, with traditions that are often too subtle to immediately discern. Excavating these layers of meaning should be (actually, *remain*) the job of the researchers concerned with media, cultural and globalization's relations to power.

Acknowledgments

Special thanks to Lee Artz, Nick Couldry, and Timothy D. Murphy for their helpful criticisms on earlier drafts.

References

Albarran, A. B. & Chan-Olmstead, S. M (Eds.). (1998). *Global media economics. Commercial concentration and integration of world media markets.* Ames, Iowa: Iowa State University Press.

Appadurai, A. (1990). Disjuncture and difference in the global economy. *Public Culture, 2* (2), 1–24.

Applbaum, K. (1998). The sweetness of salvation: Consumer marketing and the Liberal-Bourgeois Theory of Needs. *Current Anthropology, 13,* 323–349.

Artz, L., & Murphy, B. O. (2000). *Cultural hegemony in the United States.* Thousand Oaks: Sage.

Barber, B. R. (1996). *Jihad vs. McWorld.* New York: Ballantine Books.

Bhabba, H. (1994). *The location of culture.* Routledge: London.

Chomsky, N. (1998). Power in the global arena. *New Left Review, 230,* 3–27.

Curtin, M. (1999) Feminine desire in the age of satellite television. *Journal of Communication, 49* (2), 55–70.

Dahlgen, P (1995). *Television and the public sphere.* Thousand Oaks: Sage.

Downing, J. D. H. (2001) *Radical media.* Thousand Oaks: Sage.

Ekachai, D., & Thirakanont, A. (1999, November). Women in magazine advertising: Domination of Western beauty in Thailand. Paper presented at the National Communication Association Conference, Chicago, IL.

Escobar, A. (1995). *Encountering development: The making and unmaking of the Third World.* Princeton: University of Princeton.

Frank, T. (1997). *The conquest of cool.* Chicago: University of Chicago Press.

Friedman, T. L. (1999). *The Lexus and the olive tree.* New York: Farrar, Stauss and Giroux.

Fuenzalida, V., & Hermosilla, M. E. (1989). *Visiones y ambiciones del televidente.* Santiago: CENECA.

García Canclini, N. (1990). *Culturas híbridas.* Mexico, D.F.: Grijalbo.

García Canclini, N. (1999). *La globalización imaginada.* Mexico, D.F.: Paidos.

Geertz, C. (1983). *Local knowledge.* New York: Basic Books.

Gershon, R. A. (1997). *The transnational media corporation: Global messages and free market competition.* Mahwah, NJ: Lawrence Erlbaum Associates.

Gillespie, M. (1995). *Television, ethnicity and cultural change.* London: Routledge.

Gitlin, T. (2000). Prime time ideology. In H. Newcomb (Ed.), *Television, the critical view* (pp. 574–594). Oxford: Oxford University Press.

Gramsci, A. (1971). *Selections from the prison notebooks* (Q. Hoare & G. N. Smith, Trans.). New York: International Publishers. (Original work published in 1947).

Griffin, M., Viswanath, K., & Schwartz, D. (1994). Gender advertising in the U.S. and India: Exporting cultural stereotypes. *Media, Culture and Society, 16,* 487–507.

Hall, S. (1985). Signification, representation, ideology: Althusser and the post-structuralist debates. *Critical Studies in Mass Communication, 2* (2), 91–114.

Hall, S. (1995). The whites of their eyes: Racist ideologies and the media, In G. Dines & J. M. Humez (Eds.) *Gender, race and class in media* (pp. 18–22). Thousand Oaks, CA: Sage.

Herman, E. S., & McChesney, R. W. (1997). *The global media.* London and Washington: Cassell.

Jhally, S. (1995). Image based culture. In G. Dines & J. M. Humez (Eds.) *Gender, race and class in media* (pp. 77–87). Thousand Oaks, CA: Sage.

74   *Patrick D. Murphy*

Juluri, V. (1999). Global weds local: The reception of *Hum Aapke Hain Koun, European Journal of Cultural Studies, 2,* 231–248.

Kraidy, M. (1999). The global, the local, and the hybrid: A native ethnography of glocalization. *Critical Studies in Mass Communication, 16,* 456–476.

Laclau, E. & Mouffe, C. (1985). *Hegemony and socialist strategy.* London: Verso

Lewis, J. (1999). Reproducing political hegemony in the United States. *Critical Studies in Mass Communication, 16,* 51–267.

Mankekar, P. (1999). *Screening culture, viewing politics.* Durham: Duke University Press.

Martín-Barbero, J. (1993). Latin American cultures in communication media. *Journal of Communication, 43* (2), 18–30.

Mattelart, A. (1983). *Transnationals and the Third World.* Massachusetts: Bergin & Garvey Publishers, Inc.

Maynard, M. (2000, October) Image making in the global age: Communicating always (and not always) Coca-Cola to Japanese Teens. Paper presented at Global Fusion 2000 Conference, St. Louis, Missouri.

McAnany, E. G., & Wilkinson, K. T. (Eds.). (1996). *Mass media and free trade.* Austin: University of Texas Press.

McChesney, R. W. (1999, November 29). The new global media. *The Nation,* pp. 11–15.

McLeod, K. (1999). Authenticity within hip-hop and other cultures threatened with assimilation, *Journal of Communication, 49* (4), 134–150.

Miller, T., & McHoul, A. (1998). *Popular culture and everyday life.* Sage: London.

Miyoshi, M. (1996). A borderless world? From colonialism to transnationalism and the decline of the nation-state. In R. Wilson & W. Dissanayake (Eds.), *Global/local: Cultural production and the transnational identity* (pp. 78–106). Durham, N.C.: Duke University Press.

Mouffe, C. (1979). Hegemony and ideology in Gramsci. In C. Mouffe (Ed.), *Gramsci and Marxist theory* (pp. 1–24). Boston: Routledge and Kegan Paul.

Murphy, P. D. (1997) Contrasting perspectives: Cultural studies in Latin America and the United States: A conversation with Néstor García Canclini. *Cultural Studies, 11,* 78–88.

Naím, M. (2000). Editor's note. *Foreign Policy, 118,* 11–12.

Orozco, G. (1991). La audiencia frente a la pantalla. *Dia-logos de Comunicación, 30,* 54–73.

Parameswaran, R. (1999). Western romance fiction as English-language media in postcolonial India, *Journal of Communication, 49* (3), 84–105.

Rifkin, J. (1998). *The age of access.* New York: Farrar, Straus & Giroux.

Rodríguez, C., & Murphy, P. D. (1997). The study of communication and culture in Latin America: From laggards and the oppressed to resistance and hybrid cultures. *The Journal of International Communication, 4* (2), 24–45.

Rowe, W., & Schelling, V. (1991). *Memory and modernity: Popular culture in Latin America.* New York: Verso.

Said, E. (1993). *Culture and imperialism.* New York: Knopf.

Sardar, Z. (1998). *Postmodernism and the other: The new imperialism of Western culture.* Pluto Press.

Sinclair, J., Jacka, E., & Cunningham, S. (Eds.). (1996) *New patterns in global television.* Oxford: Oxford University Press.

Stephens, M. A. (1998). Babylon's 'Natural Mystic': The North American music industry, the legend of Bob Marley, and the incorporation of transnationalism. *Cultural Studies, 12,* 139–167.

Stoddard, E., & Cornwell, G. H. (1999). Cosmopolitan or mongrel? Créolité, hybridity and 'douglarisation' in Trinidad. *European Journal of Cultural Studies, 2,* 331–353.

Strover, S., Burkart, P., & Hernandez, O. (1999, June). Transnationalism in spaces and places: Global media industries in Latin America. Paper presented at the NAFTA/Mercosur Conference, University of Texas, Austin.

Tauxe, C. S. (1993). The spirit of Christmas: Television and commodity hunger in a Brazilian election. *Public Culture, 5,* 593–604.

Tetzlaff, D. (1991). Divide and conquer: Popular culture and social control in late capitalism. *Media, Culture and Society, 13* (1), 9–33.

Tinic, S. A. (1997). United colors and untied meanings: Benetton and the commodification of social issues. *Journal of Communication, 47* (3), 3–25.

Tufte, T. (2000). *Living with the rubbish queen: Telenovelas, culture and modernity in Brazil.* London: University of Luton Press.

Tuhiwai Smith, L. (1999). *Decolonizing methodologies.* New York: St. Martin's Press.

Willis, P. (2000). *The ethnographic imagination.* Chicago: University of Chicago Press.

PART II

Adjusting Hegemony
in the Globalizing North

CHAPTER 4

The "Battle in Seattle": U.S. Prestige Press Framing of Resistance to Globalization

Tamara Goeddertz and Marwan M. Kraidy

Globalization affects the wealthy industrialized countries and the developing world in different ways. According to Giddens (1990), it is the "intensification of worldwide social relations which link distant localities in such a way that local happenings are shaped by events occurring many miles away and vice versa" (p. 64). These intensified international relations lead to struggles to incorporate the meaning of global issues into the context of national and/or local life. Among the numerous concerns raised by the globalization process are the questions of the international economy, how it is presented by the First World countries into Third World areas, and its effect on global trading efforts. As a result, it is important to examine how globalization is depicted in the mass media. The World Trade Organization (WTO) meeting in Seattle, Washington, in 1999, and the demonstrations opposing it, was a key historical moment in the process of globalization, a juncture of articulation of a hegemonic process and a counterhegemonic resistance. More importantly, the examination of the coverage of the Seattle demonstrations brings issues of social class to the foreground of the discussion on globalization.

The WTO meeting and the demonstrations in Seattle, or "the battle in Seattle" as it came to be known, provides an excellent context for the examination of the framing of globalization by the so-called prestige press, opinion making, major city dailies. This chapter specifically deals with the depiction of the WTO conference in Seattle, Washington, by the *Washington Post* from November 1999 through December 1999. As the leading daily paper in the political center of the United States, and as one of the elite U.S. newspapers of record, the *Washington Post* tends to reflect the prevailing views of the U.S. political elite—what has been dubbed the neoliberal "Washington Consensus." In order to present a narrative sense of the coverage, we analyze articles in the time period prior to the advent of WTO talks, the period during the talks, and finally the aftermath and evaluation of the events discussed in the print media.

A close analysis of these articles reveals the underlying structure of hegemonic relations through the use of print media, illustrating the framing techniques employed in order to project a manufactured ideology to the general public. The stripping of layers from these articles through a critical reading poses questions about the discourses framing the WTO talks and demonstrations in Seattle. In what direction do these discourses likely sway public opinion? To what extent are the media frames compatible with the mainstream acceptance of globalization and free trade in the United States? Other questions evolving from this inquiry include: What are the reasons for the employment of media frames? How does the use of specific framing techniques shape the coverage of the WTO talks and demonstrations in Seattle? And what impact do these media frames likely have on public opinion in the United States? These questions will be considered throughout the length of the chapter, and the discussion will concentrate on the implications of the media framing of the "Battle in Seattle" as an effort of resistance to globalization.

The "battle in Seattle" is a crucial historical juncture that exposed the profound conflicts triggered by the neoliberal agenda and that unmasked the myth of the supremacy of the ideology of globalization. The protestors on the streets, the officials involved in the talks, and the political implications for a United States approaching an election year set the stage for an explosion on the global front. It is globalization in the form of a physical and visible event, the coming together of worldwide workers and officials in a struggle for meaning on several levels that becomes tangible to the public through the eyes of the *Washington Post*. This chapter will illustrate how the newspaper frames reinforce the prevailing ideology of globalization and free trade.

Hegemony, Media Frames, and the Construction of Consent

The strong private and public ties between the media and the political realm have the ability to determine the shape of public opinion. In order for hegemony to unite the public, there needs to be a majority of consent for its ideology. If the general public does not support the ideal presented by the dominant political forces, consent has to be manufactured by the framing of events through the media, in addition to the "spin" industry of strategic communications. In this way, the prestige press fulfills an important role in supporting hegemonic discourses such as globalization.

Hegemony is an adequate framework for examining the process through which the media frames stories in order to promote the dominant ideology. First coined by Gramsci as "common sense," (Brandist, 1996), the hegemonic process builds consent by discursively aligning the public interest with the interest of the elite. This process leaves only a limited number of choices for public response—choices that have been filtered and approved by the dominant ideology—from which the public then forms an opinion. However, since the options have been narrowed prior to public exposure, the freedom of choice is substantially limited, thus offering less active alternatives.

Public discourse is thus influenced to ensure the compatibility of public opinion with the viewpoint of economic and political interests. Hence, through the framing tactics of the media—the language used and "objective" reporting techniques employed—the public is led to believe in a system of free choice, while the influences of discursive communication methods help to control freedom of thought. This becomes especially important in considering the position of the media, aligned with the political interests of the industrialized West, during such a global event as the World Trade Organization talks in Seattle, Washington. Nationally, the way in which the mass media portray the talks and demonstrations and the issues at hand will influence public sentiment, thus paving political agendas for both the United States on the global level, and the future platforms of Democratic, Republican, and other politicians on the state and national level.

The mass media frame the WTO talks and demonstrations in order to mobilize public opinion in support of the interests of largely Western-controlled transnational corporations. The global industries of the corporate West depend on the labor and affect the environment where the working and middle classes of both the West and the non-West live. Therefore, the importance of the outcome of global talks, such at the WTO conference, becomes vital to the interests of the corporate West. The way in which the WTO meetings, the officials involved, and the conflicts, both without and within the walls of the conference, are presented through the media will determine the public opinion formed on critical global issues. The protestors and the global issues at stake are therefore depicted on several different fronts in line with the mainstream political agenda.

Condit (1994) modifies Gramsci's original theory of hegemony for use in modern society. Condit provides additional considerations for advanced communication technology, such as the Internet and mass media, as well as the inclusion of the multicultural population within the United States. This poses certain constraints upon the hegemonic process, requiring the accommodation of several ethnic groups and minority viewpoints within public discourse. As a result, Condit proposes the "model of concordance" to describe the American hegemonic situation of today. Condit's model of concordance replaces Gramsci's economic universalism with a mode of social concordance defined as "the active or passive acceptance of a given social policy or political framework as the best that can be negotiated under given conditions" (Condit, 1994, p. 210). However, Condit also notes the expense of mass media time required for the exposure and promotion of any ideological perspective to solicit public support. Consequentially, the ability of minority or marginal perspectives to garner support is hindered by the prohibitive cost of media time. In this way, the dominant ideology reigns without serious challenges from ethnic minorities, the working classes, and other "foreign" cultures. Thus the hegemonic process is upheld, at least in media frames.

The combination of these hegemonic ideas illustrates hegemony as in Gramsci's idea of an elite group in control of an ideology, through the rhetorical use of language (Brandist, 1996) and discourse in the mass media, including Condit's (1994) consideration of multicultural viewers. These messages are then dis-embedded from their original context and reembedded to form new meaning within society, thus becoming an acceptable commodity to the viewing public (Giddens, 1990). Meaning is now a socially constructed entity, put forth and supported by the dominant ideologies of a society through the process of hegemony. This basic understanding of the hegemonic process allows an in-depth analysis of framing tactics used in the *Washington Post*, in an attempt to examine the media frames in support of the dominant ideology at work in society.

Protestors, Power and Representation:
Media Frames of the WTO

Coverage of the "Battle in Seattle" took center stage in print news media during the months of November 1999 through December 1999. Although several main issues at the conference were covered, they were reported in such a way as to leave readers with only a vague idea as to the details and importance of each matter. In this way, the print media worked to enforce a political agenda, calling for the support of the corporate West in global economic affairs. The little information printed about the WTO issues was overshadowed by details about the protestors on the streets of Seattle, thus causing a distraction from the central concerns of the conference. In this way, the media encouraged public support of the globalization agenda while revealing very few details about these matters, positioning the readers in opposition to the demonstrators, and thus in support of the U.S. position with the WTO.

Our research, which analyzed 15 articles from the *Washington Post*, the United States' capital prestige newspaper, uncovered three main themes frame the coverage of the "Battle in Seattle," each contributing and encouraging public support of the United States in global economic affairs. The first theme presents the protests in the streets of Seattle as a misguided effort by demonstrators, concentrating on the deviance and violence occurring during the WTO meetings. The second theme equates American corporate interests to democratic representations of the United States on a global level, thus working to legitimize American involvement in the economies of Third World countries. The third theme connects and extends the second, setting up a dichotomy of the Third World versus the First World countries. This involves and underscores issues of Western-controlled transnational corporations, and presents Third World countries as a foreign "other" in the corporate quest for globalization. Each of these themes will be examined through the articulation of the demonstrations with the globalization discourse in the *Washington Post*.

Demonstrations as a Misguided Effort

The *Washington Post*'s concentration on the protestors as deviant overshadowed and dismissed the issues initiating the concern about global trade issues. The demonstrations were characterized and labeled by the *Washington Post* as nothing more than "street theater groups from all over the country" (Burgess, 1999b, p. E1), delaying talks between international officials and wasting valuable time, while the global economy spun beyond control. U.S. president William Jefferson Clinton took his stab at the protestors, while promoting the WTO, calling the demonstrations "rather interesting hoopla" noting that "the open-trade policies that triggered the outbursts . . . will benefit the average person in America and elsewhere in the long run" (Babington & Burgess, 1999, p. A1). The coverage left the average reader without adequate explanation of the reasons behind the demonstrations, leading to the conclusion that the demonstrations were nothing more than an unnecessary disturbance to important global affairs. Thus, the WTO meetings and U.S. and Western involvement within the global economy are indirectly supported by the general public through the rejection of protestors' activity. The explanation for the angry protests and demonstrations were quietly pushed aside as the media adhered to political agendas, while belittling the demonstrations as "a noisy backdrop of street protests by people who believe that the current global system destroys jobs and harms the environment" (Burgess, 1999, p. A1).

The *Washington Post* branded the protestors as the perpetrators of the trouble in Seattle, a city which is "usually the serene capital in the Pacific Northwest," leaving "wounds that city leaders say will not heal soon" (Sanchez, 1999, p. AO2). Instead of the workers worldwide as the victims of the neoliberal trade regime, it was the city of Seattle shown to have suffered throughout the WTO meetings. "Downtown businesses are reeling from vandalism and a week of lost revenue, and residents who were not partaking in the protest against the trade group are incensed that they got caught in a cross-fire of tear gas, pepper spray, and rubber bullets" (Sanchez, 1999, p. AO2). The rhetoric in this excerpt is reminiscent of stereotypical media frames of urban street gang violence, with innocent victims/citizens trapped in the violence. The cause of the protests, while at times touched upon in the articles, remains virtually unexplained to the general public, characterizing the demonstrations as pointless in both thought and action. The *Washington Post* focused on the limited violence, despite the fact that the protests were largely peaceful, and almost no effort was made to articulate the issues at the center of the demonstrations intelligibly. Similarly, no effort was made to identify the social, political, and demographic constituencies represented by the protestors, mainly the working classes.

An article claims that Clinton and other officials blamed Tuesday night's disturbance on a relative handful of violence-bent demonstrators. The quoted official said, "their actions overshadowed the peaceful messages by labor union activists and others who contend that free trade undermines environmental safeguards and workers' rights" (Babington & Burgess, 1999, p. A1). Yet no dock worker, secretary, or farm worker was substantively quoted by the *Washington Post*, not even the anarchists, those colorful protagonists so vital to the *Post's* frame, were given the opportunity to express their concerns or articulate their agenda. The only voice the protestors were given throughout the WTO talks was from the reporters concentrating on the violence, dismissing the central issues to the margins of public discourse while keeping the limited vandalism at the center. Patricia Davis, president of the Washington Council on International Trade rejected the plea from protestors, noting "the militants [are] protesting an economic system they've very much bought into . . . they all have cell phones, they all have pagers . . . they're all wearing the best of clothing from around the world . . . they're all driving vehicles that are made all over the place" (Burgess, 1999, p. E1). Again, the voices of the largely working-class and student protestors are lost in the concentration on their physical presence in the streets—their appearance, their behavior, and their exercised right to protest. The accusation of hypocrisy with the assorted use of labels such as "militants" and "parades" leaves the central issues behind the protests virtually untouched.

The following questions arise: Are the reporters relieved from their objective duties because of the supposed danger surrounding the demonstrations? And does this open the door for a more concentrated focus on corporate concerns in order to encourage the dominant ideology of Western-controlled transnational corporate interests, allowing another framing tactic to emerge to support economic globalization? The next theme found within the *Washington Post* articles addresses these questions.

Framing Trade as an Engine of Democracy

Lewis (1999) notes that the United States claims to be the epitome of democracy for the world to imitate. The American polity is held as the greatest democratic success in history, with freedom as its bottom line. In turn, the image of the United States as the epitome of democracy is used in the *Washington Post* to promote globalization and free trade as a democratizing movement in the international economy, as "WTO director General Mike Moore argued that the current world trading system benefits just about everyone . . . over 30 countries—1.5 billion people—want to join the WTO" (Burgess, 1999b, p. E1), offering the freedom of a democratic, capitalistic society to the world. President Clinton clearly supports this democratic notion, claiming that "increasing economic cooperation is in the interest of the ordinary citizens of the United States and the rest of the world" (Babington & Burgess, 1999, p. A1). Clearly, the commentary on the free trade issues is biased in favor of free trade and the promotion of the WTO. It is important to understand the meaning of this commentary and the influence it has upon public opinion. The *Washington Post* has framed the issue of world trade as an endeavor enhancing democratization around the world, invoking nationalistic feelings about being proud to export democracy.

The globalization discourse is given historical, mythical foundations: "There is a long history of this faith in open trade, proponents say. The 13 American colonies, all proud of their distinct identities, created a historic experiment in democracy; they also created one of the world's first free trade zones" (Burgess, 1999, p. A1). The democratic success of the original 13 American colonies is used to promote corporate interests worldwide, as an example of how nations around the world can imitate the achievements of the American dream and feelings of nationalism. If the public feels America is doing good by bringing capitalism to developing countries, Western-controlled transnational corporations can proceed in global business, i.e. world trade.

A prime example of this sentiment is illustrated by the American involvement with China, a Communist country and a reemerging global power. Commerce Secretary William Daley says, "It is in our best interest if we see a different China into the next century . . . a main way we can do that is to do more trade with China" (Burgess, 1999, p. A1), establishing a clear connection between democratization and the corporate interests of America. The way to democratize the world is through the American corporate interests by way of free trade among the nations of the world, exporting American ideologies and ideals to foreign countries for adoption by the local peoples. This, in turn, intensifies globalization worldwide, thus equating the notions of corporate interests to democracy, democracy to free trade, and free trade to globalization. It is the hope of the elite press to reduce globalization into this simple equation for the general public, offering the most basic understanding to garner support for this chaotic process. However, globalization is not as elementary as the *Washington Post* would have one believe; it involves a global revolution in free trade, affecting all social classes from the elite and down on the hierarchy.

To succeed, globalization has to be accepted, albeit begrudgingly, in circles beyond economists and the corporate world. It is crucial that the neoliberal trade regime be explained to the masses in terms favorable to its continuation, since "[G]lobalization is a maddeningly elusive foe. The bundle of forces that it connotes—mobile capital, mobile labor, mobile goods" are only a narrow scope of the globalization process, yet it is the focus and explanation given to the general public. The corporate interests and ideologies of the American elite initiate a rhetoric, which equates globalization, democracy, and the economy, three denotatively different ideas, for the purpose of promoting dominant ideologies befitting of their political agendas.

"Third World" vs. "First World": America and the "Others"

The preceding frames point towards the American influence on and benefits from a free trade agreement through the WTO. The political agenda in the West, and in the United States in particular, is to persuade all countries of the benefits involved in free trade in order to push public opinion in support of the World Trade Organization. As a result, the media has portrayed Western capitalistic expansion as a democratization process—an opportunity for developing countries to gain political and financial freedom. Countries rejecting this ideology have been positioned in a dichotomy, as opponents of the United States, and presented as "other" in the *Washington Post*. The contradictions inherent in globalization are also discussed, but not at length, such as in this excerpt:

> These issues are part of the paradox of a single world economy. Such an economy can generate enormous wealth, as countries specialize in products and sell to the planet at large. It can also blur distinctive food, dress and lifestyles of countries, push financial panics across borders at fiber-optic speed, and move decisions once made at home to faceless executives thousands of miles away. (Burgess, 1999, p. A1)

The outcome of the free trade agreements is framed as a trade-off. The Western-controlled transnational corporations market globalization as a process that will free underdeveloped countries from the depths of poverty, producing more jobs, more money, and more democracy. These awards, which represent the appeal of consumer capitalism, come at the unique cost of eroding cultural traditions and social standards. Ironically, while offering increased control to impoverished peoples through capitalism, these same people relinquish control of the wealth, which they produce, to the Western-controlled transna-

tional corporations. It is an interesting paradox—the price of democratic freedom is the loss of national or cultural identity.

However, the news frames in the *Washington Post* focus on overriding
these concerns with a happy face, depicting this trade-off as beneficial and
benign. Thus one reporter writes that "[I]f an agreement is reached, each
country would, in effect, undertake to trust its neighbors a bit more. At the
same time, the deal would be crafted in such a way that each country would
believe that it had defended its sovereign uniqueness" (Burgess, 1999, p.
A1). This is a definition of hegemony par excellence, as class disparities collapse into national identities, thus actively recruiting supporters from segments of the population whose interests are threatened by unfettered trade.
The means by which this "sovereign uniqueness" would be reached remains
as elusive in the *Washington Post* articles as the process of globalization—"a
maddening foe." Still, the printed word insists on a hopeful attitude towards
such vital issues in the face of resistance from Western and non-Western
countries alike.

The article also claims that "[T]here is a widespread view abroad that
globalization is being forced on the world by American corporations, that
globalization is Americanization" (Burgess, 1999, p. A1). Thus "American"
interests are equated with (mostly) U.S.-based transnational corporations,
excluding the voices of labor, environmentalists, students, and other groups
that form the U.S. polity. Also, many labor unions, some politicians, and most
intellectuals in developing countries hold different views of the free trade policies supported by the American corporate interests. "The consequences of
more trade liberalization . . . could be so negative and serious in the developing world that there will be tremendous political instability over the next five
years" (Burgess, 1999, p. E1). One complaint from smaller countries claims
unfair favoring of the United States in trade policies involving commodities
from gasoline to pharmaceutical products, as shown in the following excerpt:

> Twenty-three days after the World Trade Organization was born in 1995,
> the new agency received its first official trade complaint: Venezuela alleged
> that clean-air rules in the United States were unfairly favoring U.S. refiner-
> ies' gasoline over Venezuelan fuel. . . . In the end, the United States lost. In
> 1997 it changed its clean air rule to comply with the decision, after lengthy
> consultations with Venezuela and Brazil, which had joined the case.
> (Burgess, 1999, p. A18)

Although the complaints from the Third World countries were appeased, the
excerpt shows an obvious dichotomy between the West and the non-West
from the WTO's beginnings. In more recent years, developing nations have
not been so fortunate in the struggles of free trade and the WTO:

Developing countries say they are only beginning to appreciate the public health consequences of joining the World Trade Organization, which many have done in the 1990s. Before joining the WTO, they could avoid the high retail prices charged by pharmaceutical companies, which historically have viewed their primary market as Western nations where the price of drugs is typically covered by insurance.... But by joining the WTO, a country agrees to honor foreign patents and acknowledges it would face sanctions for dealing in generics produced before the patent expires. (Vick, 1999, p. A1)

Even at its best, the *Post*'s coverage remains abstract and reports no concrete, large-scale human and societal consequences of unfettered capitalism, such as widening worldwide income disparities and the exploitation of workers in the *maquiladoras* on the U.S.-Mexico border. These concerns, however, are ignored for more important issues, such as the deviance of protestors on the streets of Seattle or the benefits of free trade for the American public. While acknowledging these concerns, the *Washington Post* stands by its story on the benefits of free trade, propagating the need to lure underdeveloped countries into the WTO agreements under the promise of economic growth. "The president also said world trade leaders must convince poor countries, such as India and China, that they can grow economically in ways similar to what western nations did in the Industrial Revolution and afterwards" (Babington & Burgess, 1999, p. A1).

If developing countries are, indeed, convinced to join the ranks of the WTO and its alleged democratization of the world, they are forewarned that "[T]he bundle of forces that [globalization] connotes ... has no clear location or author; there is nobody to go and shout at" (Lessons From Seattle, 1999, p. A42), hence the industrialized countries will remain blameless in case the promise of unbridled capitalism is not fulfilled, as in the case of Russia's free-market disaster.

Media Hegemony and Popular Consent

The hegemonic process employs media frames as a means to expose and shape certain issues in the public eye for the purpose of garnering support for the dominant ideology. The preferred understanding in America 2000 was that of a booming economy and upward economic growth. And despite the financial slowdown beginning in 2001, wealth continues to accrue to the elite, while poverty seems to be spreading among the already poor.

A global economy is forming with America as the leader in corporate advances spurred on by international trade agreements. Consequently, it is to the advantage of the United States to control the agenda of the World Trade Organization, pushing forth trade terms that allegedly benefit all groups in the United States, while at the same claiming these agreements are for the benefit of the forthcoming global society. Hence, the talks were held on American soil, a "democratic" playing field for all countries to participate. However, not everyone is following suit on America's enthusiasm for a global economy.

The protestors and demonstrations in the streets of Seattle during the WTO talks represent resistance to the utopian neoliberal discourse about global economy. As several groups gathered in concern over environmental issues and labor unions' rights, the political agenda of the United States became threatened. The need for damage control over such angry protests became imperative, calling for the media to frame the protests, not the issues being protested. By concentrating on the violence and the appearance of the protestors, the *Washington Post* framed the events as deviant, thereby dismissing without meaningful comment the substantive issues raised and the protestors' alternative views of globalization. At times the media did shift its focus to note the peaceful demonstrations from several in the streets, however, the protesting voices were not given the media space to express their calls for international solidarity and participatory democracy. This is especially daunting because the demonstrations were a loud statement against the inevitability of globalization.

We could not find, in our research of all the *Washington Post* articles on the "Battle in Seattle," any interviews of the demonstrators, nor were their concerns made clear in any detailed positive fashion. The result was a confused public, viewing disruptive demonstrators through the eyes of the print media. Lacking other sources of information, including direct experience or contact with the protestors and their cause, public opinion was likely swayed in favor of public officials and their global concerns due to the depiction of the demonstrators as troublemakers, some of whom were not even citizens of the United States. The hegemonic process is successful in suppressing the marginalized ideas of the minority because of the elites' access to the media and its framing tactics, which purports benefits to all social classes.

The protestors were used as a distraction in another way, this time as a scapegoat. The WTO talks in Seattle were seen as an international "failure of the world's most powerful governments to launch a new round of global trade talks" (Pearlstein, 1999, p. E01). But the failure was not entirely the fault of international officials unable to come to terms on global issues. Instead, the failure was attributed to the aggressive protestors blocking the streets of Seattle and preventing several talks from occurring. Prior to the advent of the WTO conference, the media was already preparing to place blame on the protestors for any failure, "environmental militants who think [the WTO's] decisions create dirty air and water have vowed to 'shut down' the meeting with civil disobedience" (Burgess, 1999, p. A1). And delay talks they did, although in the end the blame placed on the protestors overshadowed the message they had hoped to send, leaving the political agenda free to voiceover the demonstrators' concerns.

The overwhelming media concentration on the violence of the protestors and the push for a global economy by U.S. officials can be viewed as basic news coverage. Reporters "objectively" cover stories deemed important to the American public. However, the choice of reported stories and the way these stories are presented to the public is another matter, as examined by Herman and Chomsky (1988), Gitlin (1980) and Tuchman (1978), revealing the ideological forces shaping news reports. One such revelation is the connection between the public and the private, or the link between the government agenda and the corporate interests. The framing of news along the lines of specific, private interests involved with the media was exposed by several scholars hailing from the critical (Herman & Chomsky, 1988) and agenda-setting (McCombs & Shaw, 1972) traditions, and is helpful in our analysis.

The American political system, especially during the 2000 presidential election year, is sensitive to media portrayals of issues that might affect the campaign. The way in which the media decides to frame a story for the public will help in swaying public opinion. As a result, important government affairs—the WTO conference for example—requires a positive media frame in order to shape public opinion in support of global trade. It is probable that a majority of politicians has a vested interest in positive public opinion of the global economy due to financial support from corporations. It is to the advantage of most parties involved to favor the international growth of American corporations through free trade and the issues of the global economy as discussed in the WTO talks. Thus the *Washington Post*'s coverage obstructs communication that proposes alternative policies that could provide more humane benefits to the American public. It thus "recruits" a broad base of support for unfettered capitalism. As privately owned enterprises, the mass media in the United States have financial reasons to support the political agenda and promote the dominant ideology. The result is a hegemonic circle of power between the private and the public sphere, which benefits the elite and dominant ideologies of America by shaping public opinion through media frames.

In this context, Lewis (1999) argues that the American population is not an uninformed public, but a misinformed public. According to Lewis (1999) "the process of hegemony generally involves the struggle to create consent for a system that favors certain dominant interests" (p. 263). Politicians must establish themselves on an economic level. To do so requires the financial backing of wealthy elites, pushing the candidates to adopt views of political supporters, and hence "hegemony is achieved before a single ballot is cast" (Lewis, 1999, p. 255). The American media will support the global economy and push free trade into the limelight in order to encourage a political agenda in which corporate funding and interests have vested.

The confluence of private, corporate, and government political agendas strides across the boundaries of the United States. These public and private ties affect international economies, imposing upon developing countries and shaping cultures worldwide. The Third World versus First World theme is grounded by Lewis (1999) in the notion of the United States as representative of freedom and democracy worldwide. These presumed democratizing tendencies have taken the form of global corporate interests, allowing Western powers to impose on Third World countries in the name of democracy.

The United States claims the acceptance of American products and standards will enhance other countries' economic and cultural prospects. This claim is echoed in the statement that "the deal would be crafted in such a way that each country would believe that it had defended its sovereign uniqueness" (Burgess, 1999, p. A1). In developing countries, labor unions, intellectuals, students, small business owners, and some politicians, see the extension of Western trade policies to their national and regional spheres more of an interventionist agenda than a compromise. The industrialized countries, then, are in a powerful position to hegemonically extend their trade policies to foreign nations to participate in a global economy controlled by largely Western transnational corporations. To achieve this objective, they need the support of the elite in developing countries, who take their turn "recruiting" support for the liberalization of trade policies and the privatization of public assets.

These concerns underscore the sharply different implications that globalization has for different social classes, across and within national borders. More importantly, our analysis reveals the importance of media framing in the biased construction of what globalization means for different social groups, in the United States and internationally, depending on where these social groups are located on the power spectrum. Specifically, in our opinion, the *Washington Post*'s coverage of the "Battle in Seattle," constituted a missed opportunity to bring into the fray of the debate on globalization the concerns and alternative views of the working class, labor unions, environmental activists, students—all those groups who justifiably feel they are on the losing end of globalization.

References

Babington, C., & Burgess, J. (1999, December 2). Clinton calls for open trade. *Washington Post*, p. A1.

Brandist, C. (1996). Gramsci, Bakhtin and the semiotics of hegemony. *New Left Review, 216*, 94–109.

Burgess, J. (1999, November 29). Gasoline dispute highlights environmental concerns. *Washington Post*, p. A18.

Burgess, J. (1999, November 29). WTO to meet as protestors rally forces. *Washington Post*, p. A1.

Burgess, J. (1999a, November 30). Trade-dependent Seattle of two minds on WTO. *Washington Post*, p. E1.

Burgess, J. (1999b, November 30). WTO listens to critics on eve of meeting. *Washington Post*, p. E1.

Condit, C. M. (1994). Hegemony in a mass-mediated society: concordance about reproductive technologies. *Critical Studies in Mass Communication, 11* (3), 205–230.

Edsall, T. (1999, December 9). Divisions on trade issues leave Democrats vulnerable. *Washington Post*, [on-line], p. A22. Available: *www.washingtonpost.com*.

Giddens, A. (1990). *The consequences of modernity.* Stanford, CA: Stanford University Press.

Gitlin, T. (1980). *The whole world is watching: Mass media in the making and the unmaking of the new left.* Berkeley: University of California Press.

Herman, E., & Chomsky, N. (1988). *Manufacturing consent: the political economy of the mass media.* New York: Pantheon.

Herman, E., & McChesney, R. (1997). *The global media: The new missionaries of global capitalism.* London: Cassell.

Lessons from Seattle. (1999, December 1). *Washington Post,* [on-line]. Available: *www.washingtonpost.com*.

Lewis, J. (1999). Reproducing political hegemony in the United States. *Critical Studies in Mass Communication, 16,* 251–267.

McCombs, M. E., & Shaw, D. L. (1972). The agenda-setting function of mass media. *Public Opinion Quarterly, 36,* 176–187.

Pearlstein, S. (1999, December 8). WTO talks said to send 'grim message.' *Washington Post,* [on-line], p. EO1. Available: *www.washingtonpost.com*.

Sanchez, R. (1999, December 5). After a chaotic week, Seattle eyes recovery. *Washington Post,* [on-line], p. AO2. Available: *www.washingtonpost.com*.

Tuchman, G. (1978). *Making news: A study in the construction of reality.* New York: Free Press.

Vick, K. (1999, December 4). Trade policy on AIDS drugs hurts Africans. *Washington Post*, p. A1.

CHAPTER 5

High Tech Hegemony:
Transforming Canada's Capital
into Silicon Valley North

Vincent Mosco and Patricia Mazepa

Introduction

This study investigates an often neglected but crucial side of global media hegemony. While one can understand global communication as a process of commodifying message content, the production of information and communication technology (ICT) is also implicated in the globalization of a class-based division of labor. There is a long tradition of debate about the role of communication and information technology in economic development. This was often set in the context of modernization theory that assessed the potential for using these technologies to expand the economies of Third World or less developed societies. Debates about the role of first the mass media and then telecommunications in advancing development helped shape the contours of international communication research. Today these debates are expanding as the role of communication and information technologies in developed as well as less developed societies plays a central place in research and policy analysis. Variations on the question "Are new media creating a vibrant new economy?" have taken center stage in universities, governments, and in the media itself (Thussu, 2000).

A particular form of the debate has focused on the merits of concentrating development of communication and information technologies in specific locations. Modeled after the apparent success of Silicon Valley in California or the Route 128 corridor in Massachusetts, these "technopoles" bring together a skilled workforce and large infusions of venture capital to produce new information products and applications. Technopoles have multiplied worldwide, and scholars have begun the process of assessing their consequences. A contribution to this effort, this chapter reports on research that assesses the consequence of technopole development in the Canadian city of Ottawa, one of four sites in a current research project examining a new generation of technopoles that build on the Silicon Valley model in different

93

ways. The others are "Silicon Alley" in New York's lower Manhattan (Mosco, 1999a), the Multimedia Super Corridor outside Kuala Lumpur, Malaysia (Jackson & Mosco, 1999), and the "Third Italy" in north central Italy (Mosco, 1999b). Overall, this international project addresses the political, social, and cultural consequences of technopole development, considerations which grow in importance the further away the technopole model departs from its Silicon Valley roots. In each case, government officials have made significant social, juridical, and educational adjustments to service corporate needs. This chapter presents an assessment of one of Canada's model technopoles, Silicon Valley North, in Ottawa.

The Birth of a Technopole in Ottawa

It is hard to find a city that, at least by reputation, would be less likely to embody characteristics associated with Silicon Valley than Ottawa. As a national capital, Ottawa has long been viewed as a city of bureaucrats. Furthermore, unlike some national capitals, London and Paris for example, Ottawa's economy has historically been dominated by the single industry made up of the federal government and the web of public and private institutions that are directly linked to it. Aside from the obvious differences in climate and setting, Ottawa has not been identified with a strong commercial, free enterprise ethos at least since the nineteenth-century heyday of the lumber trade. Nor has it been a center for banking and finance; historically, Montreal and now Toronto are centers of financial power in Canada. With the general economic stability provided by the federal government, Ottawa has not needed to venture into new business areas. In fact, some would see the federal government as an enormous constraint on any fundamental shift in economic activity. Persuasive as these arguments may be, they are too simple because they fail to account for the fundamental role of the federal government in giving rise to the Ottawa technopole.

The federal government has historically been the single largest user (and producer) of information technology products and services in Canada, and many of its leading technology firms, most of which remain based in the Ottawa area, grew out of government contracts. As far back as 1948, the Canadian Naval Electrical Laboratory contracted for a computer simulator to train staff in naval tactics. The contractors not only produced the simulator (a computer with 8,000 vacuum tubes occupying 1000 square meters), they also created Computing Devices of Canada, the company that anchored high technology development in Ottawa for decades. It did so largely through defense contracts that included basic management systems, sophisticated devices for command/control communication, and support for intelligence operations. Just as importantly, defense contractors created new companies to produce a network of firms with close connections to the government. As the founder of Digital Equipment Canada put it, "the government was a major user and producer of technology at the end of the Second World War. And in those days, you could fund operations out of government contracts. . . ." He goes on to note that founders of these companies "were smart enough to use that government funding to launch other businesses." (Standen, 1998, p. C1)

In essence, for economic and security reasons (but often because of political pressures), the federal government gave preferential treatment to national firms. These companies used the steady flow of federal contracts and the research from government laboratories such as the Department of Communication's Communication Research Center, to build powerful firms. For example, one of the region's leading early electronics firms, Lumonics, was created by engineers who left Computing Devices when they learned that the government was planning a major push into laser technology research and would be looking for firms to develop the technology. Similarly, secure in the protection of its telecommunications monopoly, Bell Canada reorganized its labs in 1971 to create Bell Northern Research (BNR) and its manufacturing arm Northern Electric in 1976 to create Northern Telecom (now Nortel Networks). BNR eventually gave birth to Mitel, Newbridge Networks, Corel, Mosaid Technologies, and numerous other firms that are mainstays of Canada's high technology industry and of the Ottawa technopole. Admittedly, there are alternatives to the argument that government was fundamental to Ottawa's success in advanced technology. According to Denzil Doyle, who headed the Canadian operations of the U.S. firm Digital Equipment when Digital was an industry leader, the resource industries, mainly pulp and paper, provided the foundation in much-needed capital for economic development in Ottawa. Moreover, he maintains, the absence of capital gains and stock options taxes in Canada until 1972 offered a secure base for risk-taking businesses. Nevertheless, there is little room to doubt that the federal government played an important role in launching and sustaining the Ottawa technopole.

Indeed, it is interesting to consider the comparative politics of technopole development. In the United States, where the national capital is largely a federal administrative center whose citizens only recently received the right to vote in national elections and have little more than token representation in Congress, there is practically no incentive to make Washington, D.C., anything more than a national symbol. There has been considerably more incentive to develop American technopoles in key electoral regions. Massachusetts was favored by the Kennedy administration, President Johnson backed Texas, and California received extensive support from the Nixon White House and from subsequent administrations eager to retain the largest block of electoral votes and support from the largest state congressional delegation. Unlike Washington, D.C., Ottawa's development would benefit specific members of Parliament and the government generally, especially during the past decade, when it has succumbed to intense business pressure and cut the federal workforce. Over the past decade, three successive Liberal governments, in firm control of almost every seat in the Ottawa region, have showered the local high technology sector with almost every form of support. The combination of cuts to the federal civil service and support for the private high technology industry has accentuated a state of uneven development in the Ottawa economy.

The Business of Government

Contrary to the view of information technology enthusiasts, nation-states have not been overcome nor superseded by media technology. Indeed, the Ottawa case confirms what other technopole research has demonstrated: the nation-state has been crucial to the deregulation, commercialization, and internationalization of media and technology production. As the capital of Canada and home of the federal government and its departments, the political economy of Ottawa is unique. Governance is a combination of federal, provincial, regional, and municipal jurisdiction making "local" politics more complex than anywhere else in Canada (Andrew, 1983, p.140). The local economy is less manifold, but with the federal government as the major employer and the "largest single property owner," government restructuring acutely affects the city and the surrounding region in many ways (NCC 1998, p.69). As a result of government "downsizing," for example, there has been a loss of 9,983 net federal jobs in the region over 1991–96 with all government employment falling by 8.1% (compared to 4.5% in Ontario and 2.2% in Canada) (Social Planning Council, 1999a, p. 47).

Local agencies focusing on the region's social and economic development argue that the decrease in federal employment has been more than offset by growth in the information and communication technology industry (OED, 1999). Combined with a regional concentration of related businesses in what is considered "high tech," such changes seem to signify that Ottawa is in a process of transition from a government to a high technology site conducive to the "new" economy. The city is becoming "Silicon Valley North."

In government documents and policy reports, justifications integrate government and industry under vision statements based on concepts such as "innovation" and "knowledge" (NRC, 1997). Describing both the economy and society as "knowledge-based" binds the social to the market economy in what the government calls an "innovation system" (Canada, Industry Canada,

1999a, p. 10). In this view, it is impossible to have innovation without knowledge, and since knowledge is a product of education and R&D, public services like health and education are thereby drawn into the process. "Knowledge" is filled in on the supply side of the economic equation as the new "unlimited resource" replacing natural resources (Ibid., "Message from the Minister of Industry"). As expressed in the 1999 federal budget, "commercializing knowledge" is considered mandatory, and increasingly the private sector is being drawn into decision-making to accelerate this process (Canada, Department of Finance, 1999, p. 112; Canada, Industry Canada, 1999b).

Recent private-sector involvement has been instituted through the creation of two key external advisory bodies, the Council of Science and Technology Advisors (CSTA) and the Advisory Council on Science and Technology (ACST), both made up of "experts" from private industry. The ACST immediately established the "Expert Panel on Commercializing University Research," which recommended "research and development choices [be] directed to where the highest returns are likely to be found" (ACST, 1999).

The conception of the "knowledge economy" is also translated in areas of federal and provincial control through programs and payments to post-secondary education. Government priorities based on commercialization affect research and curriculum decisions. On the federal level, the government supports university research through three granting councils whose mandates have been modified and primary activities have been restated to tie government funding directly to economic development and private sector priorities (e.g. Canada, Department of Finance, 1998, pp. 13–20). All the granting councils are located in Ottawa within the responsibility of Industry Canada (rather than Health Canada or Canadian Heritage for example) and function to promote the transfer of technology to private industry. The widely reported "skills shortage" and shift to a "knowledge-based economy" are both used to justify changes to post-secondary programs and curricula to feed into industry research and labor requirements that are primarily focused on science and technology (ACST, 2000, p. 2). Other federally created programs such as the Canada Foundation for Innovation (CFI) and the Networks of Centers of Excellence (NCE) and Canada Chairs for Research Excellence assist universities in meeting these requirements.

On the provincial level, funding through transfer payments made to the university have been drastically cut, while funding directed to building new infrastructure and particular programs has been increased. The "SuperBuild Growth Fund" (at $1.8 billion), a private-public partnership, is to build new infrastructure at colleges and universities primarily for high tech education, while the Ontario Innovation Trust established in 1999 gives a further $750 million to research institutions for new infrastructure. Additionally, the

Ontario government has made numerous financial commitments through programs such as the "R&D Challenge Fund," the "Ontario Research Performance Fund," the "Access to Opportunities" (ATOP), and "Communications and Information Technology Ontario" (CITO) that tie universities and industry. The ATOP program facilitates university-industry collaboration by matching industry donations with public funds. CITO acts to further commercialization, as its "knowledge broker" mandate is to bring together "the needs of business with the substantial resources of Ontario's universities" to create "industry exploitable knowledge" *(www.cito.ca)*. The ATOP program is the provincial government's response to "industry calls" to double their 1995 enrollment in high tech programs by 2002. (George, 1998, p. 81; *www.cito.ca;* Enman, 2001, p. D3).

All the post-secondary schools in Ottawa—Carleton University, the University of Ottawa, Algonquin College, and La Cité Collegiale—have added programs and departments dedicated to science and engineering, particularly in information and communications technology. Carleton University calls itself "High-Tech U" and aims to satisfy industry labor and research requirements. The University boasts that it has had the largest shift in enrollment in the province from arts to engineering and computer science, and it has doubled the number of students in high tech programs over the last 10 years. Both universities predict they will reach ATOP enrollment targets three years prior to the deadline (Johnson, 1999). At both universities, ICT industry donations and funding for infrastructure have established laboratories and training centers named after their corporate sponsors. Since the universities are registered charities, these corporations receive tax benefits, while the university receives funding from the provincial government in matching donations through the ATOP program, or other federal programs. What is notable about these developments is that not only are they all addressed to fulfilling the needs of the private sector, but the largest ICT companies are also involved in setting research agendas, selecting students, and directly participating in curriculum decisions.

Private sector participation was taken to the next level through government industry collaborations in the creation of the National Capital Institute of Telecommunications (NCIT). The NCIT had its conceptual beginnings as the "MIT of the North" and was established in Ottawa thanks to an initial federal government investment of $5.3 million under the CFI program. NCIT's mandate is to "foster collaborative research between academia, government and the private sector" with a total of $36 million pledged over the next five years, establishing a "training ground for high-tech grads" *(www.ncit.ca)*.

Considered as necessary infrastructure for the knowledge society, a federal government priority is to advance the incorporation of ICT through changes in its own operations and organizations, encouraging governments at all levels to do the same. While there are many progressive possibilities in the use of the technology, public policy decisions and directives are increasingly being led by the private sector. In the opening address to the Inaugural Technology Forecast Roundtable for Innovation held in Ottawa in 1996, the president of the Treasury Board told the delegates that the government has changed its role from "a doer to a facilitator." This means the continued expansion of the transfer and commercialization of technology from government research laboratories like the Communications Research Center (CRC) and the National Research Council (NRC), with additional powers and support extended to so-called public-private institutions and/or private organizations of the ICT industry. Where changes in government telecommunication regulations favoring market development end, these programs begin (Winseck, 1998). The designation "private-public" given to Ottawa-based organizations like the Canadian Network for the Advancement of Research, Industry and Education (CANARIE), the Optical Processing and Computing Consortium of Canada (OPCOM), and the Pre-Competitive Applied Research Program (PRECARN) indicates market-led and public funding. Between them, they receive over a billion dollars in public funding devoted to the application, exploitation, and commercialization of technology for Canadian business interests. If the technology does not fall within the mandates of these institutions, there is a range of programs for R&D support, tax incentives, and numerous other means of financial support, including those provided by provincial and municipal governments (Ontario, 1999).

Commercialization efforts have also been extended to the growing biotechnology industry in the region. Government support for the local industry is provided specifically to transfer technology from the NRC and local university and hospital research. Industry forecasts predict that there will be a "fusion of technologies" between this sector and the ICT industry (e.g. through electronic health services delivery), and that these "natural" linkages should be nurtured (Ekos, 1997). As can be observed by the number of federally supported ICT programs and market-led organizations, the federal government has a large stake in the maintenance and support of the high tech industry beyond the establishment of policy and regulations, as does the provincial government. With so much in the way of public resources going into commercialization, however, there is less time and space available for public alternatives. The presence of the federal government in Ottawa, its research laboratories and federally funded organizations used to stimulate and promote the ICT industry, as well as the additions of ICT research and training at university and college facilities and curricula, combine to contribute to a political economic and sociocultural environment in the region that is supportive of the industry.

The Government of Business

Following the various branches of the ICT industry genealogy from 1947 illustrates a family tree of locally created companies and offspring or spin-offs linked to government research labs, government contracts, and purchases. This helps to explain why a number of the largest companies in the Ottawa region are Canadian-owned, as their "nationality" allows them to take advantage of preferential government treatment (Mosco, 1996, p.181). Northern Telecom (Nortel) can trace its beginnings here, as can Mitel, Corel, and Newbridge as spin-offs, and SHL Systemhouse from government contracting out (Standen, 1998). These companies have been the mainstay of the industry in the region that grew by 201% from 1991 to 1998 (OED, 1999, p. 52). Approximately half of the over 1,000 companies are in telecommunications and computing, representing the largest concentration of telecommunications in Canada (CMG, 1997). A Canadian Marketing Group (CMG) study on the region's R&D per capita spending suggests that the region generates $2 billion in R&D related work in telecommunications alone, which amounts to 75% of Canada's total R&D expenditure in that industry, although 80% of this comes from Nortel alone (CMG, 1997; OED, 2000, p.5.4).

Other benchmarks illustrating ICT industry concentration in the region are the number of producer services firms. Accounting, management, consulting, and legal and venture capital firms help to achieve the "critical mass" or necessary "self-supporting" infrastructure. This infrastructure arguably includes several industry organizations headquartered in Ottawa because of the access to the federal government and the concentration of high tech businesses. The Canadian Advanced Technology Alliance (CATA) and the Information Technology Association of Canada (ITAC) take the lead in lobbying the governments at all levels. Members of the Board of Directors include CEOs and CFOs of the major high tech companies in Ottawa such as Nortel, JetForm, and SHL Systemhouse, with associate members from major legal, accounting, and banking firms. These associations have considerable clout in influencing policy in areas such as R&D Tax Policy, capital formation, human resource development, and tax and trade policy.

ICT business concentration and cross-board memberships contribute to the formation of communication links fostered through personal contacts and common political economic interests. The resulting combination of alliances and organizations advances the power to alter communication and information flows, including electronic networking, transportation, and media. At the local level, a mix of the largest company's CEOs together with local senior politicians and university faculty, head a number of public-private agencies with goals to facilitate high tech development. The Ottawa-Carleton Research Institute (OCRI) was created from just such a mix with a mandate to create a "Silicon Valley North" modeled after California's Silicon Valley. Its objective is to connect with universities, colleges, and high schools in the area to graduate potential employees for the local high tech businesses. The OCRI was the catalyst behind CITO and the development of industry-led research chairs at the local universities. Both the OCRI and CATA have established advanced communication networks for their members. OCRInet is a regional fiber optic-based communications infrastructure network with high bandwidth capability dedicated to research (OCRI, 1994, p. 2; RMOC, 1998, p. 35). The CATA networks are corporate Intranets connected to the "International Corridor" through the development of "Technogate and Virtual Business Corridors," established to help develop business in a global high tech arena" *(www.cata.com)*. Other intranets connect industry, universities, and government through the NCIT*Net, a high-speed network linking the NRC, the University of Ottawa, Carleton University, and the Canadian national optical Internet, CA*Net3.

Another local agency with the power to alter information and communication flows is the Ottawa Economic Development Corporation (OED). Local and provincial governments and corporate contributions fund the OED's mandate to foster "one vision-one voice for economic, industrial and business development" (OED, 2000, p. 1). The OED is primarily industry-led, bringing together the Board of Directors, consisting of the CEOs of the major ICT and related companies, with public representatives such as the Secretary Treasurer of the National Bank of Canada and the Mayor of Ottawa. Other councils and committees are comprised of a mix of high-tech industry, banking, insurance, legal, media and real estate personnel, and faculty of both Ottawa universities. As quasi-governmental agencies, the OCRI and the OED bring together a private-public mix, whose major decision-makers are nonelected. Where regional politics conflict in overlapping jurisdictions and complex public goals, organizations such as the OCRI and OED representing dominant interests are having increasing sway over regional planning and development decisions. Noting their influence in local decision-making, Dandy and Hunt (1998) suggest that there is a shift in local governance from elected to nonelected agencies. The power of the OED is illustrated in its success in altering both air and land transportation networks to facilitate business travel and communication links.

The OCRI and the OED, in cooperation with the NRC, also organize annual Regional Innovation Forums (RIF), bringing together top decision-makers from government, business, and education to exchange ideas and collaborate on projects for high tech sector development. The RIF is one of many conferences held to plan and promote relationships among the various "stakeholders" in the region's development, including the local media who sit on its various committees. The 1997 RIF concluded its proceedings with a set of suggestions for media coverage of high tech that remarkably came from the publisher of the city's major newspaper: "The media should tell success stories and celebrate entrepreneurial spirit. It can act as a bridge between the business community and the general public, helping to build support for changes that are required for the Region's economic development. It should continue to prod our leaders forward with editorial comments when they lose focus on the longer term interests of the Region" (Chhatbar & Darch, 1997, p.31).

This call for business "agitprop" completely ignores the view that the OED's mandate of "one-vision, one-voice" excludes the many, as alternative voices of labor and community groups are missing from its membership and decision-making. Without their participation, the local hegemony, i.e. "the taken-for-granted belief in the right to use power" is significantly strengthened (Mosco, 1996, p.189). Such conditions and practices illustrate that the globalization of privatization and the growing international division of labor in the service of media and technology producers (including education and research) further exacerbate class inequality.

A Change of Locale

Anticipating change is the goal of planning. Continued federal government downsizing, increasing government use of ICT, and corresponding changes to government operations and organization, inform regional planning decisions. Provincial downloading of responsibilities to the city without providing the money to pay for them places additional pressure on economic and social planning. High tech hegemony provides an answer: accommodate industry, and all will be well. The situation is not entirely new. In the nineteenth century regions competed with each other to attract the resource industry by supplying required water, electricity, and sewage (Magnussen, 1983, p.11). Today, regions compete to provide the necessary technological infrastructure. The region's Official Plan notes a change in context from reliance on the federal government to a region that is "increasingly tied to the high technology sector." The plan stipulates the guidelines to sustain and facilitate the industry by ensuring "servicing priorities, the provision of fibre-optic cable, supporting community telecentres," and "other measures . . . to encourage the use of new technologies" (RMOC, 1998, Section 4.2.1 [4a–4c]).

In the competition to attract business, there is an increased stress on global marketing for business. Cities within Canada compete to be known as Silicon Valley North. According to a study by Deloitte & Touche commissioned by the Greater Toronto Metropolitan Association, Toronto has more right to the title, citing lower business costs, level of R&D, larger scope and size of high tech labor force, greater access to higher education, and higher quality of life (Napier, 1999, p. D3). Furthermore, different parts of the Ottawa region compete with each other to provide the most efficient and economical infrastructure services in the hopes of attracting business to their areas. With similar financial incentives like low city taxes, rental and utility rates, appeals are increasingly supplemented by providing evidence of a high quality of life defined by such amenities as recreational facilities, quantity of open green space, availability of cultural facilities and festivals, and the existence of professional sport teams and related facilities. Of these indicators, the latter garners considerable attention in regional economic planning, as they are considered essential in marketing and tourism (Chhatbar, 1998, RMOC, 1998:Section 4.2.1 [17]). Names of key recreational facilities that were publicly owned now bear the names of premier high-tech companies, reflecting their majority owner. The $200 million "Palladium" was changed to the "Corel Center" and houses the Ottawa Senators NHL Hockey Team. The Triple-A baseball stadium, built as the "Ottawa Stadium," is now "Jet-Form Park" also bearing the name of a regionally based high-tech company. High Tech hegemony therefore works to establish regional cross-class identities, thereby disrupting working-class solidarity and more democratic social and economic projects.

In January 2001, the 11 different municipalities forming the Regional Municipality of Ottawa-Carleton merged into the City of Ottawa. Prior to amalgamation, there was heated competition among jurisdictions to attract businesses to their respective areas. In the west-end of the region, the former City of Kanata (where Mitel, Newbridge [now Alcatel], Calian Technology, and other high tech businesses are concentrated) was left to establish its own attractions in order to improve its image and marketing position. Kanata's efforts were not only directed to attract new businesses to the area, but also aimed at satisfying the requirements of key employees and already existing businesses. Without a historical town center, Kanata worked to create one. Local media reports suggested the council's logic was supported by a voter desire for a town core that would rid Kanata of its suburban image and establish itself as a city in its own right, together with a sense of residents' nostalgia for a communal meeting place or civic center. Kanata's mayor described the "Main Street Project":

> ". . . It's really exciting, the thought of having a real civic heart, a civic square." The regional shopping center will offer 800,000 to one million square feet of retail space on a 100–acre site. The 24–screen theater will feature more than just movies, with a wide variety of entertainment choices from a jazz club to a cappuccino/piano bar to a venue for live bands. The complex is expected to cater to 2.5 million to four million people a year, and will be "trendy, upscale and leading edge." (quotes from the former mayor of Kanata, in Hebert, 1998, pp. 33–34)

Visions of "Main Street" articulate the seductive hegemonic policies meant to attract business and transform citizens into consumers. Of course, in practice, the vision invariably leads to uneven local development, as employment and population patterns result in wide disparities between portions of the new city. In the west, where the majority of high tech companies are located, population and employment have increased. In the central core and near-east part of the region, where industry is primarily office and retail, population has decreased and unemployment is high. This disparity had east Ottawa planners stepping up offers to attract a Taiwanese chip plant and setting aside an area as part of the deal to attract the company.

Business was unhappy with 11 local governments in the Ottawa region because, however they may have reflected local concerns, such as the needs of francophone or new immigrant neighborhoods, they hindered making the region into a unified market. Marketing was further complicated with the varying locations of the industry with Nortel and Corel in the City of Nepean, and Mitel and Newbridge in the City of Kanata, and IBM and SHL System-house located in Ottawa. Such fragmentation was an unhealthy environment for business, so said a University of Ottawa study that suggested the area should become one megacity, or "city-region." The study explained that the municipalities needed to be "combined into one urban identity to give Ottawa a powerful national and international presence" necessary to "survive the global economy." Similar to the OED's mandate of "one voice, one vision," the University study favored amalgamation, so that the city can "speak with one powerful voice" (Centre on Governance, 1999).

The Ontario government made the decision to amalgamate the municipalities into one city of Ottawa and appointed a small group of its own "experts" to take over the elected powers of the 11 municipalities and impose a new central government conducive to its probusiness priorities. Overnight Ottawa's population "grew" from 327,000 to 750,000, the geographical area increased from 27,200 acres to 681,270 acres, and the number of elected politicians reduced from 84- to a 22-person city-council (including the Mayor) (Adam, 2000b; Denley, 2000b). The total cost of amalgamation is approximately $189 million of which $102 million is earmarked for severance pay of the 1,100 public employees who were laid off, $83 million for amalgamation of services and facilities, and $4 million for the costs of the transition board itself (Adam, 2000a). But in the eyes of the high tech community and its friends in government, Ottawa became the "Smart Capital" (Gray, 2000). Just what "smart" really means is best seen in the light of decisions made just prior to the amalgamation, including a regional rezoning of land from rural to urban of 1,000 acres around the Corel Center: Overnight, inexpensive rural property in Kanata shot from $30,000 an acre to $150,000.

> Their decision enriched a group of property owners by at least $80 million. . . . The biggest single beneficiary was Ottawa Senator's owner Rod Bryden: Council's decision raised the net value of his property around the Corel Center by at least $26 million. . . . A business park planned for land near the Corel Centre will create an employment area as large as the downtown, but will also cost the public tens of millions of dollars for roads and sewers. (Denley, 2000a, p. C1)

Bryden, a high tech executive with a strong stake in the biotechnology industry, was one of several high tech executives to benefit from the "smart" decisions of the provincially appointed transition board. Other land decisions made under the Transition Board included a $300 million plan by chipmaker Tundra Semiconductor to develop a 25-acre site within the former City of Kanata's "town center" combining high-tech office, residential, and retail space. Just weeks before amalgamation, Tundra won permission to buy the land from Kanata for $60,000 rather than the appraised value of $8.83 million in exchange for providing servicing costs such as roads, water, and sewers (Adam, 2000c). Following the "bigger is better" logic, and without public consultation, the Quebec provincial government has a similar amalgamation planned for Hull on the Quebec side of the region (Bailey, 2000; Gordon, 2000)

Whose Quality of Life?

As with the myth of the information superhighway, which disguised sharp class distinctions in access and use of media technology, so too, this corporate-written perspective obscures deep social class differences in burden and benefit. Reports on high tech Ottawa commissioned and produced by the business community emphasize labor supply and quality of life as important indicators conducive to high tech clusters (OED, 1998). As indicators, however, they tell us little about the social relations constituting these industry standards as advanced by the region's decision-makers. A closer examination of the labor environment and indicators of the quality of life not based solely on consumption, provide a clearer view.

First of all, the type of employment in the region is changing. From 1991 to 1996, all government employment in the region decreased by 8.1%, whereas employment in the high tech industry grew by 3% (SPC, 1999a, p.52). There has been job growth in the high tech sector, but when distinctions are made between full- and part-time jobs, regional statistics from 1991 and 1996 census years indicate that 78% of all new jobs created in the region were part-time (41). Another kind of work that is on the increase in the region is telework and home-based businesses (HBB) (55). The region is planning on further increases in both telework and home-based businesses, and aims to build community telecenters and adjust zoning requirements for HBB, in anticipation of growth in the federal government's use of ICT, and as corporations use telework to decrease building infrastructure costs (NCC, 1998). The growth in both part-time and telework has not corresponded with an increase in income, however. The most recent census indicates that, 12.3% of Ottawa's workers are self-employed, and over half of these (57%) earn less than $19,200 (SPC, 1999a, p.55). These types of employment follow gender lines, as women are mostly employed in part-time work, and their self-employed earnings are only about half as much as that of men (56).

The nature of employment in the region is also changing. Public sector employment tends to be stable and unionized, with wages significantly higher than the majority of self-employment, and in comparison to private sector counterparts in the blue collar and clerical occupations (SPC, 1999a, p.56). In contrast, employment in the high tech industry is very unstable. Major employers such as Nortel, Compaq (Digital), and Bell Canada have all hired and laid off workers by the thousands (Hill, 2001). Worker burnout due to overtime, stress, and dissatisfaction with work environment adds to high employee turnover (Tam, 2001; Duxbury, Dyke and Lam, 2000; Dale, 2000). The transient nature of employment can be seen in the west end of the city (in the former City of Kanata), where "resale signs can be found in neighborhoods still under construction" (Lewis, 1998, p.13). Longer working hours are sanctioned by the Ontario government with labor legislation now allowing for a 60-hour work-week in the high tech sector. According to the provincial Minister of Labor, "The extended work week should help employees adjust to the realities of the 21st century economy" (Blackwell, 2000). Regardless of the reasons, former government workers are particularly affected. According to one critical account:

> . . . Many of the region's unemployed workers—particularly unskilled and older workers—simply don't fit the needs of the rapidly growing technology firms . . . Ottawa's workforce is polarized increasingly between the highly skilled, highly educated workers who can move easily between the public sector and private industry and those without such training who have had trouble coping with downsizing. (McCarthy, 1997, pp.B1, B4)

Reports on the increase of jobs in high tech do not make distinctions among permanent, temporary, or contract employees. The high tech industry is noticeably draining workers from the service industry and health care services, as assembly-line work pays a few dollars more an hour than the minimum wage. Even the local McDonald's reports labor shortages (Salisbury, 2000). Recent immigrants are particularly drawn to high tech because it offers the promise of stock options, and strong English language skills are not as important as they are in the service sector (Salisbury, 2000; Kemsley, 2001; CCAC, 2000; OCSA, 2000).

Reports on a technology skill shortage in the ICT in Canada and in the region are generated by the industry's business organizations and are taken for granted in decision-making despite research by the federal government's Expert Panel (ACST) showing otherwise (Advisory Council on Science and Technology, 2000, p.2). Predicted shortages have resulted in changes in immigration regulations for highly skilled employees (Evans, 1998, p. B3; Anderton, 1997, p. 1), and, as previously discussed, has advanced changes to university, college, and high school curricula to satisfy industry requirements. What is key in this equation is that responsibility for the alleged skills shortage and training is directed at governments, the education system, and the individual, rather than at industry.

The emphasis on individual skills and education by industry organizations and governments, widely reported in the media, has resulted in the addition of private training facilities to the clustering effect. Unregulated private institutions offering ICT training have increased exponentially in the region, with a corresponding increase in the number of people willing to pay anywhere from $150 for a one-day course to $25,000 to train to become an "Information Technology Professional." The Algonquin College expansion is to help "compete with these organizations and the universities for students and it already has a $19,000 tuition program that promises to prepare people for computer jobs in less than a year"(Hill, 1999, p. A1). Carleton University has also added a computer science certificate consisting of five months of intensive training for a cost of $12,000 (Salisbury, 2000). The emphasis on retraining is evident in current enrollment demographics as "sixty-three percent of Algonquin's students are mature students and twenty-five percent of them already have university degrees and college diplomas" (Hill, 1999, p. A2). The Social Planning Council of Ottawa-Carleton's reports, however, that employment trends in the Ottawa-Carleton labor market indicate that employer demand has grown only for workers holding university degrees. Over the period of 1989 to 1995, the demand for workers with completed university education increased by 8%, while demand for college-trained students fell by 4% (SPC, 1999a, p.54). Moreover, the demand for university education is coming at a time when individual tuition is at an all-time high in Ontario, as government cuts to transfer payments are gradually passed on to students. Data gathered on the region by the SPC suggests it is no coincidence that the largest cohort for social assistance was people aged 25–34 (59). OED reports that Ottawa has a highly educated workforce with 26% of the population with university degrees, which is 9% higher than the rest of Canada and 13% higher than countries in the OECD (OED, 1999, p.3.7).

However, this higher level of university-educated adults has consequences for the less educated. As Osberg and Grude (1995) concluded from their case studies of labor and (un)employment in Canada, ". . . a generous supply of labour has meant that workers with university credentials are willing to take jobs that do not really use their skills, and those with poorer credentials have been pushed into marginal employment, or into unemployment" (185). As a result of these practices, education becomes little more than skills training, rationalizing the division of labor and discarding academic reflection and practical investigation of social relations and political and social consequences as unnecessary, costly, and uninteresting to students seeking degrees for industry employment.

By looking at a business report, the region appears to enjoy a relatively high standard of living. On average, individual income is higher than the rest of Canada, half the population can speak both French and English, and over 40% of local households own their own personal computer (OED, 1997). However, a more detailed studied of the region's sociodemographic and economic trends by the SPC (1999a) indicates some profound disparities:

> Income polarization for individuals is more pronounced in the RMOC and the City of Ottawa than in Ontario or Canada. . . . In the City of Ottawa, the proportion of individuals earning less than $20,000, at 47.1% is higher than the national average, and the proportion of individuals earning $60,000 or more, at 10.7% was also significantly higher than the national average. (p. 66)

Rather than focusing on the number of theaters, sport teams, or recreational facilities, a more recent study by Ottawa's Social Planning Council used different quality of life measurements to examine overall community well-being in the region including health, environment, and social indicators as well as economic. *The Quality of Life in Ottawa-Carleton* focused on the people represented by the indicators and illustrates a different picture of the region than the one marketed by business groups. The study recognizes that, while the increase in high tech is beneficial for those who are highly skilled, educated, and currently valued, there are growing numbers of excluded people. Poverty rates for all ages in the City of Ottawa are higher than provincial and national rates. The people marginalized by economic and social restructuring are the most vulnerable groups in Ottawa, those requiring extensive health care, the unemployed, those living in poverty, and more specifically, women, elderly, youth and children (SPC 1999b, p.22). While high tech hegemony gains momentum, the daily lives of this underclass demonstrate that high tech development accelerates a deepening social divide that only feeds into the globalization of social class divisions.

Driven by corporate needs, boosted by blue-ribbon business-friendly government bodies and promoted by mass media, high tech hegemony transforms communities like Ottawa into local models of private governance. Globalization means more than a world run by the World Bank, IMF, WTO, and other international private regimes. It also means transforming the local, including the neighborhood and the community, schools and governments, health care facilities and playgrounds, to reflect the singular hegemony of the market in everyday life.

References

Adam, M. (2000a, December 2). Chiarelli fuming over transition costs. *Ottawa Citizen*, D3.

Adam, M. (2000b, December 31). Ottawa's founders would be proud. *Ottawa Citizen*, B1.

Adam, M. (2000c, December 20). Tundra reinvents 'company town.' *Ottawa Citizen*, D1.

Advisory Council on Science and Technology (ACST). (1999). *Public investments in university research: Reaping the benefits*. Ottawa: Industry Canada.

Advisory Council on Science and Technology. (2000). *Stepping up: Skills & opportunities in the knowledge economy: Final report. Expert panel on skills*. Ottawa: Industry Canada.

Anderton, P. (1997, June 9). Pact no threat to Canadian jobs: CIPS. *Computing Canada*, 1.

Andrew, C. (1983). Ottawa-Hull. In W. Magnusson and A. Sancton (Eds.). *City politics in Canada* (pp. 140–165). Toronto: University of Toronto Press.

Bailey, P. (2000, November 16). PQ will be 'thrown out' over mergers. *Ottawa Citizen*, B1.

Blackwell, T. (2000, November 24). Workers perks often soften the blow of longer hours. *Ottawa Citizen, A3*.

Canada, Department of Finance. (1998). *The budget plan 1998: Strong economy and secure society*. Ottawa: Department of Finance.

Canada, Department of Finance. (1999). *The budget plan 1999: Building a strong economy through knowledge and innovation*. Ottawa: Department of Finance.

Canada, Governor General. (2001). *Speech from the throne*, 38th Parliament, Ottawa.

Canada, Industry Canada. (1999a). *Building momentum: A report on science and technology*. Ottawa: Industry Canada.

Canada, Industry Canada. (1999b). *Forging ahead: A report on Federal science and technology*. Ottawa: Industry Canada.

Canadian Marketing Group. (CMG) (1997). *Ottawa-Carleton region—Silicon Valley North, telecommunications and computing industry, leading companies, and related R&D organizations.* Ottawa: NRC.

CCAC (Community Care Access Centre) (2000). *Homemaking shortages policy report.* Ottawa: CCAC, February.

Centre On Governance. (1999). *The borough model of governance.* Ottawa: University of Ottawa Centre on Governance.

Chhatbar, A., & Darch, M. (eds.) (1997). *Inaugural technology forecast roundtable report: A summary of roundtable proceedings and issues.* Ottawa: NRC.

Chhatbar, A., & Darch, M. (eds.) (1998). *Regional innovation forum roundtable II report. The world's gateway to the next millennium: Innovation and Ottawa's information and telecommunications industry—technology and market trends.* Ottawa: NRC.

Dale, S. (2000). Lament of the silicon serfs. *Ottawa City Magazine.* February/March, 49–53.

Dandy, E., & Hunt, C. (1998). Silicon Valley North: Ottawa's new economic space and the politics of governance. Paper presented at the Annual General Meeting of the Canadian Political Science Association, University of Ottawa, Ontario.

Denley, R. (2000a, November 2). Developers donate, but "They can't buy your vote." *Ottawa Citizen,* C1.

Denley, R. (2000b, November 14). New council must forget old city battles. *Ottawa Citizen,* B11.

Duxbury, L., Dyke, L., Lam, N. (2000). *Career development in the high tech sector.* Ottawa:

Ekos Research Associates Inc. (1997). *National capital region technology forecasts for the telecommunication, software, life sciences and environmental studies:Final report.* Ottawa: National Research Council.

Enman, C. (2001, January 24). High tech's heavenly marriage. *Ottawa Citizen,* D3.

Evans, M. (1998, November 27). Easing immigration for high-tech workers called roaring success. *The Globe and Mail,* B3.

George, S. (1998). Human resource needs: An industry perspective. In A. Chhatbar. (Ed.) *Roundtable III report: Sectoral connectivity: Information and telecommunications as the enabling force for growth in all sectors* (81–83). Ottawa: NRC in cooperation with OED and OCRI.

Gordon, S. (2000, November 27). Charest joins rally against super cities. *Ottawa Citizen,* A8.

Gray, K. (2000, May 12). Ottawa wins smart-city title. *Ottawa Citizen,* D1.

Hebert, K. (1998). Kanata karma. *Ottawa Life Magazine.* March, 33–40.

Hill, B. (2001, January 26). Nortel axes 300 in new job cuts. *Ottawa Citizen,* D1.

Hill, M. (1999, February 12). Government needs high tech strategy, Auditor General says. *Silicon Valley North*.

Jackson, S., & Mosco, V. (1999). The political economy of new technological spaces: Malaysia's multimedia super corridor. *Journal of International Communication, 6*, 23–40.

Johnson, S. (1999, July). Local universities see IT programs filling to ATOP. *Silicon Valley North*.

Kemsley, H. (2001, January 30). Director, Community Care Access Centre, Ottawa. Telephone interview.

Lewis, M. (1998, April 22). High-tech's watering hole. *Ottawa Citizen*, I3.

Magnusson, W. (1983). Introduction: The development of Canadian urban government. In W. Magnussen and A. Sancton (Eds.). *City politics in Canada*. (3–57). Toronto: University of Toronto Press.

McCarthy, S. (1997, August 30). Ottawa trades bureaucrats for bytes. *The Globe and Mail*, B1 & B4.

Mosco, V. (1996). *The political economy of communication*. London: Sage.

Mosco, V. (1999a). New York.com: A political economy of the 'informational' city. *The Journal of Media Economics, 12, 2*, 103–116.

Mosco, V. (1999b). Citizenship and the technopoles. In A. Calabrese and J. Burgelman (Eds.) *Communication, citizenship, and social policy*. (33–45). New York: Rowman and Littlefield.

Napier, J. (1999, April 26). The real Silicon Valley North. *The Ottawa Citizen*, D3.

National Capital Commission (NCC). (1998). *Annual report*, Ottawa: NCC.

National Research Council (NRC). (1997). *Annual report 1996–1997*. Ottawa: NRC.

OCRI. (1994). *Annual report*. Ottawa: Ottawa Carleton Research Institute.

OCSA (Ontario Community Support Association) and OHHCPA (Ontario Home Health Care Providers' Association) (2000). *Home care worker compensation*. Ottawa: OCSA and OHHCPA, September.

OED. (1997). *Economic and community profile*. Ottawa: Ottawa Economic Development Corporation.

OED. (1998). *1997–98 Action plan*. Ottawa: Ottawa Economic Development Corporation.

OED. (1999). *Annual report*. Ottawa: Ottawa Economic Development Corporation.

OED. (2000). *Ottawa facts*. Ottawa: Ottawa Economic Development Corporation.

Ontario Government. (1999). *Ontario economic outlook and fiscal review*. Toronto: Queen's Printer.

Osberg, L., & Grude, J. (1995). *Vanishing jobs*. Toronto: Lorimer.

Regional Municipality of Ottawa-Carleton (RMOC). (1998). *Regional official plan.* Ottawa: RMOC.

Salisbury, B. (2000, December 4). Economy makes life difficult for service industry. *The Ottawa Business Journal.*

Social Planning Council of Ottawa-Carleton (SPC) (1999a). *A tale of two cities.* Ottawa: SPC.

Social Planning Council of Ottawa-Carleton (SPC). (1999b). *The quality of life in Ottawa-Carleton.* Ottawa: SPC.

Standen, K. (1998, April 6). High tech turns 50. *Ottawa Citizen.* C1–C2.

Tam, P. (2001, February 19). Special report: The changing workplace. *Ottawa Citizen.* B2–B7.

Thussu, D. (2000) *International communication.* London: Arnold.

Winseck, D. (1998). *Reconvergence: A political economy of telecommunications in Canada.* Cresskill, NJ: Hampton Press Inc.

CHAPTER 6

Britain and the Economy of Ignorance

Arun Kundnani

Over the last five years, so much has been written about the Internet and the so-called knowledge economy that it may appear as if nothing new could be said about the matter. We have heard countless times the techno-utopian argument that the Internet will change society, the economy, and politics, making the world a more efficient, peaceful, and democratic place. When these techno-utopians joined with venture capitalists in the mid-1990s, they helped create the huge enthusiasm for a "new economy" based around the idea that trade in information would replace trade in physical goods.

Barely discernible at first, then gradually getting louder, were the voices of the techno-pessimists. They counterargued that current technological changes would only bring insecurity, joblessness, and moral deterioration. With the collapse of new economy share prices in March 2000, the techno-pessimists have had a wider hearing. Their view is a mirror image of the utopian view. For each of the utopian claims that technology will cause a positive change, they counter with negative changes. Yet ironically they share a lot of assumptions with the utopian position. They share the view that technology is going to bring about large upheavals and that these are inevitable. Further, they both share the assumption that changes in society and economy can be predicted from the process of technological innovation itself.

The settled view now emerging from the more sophisticated commentators borrows elements of both the utopians and the pessimists, and emphasizes a longer-term, more complex view of technological change. On this view, today's Internet and new economy do indeed mark the beginning of a prolonged era of change. We can only know at this stage the rough outlines of how technology, economy, and society will coexist, even in the very near future. All we do know is that we need to combine attitudes of flexibility and control, to be prepared to adapt to rapid change as well as to regulate and manage it. There will be a mixture of negative and positive changes, but what is certain is the fact of change itself—that much is inevitable.

This view improves on the simple technological determinism of the techno-utopians and pessimists. However, in its own way, it remains a dangerous view, which serves the interests of particular social blocs to the detriment of others. It is a view that confidently elides social contradictions and suggests that easy leaps can be made from open technologies to open markets to open societies to open minds. But it is precisely at the join between technology and society where all the most important questions about the Internet remain to be asked, and where so many commentators remain silent.

In spite of this, the view that we are embarking on a period of inevitable rapid change towards a new economy or knowledge society has become increasingly influential. In Britain, Tony Blair has placed the transition to a knowledge economy at the center of his government's strategy and has sought to define a political Third Way, based on the imperatives of a new globalized knowledge economy. Within Blair's own Policy Units, a cadre of new economy intellectuals has been recruited to define this agenda and map out how new forms of government and public service might coexist with the knowledge economy. This new economy agenda now dominates the ruling elites of Britain to such an extent that it is difficult to imagine its weakening through a change of government. Yet the road to hegemony for the new economy idea has been remarkably smooth. The only obstacles that have been put in its way are those of falling share prices, rather than substantial intellectual critique. And plummeting share prices since March 2000 have done little to dent its confidence.

In the following pages I examine how in Britain the Internet as an idea, a way of doing business, and of organizing society, has grown in influence and come to provide one of the main ideological supports for the British government. I consider how the metaphor of a network has emerged as a new paradigm for imagining how to organize society more inclusively and openly, with less hierarchy and conflict. Yet this paradigm leads to support for the self-regulating market and neoliberalism globalization, the very processes that worsen race and class exclusion, division, and stratification. I describe the new cult of the entrepreneur, the folk hero of the new economy and how a contradiction is developing between the British state's interest in preserving the racist anti-immigration laws introduced from the early 1970s and the view that migration of skilled IT-walas from Asia may be needed to support innovation in the new economy. I discuss why the transition to the new economy brings with it greater corporatization of public services, along with competition and market values in areas previously immune to their power.

I am therefore less interested in the Internet's number of users, their social backgrounds, the number of Web pages hit or the number of e-mails sent, than I am in how the Internet is being discussed and described by policy-makers. I am less interested in how many government services are available online than in how the ruling elites are talking about the need for public sector services to be reinvented as something called "e-government." I am less interested in the rise and fall of new economy share prices than I am in the weakening of the weakest sections of society: the black and Asian communities; immigrants; and the working class, in general.

The Seduction of Silicon

During the mid-1990s, Britain had become a place in desperate need of change. Thatcher's energetic revolution-from-above, her attacks on the post-war Keynesian consensus, gentlemanly rule and the old cultural elites, and their substitution with the values of middle-class entrepreneurialism and market forces, had waned. All that was left was John Major's reassurances to an aging Home Counties audience that England would be forever village cricket, warm beer, and old maids cycling to church through the morning mist. Many now looked to Tony Blair as harbinger of a much-needed modernization.

Blair had taken charge of the Labour Party in 1994 at a time when it had not won a general election since 1977. Emulating Clinton's success in winning back the political middle ground, Blair was able to make the party acceptable to middle-class voters by dropping the historic commitment to nationalization, becoming business-friendly, and by abandoning policies aimed at redistribution of income. This was combined with a new tough stand on law and order issues that had, until then, been perceived as Labour's Achilles' heel. Denied political power for so long, most Labour Party supporters believed that Blair's shift to the political right could be justified if it won them office. In the 1997 general election the strategy paid off, as large numbers of middle-class voters in marginal seats switched to Labour, giving them a majority in Parliament even larger than the Attlee government of 1945. Meanwhile an increasing number of business managers, journalists, and intellectuals returning from visits to California had tales of a new economy based on the Internet, new ways of doing business and vast potential profits.

In the pages of the San Francisco-based information capitalist magazine *Wired,* the new economy was celebrated with a Panglossian optimism, out of kilter with the gray mood of the time. The contrast between an old, clunky, and unimaginative Britain and California's apparent light-footedness was striking. With the cold war over, and globalization of the world economy marching ahead, the future of the world seemed to be in Silicon Valley, and Britain needed to get a piece of the action.

It was inevitable that Tony Blair's Labour Party would be attracted to the Silicon Valley model, with their shared emphasis on constant modernization and penchant for all things new. The love affair was sealed through a number of go-betweens. The intellectuals gathered around the think-tank called "Demos," which played a key role in defining the Blairite agenda, articulating the Silicon Valley model into a set of policy ideas for Britain. Charles Lead-beater—who believed that Britain should emulate Silicon Valley's "network-based industrial system, which promotes rapid collective learning and flexible adjustment" (Leadbeater, 2000, p.141)—joined Geoff Mulgan, cofounder of Demos, as advocates for this agenda at the highest levels of government. Mulgan was recruited as a key adviser in the Downing Street Policy Unit once Blair was in government from 1997. Peter Mandelson, widely credited as the chief strategist of New Labour's rise, took a particular interest in the knowledge economy and, while heading the Department of Trade and Industry, was an admirer of the Californian model.

By 1999 interest in all things Internet-related reached new heights in Britain. The excitement of e-commerce infected a popular audience as a result of the massive rise in access to the Web, magazine articles on "e-millionaires," and television adverts, which portrayed a shiny new world of electronic oppor-tunity. The glamour of the new economy rubbed off on the government, which had placed the Internet at the heart of its agenda.

The Ideology of the Network

The techno-pessimists are wrong. It is not the Internet itself that is danger-ous, but the idea of the Internet as a symbol and promoter of free trade.

The Internet is an electronic communications medium. It resembles the telegraph and telephone systems in that it is a network, with each point on the network capable of both sending and receiving communications. It differs from these in that its quality of communication is far richer, offering visual as well as textual and aural elements, and its reach is instantaneously global. In the subsection of the Internet known as the World Wide Web—or Web, for short—it also allows a form of broadcast communication, analogous to televi-sion or radio, although the arrangement of the Web into generally static pages of illustrated text suggests a resemblance to print media.

But for many of our current intellectuals, the Internet is far more than a new communications medium. They have been seduced by the idea that the Internet—or, more precisely, its networked structure—is a metaphor for a new capitalism. For these writers, the network represents progress out of the old world of machine-like bureaucracy, hierarchy, and control, in favor of creativity, innova-tion, and freedom. Like earlier mythologies of capitalism, the network model explains away capital's contradictions and naturalizes its social relations, often using biological imagery. The inconvenient reality of systematic unequal distrib-ution of resources among different social or national groups is glossed over.

Nicholas Negroponte, founder of the corporate-sponsored Media Lab at the Massachusetts Institute of Technology and a major investor in *Wired* magazine, pioneered the networkist model of capitalism through the 1990s. He argues that the emergence of this new order is inevitable and organic, "like a force of nature" (Negroponte, 1995, p. 229). "The agent of change will be the Internet, both literally and as a model or metaphor. The Internet is interesting not only as a massive and pervasive global network but also as an example of something that has evolved with no apparent designer in charge" (p. 181).

Many center-left liberals have been attracted to this vision, from Manuel Castells's (1996) three-volume analysis of the "network society," to high-profile commentator Jonathan Freedland (2000), who celebrates the end of an old world of division in favor of one defined by integration and symbolised by the Web: "It is a hopeful symbol: a collection of loose, frail threads tying one individual to another" (p. 16). In Britain the two leading liberal intellectuals of the network vision are Charles Leadbeater and Geoff Mulgan, who have each crafted a version of the network ideology that has become a central theme of the Blairite script.

According to the theorists, as knowledge becomes the dominant factor in production and delivery of services, organizations will increasingly form themselves as networks. In a networked organization the emphasis is on horizontal linkages between units in a cooperative organizational structure, rather than on vertical linkages from the top downwards. The horizontal network favors initiative, responsibility, and self-organization, rather than the unthinking implementation of a superior's ideas. Knowledge is encouraged to spread across different units in the network, rather than being solely in the hands of the executive layer of a hierarchy. The network form of organization is seen as more agile and able to adjust to change. Its decent red nature allows it to evolve organically.

> As a rule the availability of more bandwidth, more communicational tools and more opportunities for horizontal communication tends to favor what I have called weak power structures, structures based on the economical, light sharing of information rather than the hierarchical strong power of mechanical systems where most of the organization's energy is used to maintain internal control. (Mulgan, 1998, p. 154)

Power is seen as withering away, as the network becomes self-organizing and dispenses with a tight command structure. Moreover networks are thought to be more inclusive, encouraging diversity and individuality. With each unit allowed some autonomy, confidence, and mutual trust grow in a virtuous circle (that is, a positive feedback loop), as different units develop their own identities. The concept of social capital, currently fashionable as a leitmotif of Third Way writing, is used to describe this reservoir of mutual trust: "Networks are not held together by hierarchy or structure but by relationships and social capital" (Leadbeater, 2000, p. 126).

Firms, economies, media, the relations between nation-states—all are becoming organized more like networks, according to Leadbeater and Mulgan, with all the associated advantages of democratization, empowerment, and inclusivity. The network concept is used as a master key to open up all conceptual barriers, in the same way that the word text was used by postmodernism. For the networkists, there is nothing outside of the network. Society itself is described as an information network. Technology and society are collapsed together so that the issue of how technology interacts with society cannot be asked: "technology *is* society" (Castells, 1996, p. 5).

For these advocates of "globalization with a human face," the tightening integration of the world economy is itself best understood as a series of networks across the world, rather than as a set of power relations. The networkists describe a world freed from structural divisions, a frictionless world, where knowledge, confidence, and wealth flow easily over dwindling national boundaries—a world without producers, without social class. The mass of communication networks across the world constitutes an information biosphere—a single, interconnected information organism of free expression and free trade. Indeed, the growth of free market globalization is presented as an inevitable result of technological progress, rather than a normative choice on the part of the ruling elites. As proven by the recent French ban on Internet sales of Nazi memorabilia, the inevitability is a concoction.

The Internet, as we have seen, is celebrated as a technology without a design, able to develop autonomously and intelligently, free of centralized control. When the Internet is taken as a metaphor for society, the same idea of an order without central points of command is powerfully suggested. Society is conceived as a set of interconnections dispersed so thinly that it no longer makes sense to speak of centers and peripheries of power—an account similar to that given in the poststructuralist thought of Michel Foucault (1988).

> Much of the baggage of sovereignty and power that we have inherited from the days when the main role of government was to protect us from danger is now obsolete, and states are now making the uneasy transition from thinking of themselves as pyramids, with clear boundaries and clear lines of command, to something more like a flotilla where no one is in absolute command. (Mulgan, 1998, p. 197)

For a world in the throes of free trade globalization, where multinational corporations occupy more and more areas of life, the postmodern image of society as a decentralized network in which there are no centers of power, is a useful enough ideology. As the subtitle to Leadbeater's (2000) book suggests, questions of power and society are obsolete—they have evaporated into "thin air." With everything on the move, power becomes meaningless, and movement is everything. Yet for all the apparent change, innovation, and movement, the grip of race, class, and corporate capital is stronger than ever.

Open Markets, Open Society, Open Minds?

The network ideology blends these postmodern themes with respect for market forces. The orthodox neoliberal interpretation of the market—where the threat of closure drives down costs—is swapped for a benign view, adapted for the knowledge economy, in which the free market is the natural font of innovation.

Information networks are imagined as free markets in ideas. If ideas are commodities, natural selection will automatically finance the most popular. Indeed, networkists see the Internet as potentially the ultimate market of ideas, with free expression overlaid on free trade in a process of near-perfect competition—ignoring the class structure and the inequality of access to the means of communication. Bill Gates is just one among many to argue that the Internet will increase market efficiencies, a view he last espoused when invited to speak at the World Economic Forum in Melbourne, September 2000 (Barkham, 2000). The globalization of e-commerce—which implies both the expansion of network infrastructure and the imposition of a legal framework protecting corporate rule across the globe—is seen as, not only contributing to economic growth, but also as inherently democratizing.

Repeating the old capitalist mythology of the nineteenth century, the networkists present the market as a free arena, open to anyone. Today in the knowledge economy, trade in goods, land, labor, and money has been eclipsed by trade in ideas. The free market in ideas is seen as an essential environment for the fostering of innovation. The usual threat to market efficiency—monopoly—is thought to be less of a concern in the new economy, since knowledge capital is regarded as having a limited lifespan of usefulness and so is less likely to lead to protection. What the networkists usually ignore is the fact that there are good reasons to think that the knowledge economy is more likely than others to suffer from monopoly distortions, as a result of economies of scale (Kundnani, 1998). Furthermore, the much-vaunted openness of the new economy belies the fact that multinational corporations—AOL-Time Warner, IBM, Microsoft—dominate the sector. In telecommunications, the top 10 firms now control 86% of the world market (Harris, 2001). In computer software and manufacture, the dominance of a handful of players is even greater.

Networkists are in awe of the corporate world that seems to them to be the only place where new ideas are thriving. The belief that creativity is the sole preserve of corporations leads to a new legitimization of corporate power, even where, as in the Microsoft case, that rule is monopolistic. Attached to this toadying to private firms is a clear message that, in an age of innovation, the state has failed to keep up. Few can now remember that the Internet itself was invented in state-funded universities.

The Cult of the Entrepreneur

At times the network philosophy appears to be nothing more than the fancies of the *digerati*, the world made over in the image of the corporate nerd who thinks about all relationships in terms of technical problems. But since the net became a target of commercial exploitation from 1995, the nerd has been replaced by the entrepreneur as the public face of networkism. The entrepreneurs have become the folk heroes of Blair's Third Way. They neither own machinery nor sell their labor power—they have nothing to sell but their ideas. According to the cult of the net entrepreneur, they are buccaneers in the fast-moving world of the new economy, never staying in one place for very long. Drivers of creativity and innovation, the power that accrues to any one of them is ephemeral, since they are only as good as their last idea. Yet many are fabulously wealthy: Jeffery Bezos of Amazon, $8.9 billion, Lawrence Ellison of Oracle, $8.4 billion, and Bill Gates of Microsoft, $71 billion (Harris, 2001).

The old yuppie image of the entrepreneur from the 1980s has given way to one of Bohemian flair and intelligence. The new entrepreneurs are casually dressed, apparently everyday folk. They appear to create wealth, not through mass production, with all its connotations of monotonous labor, alienation and exploitation, but in the knowledge economy, where workers use their brains not their hands.

The glamour of entrepreneurialism can make the sleaziest multinational smell of roses. For years Microsoft was able to present itself as the plucky entrepreneur fighting the corporate imperialism of IBM. By the time the conjuring trick was exposed, Microsoft's accumulated power reached as far as the Philippine police force, who had been ordered to conduct raids in schools for pirated copies of educational software (Kundnani, 1998). Yet Bill Gates was welcomed to Britain in Tony Blair's first months of government and recruited as a special adviser for Britain's use of technology in schools.

It is the cult of the entrepreneur that has enabled New Labor to justify a deepening process of corporatization. Indeed, a major concern of Third Way politics is the attempt to spread the values of net entrepreneurialism to the public sector, in order to save it. "'Government must behave like an entrepreneur' and create 'a vital synergy between business and government'" (Mandelson, 1999, p. 8).

Clean Capitalism?

For the Third Way intellectuals, the transition to a knowledge economy promises the Holy Grail of social democracy, a reason for thinking that capital and labor are no longer opposing forces, a clean capitalism, where conflicting interests can all be absorbed into a mutually beneficial social contract of knowledge creation. But the knowledge economy does not dispense with the dirty side of capitalism; it merely displaces it to the poorer parts of the world, where it becomes invisible (Sivandandan, 1989). The networking dream does not help the Third World sleep any easier. It is no coincidence that Nike is both Leadbeater's (2000) archetypal networking firm and a major exploiter of cheap labor. Its strategy of concentrating purely on the design of its shoes and their marketing, while their physical assembly is outsourced to the Third World, is seen as innovation in the knowledge economy. The First World concentrates on producing the knowledge, the Third World on making the economies.

One person's network is another person's hierarchy. But the new economy ideologues choose not to see what is outside their own networked universe. From their perspective, it becomes possible to imagine a politics without adversaries, yet another resurrection of the 1950s "end of ideology" thesis:

> Politics can look less like a competition between blocs to get hold of a static pool of power, and more like an information system attempting with varying degrees of success to aggregate millions of preferences, to devise common solutions and to mobilize changes in public behavior such as harder work, better parenting, or greater willingness to obey laws. (Mulgan, 1998, p.155)

Capitalism supposedly now has a vested interest in inclusivity because a knowledge economy requires everyone's talent to be valued. The reserve army of labor is a thing of the past. Labor-power itself has been replaced by "human capital." "An innovative economy must be socially inclusive to realize its full potential. If we write off 30% of the population, we are writing off a lot of knowledge, intelligence and creativity" (Mandelson, 1999, p. 155). To maximize the circulation of knowledge—Blair's mantra of "education, education, education"—is to create economic opportunity as well as political empowerment. This is a unique opportunity for the centre-left, according to Leadbeater, Mulgan, Mandelson, and Blair.

But it is also an opportunity for business. In line with the overriding promotion of market values, entrepreneurialism and network technology as panaceas for all social ills, the corporations are invited in. The contradiction between the desire for high quality comprehensive education, and the unwillingness of the rich to fund it, is resolved through commercial sponsorship.

The cost of investing in computers for schools can be paid for by supermarket chains that are rewarded with added value to their brand names. The National Grid for Learning—Blair's ambitious scheme to link all schools to the Internet—can be paid for by British Telecom, who instantly get privileged commercial access to the educational software market. In Education Action Zones—local mechanisms for bringing private money into schooling—children are supplied with resource packs produced by McDonald's. Music teachers are advised to encourage pupils to make up words for "Old McDonald had a store," to the tune of "Old McDonald had a farm" (Cohen, 1999, p. 179). Britain is moving towards the American model, where schooling is a commodity, widely traded on the stock market, and worth $650 billion (Monbiot, 2000, p. 331).

E-government

Along with the corporations comes a banal optimism, in which social problems—such as a class-ridden education system—become a matter of technical problem solving, a failure to innovate, rather than a lack of political will or democratic accountability. What is needed is a new breed of social entrepreneur, to apply a corporate approach to innovation in the public and voluntary sectors. "We need to embark on a period of sustained and intense innovation in our civic institutions, to create a new civic culture to accompany the dynamism of the new economy" (Leadbeater, 2000, p.168). Inevitably competition is seen as the basis of progress. Leadbeater suggests that the National Health Service will, in the future, compete on the Internet in a global healthcare economy (Leadbeater, 2000, p. 247).

The envisaged transformation of the public sector will, of course, require corporate expertise. More than half the places on New Labor policy task forces have been given to big business (Cohen, 1999, p179). The management consultants have been lining up to profit from the creation of e-government. Deloitte Consulting, anticipating the growing need for governments to be told how to do things by corporations, has established a "Public Sector Institute." In a report entitled "At the Dawn of E-government," consultants advise that "transformation is what e-Government is all about, and with Internet applications powering streamlined service delivery and supported by the best staff and IT infrastructure, governments will evolve into new enterprises that bear no resemblance to their structure today" (Deloitte Consulting, 2000, p. 4).

But the vast amounts of government money poured into IT projects to date—where the state has contracted firms such as Siemens, EDS, and ICL—have usually ended in disaster. There have been over 30 failed schemes since

Labor came to office, resulting in billion pound losses. Of course the public purse is expected to underwrite this risk—such is the price to be paid for introducing the spirit of entrepreneurialism to government.

Britain Rebranded

Techno-utopianism is often met with scorn by the ruling class on this side of the Atlantic; British elites have traditionally associated the right to rule with study of the arts, rather than science and engineering. But in a country that prides itself on being the home of the industrial revolution, technology is never far away from the perennial calls for 'modernization.' Like Harold Wilson before him, Blair has flung himself at new technology with boyish enthusiasm, hoping to make it the linchpin of a new national self-image, in which Britain can once again bestride the world, this time as "the world center for e-commerce." No longer happy to play Greece to America's Rome, New Labor believes that in the knowledge economy, Britain can retake its rightful place as a major economic power, taking advantage of a "tradition for inventiveness" and the spread of the English language, rather than relying on the old faiths of Empire, military strength, and sterling.

In December 1998 Peter Mandelson launched the white paper, "Our Competitive Future: Building the Knowledge-driven Economy," and made it clear that the Internet was now regarded as a vital tool for economic development. At the launch, Mandelson said that "Britain must become a leading nation on the Internet, which is now the fastest-growing market place in the global economy" (Thompson, 2001, p. 4). The following year, Blair set out his aim of making the UK "the best environment in the world for e-commerce" (Performance and Innovation Unit, 1999, p. 1). In a flurry of new initiatives, action plans and reports, the government has tried to define an agenda for techno-Britain. An "e-envoy" has been followed by an "e-minister" to oversee the development of Internet trading and to put government services online. The great hope is that London can keep a leading role on the world economic stage, through knowledge capital instead of finance capital. But whether the plan succeeds may depend on Blair tackling the deeper problems in British society—a class system that hinders creativity and leads to massive variations in the regional distribution of wealth; immigration laws that exacerbate labor shortages and legitimize institutional racism across society; a legal system that gives no protection from corporate excess; and the absence of a culture of accountability in the public services.

The solutions to these problems will not come about by applying corporate models of customer-centric government such as those recommended by Deloitte Consulting (2000): "Historically citizens' perception of government service has been less than glowing. When they think about the prospect of contacting the government in almost any way, they picture long waits and cumbersome procedures. . . . Today, leading governments are changing both perception and the reality by giving top priority to the customer" (p. 1). As Tom Nairn (2000) points out, the shift from British "subject" to "customer" should not be confused with true political citizenship: "Unable to implement a new conception of the state, Blairism had defaulted to the model of a business company. . . . This is neither ancient subjecthood nor modern constitutional citizenship. It is more like a weak identity-hybrid, at a curious tangent to both" (p. 77). The conservatism of the British state—its claim to represent an unchanging cultural essence handed down through the generations—survives this modernization and, when necessary, can be wheeled out again as the basis for a regressive nationalist allegiance (Kundnani, 2000).

The American Dream

The model, as ever, in Britain's attempts to reinvent itself, is the American variant of capitalism. In the hands of Leadbeater and Mulgan, the network philosophy is an attempt to import what are perceived as the best aspects of that country's system, a more "flexible" labor market, greater social mobility, technology-driven economic growth, more corporate "freedoms," and a more liberal immigration system. It is assumed that these can be separated from the worst aspects of the U.S. model—the huge entrenched economic inequalities and the brutal state racism by which class inequality is protected and legitimized.

A major line of fissure in this project is on the question of immigration policy, where the needs of the new economy for overseas skilled labor clash with the racism that led to the end of primary immigration following the 1971 Immigration Act. The networkists argue that migrants are likely to be enterprising and creative, a potential pool of talent not to be wasted. Their contribution to the development of Silicon Valley is highlighted. Silicon Valley itself is reckoned to support a "cosmopolitan openness" so that "many of its biggest companies are run by post-war immigrants" (Leadbeater, 2000, p. 141). Jonathan Freedland (2000), witnessing the naturalization ceremony performed by recent arrivals in the United States, comments, "It was an extraordinary sight. Immigrants, elsewhere tolerated and often loathed, were being embraced by an official of the United States government. Dark-skinned foreigners were not being cast out, but ushered in" (p. 141). The implication is that Britain could reap the advantages of following an American-style immigration policy, if only the inertia of Britain's imperial past—its racism—could be overcome. Furthermore, for Leadbeater and Mulgan, the new economy renders the rules of physical territoriality less significant than the networks of information flows. "Today the [territorial] boundaries are still there but instead you see economies, and the centers of power are not walled, but rather the hubs of creativity and exchange" (Mulgan, 1998, p. 69).

But wall-building is on the rise. The U.S.-Mexico border—a crossing that activists believe claimed the lives of at least 1,600 migrants between 1993 and 1997—is increasingly fortified with barbed wire fences, security patrols, and surveillance technologies (Barkham, 1999, p. 7). Meanwhile corporations, such as Wackenhut, profit from the industrial warehousing of immigration detainees—an estimated $500 million business, now expanded to the UK (Barkham, 2000). It is not that U.S. immigration policy is more liberal. Rather, with the gradual evolution of a system of national origin quotas, encouragement of overseas recruitment by U.S. corporations and minimal welfare provision for new arrivals, it is more finely tuned to the developmental needs of industry. The American IT industry, for example, is able to use Indian computer programmers whose education has been paid for by a poorer country. The Indian Institutes of Technology—Nehru's hopeful springboards for an independent, scientific, and prosperous India—have become finishing schools for American capitalism.

Britain, on the other hand, has moved from a period of postwar reconstruction, during which a cheap, black immigrant workforce was recruited through colonial connections, to the principle of zero immigration from outside the European Community bloc on the assumption that free movement within a 'Fortress Europe' would cater for all of Britain's labor needs. But the Fortress Europe system has failed to provide a sufficient supply of workers at the bottom end of the British economy. As a result, this gap has been filled by a growing underclass of Third World and eastern European immigrants, usually themselves exiles from the devastation wrought by neoliberalism globalization, entering Britain either without documents or through the asylum system.

> [T]he refugees, migrants and asylum-seekers, the flotsam and jetsam of latter-day imperialism—are the new under-class of silicon age capitalism. It is they who perform the arduous, unskilled, dirty jobs in the ever-expanding service sector, who constitute the casual, ad hoc, temporary workers in computerised manufacture, who provide agribusiness with manual farm labour. . . . They are, in a word, the cheap and captive labour force—rightless, rootless, peripatetic and temporary, illegal even—without which post-industrial society cannot run. (Sivanandan, 1989, pp. 15–16)

In addition, Britain is unable to fill shortages of skilled workers in nursing, teaching, and the IT sector.

The result is that immigration to Britain is unplanned and undocumented, and therefore, provides little guarantee for capital that incoming labor meets its needs. Consequently, for the first time since the early 1980s, a racialized debate on immigration is high on the political agenda, and the conservative press is calling for "the drawbridge to be raised." The alternative offered by the Blair government is a twofold modernization. First, there is to be a review of the commitment in the 1951 U.N. Convention on Refugees, which obliges the state to provide due legal process to all applications for asylum, whatever their circumstances. Second, following the American model, a limited amount of direct recruitment of overseas skilled workers is to be allowed, to meet specific needs of the economy. The economic migrants, currently abused en masse, will be screened and sectioned off into categories of skilled and unskilled, wanted and unwanted. As such, Blair's attempt to match immigration policy more closely to the needs of the economy, like his other reforms, will leave in place the substance of Britain's conservatism.

The Phony Revolution

In Britain the New Labor government has celebrated the Internet as more than just a new communications technology, but as an icon of a new globalized world of free trade, in which social and economic divisions can be easily resolved as inclusivity and multiculturalism become the norm. Yet this network ideology does not dismantle Britain's race and class divisions, but reinforces them, by intensifying the power of corporate capital.

In spite of all the pages that have been written about the Internet, there is nothing to challenge what has become a new fully-fledged capitalist ideology; as a result that ideology has almost become accepted as common sense. The real Internet debate has yet to start.

References

Barkham, P. (1999, August/September).From Schengen to La Linea: Breaking down borders. *Campaign Against Racism & Fascism*. pp. 4–6.

Barkham, P. (2000, August). The asylum system: Who profits? *Campaign Against Racism & Fascism*. p. 7.

Barkham, P. (2000, September 13). Gates rounds on protesters. *Guardian*. p. 5.

Castells, M. (1996). *The rise of the network society*. Oxford: Blackwell.

Cohen, N. (1999). *Cruel Britannia: Reports on the sinister and preposterous*. London: Verso.

Deloitte Consulting. (2000). *At the dawn of e-government: The citizen as customer*. New York: Deloitte-Touche.

Foucault, M. (1988). *Politics, philosophy, culture: interviews and other writings of Michel Foucault, 1977–1984*. London: Routledge.

Freedland, J. (1998). *Bring home the revolution: The case for a British republic*. London: Fourth Estate.

Freedland, J. (2000, January 8). Us. *Guardian Weekend*, pp. 8–16.

Harris, J. (2001). IT and the global ruling class. *Race & Class, 42* (4), 35–56.

Kundnani, A. (1998). Where do you want to go today? The rise of information capital. *Race & Class, 40*, 49–71.

Kundnani, A. (2000). "Stumbling on": Race, class and England. *Race & Class, 41*, 1–18.

Leadbeater, C. (2000). *Living on thin air: The new economy*. London: Penguin.

Mandelson, P. (1999, September 13). The new conservative enemy. *Independent*, p. 8.

Monbiot, G. (2000). *Captive state: The corporate takeover of Britain*. London: Macmillan.

Mulgan, G. (1998). *Connexity: Responsibility, freedom, business and power in the new century*. London: Vintage.

Nairn, T. (2000). *After Britain: New Labour and the return of Scotland*. London: Granta.

Negroponte, N. (1995). *Being digital*. New York: Alfred A. Knopf.

Performance and Innovation Unit. (1999). *E-commerce@its.best.uk*. London: Performance and Innovation Unit.

Sivanandan, A. (1989). New circuits of imperialism. *Race & Class, 30*, 1–19.

Thompson, B. (2001, January 22). The best an e-economy can get?. *New Statesman Special Supplement*, p. 4.

PART III

Leading the Periphery
to Media Hegemony

CHAPTER 7

"*Sábado Gigante* (Giant Saturday)" and the Cultural Homogenization of Spanish-Speaking People

Martha I. Chew Sánchez,
Janet M. Cramer, and Leonel Prieto

As the global economy mushrooms and corporate mergers become commonplace, cultural changes inevitably follow. As deregulation and international joint ventures in the media industry are in line with the increased need for an international market, global media seek to provide international advertisers with audiences that share habits, tastes, language, age, or background in order to fuel an economy largely based on economies of scale. Concentration, consolidation, and oligarchy in media are often accompanied by a recognizable process of cultural homogenization (Barbero & Jaramillo, 1999; Barbero, 1993)—especially among media conglomerates (Bagdikian, 2000; Schiller, 1989, 1996). If media corporations strive toward expansion of their markets and their profits—what might be called media without frontiers—then that logic also drives the creation of global programming and global markets that tend to homogenize audiences toward consumption of mass-produced cultural goods. We show here how the Spanish-language television show, "*Sábado Gigante*" is a prime example of this trend.

Homogenization may be defined as the decrease and obliteration in cultural and subcultural uniqueness, accomplished, by and large, through the creation of a sanitized and trivialized regional and global commercial culture. Processes of cultural homogenization, in serving the hegemonic order, often subsume culture under the narrower dimension of economics. Homogenization manifests not only in consumption patterns but also in the attitudes people have about certain values and institutions. Popular music, advertising, and television programs serve to transmit the dominant myths, ideologies, and values of the leading capitalistic countries, thus influencing how people from other countries see, experience, understand, and act in their social lives (Barber, 1995a, 1995b; van Elteren, 1996; Adorno & Horkheimer, 1972; Bryson, 1995).

131

While acknowledging the ideological weight of the mass media, it is important to also consider whether the "dialogue" that people have with multinational media shows interest from both sides to reconstruct and re-accommodate the economy, the culture, the politcal system, and the way of life. It is possible that popular desire for redefining communities may resonate in offerings by media producers, suggesting that corporate economic goals may allow a new social and cultural integration. *"Sábado Gigante"* for instance, seems to meet social needs that go beyond audience entertainment, suggesting that cultural homogenization is not merely imposed, but may also come from cultural, social, or political interests and preferences. This study thus considers the complicated interaction between audiences and media.

Two questions prompt the present research: To what extent do global media homogenize their audiences? Does this homogenization serve a capitalist social order, specifically in the sustenance of media corporations? The assumption here is that global audiences will be formed into communities defined more by consumerism than by national boundaries. In other words, the creation of a homogenous "identity" is assumed to serve a global, corporate economic structure. Here, we describe how *"Sábado Gigante"* contributes to the standardization and homogenization of Spanish-speaking people. A key concern is how the program constructs and reconstructs Hispanic identity. The present study also notes that cultural boundaries are disappearing in the process of homogenization, as new communities are created by positioning products within Spanish-speaking countries and within Hispanic communities in the United States.

Issues concerning media's role in cultural homogenization and the profit basis of such a role derive from the conceptual frameworks of cultural studies, postcolonial theory, and critical theory:

- Cultural studies scholars point to media as creators of shared meanings through representing and creating a notion of symbolic reality that serves to create a community or culture for audiences (Carey, 1988; Rodríguez, 1996; Williams, 1981, 1983).

- A critical approach to media studies seeks to identify class relations and structures of social power conveyed through media content, specifically with regard to this creation of shared community. From this perspective, media are not merely carriers of ideology that manipulate and indoctrinate; they shape people's very idea of themselves and the world—an identity construction that ultimately serves a dominant power (Althusser, 1971; Hall, 1984a; Mattleart, 1980). This identity construction is part of the ideological role of media, and it is this ideological role that is most scrutinized for how it meshes with the interests of the capitalist elites.

This notion of ideology, as Stuart Hall wrote, "sets limits to the degree to which a society-in-dominance can easily, smoothly and functionally reproduce itself" (Hall, 1984b, p. 112).

- Beyond the socioeconomic consequences of this identity creation through the media are the effects of the proliferation of negative stereotypes of other cultures that occur through idealization of the dominant culture. Postcolonial communication theorists maintain that the cultural stereo-typing in media content intensifies negative effects for minority groups (e.g., Hartmann & Husband, 1972; Said, 1992). Their concern expressed by these theorists is that the representation of other places and people affects the relation of power and knowledge between the group that is represented and the group who presents these "others."

Merging these theoretical perspectives leads to the critique guiding the present study: we recognize media contributions to the creation, reproduction, and maintenance of a global, economic social order that produces unequal relations of power and that favors dominant individuals and groups. The principle assumed here is that when global media industries create global programming for global markets, they create new communities—specifically, communities based on principles of consumerism (Tomlinson, 1991). Consequently, the consolidation and expansion of this global order privileges the type of order of the leading capitalist countries while marginalizing or absorbing other countries' orders and cultures.

This chapter presents cultural homogenization as the outcome of interactions between economic and political forces and the media that construct and reinvent an evolving hegemonic order led by socioeconomic elites. Following a brief historical background to *"Sábado Gigante,"* and its host, Don Francisco, we discuss the themes, images, and activities of the program that construct a culturally homogenized community of Spanish-speaking, pan-Latin, consumers.

Cultural Homogenization and the Media in Latin America

In Latin America, cultural homogenization must be understood in the historical context of national security as understood by domestic elites and their government agents. Politically, homogenization was a condition that, in turbulent times, helped shield national elites from internal dissension and external invasion. Economically, homogenization bolstered and protected certain elite strategies, presented as beneficial for all Brazilians, Chileans, etc., but invariably serving the elites' notion of nation in trade, production, and social norms. This is illustrated by the attitude of Latin American states towards the

North American Free Trade Agreement (NAFTA), the Free Trade Agreement of the Americas (FTAA), and other regional trade agreements secured by the socioeconomic elites that also have responded to the interest of the culture industry. Importantly, despite its history of alternating state and private controls (Waisbord, 1998), the culture industry—specifically television—may be seen as an agent in securing homogenization in service of the elites' notion of nation by featuring programs promoting the national interest and a national identity.

Of course, long before capitalist elites assumed national leaderships of states throughout Latin America, a severe form of cultural homogenization was imposed. In the course of the Spanish Conquest, national cultural unity was imposed through language, Catholicism, colonial government, and Spanish culture and customs—dictated by repression and coercion. After several hundred years, most states had nominal independence and featured national governments representing the interests of the socioeconomic elites of their countries (García Canclini, 1987, 1993; García Canclini & Monet, 1999; Monsiváis, 1981).

During the 1980s and early 1990s, capitalist economic and political forces generated free market reforms worldwide. Latin American countries—led by corporate-friendly governments—adopted neoliberal economic reforms constitutive of the aptly named "Washington Consensus" (Lowenthal, 1992). NAFTA, MERCOSUR, and an increasing number of bilateral and multilateral trade agreements have facilitated the breakdown of "frictions" to trade and economic and cultural homogenization (Fuentes, 1992; Hills, 1992; Beatriz Palacio & Olarte, 1998).

Cultural homogenization needs to be understood, then, not only as a tactic of colonial or imperial masters, but also as a mechanism by which strategic political and economic benefits have been and are produced for Latin American and other elites. In Mexico for instance, NAFTA is one major result of the consolidation of a powerful, but economically and politically narrow, free trade coalition between the state and big business elites that helped cement the neoliberal reform agenda of the governments of Miguel de la Madrid (such as achieving GATT membership and support for the World Bank and International Monetary Fund economic models), Carlos Salinas de Gortari, and subsequent governments (Prieto & Chew Sánchez, 2000).

The economic reforms of the 1980s instituted a "process of deregulation, acquisition of new technologies, and privatization of government television stations" (Crovi-Drueta, 1999). These reforms have encouraged a new cultural homogenization based on the free market, collapsing culturally distinct practices within the consumerism, advertising, and commodity entertainment. In general, throughout Latin America, radio and television has been under siege from these same processes of privatization and commercialization.

Undoubtedly, the media has been tied to the state and national elites in Latin America from its inception (Fox, 1988). In Argentina, radio was extensively used to reconcile conflicting interests and to consolidate Perón's populist policies. Radio in Mexico started in 1923 under the commercial and private model in which the government had an active role in the promotion of the capitalist class. The U.S. Marines first brought radio to Central America during an invasion of Nicaragua in the 1920s, then turned over control to the dictator, Somoza. Televisa, the Mexican media monopoly, was created in 1972 through consolidating the interests of members of Mexico's elite, including the Azcárraga and Aléman families. Televisa openly support Mexico's ruling party, the *Partido Revolucionario Institucional* (PRI), creating a strong bond between the media industry and government rule that has lasted into the twenty-first century (Fernandez & Paxman, 2000). The history of electronic communication is strikingly similar in each country of Latin America: ruling elites either monopolized the media with government protection or the state operated broadcasting directly. Meanwhile, with considerable approval from national governments, NBC, ABC, Disney, and other U.S. media investors occasionally established separate networks dedicated to entertainment and supportive of the status quo (Waisbord, 1998; Fox, 1988).

Overall, political and business elites cooperated to ensure a culture industry that could be used as a powerful socialization agent and as "an instrument . . . to rule and get the necessary concessions that allow[ed] them to achieve their objectives" (Azrur Osorio, 1996). Of course, images on TV contradicted the conditions on the ground for the continent's dispossessed, leading to widespread social protest and political rebellion. Elites unleashed military dictatorships across the continent, ensuring capitalist development and security. Under conditions of repression in the 1960s and 1970s, Latin America experienced rapid growth, diversification of industry, and an expansion of an internal market that serviced the new middle classes and the millions of peasants who had become wageworkers. Owning a television set, among other products, epitomized the notion of social development and demonstrated that Latin America was progressing (García Canclini, 1993). As the popularity of television grew, state-friendly private broadcasters established near-monopoly control in several countries—O Globo in Brazil and Televisa in Mexico, for example.

Televisa

Televisa, the media company that dominates Spanish-speaking countries and audiences, is the world's most profitable producer, exporter, and distributor of Spanish-speaking television broadcasting, film, publishing, and music recording. Televisa operates 17 radio stations with 30 national affiliates that reach

60% of Mexico's population. With four TV channels and 652 television stations in Mexico, Televisa reaches 99% of Mexican households with television and attracts 90% of the Mexican viewing audience (Malkin, 1995). Televisa has become the dominant broadcaster in Mexico through its unofficial partnership with the government, which it has aggressively supported for over 70 years (Fernández & Paxman, 2000).

While it has been consolidating and legitimizing the Mexican government, Televisa has been expanding its own power internationally—distributing programming to over 350 million Spanish speakers outside Mexico. Televisa exports soap operas, which account for 75% of all programming, to all of Latin America and 125 other countries (Ortiz Crespo, 1999; Quiñones, 2001). Televisa also owns 49% of Chile's Megavisión, 76% of the Peruvian Compañia Peruana de Radiofusión (Ortiz Crespo, 1999), and in the early 1990s, formed a joint news service with Rupert Murdoch and Brazilian media giant Organizacoes Globo to bring direct broadcast satellite service to Latin America (Malkin, 1995). In 1993 Televisa expanded to the United States, with its purchase of 25% of Univisión, the largest Spanish-language broadcaster in the United States (Romney, 2001). Eighty-five percent of Hispanics in the United States—a $350 billion a year market—watch Univisión (Consoli, 2000). In short, joined with O Globo and Univisión, Televisa dominates and defines Spanish-language television from the Canadian border to Tierra del Fuego.

Much like the rest of Latin American television, Televisa adopted the U.S. model of advertising and entertainment early on (Altamirano Celis, 1987). Seeking audiences for advertisers, this approach tends to level or absorb cultural difference—a kind of lowest common denominator broadcasting. Some scholars have noted this tendency in U.S. Spanish language media, a strategy termed "pan-ethnic marketing." According to América Rodríguez (1996):

> [T]he nexus of U.S. Spanish language media 'audiencemaking' is the notion of U.S. Latino pan-ethnicity . . . [which] holds that all U.S. Latinos, Latin American immigrants and their descendants, are one unitary group, regardless of differences of national origin, race, class, or U.S. immigration history. U.S. Latino pan-ethnicity, and its hemispheric complement, panamericanism, construct the 'Hispanic market,' and are the 'symbolic glue' that holds together the Noticiero Univisión audience for national advertisers. (p. 60)

As economic development, political stability, and the needs of media industries coalesce, cultural homogenization through language and shared experiences becomes an ever more salient factor characterizing hegemonic relations emerging in Latin American media and culture.

"Sábado Gigante":
Voice of the People?

The purpose of the present study is to examine a specific instance of cultural homogenization in the media: Univisión's *"Sábado Gigante." "Sábado Gigante"* is the longest-running TV program in the Americas. It is the only television show continuously broadcast for nearly 40 years and conducted by the same host: Don Francisco. The program is transmitted to the rest of the world via Galavisión. Half of its Latin American audience is in Mexico (Rojas, 1994), but *"Sábado Gigante"* has been consistently rated among the top ten television programs on Hispanic networks in the United States. *"Sábado Gigante"* is the most popular Spanish-language television show in the world with an audience of 10 million viewers (Martínez, 1997).

Created by Mario Kreutzberger (Don Francisco) in 1962 in Chile, *"Sábado Gigante"* was modeled on U.S. variety show television and its commercialized format. In this sense, *"Sábado Gigante"* is "a hybrid expression of a multinational phenomenon in which the United States is the hegemonic center" (Altamirano Celis,1987, p. 30). One striking indication of *"Sábado Gigante's"* alignment with cultural practices that meet the needs of international and domestic elites is Kruetzberger's accommodation to the Pinochet government, which eliminated all television that allowed "participation-representation of the masses" because they were considered "demagogic, political or subversive. . . . Participation and cultural expression was negated in the national civil society" (Altamirano Celis, 1987, p. 176). But, *"Sábado Gigante"* thrived.

Kruetzberger did not concentrate on Chile, however. Since the very early days of the program, Kreutzberger foresaw the importance of the international market and wanted to build a network in which people from all over Latin America could view the program. Venezuela, Argentina, and Ecuador were the first countries to be incorporated, soon joined by Peru and Puerto Rico. In 1986 Channel 23 of Chile partnered with Univisión, and since then, *"Sábado Gigante"* International has been produced in Miami. In 1987 the program reached all of Central America and following Televisa's part purchase of Univisión in 1992, *"Sábado Gigante"* covered the Spanish-speaking universe. Now, 40 years from its first broadcast, *"Sábado Gigante"* has a weekly audience of over 100 million people worldwide.

Given its longevity and popularity, *"Sábado Gigante"* is worthy of investigation solely as a premier example of Spanish-language television. Coupled with the outspoken consumerist ideology of Kruetzberger as Don Francisco, the program deserves analysis for its ability to successfully meld diverse cultural audiences within a homogenized, virtual culture of commercialism. Our study began with the random selection and videotaping of 10 programs totaling 40 hours of broadcasting during the period from September 1998 to May 1999. Researchers recorded the nationalities of program personalities and partici- pants whenever explicitly noted in the program. Information pamphlets from the program's producer in Miami and from the show's Web site provided addi- tional reference data.

"*Sábado Gigante*" follows a consistent program format that includes, on average, four musical segments, six grand contests, four smaller contests, four journalism spots, and three to four comic sketches. Among the 300 people present on the show, 60% live in Miami; the rest are visitors from different Latin American countries and/or different states in the United States. An average of 40 guests appear on each show, all expenses paid. Guests partici- pate in contests, games, interviews, and other parts of the program.

Our analysis followed programming divisions: contests, comic sketches, interviews, musical performances, and commercial spots. Recurring images and language were noted, as well as the performance of specific ritu- als and the nature of the participation of the in-studio audience. We sought to determine what the dominant images of Spanish-speaking people were, what program elements triggered or reinforced a group identity among audi- ence members, and what the social values were that appeared in images and program activities.

We discovered that program elements and recurring dominant themes and images indicate that "*Sábado Gigante*" contributes to the cultural homogenization of its mass audience. In particular, "*Sábado Gigante*" con- tributes to the standardization and homogenization of Spanish-speaking people as pan-ethnic consumers. This cultural homogenization would seem to be a correlate to a global culture driven by consumerism. Just as Latin American countries entered into political agreements (such as NAFTA and MERCOSUR) to secure economic and political advantages, a global culture of capitalism needs to be buttressed with a particular type of media audi- ence—an audience characterized by "sameness" and driven by the desire to consume brand-name products.

Cultural Homogenization and Consumerism

The content of the "*Sábado Gigante*" capitalizes on similarities of the common language and some superficial similarities among Spanish-speaking people to build a virtual electronic community. The program motto is "Separated by Distance but United by the Same Language." In this sense, elements of the pan-ethnic marketing strategy described earlier may be observed in "*Sábado Gigante.*" The identity of Spanish-speaking people as presented in "*Sábado Gigante*" is based on capitalist ideals of acquisition and consumerism. But these ideals are presented less as the results of engaging in political practices or hard work and more as a result of luck and chance. The program has an entertainment format designed to distract, perhaps, rather than to inform. It is thus a format shaped in relation to the demands of the global marketplace and the economic and political needs of the dominant elites of Latin American countries. Program elements have a distinct capitalist and at times, pro-United States tone, and the program may be seen as a tool of Latin American political and business elites to secure their particular reforms and agendas. It is a tool, however, used at the expense of engaged political discourse and, therefore, at the expense of its Spanish-speaking audience. Given the show's format, charismatic presenter, and style of audience engagement, this cost is not readily apparent. Rather, we are presented with an engaging, participative program that seeks to draw viewers and studio audience members into a type of ritual performance where luck, chance, community identification, and consumerism dominate, thus obscuring the subtle effects of audience homogenization and political disengagement that serve the needs of a global economic order.

Dominant Images of Spanish-speaking People

The primary image of Spanish-speaking people portrayed on *"Sábado Gigante"* is of a unified people, united primarily through a common language and undifferentiated by cultural or political differences. Though Latin America is a complex geopolitical space with significant regional cultural differences, Don Francisco and *"Sábado Gigante"* do not recognize these differences. Social, political, and economic problems are not emphasized and rarely even mentioned, as attention to ritual entertainment distracts audiences from existing controversies, such as border conflicts, immigration problems, or disagreements over U.S. policies in the region. By ignoring these issues, Don Francisco and his program take the complexity out of regional differences and present a unified picture of Latin Americans apart from their countries.

One program segment, *"Cámara Viajera,"* portrays unique regional sites as nothing more than tourist destinations or geographies that are amusing and entertaining. The audience, in other words, never sees a serious treatment of the cultural and socioeconomic conditions of the communities or citizens who live in these locations. Instead, the audience is treated to a fast-paced video clip that simultaneously isolates and synthesizes features of a particular culture or town. For example, indigenous people are invariably portrayed only as underdeveloped, nice to look at, and different from other (middle-class) Spanish-speaking people. The differences between historic Latin America and the more cosmopolitan upper-class urban population are portrayed in terms of superiority and inferiority, with the indigenous and rural portrayed as exotic and simplistic. Images do not provide the audience with any reference or meaningful discussion about the issues of the places shown, nor do these segments ever permit any images that might indicate social divisions in Latin America or unsettle the cheerful mood of the audience. Neither does any conflict appear that audiences may experience as divisive within their own communities. Our observations validate the admission by the executive director of Canal 13 in Chile, that the controlled political blandness of *"Cámara Viajera"* is intentional (Rojas, 1994).

Differences appear only as variations on the theme of similarity. Thus, actual class, ethnic, and cultural identities and concerns that contradict the ideal of pan-ethnicity never appear within the cordial universe of *"Sábado Gigante."* The studio and viewing audience are encouraged to find their identity in an artificial community hosted by Don Francisco.

Reinforcement of Community Identity

The carefully constructed and protected image of a united Spanish-speaking people forms the basis for the preferred *"Sábado Gigante"* community identity. But the program marshals several other techniques: portraying a sense of sameness regardless of geographical separation; creating rituals that serve to bond audience members; and using "family" metaphors.

Since the early days of the program, producers hired foreign correspondents to provide international coverage of news events. One function of these reports was to create community identity by showing how Spanish-speaking people around the world are the same. In an interview given to *Advertising Age,* Don Francisco said that he featured Hispanics in Alaska because showing Hispanics in the most remote part of the United States creates a positive group identity, persuading Spanish-speaking people everywhere that regardless of the geographical, economical, and political context, "We are all Hispanic!" Indeed, the stated goal is to foster "a higher level of understanding and empathy among the countries of this hemisphere" to make the show an "ideal vehicle for those who, although far way, are united by the same language" (Treister, 1988, p. 1).

Another element contributing to a sense of sameness among Spanish-speaking people is that shows feature participants, singers, and television stars from different parts of Latin America. But guest or celebrity, they dress and speak alike regardless of where they are from. The program strictly adheres to this dress and class code: it offers few representations of the diversity of races and cultures that exist in Latin America. Instead, the viewing audience sees participants and performers who (although they speak Spanish and are from

Latin America) have physical appearances and lifestyles that are distinctly middle-class white European and thus different from the majority of the program's television audience, which is undoubtedly browner and more working class. Don Francisco introduces each participant by their name and country of origin, and there is this illusion of watching multinational Latin Americans singing, acting, and joking. But most of the presenters, musicians, and journalists are characteristically middle-class professionals or celebrities. Don Francisco defends the standardized format and content, saying only that "Hispanics have to start integrating themselves into the American culture" (Rodríguez, 1996, p. 70).

Another way shared community is created by the *"Sábado Gigante"* program is through the enactment of certain rituals. Rituals are an important part of any community, providing a sense of origin and destiny. Rituals also help organize and clarify individual and group identity, as participants live out and enact certain myths (Goethals, 1986). Significantly, the myths enacted on *"Sábado Gigante"* are exceeding clear and highly ritualistic: Spanish-speaking "heroes," entrepreneurs, and business people who have gone from "rags to riches" are regularly honored; motivational speakers teach self-help; spiritual leaders visit to offer words of encouragement; and studio audiences participate in singing what amount to *"Sábado Gigante"* anthems.

Even the viewing of *"Sábado Gigante"* has ritual overtones. Every Saturday for four hours, audiences can be entertained and solaced by an expected, predictable uniformity. Songs, dances, games, audience participation, and the organization of the program itself has a ritualistic style described by Don Francisco as an "almost mystical approach" (Anonymous, 1996). Indeed, the program has a rhythm similar to religious rituals. The audience claps together, announces in unison program sections, and sings jingles related to specific segments.

Singing jingles is an essential part of the program. Jingles are about products, the program, the prizes, program characters, and participants of the contests, and the studio audience knows the tune. After one game, 300 sing in unison: *"Se lo ganó, se lleva el premio, está contento, se lo ganó, ganó, ganó."* ("He won it, he takes the prize, he is happy, he won it, he won, he won"). A more prevalent example promoting the show, recurs throughout the program itself: the studio audience sings, *"Sábado Gigante, Sábado Gigante, es un program donde hay alegría y buen humor, Sábado Gigante, es un programa que hay que ver. . . ."* (*"Sábado Gigante"* is a program where there is happiness and good humor, *"Sábado Gigante"* is a program that one must watch. . . .") Underscoring the religious aspect of these shared jingles, Don Francisco refers to the theme music for "Sábado" as the "anthem" of the program. Reinforcing the show's dedication to consumption, no distinction is made between jingles for the program and jingles for the show's sponsors, such as Mazola or Quaker Oats.

Particularly striking are jingles that link products to community, such as the jingle for Mazola Corn Oil in which audience members clap and sing together, *Con Mazola, no estás sola* ("With Mazola, you are not alone").

Audience participation in these rituals is an important component to the show's success, according to Don Francisco. "American TV has lost the connection with its people. People want to feel interaction with the shows they watch. We try and make them feel part of the show and we do so by interacting with the audiences" (Scott, 1991, p. 6). Don Francisco defines his program as a special type of entertainment in which audience participation plays a major role. Thus, host and audience interact on an ongoing basis. As Scott (1991) notes,

> It is the only program worldwide in which a studio audience of 300 partici-
> pants are so active in the development of the show. People even sing com-
> mercial jingles in unison, advertising the sponsor's products [and they] voice
> their opinions about these products throughout the show's segments. (p. 6)

Audience participation extends past studio involvement. Viewers may write to or call the program's producers, and Spanish-speakers from all over the world are part of an electronic "*Sábado Gigante* community" via the Internet. Of course, participation here can only be understood as consumer choice, audiences enamored with celebrity, interaction within the parameters of the show's entertainment and advertising dictates, and a shared community of fans and spectators.

This community has more cohesion than fandom alone provides. "*Sábado Gigante*" is a family, nurtured by the avuncular, charismatic Don Francisco. Don Francisco uses the metaphor to persuade his audience to commit themselves to certain values, lifestyles, and a variety of principles, particularly certain purchasing habits. The program has special segments related to family matters. One is called "*Tribunal Gigante*" (Giant Court) in which the audience determines the solution to the problems families present and discuss on the program. Family members agree before the show to observe the final decision of the audience. Then they provide testimonies of different family situations and discussions of how to overcome domestic problems. The program's sketches also use family situations. The concept and story lines of sketches such as "*La Familia Fernández*" are designed around family themes. The centrality of the family for Latin Americans may be explained by the absence of effective collectivistic institutions at higher lev- els (e.g., the rather narrow and self-serving notion of nation constructed by the dominant elites). So, the family has functioned, for most people, as a secure realm, as an institution providing "buffering" and compensation from the hardships of the hegemonic system.

As a type of "father figure," Don Francisco furthers an atmosphere of security and intimacy with his audience. He speaks to them as if he were their father, great-uncle, or a long-time friend. This exemplifies the authoritarian dimension present in most Latin American countries, which itself is associated with the image of the "patron," the kindly person with the wealth and power who dispenses favors. Using techniques that scholars have identified as successful in conveying trust, Don Francisco's speaking style is friendly and personal (Hall Jamieson, 1988). He communicates tenderness and candor, even when speaking from a script. The result is a communication style that closes the gap between host and audience and between different audience members, thus evoking a sense of a united community.

Moreover, Don Francisco's *"Sábado"* ethos extends will beyond the television program. He is widely recognized for his charity programs and social service activities. Since 1978 his sponsored telethons have helped an estimated 50,000 disabled children with specialized care, prosthetic and orthopedic devices, wheelchairs, and food. After the 1985 earthquake in Mexico, he organized and produced other telethons (such as "Hispanics Lend a Helping Hand") to provide relief aid. In all, he has received over 800 awards granted by charity and welfare institutions, including the United Nations' peace medal. He has been a UNICEF Ambassador and frequently speaks out on the needs of children. Additionally, Don Francisco has written some 100 songs and recorded six albums (Rojas, 1994). Kreutzberger's persona of Don Francisco has wide ethical appeal across the Spanish-speaking world. A host with such credentials has considerable authority when he offers advice.

Programming Consumerism

Concern for family and community is part of *"Sábado Gigante"* and Don Francisco's strategy to encourage consumerism—another value central to the program. Commercials are integrated into program content through transitions from family concerns. The patriarch-host, Don Francisco, frequently communicates that families can achieve happiness and strong family ties by purchasing products such as "Downy," "Nabisco," and "Quaker Oatmeal" or by going to "McDonald's" for a meal. In its content, the program advises audiences to satisfy their family's needs by purchasing brand-name goods.

In addition to being flagged as family values, commercial presentations are further enhanced by their timing, pace, and placement. *"Sábado Gigante"* proceeds rapidly, at times it is almost frenetic. Commercial spots give viewers a respite, a moment for relaxation and recovery. The tranquilizing feel to the advertising underscores the centrality of commercials to the program. Indeed, this Don Francisco readily admits. "[P]roducts are very real elements of daily life," he says, "The most successful technique is building advertising into the natural flow of the various segments of the program" (Anonymous, 1996).

Audience participation is orchestrated to further center consumerism. From the singing of commercial jingles described above, to participating in various contests that award brand-name prizes, audiences are recruited to the main theme that happiness is just a lucky purchase away. In the contests, Don Francisco appears as a mythical magician who brings ordinary people together, united in their hope for prizes. Members of the studio audience anticipate the opportunity to be game prize presenters, actors, singers, and comics. They all have the possibility of winning prizes such as cars and money. In many respects the magic has already begun for the studio audience, which is comprised of working- and middle-class Spanish speakers from the United States and Latin America who have won all-expenses paid trips to Miami to be guests of Don Francisco. Likewise, when *"Sábado Gigante"* producers reunite family members with their long-separated loved one, the reunions appear as if by magic.

This magical possibility of good fortune is wedded to notions of opportunity and success. Don Francisco repeatedly speaks of the "American Dream," and glorifies consumerism as the best way of life for Latin Americans. Guests participate in contests against a studio backdrop that reads, *"La gran oportunidad"* (The Great Opportunity). The connection between success, consumption, and good luck—rubrics of capitalist social relations—appears natural on *"Sábado Gigante."* The message of capitalism and opportunity is stressed as well through the favorable presentation of U.S. symbols, language, and values. The "Sábado Gigante" audience exists within a world of brand-name U.S. products, suggesting that Latin Americans can enjoy the North's standard of living with the strategic purchase of particular products. The program similarly sells capitalism, such as freedom of choice means the freedom to consume: We learn that Latin American families have the freedom of choosing different sizes, flavors, and packages of goods such as "Colgate" and "Kool-Aid." One commercial for a program to learn how to speak English has as its slogan, "You can make it, you can make it," and the announcer encourages the audience to "be part of the successful people." In short, on *"Sábado Gigante"* freedom is defined in terms of possession, consumption, and style—values essential to advertisers' profits.

Through its presentation of dominant images of sameness, a sense of community, and consumerism, and bolstered by the immediate gratification of contest rewards, *"Sábado Gigante"* successfully integrates these elements into an overall message of cultural homogenization in the service of capitalism and the consumer economy. After 40 years, the *"Sábado Gigante"* family album is stuffed full of thousands of light-skinned, middle-class, look-alike Latinos with smiling faces, hugging their relatives and proudly clutching their brand-name products.

Conclusion

The globalization of production and trade severely influences popular culture. The new economic order needs millions of consumers to purchase highly standardized products. This imperative of global capitalism creates the need for culturally homogenized audiences acting as consumers. Even as television networks turn to narrow-casting in an attempt to capture each niche market, corporations would prefer that people dress and eat alike, watch the same programs, listen to the same music, buy the same cars, clothes, perfumes, and so on. Popular culture contributes to this homogenization of markets when it transmits and reproduces dominant beliefs and values that socialize people toward cultural sameness. Further, this homogenization is in the service of a culture coded by consumption. In other words, this sameness is not rooted in a sense of shared values or a community spirit; rather it is a sameness created by the need to consume. As a result, community spirit is replaced by individual consumption and gain.

As the most popular Spanish-language show in the world, *"Sábado Gigante"* is a leader in the movement of popular culture toward homogenization. As shown, its content capitalizes on superficial similarities among vast numbers of people in order to create a market for its advertiser base. It thus contributes to the creation of a new electronic community of Spanish-speaking people who are united by purchasing habits and consumerism more than by class or social interests, regional similarities, or other cultural unifiers. *"Sábado Gigante"* is an element of homogenization of Spanish-speaking people because it addresses its audience, not in terms of national communities with plural identities, but as a market to purchase the world conglomerates' goods. Through content that emphasizes pan-ethnic sameness, a television community identity, and consumerism, *"Sábado Gigante"* levels cultural difference. *"Sábado Gigante"* promotes surface similarities between distinct, multiple nationalities, privileges middle-class images and lifestyles, and ignores class inequalities in social conditions and opportunities. The preferred cultural homogeneity is ripe for delivery to the global market of consumer goods.

Consumer identities come at the expense of broader political discourse and engagement. *"Sábado Gigante"* presents a world of abundance, beauty, health, free time, and happiness, in which needs are satisfied without effort or work, and where poverty and hardship are overcome by luck, individual success, status, and personal appearance. In the course of its presentation, *"Sábado Gigante"* privileges sentimental subjectivity, individualism, and consumerism over real labor and the political and economic conditions of the people.

We recall in closing, what Emilio Azcárraga, the founder of Televisa, told the entertainment industry in 1993, "Mexico is a country made of poor people, quite poor who are not going to be out of poverty. It is an obligation for television to provide entertainment to this people to get them out of their sad reality and difficult future. The middle class . . . and the rich, like myself, are not clients of television because we do not buy junk *(ni madres)"* (Esparza, 1999). Internationally, *"Sábado Gigante"* provides such entertainment—an escape from real material conditions and necessary political engagement to a land where luck, riches, consumption, and the "American way" may be seen as salvation. As such, the program is reflective of the current Latin American state where class domination prevails, an order in which the elites, whose identities, interests, and notions of nation correspond to a global elite rather than to the concerns of problems of the majority of people. As the global media strive to create a global cultural homogeneity and curtail the power of working people in all their diversity, we note the call of the nontelevised for international cultural and political solidarity.

References

Abercrombie, N., Hills, S., & Turner, B. S. (1984). *The dominant ideology thesis*. London: Allen & Unwin.

Adorno, T., & Horkheimer, M. (1972). *Dialéctica de la ilustración: Fragmentos literarios*. México, D.F.: Fondo de Cultura Ecónomica.

Altamirano Celis, J. C. (1987). *Así, así se mueve Don Francisco*. Santiago, Chile: Instituto Latinoamericano de Estudios Transnacionales.

Althusser, L. (1971). Ideology and ideological state apparatuses: Notes toward an investigation. In *Lenin and philosophy and other essays* (pp. 142–84), (B. Brewster, Trans.). London: Penguin.

Anonymous (1996). *Don Francisco*. Santiago, Chile: Editorial América, S.A.

Azrur Osorio, A. E. (1996). *El Estado y el modelo de televisión adoptado en México, 1950–1988*. México, D.F.: Universidad Autónoma Metropolitana-Azcapotzalco.

Bagdikian, B. H. (2000). *The media monopoly* (6th ed.). Boston: Beacon Press.

Barber, B. (1995a). *Jiihad vs. McWorld*. New York: Times Books.

Barber, B. (1995b). The making of McWorld: interview by Nathan Gardels. *New Perspectives Quarterly, 12*, 14.

Barbero, J. M. (1993). *Communication, culture and hegemony: From media to mediations*. Newbury Park, CA: Sage.

Barbero, J. M., & Jaramillo, J. E. (1999). *Cultura y globalización*. Bogotá: Universidad Nacional de Colombia.

Beatriz Palacio, S., & Olarte, J. G. (1998). *Análisis económico, Mercosur*. Buenos Aires: Editorial Estudio.

Bryson, B. (1995, September 8). On language: Say what? *New York Times,* p. F1.

Cabán, C. (1993). The eye of the tiger. *Hispanic, 6,* 14–18.

Cardoso, V., Martínez, C., González, R., & Castellanos, A. (1999, May 7). Carlos Slim Helú, el Tercer Socio Más importante de Televisa. *La Jornada.* [on-line]. Available: *www.jornada.unam.mx.*

Carey, J. W. (1988). *Communication as culture: Essays on media and society.* Boston: Unwin Hyman.

Consoli, J. (2000, May 22). Hispanic nets heating. *Media Week,* pp. 9–12.

Crovi-Drueta, D. (1999). Inequidades del NAFTA/TLCAN: Un análisis del sector audiovisual Mexicano. In G. Mastrini & C. Bolaño (Eds.) *Globalización y Monopolios en la Comunicación en América Latina, Colección Comunicación y Medios de Cultura* (no. 1), (pp. 151–170). Buenos Aires: Editorial Biblos.

Davids, M. (1998, June 1). Spanish steps: Brandweek. *Adweek,* pp. 24–26.

Esparza, E., (1999, September 27). La ley de herodes. *La Jornada.* [on-line]. Available: *www.jornada.unam.mx.*

Fernández, C., & Paxman, A. (2000). *El Tigre Emilio Azcárraga y su imperio televisa.* Mexico, D.F.: Editorial Grijalbo.

Fisher, C. (1992, February 3). Azcárraga looms as return player. *Advertising Age,* pp. 25–27.

Fox, E. (Ed.). (1988). *Media and politics in Latin America.* Beverly Hills, CA: Sage.

Fuentes, C. (1992). Embracing NAFTA and the 21st Century. *World Press Review, 40,* pp. 20–21.

Fuentes, C. (1995). Who is afraid of Mickey Mouse? *World Press Review, 42,* 47.

García Canclini, N. (1987). *Políticas culturales en América Latina.* México, D.F.: Editorial Grijalbo.

García Canclini, N. (1993, Septiembre-Octubre). La cultura visual en la epoca del nacionalismo. *Nueva Sociedad,* pp. 23–30.

García Canclini, N. (1995). *Consumidores y ciudadanos: Conflictos multiculturales de la globalización.* México, D.F.: Editorial Grijalbo.

García Canclini, N., & Monet, C. (1999). *Las industrias culturales en la integración Latinoamericana.* Buenos Aires, Argentina: EUDEBA y Secretaría Permanente del Sistema Económico Latinoamericano.

Goethals, G. (1986). *El ritual de la TV. Colección Popular, No. 243.* México, D.F.: Fondo de Cultural Económica.

Hall, S. (1984a). Culture, the media, and the 'ideological effect.' In J. Curran, M. Gurevitch, & J. Woolacott (Eds.), *Mass communication and society* (pp. 315–38). Newbury Park, CA: Sage. Hall, S. (1984b). Signification, representation, ideology: Althusser and the post-structuralist debates. *Critical Studies in Mass Communication, 2,* 91–114.

Hall Jamieson, K. (1988). *Eloquence in an electronic age: The transformation of political speechmaking.* New York: Oxford University Press.

Hartmann, C., & Husband, P. (1972). Race and the British media. In D. McQuail (Ed.), *The sociology of mass communication.* London: Penguin.

Hills, C. (1992). The North American Free Trade Agreement: A promise fulfilled. *U.S. Department of State Dispatch, 3,* 697–700.

Let dot-coms in: Univisión (1999, December 13). *Advertising Age,* pp. 52–53.

Lowenthal, A. (1992). *Exporting democracy: The United States and Latin America, case studies.* Baltimore, MD: Johns Hopkins University Press.

Malkin, E. (1995, December 11). The Rupert Murdoch of Mexico. *Business Week,* p. 61.

Martinez, B. (1997, March 25). Dog food, toothpaste and Oreos star on popular Hispanic television program. *Wall Street Journal,* p. B-1.

Mattleart, A. (1980). *Mass media, ideologies and the revolutionary movement* (M. Coad, Trans.). Sussex: Harvester.

Mifflin, L. (1998, September 16). Sí, no repeats. *New York Times,* p. E-8.

Monsiváis, C. (1981). *Cultura urbana y creación intelectual: El caso Mexicano.* Tokyo: United Nations Press University Project.

Orozco Gómez, G. (1992). Hablan los televidentes. In *Estudios de recepción: Cuadernos de communicación y prácticas socials.* México, D.F.: Universidad Iberoamericana.

Ortiz Crespo, G. (1999). *En el alba del milenio: Globalización y medios de comunicación en América Latina. Biblioteca de Ciencias Sociales. Volumen. 50.* Quito, Ecuador: Friedrich Ebert Stiftung, Universidad Andina Simón Bolivar.

Palmeri, C. (1995, June 5). More culture, less beach. *Forbes,* pp. 47–8.

Pate, K. (2000, October 8). Hispanic market too large to ignore. *Sunday 2D,* p. L-03.

Paz, O. (1979, September 17). Mexico and the United States: Reflections. *The New Yorker,* pp. 141–153.

Prieto, L., & Chew Sánchez, M. I. (2000, June). An overview of NAFTA's economic results. Paper presented at meeting of International Communication Association. Acapulco, Mexico.

Quiñones, S. (2001). *True tales from another Mexico.* Albuquerque: University of New Mexico.

Rodríguez, A. (1996). Objectivity and ethnicity in the production of the Noticiero Univisión. *Critical Studies in Mass Communication, 13,* 59–72.

Rojas, D. (1994). *Sábado Gigante:* El programa más antiguo del Mundo. *Don Francisco: TV y novelas.* Mexico, D.F.: Provemex, S.A. de C.V.

Romney, L. (2001, February 13) Telemundo to buy L.A.'s KWHY-TV for $239 million: Television Deal Positions the no. 2 Spanish-language network to better compete with top-ranked Univisión, *Los Angeles Times,* p. C1.

Said, E. (1992). Europe and the others: An Arab perspective. In R. Kearney (Ed.) *Visions of Europe*. Dublin: Wolfhound.

Schiller, H. I. (1989). *Culture, Inc.* New York: Oxford University Press.

Schiller, H. I. (1996). *Information Inequality: The Deepening Social Crisis in America*. London: Routledge.

Schwock, J. (1990). *The American radio industry and its Latin American activities*. Urbana, IL: University of Illinois Press.

Scott, I. (1991, August 25). Don Francisco dominates Sábado Gigante. A 3 1/2-hour extravaganza seen by 6 million people in the U.S. and millions more in Latin America. *Los Angeles Times*, p. Calendar 6.

Stern, C. (2000, December 8). Univisión to Buy Diller TV stations; Spanish broadcaster to pay $1 billion. *The Washington Post*, p. E-4.

Taras, S. (1994). Hispanic radio waves up to airwaves. *Advertising Age*, pp. 8–10.

Thompson, J. B. (1990). *Ideology and modern culture: Critical social theory in the age of mass communication*. Stanford, CA: Stanford University Press.

Tomlinson, J. (1991). *Cultural imperialism*. London: Pinter.

Treister, L. (1988, September 26). Bigger than ever, 'Sábado' sends out clear message. *Advertising Age*, p.1.

van Elteren, M. (1996). Conceptualizing the impact of U.S. popular culture globally. *Journal of Popular Culture, 30*, 88.

Waisbord, S. (1998). Latin America. In A. Smith (Ed.), *Television: An international history* (pp. 254–263). Oxford: Oxford University Press.

Williams, R. (1981). *The sociology of culture*. Chicago, IL: University of Chicago Press.

Williams, R. (1983). *Culture and society, 1780–1950*. New York: Columbia University Press.

CHAPTER 8

Television and Hegemony in Brazil

Joseph Straubhaar and Antonio La Pastina

In many countries, including Brazil, the electronic media are an increasingly complex system with powerful global and national players with hegemonic ambitions. There are global channels like CNN that reach a few people in almost every country, and there are media empires or global operations, like those of Rupert Murdoch, that reach a number of people in many countries. But perhaps just as importantly, there are powerful, hegemonic national media systems, like TV Globo in Brazil, which reach almost everyone in a country. Furthermore, all of these groups interact with the national state, which regulates, makes alliances, attempts to control content, etc.

All of these groups find their movements increasingly guided, constrained, or even sometimes enabled by a world capitalist economy, which increasingly penetrates all parts of the globe and touches almost all media. As described by Wallerstein (1979) and Chase-Dunn (1989), the world capitalist economy includes subnational, national, supranational or regional, and global economies, which all interact. In Wallerstein's analysis, core countries dominate the periphery, such as Africa, or the more developed semiperipheral nations, such as Brazil. Nation-states vary more than these categories would indicate, although they are still ultimately constrained by the boundaries of the world capitalist economy and led by the interests of the hegemonic actors in that system. However, nation-states with their own hegemonic ambitions can use private media groups as strategic allies, often against global interests. Further, various audience classes are not simply controlled by hegemonic interests. They have widely unequal access to and very varied interests in various forms of media, selecting and interpreting media to meet their own needs. While media producers and audiences act within interpretive frames that usually are shaped by hegemonic consensus (Gitlin, 1983; Gramsci, 1971), both sometimes can also be in touch with counterhegemonic media, social movements, and interpretive communities that help them escape to a more resistant way of thinking and acting.

Is Television Essentially National?

Television remains a primarily national phenomenon at some levels, but has become highly globalized at others. Most television is watched via national systems. Further, unlike the situation observed in the early 1970s by Nordenstreng and Varis (1974), much of that television is produced at the national level. However, much of this national programming is produced using regionalized or globalized genres or formats, such as the Latin American *telenovela* variation of the increasingly global commercial television reliance on soap opera. This contradiction echoes Robertson's (1995) idea that we are increasingly using globalized forms to produce the local, resulting in what he calls "glocal" culture. To take another example, TV Globo in Brazil and Televisa in Mexico are both far more powerful and important in their home markets than they are as partners in Sky Latin America, their Latin American regional broadcast joint venture with the very global Rupert Murdoch (Sinclair, 1999). The national is a layer of structure, cultural/informational production and identity that endures strongly, even when various technologies, such as satellite TV, video, and the Internet, enable new layers such as the global, the cultural-linguistic regional, and the local to potentially strengthen as well.

All of these levels of electronic media—global, cultural-linguistic regional, national, and provincial or local—are important, and they interact with each other in complex ways (Straubhaar, 1997). Castells (1997) sees the forces of globalization, based essentially in technology and economics, challenged and ultimately transformed by identity, based in "a multiplicity of sources, according to different cultures, histories and geographies" (p. 3). As our fieldwork in Brazil reflects, very few people have a primarily global identity. Identity tends to be based in language, religion, geography, history, ethnicity, collective memory, and political power apparatuses. Those elements of identity tend to be national, especially when the state has been capable of mobilizing and reinforcing them. In many cases, national governments have intervened fairly effectively to support or reinforce these cultural boundaries to define national media markets. The combination of strong states and effective national broadcast entities has helped reinforce a strong sense of national identity in countries like Brazil and Mexico.

Robertson (1995) has aptly noted that we now tend to see the global replication of ideas and models for how to express nationality and national identity. This produces contradictions, such as the expression of local identity through imported genres. A good example is how the global genre of soap opera has been transformed into the Latin American *telenovela*. Although the *telenovela* has a recognizable regional form as a genre throughout Latin America, most of the major national producers—Mexico, Argentina, Brazil,

Colombia, Peru, and Venezuela—have produced national forms of the genre that are characteristically different (Hernandez, 2001). This has been encouraged by national states in Brazil, Mexico, and elsewhere.

Radio Prelude

As Camargo and Pinto (1975) note, the Brazilian government historically has not invested directly in the ownership of media. Since private capital took the initiative to create and build up media companies in most parts of Brazil, the government tended to reserve its capital for other sectors in which private investment was judged inadequate.

The minimalist approach of the Brazilian government changed in the late 1930s. Earlier governments had been somewhat ambivalent about the commercial development of radio, but President Getulio Vargas found radio a very useful tool for mobilizing popular support for his "populist" regime. Vargas encouraged the development of commercial radio and used it extensively for the promotion of his government from 1937 to 1945 (Caparelli, 1980; Goldfeder, 1980). After Vargas, from the 1940s to the late 1950s, commercialism in broadcasting continued to be approved of, even fostered, as the Brazilian government development plans increasingly stressed the development of a consumer economy (Silva, 1982).

Broadcasting was begun by private initiative and took a strong commercial orientation in its early development, following the model of U.S. broadcasting. Some research indicates that U.S. corporations that wished to advertise in the Brazilian market played a direct role in the promotion of the commercial approach to radio broadcasting (Fejes, 1980; Schwoch, 1990). It is clear that Brazil's extensive trade and investment ties with the U.S. encouraged the adoption of the United States advertising-based approach to broadcasting in a more general way, as an aspect of the overall consumer market system. So, from both U.S. and local commercial interests, there was a strong tendency to lock Brazilian media into a commercial framework that fit nicely with an evolving capitalist global economy.

Commercial radio was successful because it fit well into the developing Brazilian market economy. Milanesi (1978) observed that "before television existed or while it was restricted to a few urban centers, radio was, above all else, the principal vehicle for advertising and selling, or if you will, the principal stimulus to the growth of the internal market" (p. 79). Radio stations were relatively cheap to start and operate, and given the advertising market, profitable. As elsewhere in Latin America, small, private radio stations proliferated rapidly throughout Brazil from the 1920s on in every town large enough to support one.

Television in Brazil

Television in Brazil is a complex blend of the national, the global, and the local. Television has contributed to the unification of a national culture and national marketplace. This signifies a great deal of success for a nationalization project begun in the 1950s, accelerated under the military regimes that ruled Brazil after 1964, and continued by subsequent civilian governments.

Television has been organized and controlled as a series of family media empires that have pursued profit and financial advantage in a variety of different ways. For most of television's history, profit has usually come from a mixture of advertising and political connection. Alliance with other key actors, such as the state, key politicians, or even more recently, churches, has been important. However, over time, the most telling issues have been the ability to organize commercial networks efficiently, understand the audience markets, and create programming. Cultural industry has a key role in politics and vice versa, but industrial dynamics, per se, have been ignored by some networks, to their harm as effective industries of culture. The most powerful television network has been the one that has best understood the political game, the need to create and maintain elite alliances, and the management of a modern commercial television network, in complex coordination.

Sérgio Mattos (1990) describes four phases in the Brazilian television. There was the elitist phase between 1950 and 1964, when television was limited to upper and upper middle classes in cities. Then came the populist phase (1964–1975), when the working-class audience expanded rapidly, and the programming became more popularly oriented. In the technological development phase (1975–1985) broadcasting expanded via microwave and satellite, and the number of networks increased. In the transition and international expansion phase (1985–1990), civilian government returned, and TV Globo and others began to export widely to the world. Since 1990, a fifth phase seems to be characterized by the advent of cable, DBS, and SMATV, and the further segmentation of the audience (Duarte, 1992)

Television was started by Assis Chateaubriand in São Paulo and spread to other major cities under his TV Tupi network (part of his larger media group, Diários e Emissoras Associados). It was the largest network for some time, covering 23 cities in 1976. Throughout the 1950s and 1960s, various other entrepreneurs, usually those who already owned other radio stations and newspapers, started rival television stations. Examples were TV Bandeirantes (the Grupo Carvalho), TV Excelsior (the Grupo Simonsen), and TV Globo (Roberto Marinho's Rede Globo Group).

Rival television stations hoped to make money from advertising or politics. With TV Tupi, Chateaubriand made much of his revenue by selling political support in his newspapers, radio stations, and television network.

Until the mid-1960s, the advertising revenues actually invested in television were not sufficient to support all the television operations that were initiated. Throughout the 1950s, the television audience was limited to an economic elite in a few cities, so advertiser interest grew slowly. However, television stations were also seen as desirable for the prestige they added to media empires, even if advertising income could not support them.

By the mid-1960s, the Brazilian economy had been growing rapidly, as the government invested in infrastructure and basic industries, such as steel, and as multinational and local manufacturing firms had been investing and growing in capacity. This led to an acceleration of the growth of a consumer economy within Brazil. With this, the television audience grew to embrace the middle class and lower middle class in an increasing number of cities. The number of television sets in Brazil went from 760,000 in 1960; 6,746,000 in 1970; 19,602,000 in 1977; to 33,000,000 in 1990 (Getino, 1990, p. 56) and approximately 38,000,000 in 2000. This growth of a mass audience for marketing mass consumption products began to attract more advertising revenues. As in other countries, television was favored by the new multinational and domestic advertisers over other media as a means to reach the mass of consumers (Tunstall, 1977, p. 56).

Roberto Marinho, owner of the Globo Group, started television operations in 1964 using capital and technical expertise from Time-Life, Inc. Although Time-Life was forced out in 1968–1971 by Brazilian government intervention, Time-Life's association with TV Globo did reinforce the commercial pattern of television use that had developed in Brazil. To a much greater degree than any of its predecessors, TV Globo reproduced a network operation on the American advertising/programming pattern, which, along with significant government support, led to TV Globo's subsequent dominance (Straubhaar, 1991).

Between 1968 and 1985, in Brazilian television's second phase, TV Globo dominated both the audience and the development of television programming. It tended to have a 60–70% share of the viewers in the major cities at any given time, and at some points in very successful programs, had over 90%. TV Globo was widely seen as consistently favoring, or at least tacitly accepting, government policies.

The financial base of television was advertising. In the 1960s to 1990s, television became very profitable. The share of advertising given to television went from 25% in 1962 to 59% in 1981 to 49% in 1991 (Duarte, 1992, p. 76) and back to 59% in 1998 (World Association of Newspapers, 2001), largely at the expense of radio and nonmass media advertising. Furthermore, these revenues have until recently been highly concentrated in the Rede Globo network, which has usually drawn at least 60% of the television audience nationwide and drew close to 75% of advertising revenue devoted to television (TV Globo, 2001).

Each of the main television networks is owned by family groups. The Telecommunications Law of 1962 actually prohibits ownership of electronic media by corporations, in order to have someone responsible for content, although that was being reconsidered in 2001. Festa and Santoro (1991) identify nine family media groups that own most of Brazil's media, particularly the networks and main stations in the major cities: Marinho (Globo), Bloch (Manchete), Civita (Abril), Mesquita (O Estado de São Paulo), Levy, Nascimento Brito (Jornal do Brasil), Frias (Folha de São Paulo), Silvio Santos (TVS/SBT), and Saad (Bandeirantes). Most operate electronic media, although Civita, Mesquita, and Nascimento Brito were prominent primarily in print media, and Frias was involved only in print.

By 2001 the number of truly dominant family media groups was smaller. The Globo Group continues to be dominant in television, newspapers, cable TV, and satellite television and is strong in publishing, radio, and music. The Abril Group leads in magazines and, together with the Folha Group, dominate both service and content provision on the Internet (with Universo Online). The other groups continue to own major media, but comprise a distinctly second-tier group.

TV Manchete was owned by Adolfo Bloch, a prominent publisher, but as of 1991–92 was sold to Hamilton Lucas de Oliveira (IBF Group) and has since hovered close to bankruptcy. TV Bandeirantes is owned by the Saad family, a family of landowners and industrialists. TVS/SBT is owned by Sílvio Santos, who started as a salesman, became a variety show host, and still hosts his own program. He has also diversified into other land and sales operations. The latest entrant into television network (re)formation is TV Record, a longstanding network that was acquired and reoriented by a fundamentalist Protestant religious group, the Universal Church of the Reign of God.

TV Globo towers over all. Whatever their origin, family connection, or content format, all of the networks have difficulty competing with TV Globo. Efforts by several networks, first TV Tupi, then TV Baneirantes and TV Manchete, to compete with TV Globo for a broad general audience failed. TV Tupi lost organizational coherence after its founder, Assis Chateaubriand, died in 1966, and the network went bankrupt in 1980. TV Tupi's licenses were broken into two groups and given to TV Manchete, linked with the weekly magazine Manchete, and to TVS, owned by Silvio Santos, a variety show host who had worked on Globo. The oligopolistic, imitative competition among commercial networks for the general audience typical of the United States never took place. Instead, TV Globo dominated, while all other networks pursued smaller, more specific audience segments largely defined by social class. Santos targeted a lower middle class-, working class-, and poor audience. That gained TVS a consistent second place in ratings in most of the 1980s and early 1990s, but big ticket advertisers were generally not interested in that audience segment (Mattos, 1990; Duarte, 1992).

The third phase of Brazilian television can be marked by its role in the transition to a new civilian republic. In 1984 TV Globo initially supported the military government against a campaign for direct election of a civilian government, while other media, including other television networks, many radio stations, and most of the major newspapers supported the campaign. Perceiving that it might literally lose its audience to the competition, Globo also switched sides and supported transition to a civilian regime, which in a compromise, was indirectly elected. This immediately reduced political censorship and pressure on broadcasters, although some censorship on moral issues remained (Straubhaar, 1988). The role of television, particularly TV Globo, as the regime's banner carrier was also diluted by the creation and effective growth of new networks. Growing television competition was marked by market segmentation, where most other networks positioned themselves around the programming strengths of the dominant network, TV Globo.

TV Globo continued to be extraordinarily successful in the late 1980s. Despite increasing competition, TV Globo still dominated in terms of revenue. TV Globo augmented its advertising in the 1980s by creating a new form of product exposure called "merchandising," especially in *telenovelas*. Specific products are either shown or mentioned in dialogue within programs in return for a negotiated fee (Ramos, 1987). In the *telenovela* "Tieta" in 1989–90, a modern, colorful branch of the Banco Itau was frequently shown in the middle of a small, traditional northeast Brazilian town. The bank branch opening was shown, characters later did business there, used its credit cards, etc. In another example, a 1990 TV Globo *telenovela* called "Top Model" contained a fashion show featuring the real-life fashion lines of a company partially owned by the daughter-in-law of Roberto Marinho, owner of TV Globo (Isto é, 1990).

In a related phenomenon, TV Globo used its various media branches to synergistically promote its products, further increasing overall revenue. *Telenovela* soundtracks are released as records, and key songs are promoted on radio, so that all three media reinforce each other—in particular the television and radio help sell the records—but also hearing the songs constantly tends to keep the audience thinking of the television program, and so on.

Roberto Marinho is now considered the second richest man in Brazil. He has branched out both vertically into all aspects of television, including research, production, marketing, and syndication, and horizontally into magazines, books, educational materials, video distribution, recording, record distribution, cellular telephony, and other telecommunications (e.g., partner of NEC of Japan), and beyond media into agriculture and other businesses.

The fourth phase of Brazilian television was its internationalization. The importation of television programs into Brazil declined in the 1980s

(Straubhaar, 1984; Straubhaar, 1991), while Brazilian exports of programming increased. The TV Globo group, in particular, expanded internationally. Globo acquired control of Telemontecarlo in Italy for several years (Netto, 1987) and in 1992 purchased one of the new private channels in Portugal (Rattner, 1992). A new phase of Brazilian television may be opening with the appearance of new technologies, especially home video systems. In the late 1980s, VCR purchases increased an estimated 250% to a total of 5,300,000 VCRs (Maiello, 1990). The extent and impact of VCR use has yet to be determined, although most videos are U.S. productions (Camargo, 1990)

Role of the State

Historically, the Brazilian government seldom directly censored the media, relying instead on "guidance" using more complex political and economic measures (Alisky, 1981). After existing censorship laws were relaxed in the late 1970s, the press has been relatively open, while radio tends to be atomized and somewhat apolitical. However, the government maintains considerable guidance in television (Caparelli, 1980; Castro, 1984). Reflecting the intimate connections between the state and civil society under capitalism, television networks have been more than complicit, offering support to governments and candidates in return for favors, particularly the granting of further licenses and placement of advertising controlled by state and federal governments (Borin, 1991).

Formally the Brazilian government followed much the same approach to the regulation of broadcasting taken by the U.S. government: minimum regulation of frequency usage and transmitter power to ensure that broadcasters did not interfere with each other. In fact, licensing of broadcast operations by private enterprises has been highly political, a means of keeping television and radio licenses among the political and economic elite. It has often been a focus of political patronage and favor trading, a way of shoring up political support and creating or rewarding alliances. In principle, private enterprises operate under government concessions or licenses for 15 years. Those licenses can, however, be quickly canceled, which gives government considerable leverage.

The Brazilian government was somewhat more active in promoting and even financing television than it had been with radio. Government has often exercised considerable control over broadcasting, both in direct censorship at times and through investments of infrastructure and advertising.

The military governments between 1964 and 1985 tended to intervene more strongly in broadcasting than preceding or succeeding civilian governments. The military governments initiated a low interest loan program for the purchase of television sets, built a microwave network, satellite, and other aspects of television network infrastructure that enabled television networks to reach the more remote parts of the country. The development of the telecommunications system, telephones, telegraph, telex, radio, and television was a high priority directly related to the military regime's perception of national security needs. The military governments saw telecommunications as vital economic infrastructure and perceived broadcasting in particular as a means of reinforcing a sense of national identity (particularly in the more remote regions of the country), communicating government development plans and messages to the people, and assuring a supportive political climate.

The military governments contributed a good deal of revenue to media through advertising by government-owned corporations and banks. The government favored certain television networks, particularly TV Globo, with government advertising, which was considerable, since government or state corporations, banks, trading companies, mines, steel mills, etc. constituted nearly half the GNP for a couple of decades. The state was the main advertiser in Brazil for a number of years.

The military governments initially tolerated, then intervened in 1968 to end a joint venture agreement that TV Globo had with Time-Life for financing and technical assistance. This enforced specific provisions of the Brazilian Constitution and the 1962 and 1967 Communication Laws that prohibited foreign ownership or decision-making input by foreign citizens in mass media. The fact that enforcement was delayed for four crucial years in TV Globo's early establishment and consolidation of its basic network was seen as a military government financial favor to TV Globo. Government loans were then used to repay Time-Life (Hertz, 1987).

TV Globo was very supportive of the first two postmilitary civilian governments, Sarney and Collor, which were conservative, as well as the current Cardoso government, which is center-left. In the early 1980s, TV Globo broadcast a Sunday evening prime time program that featured speeches and answers to questions by the president. TV Globo's news coverage has regularly reflected viewpoints preferred by the government. Many saw Collor's 1989 presidential victory as evidence of Globo's highly supportive coverage. Whatever the evidence, apparently the government has been pleased with TV Globo, as it has received considerable favor, including access to government-owned transponders necessary for nationwide broadcasting.

In the first years of television, until roughly 1968, television was local. The memorable drama experiments of the 1950s, the early development of Brazilian popular music programming, and the early *telenovelas* were primarily developed on stations limited to Rio de Janeiro and São Paulo, such as TV Rio, TV Record, and TV Excelsior. However, after the 1964 military coup, television, particularly TV Globo, helped the military create a broader sense of national identity across the diverse regions of Brazil.

Many development projects, especially those with state involvement, have been substantially changed by the post-1985 civilian governments. However, the consolidation and national extension of the television system has persisted. By 1984 the military intervention had set the essential boundary conditions for the present system: nearly complete national penetration of television broadcasts; predominance of private commercial nationally owned networks; dominance of audiences and advertising revenues by TV Globo; relatively strong minor network challengers in SBT, Bandeirantes and, more recently TV Record; development of popular program genres that reflect a nationalism favorable to the regimes; and development of a news style also essentially favorable to the regimes.

In the early and mid-1960s, while television was still turning from an elite urban medium into a truly mass medium in Brazil, several stations and networks began to turn toward a mass audience with programming that was linked to national popular culture. National music began to be more prominent on variety shows. National character types and images began to be more prevalent on the *telenovelas*, such as Beto Rockefeller, that featured a typical Rio type, the good-lifer ("boa vida") in 1968. These developments made sense within the dynamics of the commercial media system within Brazil, building on its own popular culture and history. But they were elements that the government could also use and reinforce for its own modernization and national identity projects.

The military governments encouraged this trend toward national television program production. In the early 1970s, several government ministers pushed the commercial networks hard to develop more Brazilian programming and reduce their reliance on imported programs, particularly those that contained violence (Straubhaar, 1984). TV Globo, in particular, increased national production considerably, since it had discovered that audiences, and consequently advertisers as well, preferred nationally produced musicals, comedies, and *telenovelas* over all but a few imported programs . Government also intervened to close programs that it considered to be immoral or in bad taste. In some cases, it would censor a theme from a *telenovela* but not cancel the entire program (Straubhaar, 1984).

The media build on, reinforce and, by dint of the agency of both media producers and consumers, sometimes contradict both this cultural context and the larger structural context of economics, technology, and institutions. For example, several television stations, particularly TV Rio, TV Excelsior, and TV Globo, responded to the commercial opportunity of the 1960s economic growth by changing their programming to appeal to a broader mass audience. They began to create or import programs that would sell products like soap, tobacco products, textiles, food stuffs, and fairly simple appliances (Sodré, 1978). In doing this, they were also responding to the economic policy guidance of the military government, which itself built upon the growth policies of the preceding governments. But more than anything, they were taking initiative to exploit a commercial opportunity and, for the creative producers, to produce new national programming that employed their talents and gave them an opportunity to create.

In Brazil as elsewhere, television has had a "nationalizing vocation," but Brazilian television in many ways is one of the world's most prominent national television system success stories—at least from the point of view of an advertising-driven, entertainment-based system. A number of comparative studies have noted the success of Brazilian television in producing most of its own programming, although much of it is based on foreign models (Oliveira, 1993; Schiller, 1991). Others have noted and critiqued Brazilian television's ability to mobilize support for both military and civilian regimes (Lima, 1992), including support for the elite's project of developing a market-driven consumer culture.

Television and Social Class

Economic patterns can also limit possibilities. For example, advertising as an economic system for financing television broadcasts both enables and limits the possibilities of the medium. Advertising tends to enable by increasing the money available for production. It also tends to limit broadcast program genres to certain types, predominantly entertainment, which often puts other kinds of programming, like development education, high culture, and extensive information programming, out of bounds. In Brazil, only a very small set of state government and national channels developed educational programming, while the commercial networks developed soap operas, variety shows, musical variety, comedy, talk shows, and sports, all classic commercial genres. Above all, television served the hegemonic interests of the capitalist class, which profited and ruled primarily through the militarized state. Television defended and justified the state (whether military or civilian) and, perhaps more importantly, television nurtured a supplementary culture of consumption and entertainment to disorient, disorganize, and distract the Brazilian working people.

Advertising, the dominant means of financing television in most countries, typically represents a complex interaction of forces between the state, multinational advertisers, national advertisers, and national broadcasters. In most countries outside North America, the state acts both as an advertiser (for state-owned companies) and as a regulator of advertising rules on behalf of the domestic capitalist class. In Brazil for example, effective control of much of the economy by state companies for most of the 1960s through 1980s made the bestowal or withholding of state company advertising an extremely effective lever of power over national broadcasters, enabling the state to favor national production over imported programs, favor certain genres over others, reinforce favored and cooperative TV networks (especially TV Globo), and influence news content (Straubhaar, 1988). The state could also set the macroeconomic rules within which other advertisers operated, as well as regulate certain forms of advertising.

One important impact of the dominance of advertising in Brazilian television is that it also had an impact on the representation of Afro-Brazilians on television. Critical scholars in Brazil tend to agree that Brazilian television content, particularly television advertising, tends to primarily target the richest 30% of Brazilians who consume at middle-class levels (Lima, 1993; Porto, 2001). Those Brazilian consumers are disproportionately white in a society that is largely Afro-Brazilian or mixed race. Research by Araujo (2001) shows that Afro-Brazilians have historically been underrepresented in the primary prime time television genre, the *telenovela*. Subervi-Vélez and Oliveira (1990) have shown a similar phenomenon in the underrepresentation of Afro-Brazilians in television commercials. Since race and class are heavily overlapped in Brazil, with poor people far more predominantly Afro-Brazilian, this pattern reinforces both racial and class stereotypes in Brazil.

One of the main economic constraints on new television technology and its uses is the limit placed on access to new media by the inequitable distribution of income. This is the case in most Latin American countries, where access to newspapers, magazines, books, satellite/cable television, and the Internet is limited to the upper middle class or even the elite. In Mexico 1.5 million out of 90 million have access to the Internet, and 18–20% have satellite or cable TV. In Brazil, the Internet has grown faster, to 8 million out of 170 million, but cable/satellite TV access has grown more slowly, remaining fairly static at 5–6%. In both cases there seems to be a domestic capitalist elite who can afford access to the Internet and to satellite and cable TV.

This keeps the media emphasis by the elite in Brazil on the power and reach of broadcast television. In part due to the impact of government programs to extend television distribution infrastructure and to various economic supports for broadcasting, television reaches well over 90% of all Brazilians, at home in or in public places. In the urban areas, where over 75% of Brazilians live, over 90% have television at home. That makes television a remarkably powerful medium. However, the effect of television is not necessarily direct or exclusive. Most Brazilians listen to radio, and many are closely involved with both informal and formal groups, which may serve to extend television's reach or serve as alternative sources of communication, enabling many to hear and discuss multiple meanings of messages that circulate throughout the hegemonic system of commercial mass media.

For example, the author began a long-term study of media sources and use patterns in Brazil by a national sample survey of Brazilians, conducted in cooperation with the Brazilian National Institute for Public Opinion Research (IBOPE), the main ratings and survey firm in Brazil. That study showed that in the 1989 Brazilian presidential election, Brazilians had access to and indeed used a fairly wide variety of sources of political information. In fact, talking with friends and family was the dominant source of information, especially for less-educated Brazilians. The media that most Brazilians considered dominant at the time, political ads on television and debates in TV, were in fact important, but more so to better-educated people, although television news was important to many across the educational spectrum (Straubhaar, Olson, & Nunes, 1993).

The 1989 election was considered particularly interesting as a baseline, since many Brazilian critics considered it to be the paradigmatic example of the influence of TV Globo on behalf of its allies in government. Tracking polls by IBOPE showed that the Worker's Party candidate, Lula, was gaining on the establishment candidate, Collor, leading up to the final debate. After that debate, TV Globo showed a highly edited version of the debate that accentuated Lula's negatives. The tracking polls showed a subsequent decline in Lula's support that many considered evidence of TV Globo's impact (Lima, 1993). However, both the IBOPE poll (Straubhaar, et al, 1993) and concurrent in-depth interviewing in the city of São Paulo by the author and his research team at the University of São Paulo in 1989 show that the media situation was far more complex. Lula got as far as he did in large part by skillful use of free political advertising time on national television, which resonated strongly with many of those interviewed. Furthermore, Lula got considerable support from the extensive personal and organizational networks of the progressive wing of the Catholic Church and a coalition of labor unions. The person-to-person and rally-based campaigning of those groups also showed up in both surveys and in-depth interviews as significant alternative sources of information. Lula also gained by a number of cultural industry artists (including many who worked for TV Globo) endorsing him, making songs for him, appearing at his rallies, etc. All of these channels resonated widely, too. The point here is not to deny the efforts or even the power of commercial media conglomerates on behalf of established political and economic interests, but only to indicate that counterhegemonic efforts, particularly those based on social movements, have political and communicative power that can be built upon.

Before it had television, Brazilian cultural, political, and even economic life was far more localized and regionalized. Even by the 1950s, ethnographies such as Kottak's (1990, 1994) in Arembepe showed that villagers and rural people were little aware of national holidays, national cultural figures, national foods, and even national sports. Most people now have some awareness of the world and levels of identity that correspond to global, regional, national, and local. For example, a Brazilian peasant interviewed in a remote land-reform settlement by the author (several interviews between 1995 and 1998) reflects a small level of global awareness—having in his case to do with awareness of the World Wildlife Fund, which funds a community agent who talks to him about ecological farming and provides a truck for community use. He seems very unaware, however, of the global economic forces that shape his life. He also knows a little about the Latin-American cultural linguistic region, since his wife likes Mexican soap operas, which they can sometimes see on the community TV set. He has lived in several parts of Brazil, knows quite a bit about the country and identifies himself as Brazilian. He also knows about local issues, personalities, and conditions, and thinks of himself as *Baiano* (from the state of Bahia). He knows quite a bit about Brazilian politics, some from media, some from his participation in the Landless People's Movement (Movimento dos Sem Terra, or MST), a fairly powerful national movement that helped his specific group seize the land that he currently owns and works from a major landowner. In short, his identity, like most peoples', is national and local, and that very nationalism and localism provides a source of resistance to globalization.

Even though technology now allows global and regional broadcast of satellite television with all of its homogenizing consumerist entertainment fare, other factors, such as national economics, national policy controls, and audience preferences continue to make national television broadcasts more important. However, people are increasingly acquiring identities with multiple layers that correspond in many ways to the multiple layers of world media: global, geocultural (or regional), national, provincial, and local. These layers of identity, framed by language, cultural history, and personal cultural experience, define markets for culture in ways that even global firms must respond to. Of course, emerging national identities may also be framed within consumerist terms that reflect the hegemonic interests of both global and national capital.

The state and national culture are still powerful in this process, since through schooling, national media, language policy, and national organization of institutions like militaries, education, and commercial associations, the state in many countries continues to reinforce and define these nationally based conceptual frames. In the case of the Brazil, the nation-state developed through direct government organization and intervention on behalf of national capital, relying primarily on capitalist national media to promote their mutual interests. Audiences of elites, managers, professionals, entrepreneurs, and others of the middle class, along with the working class and poor majority, receive media content created within the framework of capitalism organized by state institutions. Many Brazilian scholars focus on the dominance of coercion in this framework, but with the move to civilian rule (still "guided" by the military), the Brazilian state has made strides towards cultural hegemony, particularly due to the reach and influence of entertainment television. At the same time, as the emergence of the Worker's Party and the rise of the peasant-mobilized Landless People's Movement show, there are counter-hegemonic forces at work as well—just as Gramsci (1971) might have predicted. How strong those forces will be against the collaboration of powerful corporate media and state will be determined by their ability to independently communicate and politically organize the interests of Brazilian majority.

References

Alisky, M. (1981). *Latin American media: Censorship and guidance*. Ames, IA: Iowa State University Press.

Araujo, J. Z. (2001). A negação do Brasil.

Borin, J. (1991). Rádios e TVs crescem com o festival de concessões. *Comunicação e Sociedade, 10* (18), 19–24.

Camargo, J. C. (1990, December 30). Lista dos mais consumidos só revela quantidade. *Folha de São Paulo*, p. E-5.

Camargo, N., & Pinto, V. (1975). *Communication policies in Brazil*. Paris: UNESCO.

Caparelli, S. (1980). *Comunicação de massa sem massa*. São Paulo: Cortez Editora.

Castells, M. (1997). *The Power of identity*. Malden, MA.: Blackwell Publishers.

Castro, T. D. (1984). Padrão Global de deformação de verdade. *Revista INTERCOM, 46*, 9–10.

Chase-Dunn, C. (1989). *Global formation: structures of the world-economy*. Cambridge, MA: Blackwell Publishers.

Duarte, L. G. (1992). *Television segmentation: Will Brazil follow the American model*. Unpublished M.A. thesis, Michigan State University at East Lansing.

Fejes, F. (1980). The growth of multinational advertising agencies in Latin America. *Journal of Communication, 30* (4), 36–49.

Festa, R., & Santoro, L. (1991). Os novos rumos do espaço audiovisual latino-americano. *Comunicação e Sociedade, 10* (18), 9–18.

Getino, O. (1990). *Impacto del video en el espacio audiovisual latinamericano*. Lima, Peru: Instituto para América Latina.

Gitlin, T. (1983). *Inside prime time*. New York: Pantheon.

Goldfeder, M. (1980). *Por tras das ondas da Radio Nacional*. Rio de Janeiro: Editora Paz e Terra.

Gramsci, A. (1971). *Selections from the Prison Notebooks* (Hoare, Q., & Smith, G.M., Trans.). New York: International Publishers. (Original work published in 1947).

Hernandez, O. (2001). *Global telenovelas: Latin American cultural products in the age of globalization.* Unpublished Ph.D. dissertation, Radio-Television-Film Dept., University of Texas, Austin.

Hertz, D. A. (1987). *Historia secreta da Rede Globo.* Porto Alegre (Brazil): Tche.

Isto É, Senhor. (1990, July 2). *Enredo propício,* pp. 68–69.

Kottak, C. (1990). *Prime time society.* Belmont, CA: Wadsworth.

Kottak, C. (1994). *Assault on paradise.* Belmont, CA: Wadsworth.

Lima, V. A. D. (1993). Television and the Brazilian elections of 1989. In T. Skidmore (Ed.), *Television, politics and the transition to democracy in Latin America.* Washington, DC: Woodrow Wilson Center.

Maiello, C. (1990, February 12). Setor de vídeo está de olho no grande público. *Folha de São Paulo,* p. F-4.

Mattos, S. (1990). *Um perfil da TV Brasileira (40 anos de história: 1950–1990).* Salvador: Associação Brasileira de Agências de Propaganda.

Milanesi, L. A. (1978). *O Paraiso via EMBRATEL.* Rio de Janeiro: Editora Paz e Terra.

Netto, A. (1987, October). Exclusivo: o homen da Telemontecarlo. *Imprensa,* p. 16–22.

Nordenstreng, K., & Varis, T. (1974). *Television traffic—a one-way street.* Paris: UNESCO.

Oliveira, O. (1993). Brazilian soaps outshine Hollywood: Is cultural Imperialism fading out? In K. Nordenstreng, & H. I. Schiller (Eds.), *Beyond national sovereignty: International communication in the 1990s.* Norwood, NJ: Ablex.

Ortiz, R. (1994). *Mundialização e cultura.* São Paulo: Editora Brasiliense.

Porto, M. (2001). *Television fiction and politics in Brazil: Viewers' interpretations of the telenova Terra Nostra.* Paper delivered at Annual Conference of the Society for Cinema Studies (SCS), Washington, DC.

Ramos, R. (1987). *Gra-finos na Globo—cultural e merchandising nas novelas* (2nd ed.). Petropolis, Brazil: Editora Vozes.

Rattner, J. (1992, February 7). Globo e Opus Dei ganham canais de televisão privada em Portugal. *Folha de São Paulo,* p. C-1.

Robertson, R. (1995). Glocalization: Time-space and homogeneity-heterogeneity. In M. Featherstone, S. Lash, & R. Robertson (Eds.), *Global modernities* (pp. 25–44). Thousand Oaks, CA: Sage.

Schiller, H. (1991). Not yet the post-imperialist era. *Critical Studies in Mass Communication, 8,* 13–28.

Schwoch, J. (1990). *The American radio industry and its Latin American activities, 1939–1990.* Urbana, IL: University of Illinois Press.

Silva, L. E. P. C. (1982). *Estratégia empresarial e estrutura organizacional nas emissoras de televisão brasileiras (1950 a 1982).* São Paulo: EASP/FGV, mimeo.

Sinclair, J. (1999). *Latin American television: a global view*. New York: Oxford University Press.

Sodré, M. (1978, July 8). Interview. *Folha de São Paulo*, p. Folhetim.

Straubhaar, J. (1984). The decline of American influence on Brazilian television, *2*, 221–240.

Straubhaar, J. (1988). The reflection of the Brazilian political opening in the *telenovela* [Soap Opera], 1974–1985. *Studies in Latin American Popular Culture, 7*, 59–76.

Straubhaar, J. D. (1997). Distinguishing the global, regional, national and local levels of world media. In A. Sreberny-Mohammadi, D. Winseck, J. McKenna, & O. Boyd-Barrett (Eds.), *Media in global context: a reader*. New York: Arnold.

Straubhaar, J. D., Olsen, O., and Nunes, M. C. (1993). The Brazilian case: Influencing the voter. In T. Skidmore (Ed.), *Television, politics and the transition to democracy in Latin America*. Washington, D.C.: Woodrow Wilson Center.

Subervi-Vélez, F.A., & Oliveira, O. S. (1990). Blacks (and other ethnics) in Brazilian television commercials: An exploratory inquiry. *Georgia Series on Hispanic Thought, 28–29*, 129–151.

Tunstall, J. (1977). *The media are American*. New York: Columbia University Press.

TV Globo. (2001). *About us. www.infonet.com.*

Wallerstein, I. (1979). *The capitalist world economy*. Cambridge: Cambridge University Press.

World Association of Newspapers. Brazil. *http://www.wan-press.org.*

CHAPTER 9

Privatization of Radio and
Media Hegemony in Turkey

Ece Algan

Through the 1990s, theories of globalization and global culture have assumed increasing importance within the social sciences in general and media studies in particular. Globalization is mostly investigated in media studies with an emphasis on monopolistic practices of transnational media corporations. While some scholars (Herman & McChesney, 1997; Miyoshi, 1996; Schiller, 1991; Shohat & Stam, 1996) are skeptical about the consequences of globalization on local cultures and media, others (Appadurai, 1996; Featherstone, 1996; Hall, 1991; King, 1991) believe that globalization creates a space of resistance for the articulation of diverse voices and local identities.

In attempting to break the bipolarity of these approaches, some studies point to the complex and competing processes of globalization by locating it in its historical context (Robertson, 1992; Tomlinson, 1991) or interrogating the interaction between the global and the local (Hall, 1991; Featherstone, 1996). The concepts of creolization (Hannerz, 1987), hybridity (Bhabba, 1990; Hall, 1991; Mattelart, 1994) and glocalization (Kraidy, 1999; Robertson, 1995) have been posited to illuminate the intersection and interconnectedness of globality and locality. However, in order to understand how the local is transformed by the global, and how the global is redefined by the local, we should also consider the concept of hegemony (Artz & Murphy, 2000), which identifies dominant social forces, such as global media, and their mechanisms for manufacturing or earning the consent of subordinates, such as the local culture. This study approaches globalization as a complex process of global/local interaction, where many contrasting elements, such as nationalism, ethnicity, regionalism, diversity, homogenization, imperialism, and domination exist simultaneously and in contest. Because it questions who is dominant and for what reason, the concept of hegemony assists us in understanding the complex process of globalization and the contestation between the global and the local. Using Turkish media as a case study with a special emphasis on radio and music, I draw on the concept of hegemony to identify the ways in which the global is conceived, experienced, negotiated, and transformed by the local.

In the last decade, the Turkish media scene went through a radical transformation from a state monopoly to privatization. State-owned and controlled media—that have always broadcast with the policy of indoctrinating Turkish people with Western values in a didactic and official way—were not successful in creating a consensus among Turks about their national-cultural identities. Before privatization, media exerted little hegemonic leadership for most Turks, with the exception of elites who shared a Kemalist ideology favoring Western-style modernization under state control (originating in the policies of Kemal Atatürk, founder and first president of Turkey from 1923 to 1938). When the state monopoly was broken in 1990 and private broadcasting started, media broadcasting began to gain a hegemonic power. Private broadcasting accomplished this through the use of the dominant ideologies of globalism, whose impact was considerable since the 1980s in Turkey. In this study, in addition to the analysis of media hegemony in Turkey and the impact of globalization on national-cultural identities, I also discuss some of the consequences of global communication, such as privatization, commercialization, the impact of transnational media corporations, and deregulation of media in developing countries.

Turkey and the Impact of Globalization

As a country between Europe and the Middle East both geographically and culturally, Turkey was established on the ruins of the Ottoman Empire as a secular republic governed through a multiparty, parliamentary political system with occasional military interventions in times of crisis and some restrictions on civil liberties, including freedom of speech, violations of democratic and human rights, and oppression of the Kurdish minority and others. Some 99% of its 65 million population are Muslims. More than half of its population lives in urban areas, while the remainder lives in rural areas. Turkey's economy is a complex mix of modern industry and commerce along with traditional village agriculture and crafts. In 2001, 38% of the labor force worked in agriculture, 38% in the service sector, and 24% in industry. It has a strong and rapidly growing private sector, yet the state still plays a major role in basic industry, banking, transport, and communication. Its most important industry—and largest exporter—is textiles and clothing, which is almost entirely in private hands.

In the past two decades, Turkey has experienced the impact of globalization in almost every area, especially in media and new communication technologies. Liberalization efforts started after the military regime's third coup in 1980 with some radical economic measures and continued with former Prime Minister Turgut Özal's policies, which aimed to replace the state's protectionist approach to the economy with a competitive market economy approach. This neoliberal ideology consisted of a rejection of the previous official values (the social state, a mixed economy, protectionism, state interference, and planning) and supplanted them with an admiration for market economics, private ownership including the privatization of state property/enterprises, globalism, free trade, and interaction with foreign companies (Boratav, 1995, p. 95). This economic change also resulted in a bigger disparity in wealth, social status, and cultural practices between 1977 and 1989. During this period, the income of the working classes, such as farmers, state employees, and workers, decreased, while the income of the Turkish capitalist class increased and the capital owners shared most of the overall income. Boratav (1995) believes that this change in the distribution of income was caused by the effective promotion of a neoliberal ideology by the military regime and Özal's administration (p. 95). This "import" ideology, which went hand-in-hand with the ideals of world capitalism, corresponded with the needs and aspirations of the Turkish capitalist class, which had support from the government financially as a result of its new policies aimed at increasing exports and free trade. Some high-level bureaucrats and allied ruling elites used these policies to serve the rich in Turkey by stealing from the government both legally and illegally. During this era, "changing Turkey" slogans were promulgated by the government and leading elite politicians in a public discourse about "rising values" ("yukselen degerler" in Turkish) that carried the ideology for a capitalist consumer culture. Nonetheless, alienation and resistance grew among the working classes.

Neoliberal ideologies initiated a fundamental change not only in the economy but also in the cultural and political spheres. In this era, the popularization of liberal political ideas, rapid economic growth, and international trade resulted in an increase in imported goods, including global media products and information technologies, which advertised Western lifestyles. VCRs, video games, personal computers, imported magazines, and movie rental stores in every neighborhood (that mostly carried action and erotic movies—genres that state-run Turkish Radio and Television (TRT) does not show) became popular global media products. The military coup of 1980 dramatically underscored the need for democratization of the state and for a strong and independent political tradition, while the state increasingly relied on a conservative religious discourse.

The economic situation in recent years has been marked by serious imbalances in growth due to the widening of large government and public sector spending and debts, Russia's economic crisis, and two major earthquakes. Despite the implementation in January 1996 of a customs union with the EU, foreign direct investment in the country remains low—less than $1 billion annually—perhaps because potential investors are concerned about economic

and political stability. Currently, the government under Prime Minister Ece-
vit is implementing a major economic reform program, including a tighter
budget, social security reform, banking reorganization, and greatly accelerated
privatization—all necessary measures for Turkey's accession to the EU.

The Project of Modernization and the Role of TRT

Starting in the nineteenth century, the East's exposure to the West changed
the way the East thought about the West. The East was influenced by not
only European developments, but also the opinions that these colonizing
powers had about themselves and the societies they colonized. Turkish elites
also were inspired by Europe's "orientalist" approach in the postenlightenment
era, which created the dichotomy between the "civilized" or modern West and
"uncivilized" or primitive East. This led to an admiration and imitation of the
West among the Turkish elite. While the urban elite in Turkey mimicked a
Western style of living—*alafranka* (the European way)—and regarded it as
modern and proper, they rejected traditional living because it was *alaturka* (the
Turkish way) (Kandiyoti, 1997, p. 119). Other regions in the Middle East
underwent a similar process of Westernization—what Iranian writer Jalal Al-
e Ahmad (1982) called *gharbzadegi,* meaning "plagued by the West"—that
encouraged the rejection of the traditional and an adaptation of European
lifestyles among elites.

Atatürk was one of the leaders who saw Western-style modernization
and nation building as the only way to defeat Western imperialism (Gülalp,
1997, p. 61). Aiming to bring the country to the level of contemporary Western civilization, Atatürk attempted to change the social order into a new,
superior Western model, which he accepted as universal. This required secu-
larization of the country and modernization of social practices according to
the principles and values of the Enlightenment, which privileges progress and
change, especially change from an agricultural to an industrial society and
from religious to scientific organizing fundamentals.

Radio and the rapidly growing print media were two important venues
for the promotion of modernization. From its beginning in 1927, radio broadcasting in Turkey was instrumental in disseminating the new nation-state's
goals and ideology, and later in redefining it. In Europe public service broadcasting and state-controlled broadcasting have been considered until recently
to be the "cultural arm of nation building," which provides an agenda for citizens and a focus for the political community to unite the nation (Schlesinger,
1993, p. 10). The roles and expectations that the political community attributed to Turkish radio were quite similar. Print media and radio aimed to construct a Western national-cultural identity based upon the principles of a sec-

ular life—as opposed to traditions—in areas of education, family, health, body, clothing, and so on. Magazines and newspapers played a role in teaching Turks how to behave and dance in Western-style gatherings and receptions by showing Atatürk, his wife, other politicians, and elites in Western dress and dancing to Western music (Duman, 1997). In order to teach people Western music, dance, and culture, classical music was also played on radio and at government-sponsored ballroom dances, and free classical music classes and public concerts were offered (Tekelioğlu, 1996, p. 195). Atatürk believed that Eastern alaturka music performed by Ottoman intellectuals was unsophisticated, anachronistic, and sedative (Tekelioğlu, 1996, p. 204). In 1935, on Atatürk's order, Turkish music was banned from commercial radio for 20 months, and programmers played only Western music, such as classical, tango, waltz, and pop.

However, it was a fallacy to think that banning Turkish music and distributing only Western music through radio would actually change people's musical tastes and listening habits as if they already had a Western imagination. People began listening to Egyptian music through shortwave radio (Özbek, 1994; Tekelioğlu, 1996). Other influences, like Arab films and music, became very popular during the 1930s and 40s. Because such non-Western outside influences could not be curtailed, Atatürk moved to control its dissemination.

In 1936 all commercial radio broadcasting was abolished, radio officially became a state institution, and the ban on Turkish music was lifted. Turkish music was now dispensed by the state, but it did not prevent people from enjoying Arabic songs that the Arab musical films popularized. When the state banned Arab films and songs with Arabic lyrics in 1948, Turkish classical music performers—who were mostly unemployed due to the restrictive government policies—began performing Arabic songs with Turkish lyrics (Stokes, 1992, p. 94).

In the mid-1960s a new type of music was created from these songs. Arabesk (meaning made or done in Arabic fashion) became popular among rural migrants and laborers who lived at the fringes of urban areas in squatter neighborhoods. Despite state control of radio and the ban on arabesk, the music had a large following. Arabesk was distributed broadly via cassette, performed in most taverns, and even openly played on public transportation. Significantly, arabesk was more than a musical style: it brought many political issues to the surface, including its conflict with the state's Westernization policies (Özbek, 1997). In opposition to the state's cultivation of regional differences as buffer against political consciousness, arabesk "indirectly addressed class issues, raising an intense awareness of the migration problem and social issues connected with this on a national scale" (Stokes, 1992, p. 152). Moreover, arabesk music, which early on was dismissed as "degenerate" and "fatalistic" by cultural elites, has flourished over the decades to become even more popular today, continuing to reflect a rudimentary class critique of society.

With the establishment of Turkish Radio and Television (TRT) as a state institution in 1964, the state attempted to combat the popularity of arabesk with the promotion of more Western contemporary and politically neutral music styles. Turkish pop music, in particular, was illustrative of the Kemalist approach—it was little more than Western pop put to Turkish lyrics—a crude synthesis of East meets West. As a result, Turkish pop didn't achieved the broad appeal of arabesk until the 1990s, so TRT has never been able to gain hegemonic leadership in the cultural sphere. Defining its mission as "educating, informing, entertaining, forming a national culture, and contributing to the social, cultural and economic development of society" (Cankaya, 1995, p. 1080), TRT broadcast four radio channels nationally: a Turkish classical and pop music channel with news and magazine programs, radio plays, and children's shows (TRT-1); a Turkish folk music channel (TRT-2); a Western classical and pop music channel (TRT-3); and a channel devoted to education (TRT-4). This was radio in Turkey until 1990.

TV broadcasting in Turkey started in 1968. As part of TRT, the music and programming policies on radio that encouraged the creation of secular, modern, Kemalist Turkish people applied to TV broadcast, as well. TRT-TV devoted one quarter of its programming to news and current affairs and also broadcast some educational programs about the meaning of national holidays and events, national history, and Atatürk's reforms. Another 30% to 50% of its programming consisted of foreign films, series, and documentaries (Cankaya, 1986, p. 72). Even though TRT was set up to be independent, government control over finances and the fact that the chief TRT administrator is appointed by the president has made TRT susceptible to intervention, interference, and control.

Privatization of Media and the End of the TRT Monopoly

1990 was a turning point for commercial broadcasting in Turkey. The first Turkish commercial television station (Star 1 channel owned by a Swiss-based company called Magic Box) began broadcasting from Germany to Turkey via satellite after the prime minister declared there was no law against broadcasting abroad. Emboldened by the opening, more than a dozen commercial radio stations and 16 TV channels were operating in Turkey by 1992 (Sahin & Aksoy, 1993, p. 32). Pressured by both national and international economic and political powers to reform and privatize, Turkish elites and the government opted to forego coercion in an attempt to establish more functional hegemonic relations with the urban middle and working classes. In short order, the 1982 Constitution was amended to allow private broadcasting in 1993. Today Turkey has 16 national, 15 regional, and 229 local TV channels, some with a range of only their immediate neighborhood. There are also 36 national, 108 regional, and 1,052 local licensed radio stations throughout the country. With the boom of commercial radio and television, TRT's audience share dropped to 25%, and its advertising revenues dropped 50% (Aksoy & Robins, 1997, p. 1946). As TRT-TV livened up its programming and started covering more controversial issues, such as radical Islam (White, 1999, p. 169), TRT radio loosened its policies and opened TRT-FM, which played a new type of Turkish popular music based on arabesk and folk that emerged in the 1980s. TRT-FM and its format is a recognition by Turkish rulers that the population prefers Turkish folk and pop music, and represents a conscious decision to incorporate Turkish populism in the construction of a new capitalist hegemony in the cultural sphere.

Aksoy & Avci (1992) believe that one of the driving forces behind the emergence of commercial media channels was the widespread challenge to TRT's domination and static format, which "still champions the idea that there is a homogeneous and uniform identity that characterizes Turkish society and mentality" (p. 39). New media channels responded to the urge for an environment where many different opinions could circulate freely. With the claim of bringing listeners issues that weren't addressed before, commercial media channels welcome programs and ideas that appeal to a wide audience but could not be broadcast on TRT. Many controversial issues, such as corruption in state institutions, the head scarf dispute, and living conditions in squatter neighborhoods, were discussed by audiences on popular TV programs, such as "Arena" and "Siyaset Meydani," which were broadcast on mainstream channels owned by print media giants such as Aydin Doğan and Dinç Bilgin. As Sahin and Aksoy (1993) point out, "the global stations operating outside the constraints of the official ideology helped turn Turkey into a shooting gallery of taboos by bringing the Kurdish problem, Kemalism, secularism, religious sects, gender roles, sex, etc., into the realm of public discussion" (p. 35). Commercial media have been quite successful at reflecting the social inequities, the dysfunction of the state, and the problems of the poor and the marginal. Also, entertainment programs hosted by celebrities, Turkish dramas, sitcoms, magazine programs, and talk shows changed the TV landscape from TRT's monotonous, didactic programming full of foreign films, series, and documentaries to a lively, colorful, entertaining and "Turkish-made" broadcasting scene. Commercial media have aligned the aspirations of the Turkish people with Western programming formats. Local productions have responded to the so-called "rising values" of Turkish society by inserting specific and unique aspects of their culture into a format provided by their global media partners. Thus, commercial radio stations generally displayed a creolization or glocalization in programming. For instance, radio programs reflected the everyday realities and concerns of Turkish people from their own perspectives but presented them in the standard Western "talk radio" or "non-stop music" formats, which seemed contemporary, modern, and fresh to the audience. In short, by meeting the cultural preferences of the Turkish people on some elementary level, commercial media have managed to rapidly establish their hegemony over the cultural scene in Turkey.

Nonetheless, airing programs that depend heavily on audience participation and playing music genres that TRT radio channels do not air, such as arabesk and political pop, commercial radio dramatically affected the radio environment. Turks, who had been content with their cassette players, now listen to radio again; citizens, yearning for a voice, have some sense of the power and potential of mass communication.

This new communications space that has been opened up in Turkey with the help of global communication technologies has played an important role in the empowerment of marginal or forgotten groups and voices, and their integration to the global system. This space often functions as a public forum to question the country's modernization project and its definition of national identity, and to resist the top-down economic, political, and cultural systems. Yet, at the same time, this space makes Turkey susceptible to corporate media hegemony and cultural homogenization because it promotes commodity fetishism, mimicry of global culture and products, and consumerism.

A Space for Questioning the Modernization Project

Both the weakening of the nation-state and national-cultural identities, and the need for them exist simultaneously in any nation taking part in the global scene. The complexity of the relationship among the nation, national-cultural identities, and globalization urges us to consider the social dynamics that create contrasting responses to the process of globalization in that particular society. Turkish media, especially radio, in the 1990s illustrates clearly these contradictory manifestations of globalization, whose outcomes depend on the political struggle of competing classes and other social forces domestically and internationally.

Globalization is often blamed for the gradual disappearance of the relationship between a national-cultural identity and a nation-state (Hall, 1991, p. 22). In Turkey intervention for change has been initiated not by social movements against the repressive state but by globalization, and thus the sudden privatization and globalization of media have contributed to the dissolution of official dogma and a reevaluation of national culture and identity (Sahin & Aksoy, 1993, p. 35). Turkey's integration into the global economy and media created a space for the articulation of differences and cultural elements, such as political Islam, the acknowledgement of Kurdish identity, and non-Western cultural products like arabesk music, that are contrary to the Kemalist ideology, which grounds Atatürk's modernization project. As Appadurai (1996) points out "electronic mass mediation and transnational mobilization have broken the monopoly of autonomous nation-states over the project of modernization" (p. 10). Turkish commercial media disrupted TRT's monopoly and the way in which political elites manipulated Atatürk's modernization project. Turkish national identity, which is defined by the project of modernization, has also been redefined by these new expressions of national-cultural identity via new commercial media channels and without any input or manipulation from the state until the passage of new broadcasting laws in 1994.

Soon after the state media monopoly was broken, Islamic groups built their own TV and radio stations, and began broadcasting programs about Islam, which function to also critique the current social and political system from an Islamic perspective. Even though these media are considered Muslim or religious channels overall, they reflect the ideas and ideologies of the religious communities who own them, and thus they differ among themselves. Samanyolu TV was set up by the highly influential and controversial religious leader Fethullah Gülen's community; Mesaj TV is run by the Kadiri community; and Kanal 7 is owned by the İskenderpaşa group. TGRT belongs to a very large media group owned by İhlas Holding, a conglomerate that also owns banking, health, food service, publishing, and trade companies. TGRT was established by followers of Seyyid Abdulhakim Arvas of the Nakşibendi sect, which is another very influential Islamic sect in Turkey (Aksoy & Robins, 1997, p. 1947).

During the 1980s, Islamic groups became more organized, building their movements through 45 monthly periodicals (Güneş-Ayata, 1994, p. 254). Their response to the social consequences of rapid modernization, cultural alienation, and social rootlessness are part of the Islamic revivalism in the Middle East in the 1970s and 1980s (Piscatori, 1983). Islam in Turkey was a response to rapid urbanization and flourished as a result of the government policies that support Islamic groups with the aim of balancing the post-cold war Communist movement. The emergence of the upwardly mobile middle classes, the government's antiworking-class policies, and "the export-oriented integration of the Turkish economy into global capitalism" weakened the premises of Ataturk's nationalism. Only Islam remained as the unifying element of national identity for these groups (Keyman, 1995, pp. 112–113).

Religious media tend to utilize the global information technology but distance themselves from the global culture if it is Western-based. Because state-run radio only discusses moral aspects of Islam due to its secular politics, most religious or Islamic radio stations spend most of their air time interpreting religious doctrines and teaching how to practice Islam. They use mystic music and Islamic discourse that consists of some Arabic words and expressions in broadcast and their Web pages, which offer live Internet broadcasting and chat rooms to capture a wider audience.

Hybridity

Another significant development is the emergence of a variety of Turkish pop music genres on 24-hour music channels. Although these genres brought together many elements of Eastern and Western music, this new music confirms neither the East-West synthesis nor the "national music" that the early Westernization reforms envisioned. With its musical policies, state-run radio especially had fueled the debates about *alafranka* versus *alaturka* music and created a polarization among listeners that continued until the 1990s. However, during the 1990s opening for commercial radio, the music industry had to provide almost 2,000 radio stations with a constant supply of new popular albums that could appeal to a wide audience. The two genres of music they mostly invested in were Turkish pop, which soon became mainstream music that satisfies Kemalist sensibilities and the rising expectations of the upper classes, which look to the West for inspiration and validation, and the ubiquitous arabesk music, which has now become influenced by pop styles (Kozanoglu, 1995, p. 144). To broaden its market, the music industry has transformed traditional arabesk music into a modernized hybrid form that in content speaks to the conditions of the urban working class and middle class, and in its aesthetic is more attractive to the youth. Meanwhile in the more open cultural space, Turkish pop music has also evolved since the 1980s into what Metin Solmaz (1995) calls the 'New Wave' of Turkish pop music (p. 944). Groups such as Bulutsuzluk Özlemi, Mozaik, and Yeni Türkü have attracted a younger, upper middle-class urban audience that seeks an alternative to the more traditional arabesk or *gazino* (Turkish tavern) music environment. Soon after the East-West synthesis of music, which is another example of creolization or glocalization in Turkey, became dominant in the music industry and was applied to mainstream pop. In 1996 Sezen Aksu, Turkey's most popular composer and singer, released an album called "Light Rises from the East." The album, which combined *alaturka* with *alafranka*, became very popular, and there is a growing market for such *sentez* (synthesis) music. This contemporary synthesis of music differs from the crude, state-directed, pro-Western synthesis of cultures from years before. In other words, the music industry has accomplished *hegemonically* what the Ottoman elite failed to secure *coercively*.

This era also witnessed the emergence of political pop, rightist (ülkücü) pop, and green pop music. Political pop, performed by famous singers such as Ahmet Kaya, Grup Yorum, and Kızılırmak, addresses the tragedy of the urban working class from a leftist standpoint in a more radical way than arabesk did. In their songs, these singers point to social problems, such as the inequalities in society, life in ghettos, and restrictions on speech. On the other hand, rightist pop music—Ozan Arif, Hasan Sağındık, and Arif Nazım's albums have sold over 100,000 copies—has a radically nationalistic agenda, while green pop has an Islamic agenda. Here it is important to note the difference between the Kemalist and rightist strains of nationalism in Turkey. Rightist nationalism is based on a revival of pre-Islamic Turkic history and traditions. Hence, the rightist music's nationalistic messages differ from the mainstream pop musicians' messages. Many radio stations were built devoted to these hybrid music genres and the ideologies they represent. Hybridity of these music genres, including arabesk, comes from their use of the rhythms and instruments of Western pop music to create a contemporary but local pop music that borrows from Turkish folk music.

A Space for Resistance

Defining globalization as a "process of profound unevenness" (p. 33), Hall (1991) points to two forms of globalization that struggle with one another: The first one is "an older, corporate, enclosed, increasingly defensive one that has to go back to nationalism and national-cultural identity in a highly defensive way and try to build barriers around it before it is eroded"; the second is "a form of the global postmodern that is trying to live with—and at the same moment overcome, sublate, get hold of, and incorporate—difference" (p. 23). In an otherwise closed society, the appearance of commercial media in Turkey created an unexpected space for the articulation of national identity as negotiated between these two forms of globalization. The coexistence of contrasting responses to globalization in Turkey is, to some extent, a result of the differences among people of different social classes and status, and a consequence of the restrictions on openly political answers to state control. Theories of globalization and national identity often ignore or take for granted the impact of social class in the debate about what happens to national identity in the global era.

   In many respects, the Turkish state and international investors may tolerate, even encourage, cultural openness and variation as a site for releasing social unease and providing diversion: music on its own cannot carry a political program and in the hands of commercial broadcasters and record companies may even be diverted from its more pointed political intentions. Of course, in Turkey, musical styles, groups, and fans coalesce around aesthetic and political expressions that may viscerally or at times consciously mobilize larger social forces. The battle for cultural leadership by dominant social forces faces many challenges and unexpected contradictions, providing openings for other social classes and groups to consider more democratic relationships.

Not unexpectedly, the increasing popularity of political, rightist, and green pop music—and the accompanying lyrics and ideologies that speak to lower-middle class and working people in the urban ghettos—has prompted a response from the secular Kemalist population, which is comprised mostly by the professional, urban middle class. Mainstream Turkish pop musicians, whose music attracts the youngsters of these families, have become public proponents of secularism and Kemalist nationalism. They have pioneered the fashion of displaying the crescent moon and star symbols of the Turkish flag on necklaces and broaches. Some of them had their promotional pictures taken with the Turkish flag and in media interviews emphasized their love of contemporary Turkey. In concerts Turkish pop musicians sing songs with Kemalist nationalistic sensibilities and ask audiences to cheer "Turkiye" (Turkey). During discussions of teens and music on television talk shows such as "Siyaset Meydanı," parents approved of Kemalist pop because it promotes family and flag (Kozanoğlu, 1995, p. 152).

In short, as the struggle between various forms of globalization is exacerbated in Turkey, diverse voices in this new communication space made the national modernization ideal seem limited and impossible to achieve. On radio Turkey now has a lively and diverse music scene, but reactions to new cultural projects have been swift, as the Kemalist majority rushes to protect the ideals of a pro-Western modernism. As some of the class-based tenets of Kemalism are eroding under the impact of new forms rooted in arabesk, Islam, and working-class traditions, mainstream pop musicians champion Kemalist nationalist messages in an attempt to slow the slide. So new commercial media created a space not only for minority, religious, and ethnic groups for existence and resistance, but also for the Kemalist majority who aspire to defend and redefine their national identity in ways that diverge from the officially sanctioned parameters.

Media as Public Forum

Contrary to TRT's emphasis on educating the "Anatolian people" with a limited repertoire of music, when commercial radio was first established, it strategically situated itself to be the Turkish people's voices by realizing the need for people to express themselves after the long period of military coups and economic and political instability. These channels created an interactive broadcasting style with the slogan of "Talking Turkey" that encouraged people to call and express their opinions. Listeners, with the excitement of rebelling against the government's cultural dictation via these pirate radio stations, reached commercial channels by fax from their offices, by telephone from their homes, and by mobile phone from their cars to congratulate the stations for their broadcasts. The 1990s were the first time listeners were being asked about their opinions or song requests, and hearing their own voices broadcast, while TRT merely announced their names and song requests. This recognition of the audience coupled with friendly on-air conversation—along with more critical news coverage and previously unavailable popular music—contributed to listeners' identification with commercial radio. Listener participation also represented a mild form of public access to media, as it appeared that people could encounter and respond to social and political issues. Indeed, White (1999) argues that the historically robust oral culture in Turkey found new power through radio (and TV) because "classes of people formerly marginalized from public debates" were helping to shape the national political agenda (p. 177).

Indeed, radio stations conducted live surveys with questions such as "what do you like and dislike about the city you live in?" "What do you think about the Parliament's decision of making the four-day religious holiday a ten-day holiday this year?" "Should we take more vacation than we already have?" "Should we continue spanking our children? What kind of punishment did your parents give you, and what kind of punishment do you plan to give to your children?" People called in to express their opinions on various issues during peak hours for a couple of hours. Besides creating a public forum for attracting more listeners, this type of interaction potentially suggests that citizens might have the right to hold informative discussions that might encourage social mobility and social protest.

White (1999) argues that communication technologies such as radio and telephone have enhanced the robust oral communication culture in Turkey, leading to a national civic identity that should impact the larger national political agenda. As evidence, she reports that protests have occurred when the government has attempted to crack down on pirate TV stations. For instance, when Star TV's broadcast on government corruption was interrupted by an invasion of the Turkish police to close down the station, listeners phoned to protest and visited the station. When the government subsequently closed all commercial radio channels for violating the broadcasting law, listener support for radio channels erupted in much the same way. Then the radio stations formed an Association of Private Radio and Television Owners and Broadcasters to organize press campaigns, appeals to the Parliament, petitions, and red ribbon campaigns for many automobile and taxi antennas proclaiming "I want my radio back." Even though these protests were unable to start an effective mass movement (in part, because these stations did not emerge as a result of public efforts but rather as private enterprises) (Duran, 1995, p. 1082), the law that declared the state monopoly of television and radio ownership was quickly amended to head off further public protest.

Of course, as in any hegemonic relationship, negotiated consent seldom dislodges dominant control. In legalizing private broadcasting in 1994, the government established the Radio and Television High Council (RTÜK) to regulate radio and TV programming. Besides allocating channels and frequency bands and issuing licenses, RTÜK was also given the authority to monitor the contents of private radio and TV broadcasts, and to penalize stations that violate the new Broadcasting Law. Little of this affects the dominant media companies that represent the interests of the political and economic elite by promoting consumerism and entertainment. Rather, RTÜK monitors potentially political local, regional, and national radio and TV broadcasts through the Department of Security in every province. The Department of Security has given many warnings, stopped broadcasts for periods of a couple of days to a year, and revoked local licenses according to the severity of the violation. For instance, in 1998 Radio Karacadağ, which was a local radio station in Şanlıurfa province in Southeast Turkey, was closed for broadcasting in Kurdish. Even though RTÜK gave licenses to 10 radio stations that play Kurdish music, announcements still must be made in Turkish because the law only recognizes Turkish for radio and television broadcasts. RTÜK allows the use of foreign languages for teaching and news casting purposes because these languages "have contributed to universal works of culture and science." Although it is not explicitly detailed in the law, these accepted languages include English, French, and German. However, the law has been strictly interpreted to exclude the Kurdish language in broadcasting, and the Constitution prohibits its use in education—all in an effort to stymie Kurdish nationalism and separatism. Kurdish music stations also have to monitor and censor the songs they play because if inspectors believe that songs they play carry secret political messages that provoke separatism, their broadcasts can be stopped. TV stations mostly receive warnings and temporary closures for broadcasting shows with violent and/or sexual content as well as provocative political commentary.

Ultimately, the new law engendered consensual programming self-censorship among radio and TV stations, just as "Talking Turkey" seemed to exhaust substantive topics that were being covered on both commercial radio and TV channels. Most broadcasting in Turkey has since slid towards solely entertainment content. By the mid-90s, the novelty of social commentary was gone, as the narrow range of topics allowed on radio and TV became increasingly redundant and mundane. New topics seldom address political or economic issues, and most are not discussed with enough detail, persistence, or sophistication to elicit any social action. The dialogue is now limited to chat: shallow and repetitive. Yet Turkish radio talk (which at best provides an entertaining and cathartic experience) has established a hegemonic frame with the willing participation of the working- and middle-class audiences because it allowed the open expression of ideas that were generally off-limits in a repressive state. For now, it seems that the semblance of democracy is better than none at all. Government leaders seem to have accommodated this development, understanding the political impotence of its current form. From the perspective of the radio monopoly, radio talk attracts listeners and advertisers, lets citizens let off some steam, and positions commercial radio as champion of democracy—as occurred in 1993, when the state briefly shut down radio, but then retreated under corporate and public pressure.

Mimicry, Adaptation, and Cultural Homogenization

Turkish commercial radio demonstrates how a variety of responses to the processes of both modernization and globalization are expressed simultaneously. On the one hand, the rhetorical strategies that commercial radio uses to differentiate itself from state-run radio exemplify critical responses to the state's elitist monolithic cultural politics of modernization. These critical responses to Western modernity reflect neither society's rejection of it nor its failure to adopt it, but rather the quest to reform it. On the other hand, the diverse ways in which the project of modernization is questioned also illustrates how globalization is interpreted and experienced. In this era, mimicry of global culture and integration efforts with global media institutions became another way for Turkish commercial media to respond to the expectations of a young urban audience who wants to attune itself with global culture.

While some new radio stations featured hybrid musical styles, such as Turkish pop and arabesk, and others aired traditional music, such as folk and Turkish art music, larger commercial media—often in joint venture with international investors—took their inspiration directly from the West. They chose English to name their stations, such as Power FM, Energy FM, Hot Station, Kiss FM, Radyo Blue, Metro FM, Radio Night&Day, Show Radyo, Joy FM, Capital Radio, and Number One FM. Some hired foreign radio personalities and used English words and phrases extensively in their broadcasts, as they sought to capture the upscale, urban, professional youth enamored of all things European and American. This largely Kemalist youth market is sizeable, has considerable disposable income, and strives to keep its distance from lower- and middle-class Turkish music listeners.

Commercial radio often uses the English acronym "DJ" to define on-air personalities. The mostly 20-year-old DJs use lots of slang and English—including technology words such as e-mail, Internet, chat, fax—and have a striking inability to speak fluent Turkish. For young Kemalist Turks, English is the metonym for global modernity. As Kachru (1986) observes, "the English language is not perceived as necessarily imparting only Western traditions. The medium is non-native, but the message is not" (p. 12). English gives the young, urban Turks a new power base and elitism to negotiate with the global modernity and explore their new identities based on the rising values of capitalism as experienced in Turkey. In the 1990s columnists in mainstream newspapers started writing about their elitist lifestyles, their meals at fancy restaurants, French wines they tasted, exclusive concerts they were invited to, by using foreign concepts and words such as gusto, ambience, etc. The message was that it was crucial to know English and consume in the right places in a right way in order to feel the belonging to a global era.

We see a similar situation of a transformation of mimicry into localized hybridity in other media, as well. Joint ventures with international publishers' media have led to Turkish editions of *Cosmopolitan, Elle,* and other fashion magazines. Turkish editors have localized the content without changing the commercial, elitist, urban aspect of the magazines. Another important joint agreement was made between Turner International and the Doğan Media Group launching CNN Turk in October 1999. Doğan Group also buys Turner-owned movies for its Kanal D TV station and programming from HBO and the Cartoon Network (Peterson, 2000). Atlanta executives of CNN agreed to a 24-hour news channel in Turkish because of the prospect of reaching 7 million of Turkey's 12 million TV households. Consultants from CNN selected top Turkish journalists for its editorial team, but modeled CNN Turk on CNN in the United States and trained the reporters.

Radio Entertainment and Consumerism

Commercial radio's choice of music and the way their DJs address and engage the audience illustrate that challenges to the state's elitist politics of culture have been limited to the adoption of the readily available expressions of cultural identity subsidized by global media. While many commercial radio channels blatantly reflect Western influences in adopting English names and music, more express their accommodation through Turkish names with lively descriptions: e.g., Yasam Radyo (Radio Life), Coskun FM (Exuberant FM), and Alem FM (Good Old Fashioned Fun FM). Turkish identity only goes so far, however, as most of these stations have adopted the advertising/entertainment model dominant in the United States. For instance, Alem FM calls its listeners "Alemciler," meaning "people who want to have fun." The emergence of radio that primarily advertises fun and 24-hour music is not just a response to TRT's didactic broadcasting (which expresses the elitist idea that radio should be solely a medium of education and high culture), but reflects the dominance of the commercial/entertainment model of radio that privileges individualism, consumerism, and hedonism. The previous cultural distinction between radio, which played officially created and approved music, and the film/records/gazino industry (gazino is a Turkish tavern where you engage in "alem"), which featured popular music that was banned from TRT, disappeared in the 1990s (Özbek, 1994, p. 152), as the commercialization of culture supplied entertainment for all—according to their class taste. Arabesk and Turkish pop radio offered gazino-like entertainment for the working class and poor, while Western pop radio created a "party" atmosphere for its upscale audience. On these channels, DJs often scream, "it's party time!" in both English and Turkish. Dominated by commercial concerns, freedom in broadcasting in Turkey reveled in the constant demand for more entertainment—according to clear social class distinctions—demonstrating the hegemonic pull of global capitalist values. As Herman & McChesney (1997) suggest, "the commercial model [of media] has its own internal logic and, being privately owned and relying on advertiser support, tends to erode the public sphere and to create a 'culture of entertainment' that is incompatible with democratic order. Media outputs are commodified and are designed to serve market ends, not citizenship needs" (p. 9).

Commercial TV and print media in Turkey promote this culture of entertainment (which radio successfully creates) even further in ways quite familiar in the celebrity-obsessed West: featuring reports on where pop stars shop, which brands they prefer, where they go on holiday, etc. Television magazine programs regularly publicize entertainment events and trendy clubs, where celebrities perform or frequent, and describe how the hip crowd has fun. Weekend newspaper and magazine supplements (owned by television stations) also feature celebrity lifestyle stories. An eager audience of Turkish youth willingly learn cultural sophistication according to Westernized global norms, while eager advertisers willingly pay media producers for time and space. Entertainment programs have high ratings in part because they introduce and feature cultural products offering new pleasures and identities to a previously culturally-restricted society, and in part because the only alternative to this entertainment-laden programming is the stilted state-run Kemalist media. Perhaps more importantly for the future of Turkey, this new entertainment culture saturates society with seductive appeals for participation in this new, globalized world. Above all, these programs indicate that one must become a good consumer of both popular culture and new cultural products/services. Thus, although many viewers—especially older ones—may express dissatisfaction with the culture of entertainment and consumerism, commercial media maintain hegemony because for now younger Turks are satisfied with the social and cultural benefits that come from participating in such a culture. Given the quickly established structure that evolved in the radio and television industry following the reforms of 1994, more creative, democratic cultural and political models for broadcasting will require increased social consciousness and political mobilization.

From the State's Media Monopoly to Corporate Media Monopoly

The broadcasting law passed in 1994 restricts ownership of private radio and television to corporations, which can only own one radio and one TV station, no shareholder is allowed more than 20% ownership, and foreign ownership is limited to 20% as well (Aziz, 1995, p. 20–1). Additionally, 20% of weekly broadcasting had to be educational and cultural, and include traditional Turkish music (p. 318). Even though the law sought to prevent media monopolies, the new owners quickly found ways around the restrictions, and media ownership rapidly narrowed, even as the number of stations increased. The larger players soon bought the smaller ones. Today more than 60% of the media in Turkey are owned by two conglomerates, the Doğan Group and the Sabah Group, while some 80% of the media are owned by only 5 corporations. In addition to holdings in banking, tourism, insurance, and energy, the Doğan Group owns 8 newspapers (which account for 66% of the country's print advertising revenues and almost 50% of daily circulation in Turkey), 35 magazines, 3 radio stations, printing and book publishing businesses, and an Internet portal (Boulton, 2001; Peterson, 2000). Using proxy companies, Doğan owns more than 20% of his television and radio stations. Other major media groups have similar dominant individuals or families.

Even as they flaunted the spirit and letter of the law, dominant media in Turkey have been challenging the few remaining restrictions on media ownership, spurred on by global capitalism's insistence on international deregulation of trade. The European Union has insisted that Turkey lift restrictions on international investment, and the IMF is withholding needed credit unless Turkey privatizes its entire telecommunications system. In the fall of 2001, the Turkish Parliament obliged domestic and international capitalists by raising individual ownership restrictions to 50% and opened the bidding on government holdings. The new law maintains restrictions against negative media coverage of official policies, a condition unreported in the major media, and of little immediate consequence to the commercial media devoted exclusively to entertainment and advertising

Media Hegemony and Commercialization in Turkey

Until the broadcasting law of 1994, nonstate media in Turkey enjoyed an unregulated, independent broadcasting climate with large urban audiences seeking democratic public discourse. A political consciousness was forming, and many civil society organizations were gathering around issues such as human rights, women's rights, the environment, and labor issues. The political and social activities of the 1980s created an environment of relative freedom, and many of the groups were already seeking ways to reach a mass audience and gain public recognition, when several private radio and TV stations began broadcasting (Alankuş-Kural, 1994). Commercial media, aiming to increase their ratings, sought to air what state media did not. Many competed to provide air time to the civic organizations, ethnic minorities, and others that had been politically and socially marginalized by the Turkish state. Access to media by groups challenging the Kemalist political and social agendas, including its promotion of a Westernized Turkey, helped legitimate diverse local identities and disrupted the class presumptions of the nation-state and its national culture. As Alankuş-Kural (1994) puts it:

> [those] who had been assimilated, oppressed and targeted as "enemy" by the dominant classes throughout the history of the Republic, have also taken an opposing/challenging stance to the system. They have loosened/given up their reluctant/forced "consent" to the system and their reaction has been to resort to a self-definition of their identity instead of the one which is imposed upon them via hegemonic ideology. In other words . . . the deadlock emerged in the economic aspect of such a total project—the Western path of modernization dominated by capitalism—demonstrated its impacts on the political sphere as potential "regime/system crisis," while as an identity crisis on the cultural sphere. (pp. 2–3)

Commodifying the new cultural scene as it simultaneously created a cultural space to experience the identity crisis, commercial media built their hegemonic presence within the context of global capitalism. Commercial media gained the willing support of an urban middle-class majority eager to expand their participation in society and also attracted those working-class and ethnic groups so marginalized and repressed by the corporate state who were happy just to come out on the surface of society.

Even though after the 1980s and with the emergence of the new media, the Turks are thought to reject the "official culture" that is dictated by the state ideology and return to their "real culture," which is traditional and/or local (Stokes, 1992; Robins, 1996; Aksoy & Robins, 1997), the popular culture in Turkey today is neither traditional nor solely local, and the majority's preferences are not necessarily more traditional compared to the Western culture that the modernization project dictated. Popular music genres in Turkey today, such as arabesk and Turkish pop, are hybrid forms played by Western instruments. Nevertheless, the traditional elements of these music genres, such as arabesk, have been transformed in a way that reflects the dilemmas of modern life (Özbek, 1994, p. 210) and therefore cannot be regarded as traditional. In that sense, commercial radio stations should not be perceived as providing people with music that is less Western and more traditional, since the music genres that are mostly played by commercial channels, such as Turkish pop, arabesk, fantezi, rightist music, pop (especially American and Latin American pop music), are not traditional at all.

Until the mid-1990s, nonstate radio in Turkey was crucial in aiding people to question the essentialist identity that the state and its institutions dictate by offering a forum for audience expression and conversation as well as sanctioning the popular taste in music. The rapid commercialization of radio, which is linked to its rapid monopolization, resulted in broadcasting formats that emphasize entertainment through music and chat, almost exclusively aimed at urban youth. Today, the privatized, commercialized media are widely criticized for their weak, sensational, and distasteful content by not only elites but also a majority of the population. Commercial television channels also are criticized for invoking a racist nationalism. These commercial media outlets do not function as public broadcasting channels, as they once claimed. Indeed, most of these stations exclusively emphasize the values of a consumerist culture and promote a lifestyle that is practiced in the capitalist West.

What undercut and strangled the diversity, creativity, and independence of the new media was its commercialization by monopolies willing to broadcast any style attractive to advertisers seeking particular audiences. Turkish audiences have tolerated, even sought out, this capitalist commodification of culture because it permits positive representations of their ethnicity and class culture and/or identity. As a hegemonic apparatus, the Doğan-Sabah media monopoly (apparently distanced from the state) poses no threat to capitalist Turkey or its investing suitors. The state chooses to ignore the monopolistic practices of these new media corporations, as long as their broadcasts do not conflict with the state's official stance on critical issues, such as the Kurdish struggle and the Cyprus problem. The new corporate media of Turkey advance their hegemony in tandem with the rule of the state: not only do they prosper from existing regulations in commerce and labor, they share similar interests (and often investments) with other capitalist enterprises. Yet, as Artz and Murphy (2000) observe, "hegemony exists only when dominant social forces represent and incorporate some very real material interests of subordinate groups into their social relationships" (p. 23). Since a politically conscious social movement or organized class intervention are absent in Turkey today, the democratic opening in the media has been commandeered by the corporate privateers. Corporate media hegemony (with or without global direction) has been constructed on global terms, because commercial media offer multiple rewards to its audiences: entertainment, a semblance of public voice, positive representations of cultural diversity, and variety in musical styles—all in the guise of antigovernment posturing. In Turkey globalization has threatened and weakened state control and official ideologies, but the relentless privatization/commercialization of media as entertainment is providing a new hegemony.

The commercial media continue to weaken the TRT's cultural and sociopolitical influence. What had been instrumental in maintaining an essentialist monolithic Turkish identity (Kadıoğlu, 1996, p. 190) is losing its value as a means of communication for the government, leading communication scholars in Turkey to suggest that TRT become a public broadcasting channel operated independently from the state (Kültür politikaları, 1998, p. 7). Independent of the state control, and domestic and international corporate influence, such a public channel could provide an opportunity for representation and democratic participation by the working classes and other marginalized groups in Turkey.

References

Ahmad, J. A. (1982). *Gharbzadegi: Plagued by the West* (trans. P. Sprachman). Delmor, NY: Center for Iranian Studies, Columbia University Press.

Aksoy, A., & Avcı, N. (1992). Spreading Turkish identity. *Intermedia, 20* (4–5), 39–40.

Aksoy, A., & Robins, K. (1997). Peripheral vision: Cultural industries and cultural identities in Turkey. *Environment and Planning, A* 29 (11), 1937–52.

Alankuş-Kural, S. (1994). Mass media disorder and the representation of the other in Turkish media. Paper presented at the *Turbulent Europe: Conflict, Identity, and Culture; European Film and Television Studies Conference,* London.

Appadurai, A. (1996). *Modernity at large: Cultural dimensions of globalization.* Minneapolis, MN: The University of Minnesota Press.

Artz, L., & Murphy, B. O. (2000). *Cultural hegemony in the United States.* Thousand Oaks, CA: Sage.

Aziz, A. (1995). *Radyo ve televizyon: Yasal Düzenlemeler.* Ankara: A. Ü. İletişim Fakültesi Basımevi.

Bhabba, H. (Ed.) (1990). *Nation and narration.* London: Routledge.

Boratav, K. (1995). *İstanbul ve Anadolu'dan sınıf profilleri.* İstanbul: Tarih Vakfı Yurt Yayınları.

Boulton L. (June 5, 2001). Turkish tycoon strikes back. *Financial Times*.

Cankaya, Ö. (1986). *Türk televizyonunun program yapısı (1968–1985)*. İstanbul: Mozaik.

Cankaya, Ö. (1995). Türk radyoculuğunun gelişimi . In M. Belge (ed.), *Yüzyıl biterken Cumhuriyet dönemi Türkiye ansiklopedisi* (pp. 1078–1086). İstanbul: İletişim Yayınları.

Curran J., & Park, M. (2000). Beyond globalization theory. In J. Curran & M. Park (Eds.), *De-westernizing media studies* (pp. 3–18). NY: Routledge.

Duman, D. (1997). Cumhuriyet baloları. *Toplumsal Tarih VII* (37), 44–48.

Duran, R. (1995). Ticari, hür ya da yarı-resmi özel radyolar. In M. Belge (ed.), *Yüzyıl biterken Cumhuriyet dönemi Türkiye ansiklopedisi* (pp. 1082–3). İstanbul: İletişim Yayınları.

Featherstone, M. (1996). Localism, globalism, and cultural identity. In R. Wilson & W. Dissanayake (Eds.), *Global/Local: Cultural production and the transnational imaginary* (pp. 46–77). Durham, NC: Duke University Press.

Gülalp, H. (1997). Modernization policies and Islamist politics in Turkey. In S. Bozdoğan & R. Kasaba (Eds.), *Rethinking modernity and national identity in Turkey* (pp. 52–63). Seattle, WA: University of Washington Press.

Güneş-Ayata, A. (1994). Pluralism versus authoritarianism: Political ideas in two Islamic publications. In R. Tapper (Ed.), *Islam in modern Turkey: Religion, politics and literature in a secular state (2nd ed.)* (pp. 254–279). NY: I. B. Tauris.

Hall, S. (1991). The local and the global: Globalization and ethnicity. In A. D. King (ed.), *Culture, globalization and the world-system: Contemporary conditions for the representation of identity* (pp. 19–40). London: Mcmillan.

Hannerz, U. (1987). The world in creolization. *Africa, 57* (4), 446–59.

Herman, E. S., & McChesney, R. W. (1997). *The global media: The new missionaries of corporate capitalism*. London: Cassell Academic.

Kachru, B. B. (1986). *The alchemy of English: The spread, functions and models of non-native Englishes*. Oxford: Pergamon Institute.

Kadıoğlu, A. (1996). The paradox of Turkish nationalism and the construction of official identity. *Middle Eastern Studies, 32* (2), 177–193.

Kandiyoti, D. (1997). Gendering the modern: On missing dimensions in the study of Turkish modernity. In S. Bozdoğan & R. Kasaba (Eds.), *Rethinking modernity and national identity in Turkey* (pp. 113–132). Seattle, WA: University of Washington Press.

Keyman, E. F. (1995). On the relation between global modernity and nationalism: The crisis of hegemony and the rise of (Islamic) identity in Turkey. *New Perspectives on Turkey, 13*, 93–120.

King, A. D. (ed.). (1991). *Culture, globalization and the world system*. New York: MacMillan.

Kozanoğlu, C. (1995). *Pop cagi atesi* (4th ed.). İstanbul: İletişim Yayınları.

Kraidy, M. M. (1999). The Global, the local, and the hybrid: A native ethnography of glocalization. *Critical Studies in Mass Communication, 16,* 456–476.

Kültür politikaları ve iletişim sempozyumu. (1998). *İletişim Araştırma, 13* (11), 1,6–7.

Mattelart, A. (1994). *Mapping world communication: War, progress, culture* (trans. S. Emanuel & J. A. Cohen). Minneapolis, MN: University of Minnesota Press.

Miyoshi, M. (1996). A borderless world? From colonialism to transnationalism and the decline of the nation-state. In R. Wilson & W. Dissanayake (Eds.), *Global/Local: Cultural production and the transnational imaginary* (pp. 78–106). Durham, NC: Duke University Press.

Özbek, M. (1994). *Popüler kültür ve Orhan Gencebay arabeski* (2nd ed.). İstanbul: İletişim Yayınları.

Özbek, M. (1997). Arabesk culture: A case of modernization and popular identity. In S. Bozdoğan & R. Kasaba (Eds.), *Rethinking modernity and national identity in Turkey* (pp. 211–32). Seattle, WA: University of Washington Press.

Peterson, L. (2000). Difficulties abroad: CNN meets the Turkish High Council. *http://www.dorduncukuvvetmedya.com.* (15.5.2001).

Piscatori, J. P. (1983). Introduction. In J. P. Piscatori (Ed.), *Islam in the political process.* London: Cambridge University Press.

Robertson, R. (1992). *Globalization, social theory and global culture.* London: Sage.

Robertson, R. (1995). Glocalization: Time-space and homogeneity-heterogeneity. In M. Featherstone, S. Lash, & R. Robertson (Eds.) *Global modernities* (pp. 25–40).

Robins, K. (1996). Interrupting identities: Turkey/Europe. In S. Hall & P. du Gay, *Questions of cultural identity* (pp. 61–86). NY: Sage.

Şahin, H., & Aksoy, A. (1993). Global media and cultural identity in Turkey. *Journal of Communication, 43* (2), 31–41.

Schiller, H. I. (1991). Not yet the post-imperialist era. *Critical Studies in Mass Communication, 8* (1), 13–28.

Schlesinger, P. (1993). Wishful thinking: Cultural politics, media, and collective identities in Europe. *Journal of Communication, 43* (2), 6–17.

Shohat, E., & Stam, R. (1996). From the imperial family to the transnational imaginary: Media spectatorship in the age of globalization. In R. Wilson & W. Dissanayake (Eds.), *Global/Local: Cultural production and the transnational imaginary* (pp. 145–170). Durham, NC: Duke University Press.

Solmaz, M. (1995). 1980'den günümüze Türkiye'de pop müzik [Pop music in Turkey since 1980]. In M. Belge (ed.), *Yüzyıl biterken Cumhuriyet dönemi Türkiye ansiklopedisi* (pp. 943–947). İstanbul: İletişim Yayınları.

Stokes, M. (1992). *The arabesk debate: Music and musicians in modern Turkey.* New York: Oxford University Press.

Tehranian, M. (1999). *Global communication and word politics: Domination, development, and discourse.* Boulder, CO: Lynne Rienner.

Tekelioğlu, O. (1996). The rise of a spontaneous synthesis: The historical background of Turkish music. *Middle Eastern Studies, 32* (2), 195–215.

Tomlinson, J. (1991). *Cultural imperialism.* Baltimore, MD: John Hopkins University Press.

White, J. B. (1999). Amplifying trust: Community and communication in Turkey. In D. F. Eickelman & J. W. Anderson (Eds.), *New media in the Muslim world: The emerging public sphere* (162–179). Bloomington, IN: Indiana University Press.

Wilson, R., & Dissanayake, W. (Eds.) (1996). *Global/Local: Cultural production and the transnational imaginary.* Durham, NC: Duke University Press.

PART IV

Cultural Variations in Global Media Hegemony

CHAPTER 10

Globalization and the Mass Media in Africa

Lyombe Eko

Introduction

Despite its relative isolation—some would say marginalization—from international telecommunications centers and markets, the African continent is in the vortex of globalization. Indeed, Africa is flooded by mass media content and, with it, the attendant philosophy, values, and worldviews from several parts of the world, most notably, the United States. Among other characteristics, globalization enables images, representations, and even entire programs from a dominant cultural industry to recruit fans among heterogeneous language groups and cultures around the globe.

Consider a few instances of the cultural reach of recent global communication:

- The "Jerry Springer Show" moves from studios in downtown Chicago to international programmers such as MIP-TV in Cannes, France, which reaches audiences throughout Europe and into Africa, so that in the slums of Lagos, Nigerians regularly witness American public confession television culture.
- From Moyabi, Gabon, located in the heart of the equatorial rain forest, Africa's most popular commercial FM and short-wave radio station, Africa No. 1, broadcasts to millions of Africans some of the most popular American and European commercials for products ranging from automobiles to cigarettes, including the ad that depicts the Marlboro Man on horseback, rounding up cattle in the mythic American West, exhorting Africans in a gravelly voiced, Parisian-accented French, to "Come to Marlboro Country."
- On the edge of the Saharan desert, lies one of the most inaccessible places on the globe, the ancient city of Timbuktu, Mali. Timbuktu was one of the first places in Africa to be wired for the Internet, as part of the United States Agency for International Development's (USAID) Africa Global Information Infrastructure project (Thussu, 2000).

195

- African television has been overtaken by the regular transmission of American, European, and even Asian programming on stations across the continent.

- From Algeria to Zimbabwe, American popular music, most notably rap, blares from radios, public transport vehicles, and nightclubs.

Yet, while these conditions indicate an Africa assaulted by Western media and concomitant values, the cultural exchange in Africa is hardly unidirectional, and Africans are far more than passive receivers of Western messages. Rather, despite a nearly overwhelming exposure to Western programming, and African government controls on the media that have their basis in coercive models of European colonialism, African media are active participants in the cultural hegemony that accompanies globalization.

The aim of this paper is to survey the mass media in Africa within the framework of globalization to briefly consider the significance of transnational media content on African cultures. As shall be illustrated, African media across the continent engage in a certain cultural eclecticism, a practice that promises to preserve African culture and values while popularizing the Western messages that inundate the African media market. Such a method cannot hope to successfully preserve "Africa" in a globalized world, unless African governments and social movements foster the growth of indigenous broadcasting and resist the slide towards commercialization and privatization that drives current global media activity.

Globalization and the African Mass Media

The common concern in most discussions of globalization is the disparity of power among different nation-states, regions, cultures, and civilizations, and the economic, political, and cultural domination that results from such disparity. Of particular concern is the commonly voiced perception that globalization tends to allow the exploitation of power differentials to the advantage of the powerful and detriment of the powerless. In this view, the operation of power appears agentless; thus analysis of globalization seems nearly impossible. In a treatment typical of this approach, one scholar calls globalization "hegemony without logic" because its apparent complexity obscures its ideology, its exercise of power is not rational, and there appears to be no central force guiding globalization in specific directions (Bamyeh, 2000, p.64).

The phenomenon of globalization has also been defined as cultural politics and cultural economics expressed in solidarities, common habits, and shared standards of behavior and norms. In this view, global culture is a common culture that presupposes a common knowledge system transmitted across vast distances by the transnational media and mass travel (Baymeh, 2000, p. 89). Yet, such a notion of global cultural exchange appears at least a bit disingenuous, for, with rare exception, the most visible manifestations of cultural globalization can be traced to American origins: the most frequently cited indicators of cultural globalization are ubiquitous "western" information and communication technology, films and television programs, video games and other culture industry products, ranging from Coca Cola, McDonald's, and the Marlboro man, to basketball, baseball caps, and rap music.

The reality is that multinational mass media conglomerates like Disney and AOL/Time-Warner increasingly practice what Juan Somavia of the International Labour Organization (ILO) has called "the industrialization of cultures . . . through the absorption of smaller players, the weakening of national and local cultures and enterprises . . . and a growing standardization of media products and performances sold around the world" (Buhrer, 2000, p.1). Disney is only one of several American companies that actively use aspects of African culture to create culture-neutral mass media content and advertising products for world consumption. Disney "de-Africanizes" African motifs, music, landscape, and wildlife, reducing them to clichés and stereotypes to make them appealing to a mass audience. The resulting fantasy of a neutral, marketable Africa is evident in feature films such as "The Lion King." Such globalization and merchandization of African symbols for corporate profit is obviously not intended to promote authentic African cultures.

Some theorists have characterized globalization as the outcome of relationships between the international and domestic political and cultural environment. According to this perspective, globalization occurs when national interests and institutions are structured in such a way that they become intertwined with international structures of power and authority in a circular and self-propagating arrangement. National interests are in part a product of international structures, institutions, and processes, which were created and set in motion to protect and promote state interest and identity in the first place (Wendt, 1992; Geske, 2000). Thus, the United Nations and its specialized agencies, such as United Nations Education Scientific and Cultural Organization (UNESCO), The World Bank and the International Monetary Fund (IMF), and the International Telecommunications Union (ITU), have served as platforms for the furtherance of the political, economic, and cultural interests of the major world powers—with the cooperation of domestic elites representing their particular developing nation-state.

Through their communications activities, the United Nations and its specialized agencies have been catalysts for this globalization. At its creation, the UN was viewed in part as a "communication operation of explicit global purpose" (Lerner, 1976, 50). During the period after World War II, development of the communications industry was identified as the means of transforming the poor countries of the world, with their active participation and consent, into partners in transnational communication under the aegis of the UN, but clearly under the sway of the United States (Lerner, 1976).

The UN's vision of global communication is most evident in the operations of the International Telecommunications Union, an intergovernmental specialized agency that cooperatively regulates international communication, including satellite broadcasting. The ITU is perhaps the single most effective promoter of globalization of telecommunications and mass media content. Through its World Radio Communication Conferences (WRCs) the ITU has embraced a market-oriented approach that has opened up electromagnetic spectrum bands for mobile telecommunications and broadcasting satellites, in addition to other radio communication services. In 1998 the ITU changed its constitution to admit private corporations as members with rights equal to nation-states (Thussu, 2000).

In keeping with its new privatization agenda, the ITU's most recent broadcasting satellite plan for Africa, which was adopted in 2000, is aimed at facilitating the delivery of direct satellite TV broadcasting to all countries on the continent. Each country is granted one orbital position from which up to 10 analog channels can be delivered (ITU, 2000). Of course, with the exception of South Africa, none of the 53 African countries have the legal framework, infrastructure, resources, or economic base to support such satellite broadcasting. Thus, most of these channels will eventually be leased or granted to multinational media conglomerates that will use them to deliver programming content from the United States and Europe to African countries.

Ultimately, the effects of globalization on African mass media are manifest in a wide array of inseparable form and content variables: organization, structures, infrastructures, venues, control of and access to all forms of telecommunications, mass media and information technology networks, the electromagnetic spectrum (airwaves), satellites systems, databases, as well as storage and retrieval systems (Bamyeh, 2000, p.132). The private, non-African entities that control the African communications infrastructure also control the software that makes the system function and much of the content that is transmitted on this infrastructure. The needs and concerns of nonelite Africans are reduced to issues for consideration by the marketing departments of these enterprises and their advertisers. Such "liberalization" of the media in Africa has brought little increase in public access, public service, or public decision-making on content and control.

Cultural Hegemony

Globalization is a controversial phenomenon because it is generally perceived as the vehicle for political, economic, and cultural domination. Groups, organizations, and institutions ranging from the Vatican to UNESCO have been critical of globalization of the mass media (Tinq, 2000). Indeed, to many, globalization is synonymous with wholesale Americanization or Westernization of the world. It has become a byword for the homogenization of global culture (Meunier, 2000; Tehranian, 1999; Giddens, 2000). For the French, globalization is Americanization, or the "Anglo-Saxon" homogenization of world culture, language, and values (Meunier, 2000). According to UNESCO Director General, Koichiro Matsuura, globalization is a dangerous phenomenon because flooding the Third World with "cultural products" from the industrialized countries could lead to homogenization and subsequent global cultural impoverishment (Caramel & Laronche, 2000).

These critiques warn that the cultural riches and creations from Africa and elsewhere will be transformed into homogenous commodities that primarily benefit the dominant classes at the expense of workers, artists, and the wider citizenry. Or, as Giddens puts it, a more accurate description for the "global village" would be, "global pillage" (Giddens, 2000, p.34). However appealing this conceptualization of globalization may be, its construction of political and cultural domination is overly simplistic and inaccurate.

A more apt explanation for global media's entrance to Africa is provided by Antonio Gramsci's notion of hegemony, which recognizes the consensual political and cultural relationship that oftentimes may be constructed by a leading, dominant class or culture and subordinate cultures or social groups, in which the latter accept the leadership, initiative, and interests of the former as preferable to other arrangements. However, since the subordinate class or culture gives its active consent to the relationship—often for reasons of cultural prestige—the leading roles cannot be reduced to domination or coercion, nor are the subordinate simply submissive (Gramsci, 1996, p. 21, p. 91). Hegemony, in Gramsci's sense, is a negotiated process: dominant political and cultural leaderships provide values, worldviews, and cultural and political meanings that speak to and recruit adherents from diverse subordinate classes and groups, socially, psychologically, and cognitively (Gramsci, 1985). In the realm of mass culture, the terms of this social relationship are popularized by the mass media of the elite, which provide entertainment that resonates with the experiences and expectations of working class and other subordinate audiences in Africa and internationally. Thus, the cultural transformation augured by the influx of Western programming into Africa is, in a very real sense, achieved with the consent of African peoples. Bilateral agreements between African and Western governments bring cheap reruns and movies on television, and free programming and news features on radio to an eager African mass audience.

For example, news and current affairs programming is distributed free of charge by WorldNet, the U.S. government broadcaster. Similarly, the French-led Organisation Internationale de la Francophonie (The International Organization of French-speaking Countries), whose main aim is the promotion of French language and culture, provides to the French speaking-countries of Africa satellite reception antennae as well as video recorders to record and rebroadcast French programming produced by the French government broadcaster Canal France Internationale (French International Channel). Occasionally, funding is also provided for "coproductions" between French and African producers. In either case, audiences in most African countries are regularly exposed to programming from France and other Western nations. Recently, joint ventures between international media and their African partners have inserted African languages, scenes, and cultural markers into standardized formats and genres in radio, television, and film—creating a foundation for a new cultural hegemony that favorably represents African influences.

In other words, the dominance of international media interests and their preference for Western-style commercial programming has not been physically coerced. Rather, the new media landscape has been rendered according to terms agreed to by global media players and numerous African governments and African investors. This reality suggests the consent of the "oppressed." Yet, it has been the political and cultural elite in each nation that has explicitly agreed to new media practices. The larger population of workers, shopkeepers, farmers, and urban and rural poor have given their "consent" in a less direct fashion—to the extent that they have been attracted to the music, movies, programming, and other media commodities of the newly privatized, commercialized communication system. Nonetheless, one must recognize that African nations (at least as represented by their elites) are making conscious decisions regarding media, and for now they must be considered junior partners in the emerging cultural hegemony, actively contributing to (but not leading) the construction of a negotiated global culture.

Globalization and cultural hegemony are thus inextricably linked: globalization of the cultural, political, and economic hegemony of Western capitalism overwhelms the resources and perspectives of developing countries. An important tool for establishing Western leadership is also its most attractive offering—the mass media. The global media and the commercially driven, entertainment-based cultural industry it promotes is appealing, gratifying, and informationally rewarding to diverse international audiences, including those in Africa. A key tenet of the new cultural hegemony is the preference for a free-market, deregulated, commercialized world: a global culture of consumerism.

Globalization and Hegemony in Perspective: Colonial Antecedents

For hundreds of years, the African continent was under colonial domination of European powers. Though colonialism took several forms, its most common characteristic was its attempt to eradicate African cultures and transform Africans into shadows or poor imitations of the colonizing power. This was accomplished by melding the mosaic of cultures within each colonial empire into a single, identifiable, junior model of the colonial center model that steadfastly looked to Europe and Arabia for inspiration.

The assimilationist colonial policy of France is a case in point. French policy was to eliminate indigenous African cultures and to assimilate all Africans into French culture, with Parisian accents to match (Betts, 1961). To this end, the colonial administration was the sole authorized newspaper publisher in most territories, and the French colonial press, strictly controlled from Paris, was charged with advancing assimilationist policy through the "Frenchification" of Africans. No taxes were levied on the import of newspapers published in France, while taxes were assessed on the importation of newsprint and printing machinery into the African colonies. As a result, local production of newspapers was penalized, and the circulation of French newspapers encouraged. Even the French Roman Catholic educational institutions and newspapers in Africa complied with the official policy of assimilation.

To stifle dissent, French official policy required that all publication in the French colonies had to be under the control of a European-born French citizen. Yet, tight controls sowed the seeds of "guerrilla" or "combat" journalism and the flowering of an underground press, which remains prevalent in many French-speaking African countries to this day (Palmer, 1997). In contrast to Liberia and British colonial South Africa and Sierra Leone, where an independent indigenous press had been in existence for over 80 years (Ainslie, 1966), it was not until 1881 that the French government extended the right to independent publishing to all French colonies.

The development of African broadcasting followed a slightly different trajectory, exemplified by the British imperial model. In the 1920s and 1930s, the British colonial administration decided to develop radio as a public service in its African colonies. The British formed statutory public broadcasting corporations, similar to the BBC, which targeted an audience of European settlers in Africa. Since adequate funding could not be raised from license fees due to the limited number of radio sets in the colonies, funding was culled from a combination of government grants and advertising. This was the system inherited by most African countries upon independence (Kasoma, 1997). In the early 1960s broadcasting companies in the former British colonies of East and West Africa resembled a "brood of more or less dutiful offspring" with the BBC as mother hen (Kasoma, 1997, p. 158).

Thus, from the moment they obtained independence from their colonial overseers in the late 1950s and early 1960s, virtually all African countries were connected to the nascent international communication system: literally, via purchased and "free" European programming, and more figuratively, via systems and practices inherited from the former colonizers. The first satellite broadcasts of an international event, the 1964 Tokyo Olympics, showed the newly independent African governments the potential of instantaneous international telecommunications. Their desire to belong to the family of nations led them to join the International Telecommunications Satellite Consortium (INTELSAT), the U.S.-based organization that controls virtually all international nonmilitary satellite communications in the world. Most countries built expensive international communication satellite tracking stations and linked their capitol cities to the rest of the world. Thus inhabitants of African capitals found themselves in constant and instantaneous contact with points around the globe. Ironically, communications within and between individual countries in Africa remained tenuous at best, a situation that remains only slightly improved today.

Globalization and Cultural Hegemony: The Contemporary Situation

At first glance, African mass media are exemplary of globalization and cultural hegemony. In movie theaters, on television, and on the radio, in the course of a single week, the casual observer can watch Jesse Ventura on World Wrestling Federation (WWF) reruns in Kenya, "Larry King Live" in Ghana and several other countries, and rebroadcasts of French television programs in Francophone Africa. Reruns of "Football Made in Germany," "Dallas," "Dynasty," and "The Cosby Show" dubbed in French or Portuguese rival Brazilian and Mexican-produced *telenovela* soap operas dubbed in English by Latin actors speaking with contrived American accents. Action-packed martial arts films from Hong Kong and Hindi melodramas from Bombay add to the mix.

With the end of the cold war and the collapse of bureaucratic states in Eastern Europe, a wind of capitalist liberalization swept through Africa. Under pressure from dissatisfied populations, press and media laws were "liberalized" across the continent. Private radio stations broadcasting in several African and European languages appeared across the continent. It should be noted that the continent has always had one of the highest rates of listenership of international shortwave broadcasts. The BBC, the Voice of America, Radio Moscow, Radio France Internationale, Radio Deutsche Welle, and others have long broadcast hundreds of hours of programming to Africa. Today, international broadcasters have expanded their African services to include direct broadcasting by satellites, relays, rebroadcasts, and the Internet.

Most recently, the "good governance" programs of the IMF and the World Bank called on African countries to create legal frameworks and privatize their telecommunications infrastructure and industries with the goal of making them attractive for foreign investment. Indeed, in Kenya, Nigeria, South Africa, and other countries with a potential mass market for consumer goods, multinationals invested in the mass media, but the influx of foreign capital has done little to improve the lot of the Africans served by the media— and nothing to improve media access by African middle classes, working classes, or the millions of disenfranchised. Rather than providing a forum for African free speech, these foreign-supported media are purely business concerns that serve as conduits that introduce American and European programming to the African mass audience.

Since the "liberalization" of the mass media got underway in Africa, several international broadcasters who used to broadcast only on shortwave radio to Africa have been allowed to broadcast directly to African audiences on the FM band. Indeed in many African countries it is easier for political reasons, for international broadcasters to obtain broadcast licenses than Africans. In a bid to take advantage of this historic opening up of the African media landscape, many Western international broadcasters have lined up affiliates and are actively seeking others to broadcast or rebroadcast their programming to African audiences. In short, global media have mentored local partners as a means of entry to the African market.

The international broadcasting arm of the American government, Voice of America (VOA), is one such presence in Africa. The U. S. House of Representatives recently passed the "Promoting Independent Broadcasting in Africa Act" (House Resolution 415, 1998) in support of the VOA's "Radio Democracy for Africa" project, which is aimed at creating "surrogate" or affiliate radio operations throughout Africa. The bill, which is based on the premise that the promotion of independent radio in Africa is a useful tool for advancing democracy and human rights, provides VOA's African affiliates with the necessary means to relay or rebroadcast American programming. The broadcasts of VOA "affiliates" are received in neighboring countries, as well. In addition to broadcast by surrogates, and regular VOA shortwave and satellite broadcasts to the African continent, VOA simulcasts on FM in a number of African countries, and in some cases, several cities within the same country.

Other international broadcasters with affiliates on the African continent include Cable News Network International (CNNI), BBC World Service & BBC World Service TV, Radio Vatican, Radio France Internationale, Canal France Internationale, Canal Horizon, Radio Deutsche Welle, Deutsche Welle TV (Voice of Germany Radio and Television), Radio Television Portuguès International (RTPI), and others. The BBC is the leader in surrogate broadcasting on the continent (Médias, 2000).

However, while American and European broadcasters have been able to use political and economic inducements (including joint ventures with key

African elites) to secure frequency bands for broadcasting or rebroadcasting their programming, most African countries do not grant the same degree of access to their own citizens. In the Ivory Coast, Gabon, Senegal, Benin, Mali, and other countries, international broadcasters were granted FM broadcast licenses before Africans. In Cameroon production companies and potential broadcasters need licenses to operate. The process is so complicated and stringent for Africans that a number of pirate FM stations have sprung up in the capital, Yaoundé, in defiance of the government.

Globalization and Cultural Eclecticism in Africa

To some researchers, African radio, television, and telecommunications are the picture of "cultural imperialism" and run riot. Indeed, some have described African television stations as vectors of cultural imperialism and domination (Land, 1992; Bourgault, 1995). The question that needs to be asked, however, is whether the visible prevalence of non-African media content on the mostly government-controlled African mass media scene has transformed African countries into passive, unwitting victims of Western cultural and corporate control. A cursory look at media content in African suggests a significant African influence, evidence of negotiation by Africans, and potential points of contradiction within the cultural hegemony now led by the global media.

"Liberalization" of the airwaves in Africa and termination of government monopoly on broadcasting released fierce competition from new, private commercial radio and TV stations that soon surpassed state-controlled stations in the creation and promotion of popular culture. These commercial stations were both the catalysts and the result of political "democratization." They tapped financial resources that had been considered nonexistent and revolutionized broadcasting by campaigning for multiparty democracy and championing the cause of opposition political parties. The arrival of independent stations blurred the lines between commercial and public broadcasting in the traditional sense.

For instance, Africa No. 1, based in Gabon, is the continent's premier French-language commercial radio network. When it was launched in 1981, it was the first pan-African commercial station with broadcasts reaching most of Western Africa. Sixty percent of the network's shareholders are Africans, while the rest of the capital is provided by a French government investment group, La Société de Financement de Radiodiffusion (SOFIRAD, or Broadcast Finance company), and two French companies, Sofrea and Havas, the international news and financial agency. It is not unusual to hear an advertising jingle or product commercial—signs of encroaching American culture— follow a serious ethnographic or historical documentary on the rainforest Pygmies or the Bantu peoples of Central Africa. Yet, with its well-researched radio documentaries and credible news and features, Africa No.1 represented a refreshing balance of news, sports, and popular African music.

Some tightly controlled government broadcasting stations, such as Radio Mali, which had been stuck in the monolithic development communication model for three decades, had no choice but to adapt and began to show signs of becoming public or even public service radio and television (Senghor, 1996). As a result of political liberalization, and IMF and World Bank-imposed structural adjustment programs, governments across the continent gave state-controlled broadcasters more autonomy. Simultaneously, they reduced their already inadequate funding, thereby forcing them to sacrifice some public service programming for advertiser-sponsored specials, underwriting and mass appeal musical formats favored by advertisers. Some stations have been successful with local programming that is both consistent with traditional practices and relevant to contemporary audiences. Meanwhile, because private commercial and noncommercial independent stations need to deliver audiences to advertisers, radio programming shows signs of being Africanized and localized anew.

During colonialism, Africans practiced various forms of cultural eclecticism as a means of survival and a way to preserve their traditional practices. For years, African media have recontextualized American and other Western cultural codes and idioms, to give new perspectives and forms to African culture. Contemporary global media offers similar multilayered cultural practices. Indeed, global media producers strive to fuse elements of diverse African cultures with the forms and genres developed for commercial broadcasting—such as the situation comedy, soap opera, and talk radio—along with the attendant "pause" for advertisements.

The outcome of this social battle over meaning has not been decided. One can hear American-style disc jockeys spinning and "scratching" African music in African languages from the Sahara to the Kalahari. Some West African FM radio stations like Radio Bamakan in Mali try to replicate real life village situations: hosts and guests use multiple languages—Bamanan, Bambara, Moré, Toucouleur, Hausa, Wolof, and others—and switch dialects in the course of the program. Sometimes the multiple languages themselves become the topic of discussion (Senghor, 1996). These "palaver trees" of the air are Africa's answer to talk radio.

However, this type of local, grassroots programming is shunned by some newly launched urban commercial broadcasting stations that increasingly opt for American-style, popular music formats (Zulu, 1996). Radio Nostalgie in Abidjan, Ivory Coast, Radio Horizon in Ouagadougou, Burkina Faso, Sud FM in Dakar, Senegal, and dozens of other stations are examples of this phenomenon. These new commercial stations have not completely discarded their local connection, yet they still publicize community activities, events, and news.

Government-owned television stations have proved that they can be as culturally eclectic as their private radio counterparts. For instance, a Kenyan station exemplifies one of the most notable uses of American cultural forms and advertising techniques to reflect African cultural images and values. In the 1990s, the most popular program on the government-owned Kenya Broadcasting Corporation was a Swahili-language situation comedy called "Vitimbi." More popular than CNN, which, together with other American programs, was being rebroadcast 24 hours a day on the rival Kenya Television Network (KTN), "Vitimbi" was sponsored by Wellcome Kenya, Limited, a branch of a British multinational company. The weekly program started with this sponsorship announcement in Swahili: "'Vitimbi,' brought to you by Wellcome Kenya Limited, makers of 'Strike' the spray that gets rid of ants, cockroaches, mosquitoes, flies and other insects, fast!" Then, a humorous commercial skit full of double entendres about a killer cockroach that is neutralized by "Strike" would be performed by the actors of "Vitimbi." The hour-long show adapted ancient African arts such as free-wheeling and loosely structured village masquerades, theater masked dances, and cultural festivals to the highly structured, time-constrained environment of multinational corporate-sponsored television. This content, spiced with a skillfully combined mixture of improvised dialogue, deliberate Swahili grammatical mistakes and mispronunciations, overacting, and off-color humor peppered with Swahili slang, African sayings and proverbs, held the audience spellbound until another Wellcome Kenya, Limited, commercial, featuring the same actors on the same set with the same sponsorship message, signaled that the show was over.

"Vitimbi" exemplifies the contextualization and Africanization of an American cultural idiom, the televised situation comedy, complete with a multinational corporate sponsor, in an African cultural framework. Other African broadcasters, such as Uganda Television (UTV), attempt to recontextualize American cultural idioms according to African values and cultural norms. UTV's successful show "The City Game" satirized the country's Westernized urban elite. For instance, one episode pokes fun at the British colonial practice of hiring manual laborers because of their brawn not their brains, making fun of absentee multinational corporate executives and their African subordinates. In this episode, an unemployed young man goes to an African subsidiary of a multinational corporation to interview for a job. Sitting nervously in the waiting room, he questions the janitor, an older man who busily cleans the office windows, about the company and the managing director. The janitor replies that he is not supposed to know such things. He was hired to work with his hands not with his head. He then reveals, via wild gestures, that everything in the company was done "for and on behalf of" a nameless absentee managing director. At intervals throughout their conversation, an overdressed African supervisor floats in and out of the office with a huge pipe, barking orders at imaginary employees. Similar to the U.S. sit-com, "Fresh Prince of Bel-Air," the program finds humor in the urban working-class critique of black accommodation that pleases mass audiences and avoids serious political challenge to existing social relations.

African television dramas reflect a different accommodation to global media practices. Traditional village theater has never been bound by the time constraints that are assumed on Western television programming. A 1980s survey of television dramas sent to the Program Exchange Center of the Union of National Radio and Television Organizations of Africa (UNRTA) shows that most of programs had, by American standards, "nonstandard" duration. The duration of single programs and episodes ranged from 37 minutes to over 122 minutes. The Gabonese anti-Apartheid drama "L'Etudiant de Soweto" ("The Student of Soweto") is 78 minutes and 29 seconds long. The Senegalese historical drama "Dialawali, Terre de Feu" ("Dialawali, Land of Fire") is 84 minutes and 18 seconds long, while the Algerian anticolonial drama "Les Enfants de la Casbah" ("Children of the Casbah") is 120 minutes and 16 seconds long. With the advent of globalization of the media, however, program times and lengths have become increasingly structured and standardized according to the demands of corporate sponsorship and the wide availability of American situation comedies.

Overall, the amalgamation of African and American cultural idioms and styles has led to the Africanization of many American television program formats. This represents a beneficial cultural synthesis that serves Western corporate needs while satisfying African cultural aspirations. Indeed, African television represents hegemony at its finest—absent alternatives, local audiences willingly consent to global media standards.

Nigeria is the quintessential example of the Africanization of television and video production and content. Over the years, it has developed a booming home-grown video production industry that has, with the support of local entrepreneurs and sponsors, drawn from the country's rich African oral culture and village theater tradition. Indeed, Nigeria has given the world a new horror genre, the cult "juju" video. The stock-in-trade of juju video is computer-generated special effects that highlight stories of evil sects, black magic, witchcraft, disappearing sexual organs, ritual sacrifice, bad children being transformed into animals, greed, corruption, and spiritual punishment (Servant, 2001). Juju video, which is produced in the widely spoken African lingua franca like pidgin, is also produced in Igbo, Yoruba, and Hausa, and subtitled in English, French, or pidgin. Juju video, the marriage of computer graphics, Western cult horror film traditions and the African occult, is almost always accompanied by the danceable polyrhythmic juju music that was pioneered by King Sunny Ade and other Nigerian musicians. According to the Nigerian Censor Board, the government agency responsible for vetting all film and video material before it is distributed, 1,080 video productions, some of which have gone on to sell more that 300,000 copies, have been produced and submitted to the board since 1997. Produced by the Independent Television Producers Association of Nigeria, these videos are distributed across Africa through informal trading channels by dealers and petty traders (Servant, 2001).

Nigerian private sector video production is the latest manifestation of the country's cultural dynamism. Juju videos provide a fantasy forum for addressing issues that are elsewhere addressed more realistically. Meanwhile, shows such as the Nigerian Television Authority's situation comedy, "The Village Headmaster," routinely deal with subjects like the clash of cultures, polygamy, corruption, Westernization, and cultural alienation—providing voices of resistance and critique, which are then resolved within the confines of the small screen.

The rewards for following the leadership of the global media and creative contributions of Africans to world culture are perhaps most strikingly revealed in the global marketplace itself. African music has become one of the pillars of the "World Music" phenomenon that resonates in dance clubs, on new "hit" albums, and is aired by DJs around the world. The internationally known "authentic" South African dance music style, "Township Jive," or Mpaquanga, as well as other types of African music, have secured a distinct place on the charts of international popular music.

Conclusion

The overview presented here of simultaneous use of African cultural representations by global media and in turn the often canny use of the Western media products for portraying favorable African representations fosters an uneasy, but nonetheless workable hegemonic relationship.

There is ample evidence of the agency of African media in negotiating a new expression of African culture in a global community. Many African radio and television stations have adapted a superficial resemblance to Western languages, motifs, idioms, and even commercial sponsorship, but these impulses are still propagated by diverse, yet recognizable, African cultural values. These include respect for older people and individual responsibility to one's social group—both of which stand in stark contrast to the culture of youth, individualism, and consumerism that characterizes most American programming. While one suspects that the West could learn a lot from

African adaptation of Western idioms, it is abundantly clear that the global media has already learned to ingratiate itself into the African media world.

There is no denying the tremendous impact of globalization upon Africa's media. On the one hand, globalization means that Africans are daily barraged by the messages and values of advertisers, global media interests, and even international governmental broadcasters, such as Voice of America. Likewise, the telecommunications sector—including Internet access—is now controlled by a handful of multinational corporations. Yet, globalization has also spurred the opening of state-controlled airwaves to private commercial stations, leading government broadcasters to offer more culturally relevant, noncommercial programming in order to attract listeners and viewers. In addition to long hours of American and African popular music, many stations also attract appreciative audiences by broadcasting a fair amount of local programming—validating their legitimacy as leaders of a new cultural hegemony that blends Western media idioms and values with formerly distinct African cultures and images.

The emerging hegemonic relationship among the global media, their domestic African elite partners, various African nation-state governments, and the millions of African workers and farmers in all their ethnic and national difference has yet to be fully constructed. At this point, despite the attraction and the apparent space for African voices, one must caution that African cultures, even in modified form, can survive globalization only if the broadcast spectrum is not dominated by multinational and international broadcasters. The airwaves must be filled with independent African broadcasters representative of diverse social constituencies, uncurtailed by advertisers, investors, and government bureaucrats. To flourish, authentic African cultural practices must have the opportunities, resources, and environments that emphasize democratic participation in each country and across the continent.

References

Ainslie, R. (1966). *The Press in Africa: communications past and present.* London: Victor Gollancz.

Bamyeh, M. (2000). *The Ends of Globalization.* Minneapolis: University of Minnesota Press.

Berger, S., & Dore, R. (Eds.). (1999). *National diversity and global capitalism.* Albany: State University of New York Press.

Betts, R. F. (1961). *Assimilation and association in French colonial theory.* New York: Columbia University Press.

Bourgault, L. (1995). *Mass media in Sub-Saharan Africa.* Bloomington, IN: Indiana University Press.

Buhrer, J. C. (2000, March 1). Le BIT souligne l'eneu d'Internet pour les pays and dévelopement (The ILO stresses the Internet challenge for developing countries). *Le Monde*, 1.

Caramel, L., & Laronche, M. (2000, March 1) Il faut mener un combat pour la diversité culturelle (We must fight for cultural diversity). *Le Monde*, (DOSSIER).

Deibert, R. (2000). International plug and play? Citizen activism, the Internet, and global public policy. *International Studies Perspectives, 1*, 255–272.

Eribo, F. (1997). Internal and external factors affecting press freedom in Nigeria. In Eribo, Festus, & Jong-Ebot, William (Eds.). (1997). *Press freedom and communication in Africa* (pp. 51–74). Trenton, NJ: Africa World Press.

Eribo, F., & Jong-Ebot, W. (Eds.). (1997). *Press Freedom and Communication in Africa*. Trenton, NJ: Africa World Press.

Geske, M. (2000). Globalization is what states make of it: Constructivism, U.S. foreign economic policy and the peso crisis. *International Policy, 37*, 301–322.

Giddens, A. (2000). *Runaway world: How globalization is shaping our lives*. New York: Routledge.

Gitlin, T. (1980). *The whole world is watching*. Berkeley: University of California Press.

Gramsci, A. (1985). *Selections from the cultural writings*. D. Forgacs & G. Nowell-Smith (eds.). W. Boelhower (trans). Cambridge, MA: Harvard University Press.

Gramsci, A. (1996) *Prison notebooks, vol. II*, (Original published 1975). Joseph Buttigieg, ed./translator). New York: Columbia University Press.

House Resolution 415, 105th Cong., 2nd Session, 144 Cong. Rec. H7655 (1998).

Hurrell, A. (1999). Security and inequality. In A. Hurrell & N. Woods, *Inequality, globalization, and world politics* (pp. 248–271). Oxford: Oxford University Press.

ITU (2000). World Radiocommunication Conference concludes on series of far-reaching agreements. [on-line]. Available: <*http://www.itu.int*> (March 10, 2001).

Kasoma, F. (1997). Press freedom in Zambia. In Festus Eribo & William Jong-Ebot, *Press freedom and communication in Africa* (pp.135–156). Trenton, NJ: Africa World Press.

Krasner, S. (1985). *Structural conflict: The Third World against global liberalism*. Berkeley: University of California Press.

Land, M. (1992). Ivoirien television, willing vector of cultural imperialism. *The Howard Journal of Communication, 4* (3), 10–27.

Lerner, D. (1976). Is international persuasion sociologically feasible? In Ronald McLaurin, Carl Rosenthal, & Sarah Skillings (Eds.), *The art and science of psychological operations: Case studies of military application*, vol. 1, (pp. 47–52).

Médias. (2000, July 24). Medias, La BBC tisse sa toile (Media: The BBC weaves its web in Africa). *Jeune Afrique/L'intelligent*, 2062, p. 14.

Meunier, S. (2000, August 3). The hegemonic hamburger. *Wilson Quarterly, 24,* 120–121.

Moulson, G. (2000, August 3). Big tobacco documents show WHO targeted. *Bangor Daily News* (Maine), A5.

Palmer, A. (1997). Reinventing the democratic press in Benin. In Festus Eribo & William Jong-Ebot. *Press freedom and communication in Africa* (pp.243–261). Trenton, NJ: Africa World Press.

Rodrik, D. (1997). *Has globalization gone too far?* Washington, DC: American University Press.

Schlosser, J. (1999, July 12). Springer pulls a Leno in England. *Broadcasting & Cable, 129,* 61.

Senghor, D. (1996). Radio stations in Africa, issues of democracy and culture. In P. G. Altbach & S. Hassan (Eds.), *The Muse of modernity: essays on culture as development in Africa* (p. 79–108). Trenton, NJ: Africa World Press.

Servant, J. C. (2001, February). Boom de vidéo domestique au Nigeria (Home Video Boom in Nigeria). *Le Monde Diplomatique, 6.*

Soudan, F. (2001, April 3). Biya et l'armée (Biya and the Army). *Jeune Afrique, 2099,* 10.

Tehranian, M. (1999). *Global communication and world politics: Domination, development, and discourse.* Singapore: Institute of Southeast Asian Studies.

Thussu, D. (2000). *International communication.* London: Arnold.

Tinq, H. (2000, June 3). Le Vatican réclame une éthique de l'information. (The Vatican demands an ethic of information). *Le Monde, 7.*

Watremez, E. (1992). The Satirical press in Francophone Africa. *Index on Censorship, 21,* 34–36.

Wendt, A. (1992). Anarchy is what states make of it: The social structure of power politics. *International Organization, 46,* 391–425.

Ziegler, D. (1992). *Thunder and silence: The mass media in Africa.* Trenton, NJ: Africa World Press.

Zulu, B. (1996). Rebuilding Africa through film video and television. In P. G. Altbach & S. Hassan (Eds.), *The Muse of modernity: essays on culture as development in Africa* (pp. 63–78). Trenton, NJ: Africa World Press.

CHAPTER 11

Media Hegemony and the Commercialization of Television in India: Implications to Social Class and Development Communication

Robbin D. Crabtree and Sheena Malhotra

Introduction

Reductionist notions of cultural imperialism predicted a global monoculture would inevitably result from global media dominance. Ample evidence demonstrates such a prediction was naïve. Myriad quantitative analyses failed to demonstrate significant (or even measurable) effects on international audiences (Salwen, 1991; Elasmar & Hunter, 1997). While these scholars provide apologia for globalization and media hegemony, American cultural products are only becoming more popular and more globally dominant (Olson, 1999). Yet our dominant theoretical paradigms and research methods continue to fall short of revealing the complexities and implications of media and cultural hegemony. From the other side of the epistemological (and often ideological) fence, cultural studies critics have persuasively argued that cultures are sophisticated and resilient, and that individuals within cultures produce alternative and resistant readings of media texts. Combining both empirical and critical analysis, our study of commercial television in India provides evidence of the multifaceted processes and implications of media hegemony at the macrosocietal, organizational, and individual levels.

Based on research ongoing since 1993, our study of the commercialization of television in India illustrates three important trends related to globalization and media hegemony in this developing nation. First, interviews with commercial television personnel and examination of new programming clearly demonstrate the ways hegemonic media philosophies and practices become embedded in the discourse of indigenous media systems. Despite an effort to create enlightened alternative programming by personnel at one new commercial network, for example, unimaginative, sexist, and Western "recombinant" (Gitlin, 1983) programming results (Crabtree &

Malhotra, 2000; Malhotra & Rogers, 2000). What is really at stake here, then, is "the capacity of a collectivity to generate any satisfying narratives of cultural meaning" (Tomlinson, 1991, p. 24).

Second, our focus groups with young audiences revealed the development of Western media tastes and consumer attitudes. Highly articulate and deeply ambivalent about the new media in India, young and middle-class audiences remarked on the effects of globalization and commercialization, providing evidence for hybridity as an alternative model of global media effects. We have previously discussed these complex interrelationships between hegemonic media texts and subaltern identity negotiation (Malhotra & Crabtree, in press).

Third, given the long history of education media and communication-for-development in India, we cannot help but notice the effects of media commercialization on national development efforts. India's state television network, *Doordarshan,* is scrambling to compete in a rapidly changing television/market landscape including increased commercialization and entertainment orientation. In the latest spin-off of Modernization Theory, globalization and commercialization of media in India increase the gap between the elite and the periphery, posing consumerism as the road to development. As Petras has argued, media hegemony "promotes the cult of 'modernity' as conformity with external symbols . . . [a] false intimacy and an imaginary link are established between the successful subjects of the media and the impoverished spectators in the 'barrios'" (Petras, 1993, p. 141–142).

As we have tried to illustrate with our ongoing analysis, media hegemony produces a constellation of related processes and effects. By charting these processes over time, in a single media system within one developing nation, we hope to illustrate how these processes manifest within the practices and discourse of indigenous media systems, in the programs themselves, and from the perspectives of audience members. While India is a unique culture and context, it provides an excellent illustration of some of the implications of globalization and media hegemony on gender, class, culture, and nation. In this chapter, we concentrate on the Indian media industries and the programming they produce using the analytical lens of media hegemony and its impact on social class issues.

Theoretical Frameworks for
Understanding Commercial Television in India

"Hegemony, as a mechanism of dominance, enables a culture or group to extend its influence and direct the consciousness of the public" (Real, 1989, p. 53; also see Hall, 1982). In their book on cultural hegemony in the United States, Lee Artz and Bren Ortega Murphy argue that "hegemony as a process is neither good nor bad. Hegemony is about hierarchical relations and vested interests. The most important question is, Who is dominant and for what purpose, and who is subordinate and what do they gain or lose?" (Artz & Murphy, 2000, p. 4). Using this neo-Marxist framework, we examine the diverse and interconnected forces that are operating in India, and whether the new commercial media represent, in essence, a neocolonialist force in Indian society. In addition to the concerns of media and cultural imperialism (e.g., Schiller, 1976, 1991) as an outgrowth of global media dominance by the West, the cultural hegemony framework incorporates the ways that Indian media organizations and viewers "consent" (Herman & Chomsky, 1988) to the development of Westernization in India and within the new media there. In this chapter we explore the ways hegemonic discourses pervade the new commercial television production practices and programming, as well as the impact this new media environment has on public television and development communication.

Given our specific concerns with gender roles and identity, a feminist perspective further informs our research. Feminist media criticism evolved as a field of study that deconstructs gender images in popular culture in an attempt to illuminate particular discourses of dominance (see Penley, 1988). It is arguable that new constructions of gender represent one of the greatest impacts of the 1990s television revolution in India. Gender role constructions have undergone a drastic change since 1991 and are being rearticulated through new television imagery in the late 1990s (Malhotra & Rogers, 2000; Malhotra & Crabtree, in press). These changing gender roles intersect with evolving systems of class, as Indian media are increasingly incorporated into the spread of global capitalism. The majority of the Indian population is poor and lives in rural areas and small villages; obviously, at least half of these are women. Thus, Indian women face an intersection of gender and class issues, such as the persistence of "bride burnings" and "dowry deaths" still prevalent in rural areas as well as the differential birth rates and treatments of female infants ("Woman kills daughter," 1995; Man kills wife," 1995). It is our contention that the class differences in India are being exacerbated by the increasing emphasis on consumerism and commercial culture, which also creates a growing disparity among Indian women based largely on a social class divide. This undermines a common cultural identification among Indian women, the possibility of which seems to be diminishing.

The Commercialization of Television in India: A Brief History

It was the introduction and increased use of color television by Indira Gandhi in the mid-1980s that has been credited with whetting the appetites of Indians for better television software (Pheroza Bilimoria, personal communication, 8 June 1995). At that point, as much as 80% of the Indian population had access to television but, similar to most non-Western nations before the propagation of the Reagan-Thatcher deregulation/privatization agenda, the state-funded *Doordarshan* (DD) network was a public broadcasting monopoly similar to the BBC of Britain.

In this climate of the mid-1980s, DD launched the serial, *"Hum Log,"* which became one of the highest-rated programs in the history of Indian television. *"Hum Log"* was an entertainment-education program, a prime-time soap opera with socially relevant messages on topics like family planning (Singhal & Rogers, 1989; Sood & Rogers, 2000). This program enjoyed phenomenal success, thus demonstrating that television—even development programming—could be commercially viable in India (Singhal & Rogers, 1989).

The 1990s signaled a drastic change in the national economic policies of India, which enabled the commercialization of television. The finance minister, Dr. Manmohan Singh, developed a new economic policy to "liberalize" and "open" the Indian economy in order to strengthen India as a force on the global scene (Melkote, Shields, & Agarwal, 1998). India thus moved rapidly from a "protected" economy with little or no foreign investments to an economy that had very few restrictions for multinational corporations. An influx of multinational corporations like Nike, Kentucky Fried Chicken, Puma, AT&T, and others has had multiple and important effects on the Indian urban population. One effect was the novel availability of the consumer products that were advertised on Western-oriented satellite television. With large foreign investments came a need to create a corresponding large consumer market if the investments were to be profitable.

The sea change in Indian television may be marked by the moment when the Taj Mahal Hotel in Bombay, among others, put a satellite dish on its roof to catch CNN's signal during the Gulf War. This instantaneous access to images and news from afar was a manifestation of the discernible power and qualitative difference satellite broadcasting would come to represent in India (also see Contractor, Singhal, & Rogers, 1988). Soon thereafter, in 1991, Satellite Television for the Asian Region (hereafter STAR-TV) was established in Hong Kong. This represented a sudden influx of Western programming into India, particularly to the urban areas where it is most easily available (Rahman, 1992; also see Malhotra, 1993). In response to a growing foreign satellite/broadcasting presence, would-be Indian broadcasters challenged the government's monopoly of broadcasting, eventually winning a Supreme Court case that overruled the Indian law prohibiting nongovernmental entities from uplinking to Indian satellites (Agarwal, 1995).

While external satellite services seemed to be proliferating over Asian skies, small-time cable operators were developing an extensive ground distribution network that also played a pivotal role in the development of private broadcasting in India. Even before commercial television operations were initiated in India, local entrepreneurs found they could purchase a small satellite dish and charge their neighbors for additional hook-ups. These cable networks have since multiplied, so that most major cities and many villages are now wired to receive satellite television (for an elaborated discussion of this phenomenon, see Crabtree & Malhotra, 2000; also see Boyd, 1988; Boyd & Straubhaar, 1985).

Since the early 1990s then, about 30 to 45 channels have come on the air in India (depending on the location and individual cable distribution network). The selection includes the different regional channels launched by the government network *Doordarshan* (DD), in addition to Western channels, such as CNN, the STAR network, Discovery, ABC, MTV, NBC, and ESPN all of which began broadcasting in India in the 1990s. However, it is the private, Indian commercial television networks that represent the phenomenal boom this industry has experienced. ZEE was the first private Indian network and was started in 1992 with an original entertainment channel and a pay-per-view movie channel. SONY launched a general entertainment channel in October 1995. There are also several city-specific and regional language channels. This remains a constantly shifting constellation, as new channels are announced and other channels go off the air on almost a monthly basis (Crabtree & Malhotra, 2000). It is noteworthy that most of the global media giants are present here. For instance, STAR-TV, ostensibly an Asian regional channel, is actually now owned by Rupert Murdoch, who also owns a considerable interest in ZEE. Thus, while one aspect of this trend shows Indian broadcasters becoming prominent both nationally and regionally, creating a real challenge to the *Doordarshan* state monopoly, we see the co-occurring trend of global media convergence, wherein fewer and fewer large corporations control the majority of information and entertainment production and distribution (Thussu, 2000). While media corporations are finding Indian television networks attractive partners and gaining access to the largest consumer market and middle-class in the world, the interests of working-class urban and poor rural Indians are likely to go unserved.

Hegemonic Discourses in Private and State Indian Television Organizations

Western and capitalist discourses of media professionalism and production processes are very much in evidence in the new Indian commercial television industry, as well as in the priorities and production values of *Doordarshan*. It is important to note that while most of the television executives and programmers we interviewed avowed a distinctively Indian identity, many were educated in the West. While their stated goals were to construct television organizations and programming that reinforced and perpetuated a distinctly Indian and South Asian identity, they often evoke Western ideas, organizational processes, and programs in their talk. For example, one programming executive at a new private commercial television network said:

> Every time you give an idea for a show, if he's undecided about it, [the Vice-Chair] says, "is there a precedence in the West?" That's exactly how he asks—in plain terms, unabashedly. Because he feels that's what we should be doing. And he says, "can that just be dubbed into Hindi? Why do we need to go through the whole experience of creating something else? (Anjum Rajabali, personal communication, 18 June 1995)

Discussion in production and programming meetings reveal a tendency to mimic American series by merely substituting names and dialogue and making minor plot adjustments. This phenomenon even prompted one of the new television networks to develop a series based on the 1970s show "Charlie's Angels" (U.S., ABC), a move motivated by a feeling among some top executives and programmers that there was not enough "skin" or "glamour" at their network. The show was to have four "girls," wearing minimal clothing, and fighting crime while performing in a rock group as a cover. According to the executive who proposed it, this program would help to glamorize the network as well as to create marketing and merchandizing opportunities (such as a sound track recording). This scenario sounds all too familiar to Western consumers and coordinates perfectly with the synergism apparent in the larger global media landscape (Olson, 1999). Thus, we argue that the influence of foreign programming on the domestic television production industries is in fact more insidious than the more direct influence of imported or satellite-fed foreign programming on audiences. The above examples also demonstrate the ways media hegemony works through a process of consent and cooptation rather than outright dominance.

The use of foreign consultants is a novel strategy adopted in India during this period of commercialization. These media consultants, from firms such as Frank Magid Associates, are having a noticeable impact on the development of the new television services in India (Crabtree & Malhotra, 2000). While ostensibly helping Indian broadcasters "avoid the learning curve" (Reagan Ramsey, personal communication, 14 June 1995), these consultants suggest and teach production techniques and news values as if they are neutral, value-free aspects of programming. Given that the growing presence of slick foreign programming raises the standards for local productions, consultants are seen as necessary. Since locally produced programs are increasingly forced to compete against imported ones, the motivation to mimic Western genres and production values will likely persist. Imported programming and local programming alike compete in a high-stakes commercial environment, where cultural values and social goals are subordinated to profit.

The impact of commercial television in India also can be seen on the state television, *Doordarshan* (DD). *Doordarshan* has evolved substantially with the proliferation of its competition. The development of multiple commercial entertainment options has impacted the form, content, popularity, and impact of DD's educational and development programming. For example, DD Metro bears marks of influence from STAR-TV and the other commercial stations in its slick new programming and attempts to appeal to a young, urban, middle-class audience. Increasingly, DD uses commercial financing to supplement its public broadcasting budget, which is insufficient to the task of competing with foreign and local commercial programming. Threatened by the proliferation of satellite television networks and despite its successes (e.g., *"Hum Log"*), DD's emphasis on development programming (targeted to poor, rural audiences) has waned, as its programming increasingly vies for the middle-class, urban audience. In the global climate of deregulation and privatization, state-funded public television in the West has been diminished (in funding and quantity) and become more conservative; the same trend can now be noticed in India.

In 1995 DD arranged to carry CNN as a 24–hour DD channel on which DD has a 2–hour slot ("24–hour CNN," 1995). This deal afforded DD access to other programming owned by Turner Incorporated, as well. CNN subsequently launched an Indian service, so this arrangement has gone by the wayside. Then, in 2000, DD signed a deal with Nine Gold, an Australian-owned software company for prime time programming (the 7 to 10 p.m. slot) on DD Metro in order to appeal to the "satellite television" homes (Saxena, 2001). *Doordarshan's* improved transmission quality and 1999 legislation that made it compulsory for cable operators to show DD has combined with slick programming on the Nine Gold band to increase DD visibility (Saxena, 2001). It is a strategy that is paying off, particularly as the ratings for DD Metro are rising steadily among cable and satellite television homes, even topping the ratings of ZEE and SONY programs in some instances (Saxena, 2001).

Despite the recurrent evocation of Western programming ideas and strategies in Indian television programming discourse, there are also some interesting signs of resistance on the part of certain Indian programming personnel. For example, there is open criticism of the tendency to imitate Western television programs:

> I think that we shouldn't hold the West as some kind of ideal. India's a crazy place, and it has its own personality, no matter what else can be said of us.

> We're a mad bunch. And we have our own sort of problems. We should just pick up our own flavor and stick to it instead of trying to see what the West is doing and then zeroing in on those programs. (Ilham Khan, personal communication, 7 June 1995)

New Indian broadcasters are also quite aware of the broader cultural implications of their new industry, and there is open critical analysis of the potential cultural effects of Western and commercial television in India. One Indian broadcaster's comments demonstrate keen awareness of the concerns and processes of cultural imperialism itself: "I don't believe that cultural imperialism, whether from inside or from outside, can eventually destroy a race. I think that there are also deeper instincts which are more innate. Self-preserving sorts of mechanisms which we have. [These] will seek out their own levels and own forms of expression" (Anjum Rajabali, personal communication, 18 June 1995).

Thus, we can see that hegemony is the result of complex dialectical tensions between forces such as neocolonialism and local initiative, acquiescence and analysis, consent and resistance. Personnel in the new commercial television industry in India are conscious and articulate about their struggle between conformity to formulaic Western-style programs and their resistance to reproducing culturally and/or ideologically problematic genres and series.

Hegemonic Representations in Television Programming

When certain axioms become hegemonic among television programmers and then are perpetuated through the programming, they become increasingly normative. An examination of new programming on commercial networks in India illustrates the growing normativity of capitalist values, lifestyles, and dreams. While India's Constitution defines it as a socialist country, these ideals are increasingly being replaced by a consumerist capitalist ideology.

The recent phenomenal success of *"Kaun Banega Crorepati?"* (KBC)—modeled on the ABC show "Who Wants to Be a Millionaire" translates literally to "Who Wants to Be a 100 Millionaire?" as one crore is one hundred million rupees—on STAR is one example of the increasing valorization of wealth in India. The show offers the highest amount of money ever offered on Indian television and is hosted by Amitabh Bachchan, one of India's biggest superstars (Aiyar & Chopra, 2000). KBC is a crucial part of STAR's strategy to regain advertising and ratings ground lost to ZEE and SONY and is being positioned as STAR's "Unique differentiator. A killer program with killer content" (Sumantra Datta as quoted in Aiyar & Chopra, 2000). According to Siddharth Basu, the designer of questions for the show, "It is not just another quiz game. It's really about human drama. About hope and disappointment" (Basu as quoted in Aiyar & Chopra, 2000). Perhaps more to the point, it is about human hope and disappointment hinging on money. It is a show where "anyone from anywhere can win a jackpot, become a star" (Aiyar & Chopra, 2000) and on the show, the specific route to stardom is wealth.

While KBC is a recent and particular phenomenon that celebrates wealth overtly, it is only one example in a growing trend towards consumerism. Hegemonic class ideals are being perpetuated through new programming for satellite television channels. Berger (1992) suggests that when analyzing television from a cross-cultural perspective, it is important to examine the characters' values, social class, and other characteristics; those of protagonists are especially significant. It should be noted that, in many cases, the Indian protagonist has evolved from the poor or lower-class Indian, someone referred to in the popular imagination as the "common man" whose "goodness" derived from his values and his virtues, to an upper middle-class or wealthy man who gains respect for his power, and that power is derived from his wealth.

Previously, Malhotra and Rogers (2000) conducted a content analysis of some of the top-rated television programs broadcast by private television networks in India using the lens of gender. They analyzed the five top-rated programs on private, Indian networks (all on ZEE-TV and the SONY networks), along with five comparable programs on STAR-TV because of its role as a catalyst in the privatization of television in India. The programs represented five major genre categories: (1) situation comedies, (2) soap operas, (3) game shows, (4) night-time drama, and (5) music countdown shows. While they found that women are gaining greater visibility in television programming, as evidenced by the greater number of female characters in the 10 television programs analyzed, women remain in primarily traditional roles, only working outside the home 10% of the time. In sum, that analysis clearly demonstrated the ways characters in the new Indian commercial television programs are constructed primarily through patriarchal interests and nationalist discourses (Malhotra & Rogers, 2000).

When we analyze the same programs through the lens of class, we find an increasing trend towards middle-class values, and a move to equate money with power and progress. As programmers try to emulate the West, they have realized that one way to produce glamour on the television screen is to set soap operas and television series in wealthier settings than was typical of Indian soap operas in the past. For example, all 10 programs analyzed from the 1998 season either had glamorous sets if they were nonfictional or were set in middle-class or wealthy settings. There are still some characters who are poor or working class, but they are usually not the main protagonists. Normalizing and valorizing wealth, these new programs create a televisual reality that is unachievable for most Indians, and it has become increasingly hegemonic in the television programming broadcast in India since the onset of privatization and commercialization.

Equating consumerism, Western lifestyles, and progress is another conflation evident in the programming we examined. As the West becomes glamorized and equated with progress, India becomes equated with tradition. Thus, the growing middle class strives to break out of traditional cultural frameworks; the mechanism for this escape from traditionalism is found in manifesting a consumerist mentality. A recent content-analysis of advertisements from the United States and advertisements from India compared the consumption values portrayed by commercials in the two countries. This study found that while the U.S. advertisements still had more materialistic appeals than Indian advertisements did, material values were becoming more important to Indians (Sengupta, 1996).

It is well worth mentioning that Indian commercial broadcasters reflect on these same concerns. For instance, this excerpt from an interview with Indian film director and television producer for one new network, Shekar Kapur, illustrates a thoughtful and even sorrowful concern for the implications of advertising:

> The sinister thing is that advertising is really aimed at trying to change your psychology. . . . What is a kid in a village going to do, or even a kid that's watching television here [in Bombay]? Let's take a bar of chocolate. It costs 10 rupees. He's never going to be able to buy a bar of chocolate in his whole life. But the commercial is telling him that if his parents love him, they'll buy him that bar of chocolate. And he's going to feel seriously left out of this world. And he, or she, is probably going to resent the fact that his parents never bought that bar of chocolate. This is the kind of thing the ethics of television has to look at. (personal communication, 16 June 1995)

The conflation of love and consumption is a dangerous one in a poor country, but it is a conflation that is crucial for the survival of a capitalist system.

Implications to Social Class Issues in India

It is apparent from our ongoing analysis that the privatization and commercialization of television have significant, severe, and far-reaching consequences for social class relations in India. Development in India—ostensibly and potentially a process of equalization of access to natural resources, technology, economic and political participation, and general improvements of material conditions—has been deeply affected by the growing climate of consumerism. We can see these effects on development communication efforts, in the commercialization of culture, and in what appears to be a return to the tenets of Modernization Theory.

While the presence of VCR technology has been of concern to development communication scholars for years, the move to commercial television is likely to have a more devastating impact on the development communication efforts of the Indian government and international NGOs. The development of private, commercial television in India has been, in many ways, a national response to a growing foreign commercial media presence in India. This incursion of transnational media systems (such as CNN, SONY, STAR-TV, and Murdoch) "defines the path that will be taken and brings the country in question into the orbit of interests of the dominant powers. This is the 'neo-imperialist' form that has replaced the older, cruder, and obsolete methods of colonialism" (Herman & McChesney, 1997, p. 154). In other words, earlier concerns about media imperialism are renewed in the current "satellite invasion" of India and the domestic media industries' response to it in the form of private, commercial broadcasting.

The influence of the commercialization of broadcasting may in fact be more far-reaching than the values and beliefs of any particular imported or domestic programming itself. On one level, there are anticipated effects on the configuration of the Indian economy. The increased presence of multinational companies as discussed earlier, along with their coexistence with the new commercial media, causes local artisans and manufacturers to compete on an uneven playing field (see, for example, Shriver, 1997, for a discussion of a similar situation in Nicaragua). Similarly, the consumer market in India increasingly comes under the influence of global forces; middle-class Indian youth are already enamored of Levi's, Ray-Ban's, and Kentucky Fried Chicken, all introduced about the same time as commercial television. Thus, as Bagdikian (1996) warned, the transnational media giants operating in countries across the world ultimately aim to maximize profits by "conditioning the world to buy compulsively," thereby creating worldwide markets for their products (p. 8). Media and advertising campaigns normalizing conspicuous consumption and promoting capitalist lifestyles were almost inevitable once Indian television was no longer controlled by the DD monopoly. The combination of Western television programming and the presence of multinational corporations in India have led to a reinforcement of Western culture never witnessed before in Indian cities.

In this sense, we can see that "out of the 'incorporation' of all national cultures into the global capitalist economic system is arising an overarching culture of capitalism" (Tomlinson, 1999, p. 81). Whether or not this capitalist culture is characterized by the global dominance of Western culture almost becomes a moot concern when compared to the commercialization, consumerism, and commodifying practices that threaten all cultures, including those of the West. "If cultural performance is going to follow this road, then we have little to be content about. Not because the show is "cultural," but because it is a "show" in the worst sense of the word" (Eco, 1986, p. 156). Similarly, Tomlinson argues that commodification effectively colonizes "a moral-cultural space left by other developments in modernity" (Tomlinson, 1999, p. 136). In this sense, the effects of globalization do indeed weaken dominated and dominating cultures alike.

In many ways, the current situation in India is like revisiting "Modernization Theory" (e.g., Lerner, 1958), which, like globalization, urged a particular vision of progress and development. Consistent with the subsequent and prolific critique of this ethnocentric development model (e.g., Rogers, 1976), current critiques of globalization identify a growing gap between the few beneficiaries and the many who are marginalized or victimized by the process. In a country where disparities between the "haves" and the "have nots" seem to be increasing, the cultivation of a consumerist ideology implies grave consequences: "The TV 'table of plenty' contrasts with the experience of the empty kitchen; the amorous escapades of media personalities crash against a houseful of crawling, crying hungry children. . . . The promise of affluence becomes an affront to those who are perpetually denied" (Petras, 1993, p. 147).

Thus, the new economic system and the media that service it "organize and structure much of modern cultural life within certain narrow commercial parameters" (Tomlinson, 1999, p. 83). We can see that the trappings of modernity itself now have largely been commodified, and the "shopping element" is present in virtually all leisure activities that are considered the fruits of modern life; this life becomes, by definition, the life of the few and merely the "dreams, nightmares, and skepticism" of the rest (Tomlinson, 1999, p. 71).

The "communication effects gap" first identified by Rogers (1962/1995) predicts and explains the current situation in India (Shingi & Mody, 1976), where an increasing cultural divide exists between those who identify with Western/consumerist values and lifestyles and those who adhere to traditional beliefs and values. The epidemic of interethnic and interreligious violence in India may also be a symptom of this; Hindu fundamentalists destroy artifacts they believe reflect Western and Christian ideas, Moslems throw their television sets out of their apartment windows ("Bombay," 1994, pp. 1, 7).

Another old theory comes to mind, as well, regarding "a revolution of rising expectations" (Lerner, 1958). When these expectations, nurtured by commercial television programming, advertising, and the increased presence of luxury consumer products, go unmet for the majority of people in India (and/as elsewhere), we can expect to see increased disaffection and rising unrest.

Thus, in addition to providing fuel for growing ethnic and religious intolerance in India, this growing lifestyle chasm is likely to reflect and exacerbate age-old divisions in social class, as well as the urban/rural dichotomy that is already striking in India. In the end, it is the commercialization of media in India, within the larger framework of globalization, that pushes the argument far past any previous concerns over ideological incorporation and cultural domination, "towards a vision of a world dominated entirely by the single, systematic principle of consumerism" (Tomlinson, 1999, p. 87; also see Baudrillard, 1988). Service and industrial workers, women, the poor—all those already marginalized in complex ways in India, join the ranks of indigenous cultures, languages, and landscapes (Davis, 1999), as those who are deeply endangered by the contemporary configurations of media and cultural production.

The question remains, then, whether the particular configurations of hegemony in India at this time will evoke a movement to define common interests among those Indians most marginalized by processes of economic and media privatization and convergence, rampant consumerism, and the larger forces of globalization. Identifying the many innovative strategies of Third World women workers in their struggles to build community life, form unions, share resources, and in myriad ways otherwise resist patriarchy, colonialism, and capitalist domination, Chandra Mohanty (1997) writes about the possibility for potentially revolutionary collective action. We close with her optimistic presentiment: "The end of the twentieth century may be characterized by the exacerbation of the politics of global capitalist domination and exploitation, but it is also suggestive of the dawning of a renewed politics of hope and solidarity" (p. 26).

References

Aiyar, V. S., & Chopra, A. (2000, July 17). Great Gamble. *India Today*. [on-line]. Available at: *http://www.india-today.com*. Accessed March 3, 2001.

Agarwal, A. (1995, March 15). A judgement opens a door. *India Today*, 202–205.

Artz, L., & Murphy, B. O. (2000). *Cultural hegemony in the United States*. Thousand Oaks, CA: Sage.

Bagdikian, B. (1996). Brave new world minus 400. In G. Gerbner, H. Mowlana, & H. Schiller (Eds.), *Invisible crises: What conglomerate control of media means for America and the world* (pp. 7–14). Boulder, CO: Westview.

Baudrillard. J. (1988). In M. Poster (Ed.), *Selected Writings*. Cambridge: Polity Press.

Berger, A. A. (1992). Analyzing media and popular culture from a cross-cultural perspective. In F. Korzenny & S. Ting-Toomey (Eds.), *Media effects across cultures* (pp. 11–22), Newbury Park, CA: Sage.

"Bombay turnoffs: Sex, violence go out window." (1994, December 26). *Contra Costa Times*, p.1, 7.

Boyd, D. (1988). Third world pirating of U.S. films and television programs from satellites. *Journal of Broadcasting and Electronic Media, 32,* 149–161.

Boyd, D., & Straubhaar, J. (1985). Development impact of the home video cassette recorder on third world countries. *Journal of Broadcasting and Electronic Media, 29,* 5–21.

Contractor, N., Singhal, A., & Rogers, E. (1988). Metatheoretical perspectives on satellite television and development in India. *Journal of Broadcasting and Electronic Media, 32,* 129–148.

Crabtree, R. D., & Malhotra, S. (2000). A case study of commercial television in India: Assessing the organizational mechanisms of cultural imperialism. *Journal of Broadcasting and Electronic Media, 44,* 364–385.

Davis, W. (August 1999). Vanishing Cultures. *National Geographic, 196/2,* 62–89.

Elasmar, M., & Hunter, J. (1997). The impact of foreign TV on a domestic audience: A meta-analysis. In B. Burelson (Ed.), *Communication yearbook, 20* (pp. 47–69). Thousand Oaks, CA: Sage.

Gitlin, T. (1983). *Inside prime time.* New York: Pantheon.

Hall, S. (1982). The rediscovery of 'ideology': Return of the repressed in media studies. In. M. Gurevitch, T. Bennett, J. Curran, & J. Woollacott (Eds.), *Culture, society and the media* (pp. 56–90). London: Methuen.

Herman, E., & Chomsky, N. (1988). *Manufacturing consent.* New York: Pantheon.

Herman, E., & McChesney, R. W. (1997). *The global media: The new missionaries of corporate capitalism.* London: Caswell.

Lerner, D. (1958). *The passing of traditional society.* New York: MacMillan.

Malhotra, S. (1993). Satellite television viewership and perceptions of women's gender roles in India. Unpublished master's thesis, Pepperdine University, Malibu, CA.

Malhotra, S., & Crabtree, R. D. (in press). Gender, (inter)nation(alization), culture: Implications of the privatization of television in India. In M. J. Collier (Ed.), *International and Intercultural Communication Annual, 24.* Thousand Oaks, CA: Sage.

Malhotra, S., & Rogers, E. M. (2000). Satellite television and the new Indian woman. *Gazette, The International Journal for Communication Studies, 62,* 407–429.

Man kills wife, self over dowry. (1995, July 1). *The Asian Age,* p. 4.

McBride, S. (1984). *Many voices, one world* (abridged edition). Paris: UNESCO International Commission for the Study of Communication Problems.

Melkote, S. R., Shields, P., & Agarwal, B. C. (Eds.). (1998). *International satellite broadcasting in South Asia: Political, economic and cultural implications.* Lanham, MD: University Press of America.

Mohanty, C. T. (1997). Women workers and capitalist scripts: Ideologies of domination, common interests, and the politics of solidarity. In M. J. Alexander & C.
T. Mohanty (Eds.), *Feminist genealogies, colonial legacies, democratic futures* (pp.
3–29), New York: Routledge.

Olson, S. (1999). Hollywood Planet: Global media and the competitive advantage of
narrative transparency. Mahway, NJ: Lawrence Erlbaum Associates.

Penley, C. (1988). *Feminism and film theory*. New York: Routledge.

Petras, J. (1993). Cultural imperialism in the late 20th century. *Journal of Contemporary
Asia, 23*, 139–148.

Rahman, M. (1992, November 15). The new TV superbazaar now at your fingertips.
India Today, 17 (21), 22–36.

Real, M. (1989). *Super media: A cultural studies approach*. Newbury Park, CA: Sage.

Rogers, E. M. (1976). Communication and development: The passing of the dominant
paradigm. *Communication Research, 3*, 213–240.

Rogers, E. M. (1962/1995). *Diffusion of innovations* (4th edition). New York: The Free
Press.

Salwen, M. (1991). Cultural imperialism: A media effects approach. *Critical Studies in
Mass Communication, 8*, 29–38.

Saxena, P. (2001, 10 January). Old is gold: Top 20 are all on DD. *The Hindustan Times*,
New Delhi, India, p. 1.

Schiller, H. (1976). *Communication and cultural domination*. New York: Augustus M.
Kelley.

Schiller, H. (1991). Not yet the post-imperialist era. *Critical Studies in Mass Communication, 8*, 13–28.

Sengupta, S. (1996). Understanding consumption related values from advertising: A
content analysis of television commercials from India and the United States.
Gazette, The International Journal for Communication Studies, 57, 81–96.

Shingi, P., & Mody, B. (1976). The communication effects gaps: A field experiment on
television and agricultural ignorance in India. In E. Rogers (Ed.), *Communication and development: Critical perspectives* (pp. 79–98). Beverly Hills: Sage.

Singhal, A., & Rogers, E. M. (1989). Prosocial television for development in India. In
R. E. Rice & C. K. Atkin (Eds.), *Public communication campaigns* (2nd ed.).
Newbury Park, CA: Sage.

Shriver, J. (1997). A view of the global village from the South. *Nicaraguan Developments, 5*, 1.

Sood, S., & Rogers, E. M. (2000). Dimensions of parasocial interaction by letter-writ-
ers to a popular entertainment-education soap opera in India. *Journal of Broadcasting & Electronic Media, 44*, 386–414.

Thussu, D. K. (2000). *International communication: Continuity and change.* London: Oxford University Press.

Tomlinson, J. (1991). *Cultural imperialism.* Baltimore, MD: Johns Hopkins University Press.

Tomlinson, J. (1999). *Globalization and Culture.* Chicago: University of Chicago Press.

24-hour CNN in India now via *Doordarshan.* (1995, July 1). *The Asian Age,* p. 3.

Woman kills daughter, herself. (1995, June 11), *The Hindu,* p. 3.

CHAPTER 12

MTV Asia:
Localizing the Global Media

Stacey K. Sowards

MTV Asia, broadcast from Singapore to homes in Southeast Asia, has become increasingly popular in the last few years, especially among middle- and upper-class youth. Initially founded in 1991, MTV Asia broadcast for three years, before ceasing programs in 1994 because of disputes with Murdoch's Star TV (Shuker, 1994). In April of 1995, MTV Asia was launched again, reaching over 40 million viewers, more than the 28 million MTV viewers in the United States (Thussu, 2000). One of the unique aspects of MTV Asia is that it has made substantial efforts to modify programming to reflect and attract Southeast Asian youth culture (Einhorn, 1997). For example, the programming includes VJs (video jockeys) of Southeast Asian descent, Asia's Top 20 Hitlist, request and interactive shows, and the promotion of Asian bands both in commercials and in airplay. These examples ostensibly indicate that American programming marketed to Asia has become less culturally imperialistic in nature in comparison to past marketing efforts and exports (Colista and Leshner, 1998; Goodwin, 1992: Goodwin & Gore, 1990; Jakubowicz, 1995; Mohammadi, 1995; Stevenson, 1994).

In the past, the American media industries have been successful in Asian markets, which in turn have increased appetites for American popular culture. MTV seeks to satiate that demand in popular music. The effects of popular music on a particular audience can be wide ranging, especially in conjunction with television broadcasting (Frith, 1996; Jhally, 1987). In this essay, I argue that MTV Asia is essentially a cleverly repackaged and redisguised form of Western narratives of class, culture, values, and consumerism that shapes and influences Southeast Asians across class and culture in a potentially culturally disruptive manner. MTV Asia effectively demonstrates how middle-class and elite Southeast Asians accept and participate in media hegemony of Western popular music and ideologies.

Identity Construction and Popular Music

Several authors contend that narratives are the basis for how individuals make sense of their surrounding environment (Bhavnani & Phoenix, 1994; Frith,

1996; Hall, 1996; Novitz, 1989; Somers, 1992; Vila, 1996). Novitz (1989) contends that narratives are based on past experience and are capable of changing human thought patterns. Narrativity can also legitimize normativity. Narratives are, according to Novitz, a critical element in the formation of group and individual identities. Bhuvnani and Phoenix (1994) argue that the discourses of narratives are the product of human interaction in which individuals construct materialized plots to which others can relate. Stuart Hall (1996) argues that because human identity derives from historical experience, identity is in constant flux in response to new conditions. Hall explains that identity is conceived from the human interiority that is constructed on the basis of historical experience. Furthermore, identity is constantly changing, because it is a temporary attachment.

Frith (1996) and Vila (1996) maintain that music, especially popular music, provides narratives that have a powerful effect on audiences. In fact, Vila (1996) writes that the narrative is the bridge between music and the formation of identity. Frith (1996), instead of viewing the composition of music as something created by the individual, examines the role that music, as a performance, story, or narrative, plays in both self and group identity. Music, according to Vila (1996), is a cultural artifact that, in part, constructs these identities. Music brings satisfaction to the listener and self-definition to the listener. Both Vila and Frith contend that music is not just the affectation of the single individual, but also creates group identity. Frith writes that:

> social groups [do not] agree on values which are then expressed in their cultural activities (the assumption of homology models) but that they only get to know themselves *as groups* (as a particular organization of individual and social interests, of sameness and difference) *through* cultural activity, through aesthetic judgment. (1996, p. 111, emphasis in original text)

Vila also suggests that music is a means for group identity by claiming that music facilitates the forging of relationships with others and can furthermore affect the listeners' emotional state, by creating feelings of happiness, friendship, and solidarity. Thus, music is capable of articulating an understanding of both self and group solidarity by creating an emotional alliance with an individual's interiority and with others.

Popular Music and MTV

Several authors have argued that MTV and music video have fundamentally changed not only the music industry, but also the way in which audiences relate and construct meanings from popular music (Jhally, 1987; Pettegrew,

1995; Shuker, 1994). Additionally, MTV has had substantial influence on the 18–34 age group; before MTV, advertisers had difficulty in targeting this particular age group (Jhally, 1987).

There are several implications of such a large viewership for popular music and its audience. First, MTV has created a music industry that makes it nearly impossible to achieve success without a music video and extensive airplay on MTV to increase exposure. In fact, Jones (1992) and Shuker (1994) contend that MTV airplay is the most effective way to break a new artist. MTV Asia has reserved a 20% quota for Asian videos, but as Banks observes (1997), 90% of the videos broadcast on MTV Asia are non-Asian videos. This potentially means that Southeast Asian artists are crowded out of the popular music markets or undesirable in comparison to the choices available from Europe, Australia, or North America.

Jhally (1987) and Nash (1999) also argue that MTV plays videos that are targeted for white suburban youth. While MTV in the United States currently airs African-American or Latina/o artists, the primary audience remains white, middle-class viewers. Additionally, Banks (1997) has observed that MTV Latin America has refused to play salsa or cumbia videos even though such styles of music are high in viewer demand. Unfortunately for musicians without videos or that fail to target white, middle-class youth culture, widespread success in the United States is difficult to obtain without MTV airplay. Furthermore, the American MTV program "Total Request Global," which features the top 10 countdowns from around the world, demonstrates that most songs requested in each region are American or European. While this program attempts to diversify its programming through more global music exposure for American audiences, these global trends are in fact very much American (Banks, 1997; 1996).

A primary purveyor of popular culture, MTV is above all a commercial enterprise that bases decisions on its advertising projections—which music will attract the largest audience that can in turn be sold to the most advertisers. In essence, MTV is one large, continuous advertising scheme (Grossberg, 1993; Pettegrew, 1995; Shuker, 1994). Not only does MTV fund its endeavors through advertising of commercial products, but each music video functions as an advertisement for the band or musician in the video. Additionally, musicians also advertise products within videos, by wearing advertisers' clothing or using other products, such as Coca Cola, Pepsi, and clothing (such as Nike, Phat Farm, or famous designers). Musicians or their songs often are used in commercial advertising. Rather than serving as an arena for musical talent, MTV has "fetishized" popular music by conferring cultural significance to videos that they do not possess (Jhally, 1987). Thus, music videos provide a marketing tool, not just for the music, but also for other commercial products, including the rhetorical power of celebrity conferred on chosen musicians. Pettegrew emphasizes that this fetishization has caused MTV, which claims to be a text of subversion or rebellion, to perpetuate corporate hegemony, where viewers believe they are buying into underground culture of subversion, but in reality, legitimizing the ideologies of white, middle-class cultures and consumerism.

Finally, audio texts and simultaneous visual texts often change the viewers' or listeners' interpretation of songs. Frith (1996) and Vila (1996) both contend that popular music acts as part of the identity formulation process. Interpretation of music allows individuals to construct multiple meanings and contribute to their own identity, as well as allows them to formulate ties with others through the social construction of meaning. However, the nature of MTV and music videos change this process because the visual text more clearly embeds the meaning of the music in a visual framework in which viewers are less likely to develop alternate interpretations of the audio text. Gehr argues that "MTV is a context that seems to abolish context, removing the freedom of the record listener to edit his or her experience, or the radio listener to imagine the music as playing some indirect part of his [or her] life" (1983, as quoted in Jhally, 1987, p. 99). The presence of the visual text cements a visual image and prevents listeners from developing their own interpretations. In essence, the video fixes the narrative for the viewer by superimposing a story that accompanies the music.

MTV represents an important amalgamation of popular culture for youth. It functions as an acculturation of popular music, fashion, and an ideology of consumerism (Pettegrew, 1995). MTV is a central component of American popular culture, affecting how audience members construe meanings of music, how music becomes commercialized, and musicians achieve success in the industry. Banks (1997, 1996) argues that these effects change across cultures. MTV Asia in particular, seeks to develop an international youth culture, based on a shared affinity for consumerism. Banks concludes that this international identity becomes one of consumption.

Popular Music and Hegemony

Because popular music has the potential to play a large role in the social construction of identity for its audiences, the effect of MTV and popular culture across cultures has important implications for viewers, listeners, and identity (Hamelink, 1994; Jones, 1993; Mohammadi, 1995; O'Connor & Downing, 1995; Wasko, 1994). Culture industries often reflect economic exploitation and an ideology of consumerism rather than social culture or identity (Ang, 1995; DeFleur & Dennis, 1994; Negus, 1995; O'Connor & Downing, 1995). This is especially true of popular music genres (Goodwin & Gore, 1990;

Malm & Wallis, 1992; Straubhaar, 1991). According to Petras, cultural imperialism is "the systematic penetration and domination of the cultural life of the popular classes by the ruling class of the West in order to reorder the values, behavior, institutions and identity of the oppressed peoples to conform with the interests of the imperial classes" (1993, p. 140). Colista and Leshner (1998) argue that discussions of imperialism are too simplistic because audiences are active rather than passive; the entirety of the system should be examined. Media do not dominate or influence people because of blind or passive acceptance; in fact, audiences have the capacity to accept, censor, or reject Western popular culture. As argued elsewhere in this book, hegemony is a process in which a dominant group acquires the consent of other social groups by including (in political, social, economic, and cultural ideologies) some minimal interest of other social groups (Crabtree & Malhotra, this volume; see also Artz & Murphy, 2000).

Pettegrew (1995) argues that MTV specifically represents interests of big business and capitalism far more than its cutting edge, adventurous image leads viewers to believe. He also contends that the viewers buy into the hegemony of the MTV culture, because MTV promotes consumerist and capitalist ideologies, under the guise of something that viewers find more appealing. The effects cross-culturally are much more influential when considering one-way exportation of media. Individuals in other parts of the world may consume Western popular culture specifically because it is Western and the way in which all Western media have advertised their programming, illustrating the hegemonic effects of popular culture. Additionally, producers rarely make accommodations to the local cultures of the region where these shows are viewed, and the shows may not even be translated into other languages. MTV's regional adaptation efforts seem substantial in comparison to the nature of other Western programming exports that have little, if any, modification for their international audiences.

MTV Asia:
Cultural Hegemony and Music Videos

Singapore Investment News (1996) reports that MTV Asia's efforts to broadcast with local interests in mind follow the "think globally, act locally" MTV philosophy. However, this study of MTV Asia's programs reveals that there is very little inclusion of Southeast Asian "local action" or music. Based on several hundred hours of MTV Asia's programming from 1997 to 2000, five main categories for cultural identity were distinguished for further analysis: (1) the language (English, Thai, Indonesian, etc.) of the programming; (2) the number of songs from East Asian or Southeast Asian singers or bands (some in English and some in other languages); (3) the number of songs from Europeans or American singers or bands (all in English); (4) nationality/ethnicity of VJs; and (5) the origin and content of the programs (Southeast Asia, Europe, or the United States). MTV Asia adds new programs and removes old programs regularly. While some shows have aired since the inception of MTV Asia, other programs are constantly revised, and the schedule changes frequently. For this ongoing study, I have reported scheduling hours that range from April 1999 to April 2001. Total viewing hours and percentages are based on April 1999 schedules as reported on the MTV Asia Web page.

Although many of MTV Asia's shows are produced in Singapore rather than exported from the United States or Europe, there are few that play only Southeast Asian music. For example, Thai music is aired on two shows, "Bangkok Jam" (aired for one hour late Sunday night, Saturday morning) and "MTV Wow" (aired late Tuesday through Friday nights and 3 a.m./4 a.m. on Wednesday and Friday). However, "MTV Wow" is a mix of Thai and international music, meaning that the four hours of music videos are only part Thai. Another show filmed in Thailand, "Life's a Beach," is a guest talk show that takes place on a Thai beach (aired in the late evening on Thursday, Friday, and Saturday). "Para Bos," a show filmed in Manila, is aired three times a week, in the late evening, Sunday through Tuesday. A VJ travels around Manila to find the most popular clubs and hangouts for Filipinos, sometimes discussing music. Neither "Life's a Beach" nor "Para Bos" are music video programs, although seemingly more reflective of Thai and Filipina/o popular culture than imported programs without modification.

Indonesian music programs include "MTV Ampuh" (aired late Monday night, Saturday afternoon) and "Seratus Persen, 100% Indonesian" (aired late Saturday afternoon for one hour). Both of these programs play entirely Indonesian artists. "Getar Cinta" (Love Vibrations) is also an Indonesian program, but is a talk show on relationships aired late Sunday night and Friday afternoon. A new program that features Dangdut music (a style heavily influenced by Indian popular music that is favored by Indonesian working classes) is aired on Thursday at 3 a.m., but in Indonesia airs on a public channel (ANTV) on Friday afternoons. Another program that focuses on Southeast Asian artists is "Live and Loud," which each week features a different band or musician from Southeast Asia performing live and is aired late Thursday afternoon, Friday evening, and late Sunday night. Finally, "MTV Syok" is a Malaysian music video program aired late Sunday night.

These localized and adapted programs air for a total of 14.5 hours a week, representing 9.2% of all MTV Asia programming hours. However, if only the programs that play Southeast Asian music videos are counted, the total number of hours is reduced to 8.5, or 5.4%. Additionally, most of these programs are aired after midnight. Although MTV's primetime hours are usually different from other networks, programs aired after midnight more than likely occur during low viewing hours.

In other MTV Asia programs, music videos are predominantly European or American. The most frequently aired programs are: "Non-stop Hits" (56 hours/week), "MTV Hanging Out" (9 hours/week), "MTV Most Wanted" (6 hours/week), "MTV Asia Hitlist" (6 hours/week), "MTV Land" (5 hours/week), and "Classic MTV" (3 hours/week). Together, these programs represent almost 60% of MTV Asia's weekly programming and are aired during prime viewing hours, except for "Non-stop Hits," which is aired during both on and off hours. Furthermore, all of MTV Asia's shows are in English with the exception of a few programs. Thus, 91.5% of the week's programs are broadcast in English, although only 5 hours (3.2%) of programming has been imported directly from MTV in the United States or Europe. These findings also confirm Banks's (1996) contention that 90% of the programming features non-Asian music or television shows. He also reports that an MTV Asia representative claimed that as much as half of some programs throughout various times during the day are devoted to Asian artists. This study demonstrates that this claim is somewhat spurious and misleading. Clearly, the number of programs that dedicate at least half of the show to Southeast Asian artists is very minimal.

Commercial slots are one area in which Southeast Asian musicians have received exposure on MTV Asia. In translated interviews during commercials and programs, musicians report their musical influences and favorite bands. The bands almost always report that they are influenced mostly by Western musicians, usually American bands. These include bands such as Pantera, Public Enemy, Rage Against the Machine, Metallica, and others, usually various forms of American rap, grunge, heavy metal, and pop music. Furthermore, the Southeast Asian musicians that do receive airplay, almost always play Western style music (pop, alternative, rap). Generally, Southeast Asian artists featured on MTV Asia follow North American or European trends in popular music. In essence, MTV seeks regional bands that demonstrate Western musical tendencies for air time. Often, local bands popularize Western musical genre and values. This practice demonstrates how MTV Asia is able to attract subordinate participation and consent to this globalized, hegemonic relationship.

In a representative sample of MTV Asia's most popular programming, including one "Live and Loud" episode in which all the videos were Indonesian, 22 of 181 videos analyzed were from Southeast Asian musicians, representing 12.2% of the total number of videos. Of both the 9.2% of programs and 12.2% of videos that are distinctly Southeast Asian, neither percentage is close to the 20% quota MTV Asia claims (Shuker, 1994). Many of the most popular programs are request shows or videos that are selected based on record sales, demonstrating that Southeast Asians participate in selecting the music aired. For example, "MTV Asia Hitlist" is a top 20 countdown program that selects videos based on record sales, radio airplay, viewer requests, and video airplay in Southeast Asia. Almost every single week, all 20 videos on the hit list are or have been European or American. Similarly, on the Filipino countdown program "Dyes 10," the top 10 videos for the week are nearly always Western videos, even though the MTV Asia Web page claims that the show heavily features local acts. The selection process of videos through its viewers signifies that viewers prefer North American or European music to their own local music. Another possible explanation is that many Southeast Asian musicians do not have videos for airplay, which can lead to failure in a saturated market of videos (Jones, 1993; Shuker, 1994). However, this explanation does not explain why those Southeast Asian artists with videos are not as requested as are their North American or European counterparts.

Video request shows such as "MTV Most Wanted," "MTV Select," and "Lili and Bebe" allow viewers to request videos via letter, e-mail, fax, telephone, or hand phone. Viewers can send letters, faxes, or e-mail at any time before the program airs, and during some programs, such as "MTV Interactive," viewers can make live requests. On "MTV Most Wanted," there is a daily contest for the best request that a viewer has sent via regular mail. These requests are often elaborately and artistically constructed cardboard cutouts in some form of the letters MTV. The VJ then selects from these requests the "Request of the Day." VJs invite viewers to participate via these sorts of requests as part of MTV Asia's attempt to incorporate local music preferences. Viewers often call in or send a request because they would like to see a particular video, but also as part of a social network. Often, viewers who request videos ask the VJ to say hello to numerous friends and family. For the viewer, having a request played on MTV is sort of like winning a contest.

However, almost all of the music requested on "MTV Most Wanted" is North American or European, and almost all of the requests in general are for non-Asian music. "MTV Select" only allows viewers to choose from a short list of 35 songs, almost all of which are North American or European. These programs, reliant on communication technology for sending requests, demonstrate how MTV Asia perpetuates consumer ideologies by requiring requests from hand phones, faxes, or e-mail. Other programs, such as "Non-stop Hits," "MTV Hanging Out, " and "MTV Land" also primarily broadcast Western music. "Classic MTV" airs virtually no Southeast Asian videos, since the focus of the program is on videos from the 1980s and the early 1990s, before Southeast Asian musicians had access to music television. These programs that air few Southeast Asian videos, comprise 60% of MTV Asia's total programming. They are also all broadcast in English, a language mostly accessible to the middle class and elite. These programs that require requests or participation through purchases illustrate how viewers consent and participate in this cultural and globalized hegemony. Viewers desire and even prefer Western artists over Southeast Asian artists, perhaps because such a preference, and access to the English language and communication technologies distance them from traditional cultures, lower classes, and the "uneducated."

"MTV Interactive" also demonstrates how Southeast Asian viewers participate in media hegemony. The hosts of the program play videos and discuss comments from the MTV chat line, which is broadcast simultaneously at the bottom of the television screen. This program represents Southeast Asian viewers' opinions on chosen subjects of the day, such as the dangers of the Internet, which bands should be reunited, and what one would do if she or he were president. The entire show is broadcast in English, including the interactive chat. Additionally, because it is a chat line, to participate in the program, participants must have access both to a computer and the Internet. Southeast Asians (with the exception of Singaporeans) rarely own their own computers, and the Internet is generally accessible and affordable only to the middle and upper classes. Poster (1995) indicates that the effects of the Internet and English as the predominant language illustrate the "extension of American power" in other nations, noting that the Internet and new communication technologies undermine other nation-states, as the predominant users of the Internet are still wealthy, white, and male.

MTV Asia's VJs are mostly Southeast Asian, Australian, or North American. However, the shows are always in English, meaning they all speak in English, rather than in Indonesian, Tagalog, Thai, or Tamil. Some Western VJs have seemed generally culturally ignorant of Singaporean and Southeast Asian cultures. For example, when reading requests, they may mispronounce words in non-English languages, even simple words, such as *terima kasih* (the Indonesian words for thank you). On one show, for example, the VJ demonstrated his lack of knowledge about Southeast Asian fruits and his disdain for the durian, a particularly pungent, but very popular, fruit in Southeast Asia. All current VJs are Southeast Asians, but in the past they have not always been. However, all the VJs (Western or Southeast Asian) represent Western values and ideals through their dress, speech, and musical preferences, demonstrating their own consent and participation in this media hegemony. The program seems largely focused on Western popular culture, both through the VJs' interactions, and music requested and broadcast.

Finally, the show "It's My Life" (fashioned after U.S. MTV's "Road Rules" and "Real World") features the lives of seven so-called typical Southeast Asians, generally ranging from 18 to 24 years of age. While this show is not a music focused show, the popularity of its American counterparts illustrates its potential in Southeast Asia. Although the participants for the show are Asian (coming from countries such as India, China, the Philippines, Singapore, and

Indonesia), the participants are not typical Southeast Asians. Diani (2000) observes that these participants are often professional models, actors, or singers, or else hold jobs that require high educational backgrounds, such as journal editors or magazine reporters. These so-called representatives are typically middle or upper class. Diani writes,

> judging from their outfits, houses, and cars, it is clear that the monetary crisis which battered the region in recent years had nothing to do with their privileged lives . . . [one character] sure has a fun life as a reporter, and she really filled her spare time with exciting activities like diving, bungee jumping, traveling abroad and stuff. Then again, how many young people can afford such activities? (Diani, 2000, p. 12)

Diani's observation demonstrates MTV Asia's attempts to target middle- and upper-class Southeast Asian youth and values to create the consumerist culture that Jhally (1987) and Pettegrew (1995) describe.

MTV Asia's advertising especially illustrates an ideology of consumerism. Almost all of the advertisements are for hand phones, CD players, Western movies, or an MTV Asia promotion. The request show "Lili and Bebe" is "powered by Ericsson," a Swedish hand phone company, and commercials for Nokia hand phones are also frequent. One 2001 contest commercial only allows entry by hand phone; in order to enter, viewers must go to the MTV Asia Web page to get detailed instructions for entering by hand phone. Such contests are clearly targeted to the middle class and elite in Southeast Asia. Most Indonesians, Thai, and Filipinas/os are entirely too poor to even own a telephone or send an MTV Asia request by regular mail, let alone via a hand phone, fax, or e-mail.

Cultural Implications of MTV Asia's Hegemony

The nature of MTV Asia's programming and selection of music videos fails to include indigenous music, culture, and representation. This cultural exclusion and resulting media hegemony have several implications. First, MTV Asia's programming perpetuates Western narratives in music in Southeast Asia. As Frith (1996) and Vila (1996) have argued, narratives in music play an important role in both group and self-identity. MTV Asia's videos fix the meaning for songs and Western cultural narratives for Southeast Asians. Southeast Asians develop new group and self-identities based on the extensive influence of Western music. They are attracted to MTV Asia because it represents success, cosmopolitan and Western lifestyles, wealth and consumerism, the pinnacle of fashion, and the cutting edge in technology, while presenting highly stylized and technical products and music. Because South-east Asian musicians and VJs are recognized as spokespeople for Southeast Asian youth, MTV Asia appears and develops as a unique and trendy Southeast Asian cultural experience. Unlike MTV India or MTV Mandarin, where many videos and programs are based on local music and culture, MTV Asia has a much more pervasive cultural hegemonic relationship with its viewers. Diani argues that MTV is "hip among young people and sets trends for them" (2000, p. 12).

MTV Asia also popularizes globalization and Western lifestyles and cultures. As one of the "It's My Life" participants says "I want to [live] in the United States for the rest of my life" (Diani, 2000, p. 12). Clearly, MTV Asia is influential with Southeast Asian middle-class youth, and they consent to what they see on MTV Asia. MTV Asia plays a significant role in the development of a globalized, music culture through a process, as Frith argues, of getting to know themselves as a group with similar interests. MTV Asia functions as a key component of global youth culture because it differentiates the middle class and elite from their poorer counterparts through an ideology of consumerism, a global language of English, education, fashion, and music.

For poorer or lower-class communities, globalization has a somewhat different effect. For Southeast Asian middle-class and elite youth, MTV Asia reinforces globalization and abandonment of traditional or local values, culture, and language. However, because the middle and upper classes have more mobility and access to globalization through satellite television, education, movies, the Internet, and consumerism, globalization has the ability to create a widening chasm between classes. MTV Asia reinforces the manifestations of this developing globalized youth culture. In Indonesia for example, MTV Asia is widely watched by Jakartan youth of all classes. In more rural and other urban communities, MTV Asia is seen only by those who have access to satellite or cable television. MTV Asia audiences participate in a global, popular culture in part through music television, whereas members of lower classes do not or cannot afford to participate in such a culture. Furthermore, younger members of lower classes may develop a sense of consumerism that they cannot afford. Certainly among the middle class in Southeast Asia, credit card debts related to consumerism are increasing problems. Not only does MTV Asia function as an advertising scheme for Western music, but it also relies on advertisements for movies, cellular phones, CD players, and other technology often unavailable and unaffordable for the poorer classes. This ideology of consumerism leads to the potential development of societies filled with unsated desires and dreams.

In addition, MTV Asia reinforces globalization through its predominant use of English both in music and with its VJs. Because those who have access to English education in Southeast Asia tend to be middle or upper class, MTV Asia perpetuates the divide between the rich and the poor by creating a youth culture in music that is accessible only to those who speak English. English as a global language may connect cultures, but it also disenfranchises those who do not have access to English education (Asuncion Lande, 1999; Crane, 1991). MTV Asia, even though members of poorer classes can watch it, functions as a global culture that unites the middle and upper classes across Southeast Asia, but widens the cultural gap between the elite, the middle class, and the poor.

Finally, the MTV Asia phenomenon globalizes and sanitizes Southeast Asian music. Southeast Asian musicians often emulate Western styles of music, particularly those who receive airtime on MTV Asia. Furthermore, MTV Asia only plays Southeast Asian music that is Westernized to some extent. Southeast Asian musicians adopt a Westernized or globalized style either because they are attracted to Western music in the first place, perhaps because of influence of MTV Asia or radio air play of Western music or because they know it is the best way to become well known. Musicians that receive airtime on MTV Asia or other music channels are more likely to gain a wider audience than those who do not receive similar exposure.

In effect, MTV Asia facilitates the construction of a globalized, consumerist culture for middle-class Southeast Asians based on their consent and participation of MTV's cultural hegemony. MTV Asia demonstrates that many Southeast Asians embrace Western music and its effects of globalization, particularly in the middle and upper classes. Southeast Asians surely can choose to reject Western music and its influence, but many do not. For viewers, there is an attraction in music globalization. It represents class status and education because it can create a music culture that is based on identification with Western music, consumerism, and the ability to speak English. The fact that 40 million Southeast Asians watch MTV Asia illustrates the very nature of cultural hegemony. The effects of media hegemony result in consequences in Southeast Asia that may include loss of culture, usurpation of local music groups and concerts, elitism among those who speak English and have regular access to the Internet, and the promotion of consumerist ideologies. It may also further widen the gap of cultural understanding as the middle class and the wealthy become part of a globalized culture, and the poor remain isolated within traditional communities. Although MTV Asia purports to think globally and act locally, they really reinforce a globalized, consumerist culture enjoyed by the middle class and elites in Southeast Asia that functions to exclude or transform local music and cultures. The effects of such cultural hegemony are complicated to be sure, but MTV Asia is a culturally powerful phenomenon with far-reaching influence on youth cultures in Southeast Asia.

References

Ang (1995). The nature of the audience. In J. Downing, A. Mohammadi, & A. Sreberny-Mohammadi (Eds.), *Questioning the media* (pp. 207–220). Thousand Oaks, CA: Sage.

Artz, L., & Murphy, B. O. (2000). *Cultural hegemony in the United States.* Thousand Oaks, CA: Sage.

Asuncion Lande, N. C. (1999). English as the dominant language for intercultural communication: Prospects for the next century. In M. H. Prosser & K. S. Sitaram (Eds.), *Civic discourse: Intercultural, international, and global media.* Westport, CT: Greenwood.

Banks, J. (1996). *Monopoly television: MTV's quest to control the music.* Boulder, CO: Westview.

Banks, J. (1997). MTV and the globalization of popular culture. *Gazette, 59* (6), 43–60.

Bhavnani, K. K. & Phoenix, A. (1994). *Shifting identities, shifting racisms.* Thousand Oaks, CA: Sage.

Colista, C., & Leshner, G. (1998). Traveling music: Following the path of music through the global market. *Critical Studies in Mass Communication, 15,* 181–194.

Crane, D. (1991). *The production of culture: Media and the urban arts.* Newbury Park, CA: Sage.

DeFleur, M. L., & Dennis, E. E. (1994). *Understanding mass communication: A liberal arts perspective* (5th ed). Boston, MA: Houghton Mifflin Company.

Diani, H. (2000, December 10). Up-close and not so personal with 'MTV It's My Life.' *The Jakarta Post,* p. 12.

Einhorn, B. (1997, June 27–July 3). MTV cranks up. *The Economic Times.* [on-line]. Available at: *http://www.economictimes.com.*

Frith, S. (1996). Music and identity. In S. Hall & P. duGay (Eds.), *Questions of cultural identity* (pp. 108–127). London: Sage.

Goodwin, A. (1992). *Dancing in the distraction factory: Music television and popular culture.* Minneapolis, MN: University of Minnesota Press.

Goodwin, A., & Gore, J. (1990). World beat and the cultural imperialism debate. *Socialist Review, 3,* 62–79.

Grossberg, L. (1993). The media economy of rock culture: Cinema, post-modernity and authenticity. In S. Frith, A. Goodwin, & L. Grossberg (Eds.), *Sound and vision: The music video reader.* New York: Routledge.

Hall, S. (1996). Introduction: Who needs 'identity'? In S. Hall & P. duGay (Eds.), *Questions of cultural identity* (pp. 1–17). London: Sage.

Hamelink, C. J. (1994). *The politics of world communication.* Thousand Oaks, CA: Sage.

Jakubowicz, A. (1995). Media in multicultural nations: Some comparisons. In J. Downing, A. Mohammadi, & A. Sreberny-Mohammadi (Eds.), *Questioning the media* (pp. 165–183). Thousand Oaks, CA: Sage.

Jhally, S. (1987). *The codes of advertising: Fetishism and the political economy of meaning in the consumer society.* New York: Routledge.

Jones, S. (1992). *Rock formation: Music, technology, and mass communication.* Newbury Park, CA: Sage.

Jones, S. (1993). Who fought the law? The American music industry and the global popular music market. In T. Bennett, S. Frith, L. Grossberg, J. Shepherd, & G. Turner (Eds.), *Rock and popular music: Politics, policies, and institutions* (pp. 83–95). New York: Routledge.

Malm, K., & Wallis, R. (1992). *Media policy and music activity.* London: Routledge.

Mohammadi, A. (1995). Cultural imperialism and cultural identity. In J. Downing, A. Mohammadi, & A. Sreberny-Mohammadi (Eds.), *Questioning the media* (pp. 362–378). Thousand Oaks, CA: Sage.

MTV Asia. (1997, December 1). [on-line]. Available: *http://www.scv.com.*

MTV Asia. (1999, May). [on-line]. Available at: *http://www.mtvasia.com.*

MTV Mandarin. (1997, December 1). *http://www.scv.com.sg.*

MTV sets up broadcast base and regional HQ. (1996, November). *Singapore Investment News.* [on-line]. Available at: *http://www.wedb.com.sg.*

Nash, M. (1999). Beavis is just confused: Ideologies, intertexts, audiences. *Velvet Light Trap, 43,* 4–22.

Negus, K. (1995). Popular music: Between celebration and despair. In J. Downing, A. Mohammadi, and A. Sreberny-Mohammadi (Eds.), *Questioning the media* (pp. 379–393). Thousand Oaks, CA: Sage.

Novitz, D. (1989). Art, narrative, and human nature. *Philosophy and Literature, 13* (1), 57–74.

O'Connor, A. & Downing, J. (1995). Culture and communication. In J. Downing, A. Mohammadi, and A. Sreberny-Mohammadi (Eds.), *Questioning the media* (pp. 3–22). Thousand Oaks, CA: Sage.

Petras, J. (1993). Cultural imperialism in the late 20th century. *Journal of Contemporary Asia, 23,* 139–148.

Pettegrew, J. (1995). A post-modernist moment: 1980s commercial culture and the founding of MTV. In G. Dines & J. M. Humez (Eds.), *Gender, race, and class in media* (pp. 488–498). Thousand Oaks, CA: Sage.

Poster, M. (1995). *The second media age.* Malden, MA: Blackwell.

Shuker, R. (1994). *Understanding popular music.* London: Routledge.

Somers, M. R. (1992). Narrativity, narrative identity, and social action: Rethinking English working-class formation. *Social Science History, 16* (4), 591–630.

Stevenson, R. (1994). *Global communication in the twenty-first century*. New York: Longman.

Straubhaar, J. (1991). Beyond media imperialism: Asymmetrical interdependence and cultural proximity. *Critical Studies in Mass Communication, 8,* 39–59.

Strauss, A., & Corbin, J. (1990). *Basics of qualitative research*. Newbury Park, CA: Sage.

Thussu, D. K. (2000). *International communication: Continuity and change*. London: Oxford University Press.

Vila, P. (1996). *Narrative identities, interpellations and the imaginary essential identities of different musical practices materialize*. Available from the author at the University of Texas at El Paso, Sociology and Anthropology Department, El Paso, TX 79968.

Wasko, J. (1994). *Hollywood in the information age*. Austin, TX: University of Texas Press.

CHAPTER 13

Political and Sociocultural Implications of Hollywood Hegemony in the Korean Film Industry: Resistance, Assimilation, and Articulation

Eungjun Min

Introduction

Hollywood is an industry with its own standardized product, marketing and management practices, specific conventions governing film structure and content, and a combination of economic and political power rationalized by free trade and political considerations. In addition to this apparatus, the mass market for films in the United States enables major film companies to dominate overseas markets. In most film-producing countries outside the United States, it is difficult if not impossible to generate investment from local markets because the markets lack capital or consumers. Despite the fact that the number of American moviegoers has declined since 1990, American films usually are amortized in the home market, which has about one-third of the world's theaters. Besides, Hollywood's genius for tapping broadly (albeit tritely) into the common elements of experience that bind humanity together attracts foreign audiences.

South Korea is one of only a few countries that have resisted Hollywood's hegemony with some success. Yet "Hollywood" is a palpable presence in South Korean culture, and substantial fears about Hollywood's cultural influence still exist. This chapter examines three related questions. First, I consider how Hollywood films have affected the modes of production and construction of narratives in both Korean mainstream and nonmainstream films. Second, I indicate how Hollywood's dominance has spurred Koreans—workers, students, and intellectuals—to create resistant film discourses. Finally, I argue that Korea's internal political and structural constraints have forced the formation of complex relationships among Hollywood films, and the mainstream and nonmainstream Korean film industries.

First Commercial Appeal:
Foreign Films in the Early Years

Opinion varies as to when the first motion picture was publicly screened in Korea. Early accounts indicate that in a barn on South Gate Street *(Nam-daemoonro)* in Seoul, in October 1898, Mr. Asthouse, an American in the oil business, showed a film to the public (Junger Lee, p. 20–21, 1992). A short documentary produced by the French company, Pathê, the film was projected using gas lamps, and the price of admission was a piece of nickel or ten empty cigarette packs. In fact, showing the motion picture was a sales gimmick and advertisement for these cigarettes, which had been newly introduced to the Korean market. The account of this 1898 film showing has been handed down by word of mouth from the earliest Korean filmmakers and Japanese film historians.

Official records indicate that Hansung Electric Streetcar Company showed a few American one-reel films to advertise their product in Korea in 1903. With the Japanese annexation of Korea in 1910, more American and European films were introduced, including feature films. Koreans were mesmerized by historical dramas like *Quo Vadis* (1913) and *New General Othello* (1913) no less than American short newsreel documentaries such as *Niagara, The Big Fire of New York,* and *The Practice of Horse Racing* (Lee, p. 342, 1988).

Simultaneously, indigenous film production was hampered by the Japanese Occupation from 1910 to 1945, which imposed various forms of censorship and economic restrictions on the Korean motion picture industry (Lee, p. 324, 1988). During the occupation, domestic film scripts were subject to the approval and censorship of the Japanese general governing authority, the *Chongdokbu.* These "Korean" films were produced by Japanese companies and private citizens who retained distribution and exhibition rights. A few films, such as *Arirang* and *The Bird in Her Cage* by legendary director Woonkyu Na, depicted Koreans' anger about and resentment of Japanese oppression metaphorically, but there was little direct criticism in film. The expression of Korean sensibilities became even more limited as the occupation continued. By the 1930s, for example, the *Chongdokbu* increased censorship and limited production of films to two or three (Lent, 1990, p. 125). During World War II, the *Chongdokbu* closed down film companies that refused to produce pro-Japanese propaganda films (Lent, 1990, 125).

With the liberation in 1945, the Korean film industry rebounded briefly by producing numerous uncensored films. A favorite focus of films of the era was the realistic portrayal of the independent resistance movement against the Japanese typified in films such as *The Patriot,* a true story about Joongkun Ahn, the man who assassinated Hirobumi Ito, the first governor of the *Chong-*

dokbu. In spite of this brief post-War flowering of the Korean film industry, production was severely restricted in the period from 1945 until the outbreak of Korean War in 1950 due to political instability, lack of equipment, and the disorganization of the fledgling Korean film companies.

Political and Economic Resistance to Hollywood Films

After the Korean War (1950–1953), foreign films, including Hollywood films, suffered a sharp decline in box-office income in Korea as the result of a shrinking market, although they still had dominant presence. As part of the government's measures to encourage production of domestic motion pictures, a 115% admission tax was imposed on all imported Western films, and it was practically impossible for foreign film distributors to expect any reasonable revenue. Only 10 theaters—mostly in Seoul—were showing foreign films. Tickets were printed at the government mint to prevent fraud in tax payment. Furthermore, the government imposed a quota on foreign films at 165 films per year, although the annual quota usually consisted of about 180 films with a bonus quota of 20 additional films (Junger Lee, 1992, p. 356).

Despite restrictive policies, imported foreign films remained economically more viable than domestic film production: it cost almost five times more to produce a domestic film than it did to produce the average foreign film. Although a few domestic films occasionally beat out foreign films at the box office, block-booking tactics of Hollywood distributors privileged two-year leases for their own products.

Recognizing Hollywood's economic advantage in the Korean film market, during the 1960s the government further limited the number of foreign films admitted in an effort to promote increased domestic production. In 1968 some 200 Korean films were produced. The government also introduced a screen quota system under which theaters showing foreign films were required to exhibit domestic films for 60 to 90 days per year. As added motivation, the government granted an additional import quota to any film company that produced two domestic films (Joo, p. 50–87, 1990)—and domestic film production increased.

In the 1970s, revisions to the Motion Picture Law, along with modifications to the government policy on export promotion, enabled the establishment of the Korean Film Union. The Korean Film Union was designed to promote exportation of films and to strengthen the requirement for import quotas, increasing from two to five the number of domestic films produced per one foreign import. However, the economic recession and martial law during the 1970s crippled the Korean film industry: 20 out of 23 film production companies went bankrupt in 1972. Unable to fulfill its mission in these tough economic and political times, the Korean Film Union was dissolved in 1973 and incorporated into the Motion Picture Promotion Corporation (MPPC), when another revision of the Motion Picture Law in 1973 loosened requirements for new film production companies, increased import rights, and limited censorship. The industry slowly recovered by the end of 1970s (Joo, 1990, p. 56–59).

Despite efforts to stimulate domestic film production and to lessen the impact of Hollywood film on local culture and audiences, the presence of Hollywood narrative modes in domestic films has been extensive. As the closest ally of the United States in East Asia, the Korean government has had little power or inclination to control the flow of Hollywood films, or any other American cultural product. Korea is only one of many nations that has been force-fed American culture through the consistent commercial and political intervention from U.S. business and government. Yet, domination is never just economic or political; rather, domination is also enacted, sustained, and enabled by artistic and cultural means as well.

In culture and art, the domination that some scholars may call "cultural imperialism" is perhaps better understood as hegemony: an exchange in which both parties benefit in some way—albeit one that is structured by uneven access to power. The element of exchange, perhaps even of homage, clearly informs Korean films in which Hollywood films are echoed; conversely, Hollywood's narrative structures are translated as form vehicles, driven by Korean sensibilities and Korean concerns. Significantly, Korean films that refuse to exploit or develop Hollywood-style conventions, have often failed in the box office. It seems that Western leadership offers substantial rewards.

Hegemony in Tragedy and Tradition

Hollywood conventions most apparent in Korean films include structural properties such as parallelism, repetition, contrast and variation, a reliance on continuity editing, a preoccupation with individualism, and the use of the *mise-en-scène*. Film scholars (Bordwell & Thompson, 2001, 3–24.) have also identified seven narrative conventions that dominate Hollywood films, including:

1. Temporal and spatial coherence in stories;
2. A powerful beginning that provides the basis for regular audience involvement through hypothesis-forming and subsequent narrative cues;
3. Goal-oriented, individual character-centered plots;
4. Patterned narrative tempos—repetition and delay;

5. Bipolar dichotomy (good vs. evil) and excessive emotion;
6. Multiple causes-effects that reveal the narrative process;
7. Emphasis on the climax and the resolution.

These conventions are apparent even in a traditional Korean film like *Sopyonje* (1993), a winner of the Silver Bear Award in the 1994 Berlin International Film Festival and arguably the best Korean film ever produced.

Sopyonje follows the life of a post-World War II Korean *P'ansori* performing family. *P'ansori (p'an* = playground, stage, abstractive open space or a site of affairs; *sori* = singing or sound) is a story-telling musical form performed by two individuals: a singer *(kwangdae)* and a barrel drummer *(kosoo)* (Pihl, 1977, p. 15–18). *P'ansori* performance is based on plaintive refrains and chilling voice vibrato, and the philosophical belief that one can only express the necessary emotive power of a great *P'ansori* singer by living and enduring grief and sorrow. Trainees not only sing themselves hoarse, but actually vocalize in the wilderness or under a waterfall in an attempt to produce a voice of great power, often spitting up blood in the process. The peculiarly Korean subject matter invites interpretation of the film as the director's search for Korean identity: Yubong's *P'ansori* family becomes a painful and tragic metaphor for Korea's struggle to keep its identity in the wake of the Western cultural domination. On yet another level, the division of brother and sister enacted in the film seems to be a metaphor for the division of North and South Koreas by the super powers (United States and Russia) and the subsequent ideological differences that arise from the forced parting of the "brother" and "sister" nations. Yet, even with a subject matter so peculiarly Korean, *Sopyonje* uses conventional Hollywood film narrative conventions.

The initial appeal of a typical Hollywood film often resides in its ability to involve audiences by positing character-centered and goal-oriented plots. *Sopyonje* draws our attention by beginning with a young man, Dongho, getting off a bus and entering a small inn in search of a famous *P'ansori* singer. The next scene takes the film back 21 years (from 1965 to 1946) with a close-up of young Dongho in slow motion. A *P'ansori* master, Yubong, who is determined to transfer his art of *P'ansori* to a female prodigy, adopts Dongho and his sister Songwha. To insure his plan, he feeds Songwha a drug that makes her blind so that she will remain at his side and experience the grief and sorrow *(Haan)* essential to become a true *P'ansori* singer. Yubong teaches *P'ansori* singing to Songwha and drumming skills to Dongho, and they travel from village to village, earning a living by performing at market places, restaurants, and private dinner parties. As we follow their painful and sometimes joyful journey from the adoption to the *P'ansori* tour, the film's narrative process clearly encourages the successive formation of hypotheses concerning future development, hypotheses that are essentially based on audience expectations that may be formed or learned through repetitive narrative conventions.

The director, Kwontak Im, utilizes Hollywood visual styles such as the eye-level shot, the point of view shot, reverse shot, multiple shot, graphic/temporal/spatial editing techniques, and changing locales to achieve a tight cause-effect relationship, and to convey internal coherence and motivations. For example, unable to tolerate his adoptive father's tyrannical treatment, Dongho decides to run away. This moment is conveyed through three shots: 1) Songwha stands still next to a huge dark tree and stares at Dongho's back (medium long shot, static, dark in high contrast); 2) Dongho runs away (extreme long shot, fast-moving, bright in low contrast); 3) return to the first shot. There is no music to underscore the emotional parting of brother and sister, and Songwha does not desperately attempt to stop Dongho. Instead the shot focuses our gaze on the hanging branches of the tree moving in the wind as the correlative of Songwha's grief. Thematically, this scene functions as a typical Hollywood narrative bridge that encourages the spectator to travel with eager anticipation to the end of the narrative.

As Bordwell (1985) demonstrates in his study of Hollywood narrative conventions, three motivations expose the narrative process: realistic motivation (plausible explanations), generic motivation (dramatically logical), and causal motivation (compositional). The causal motivation is the most significant, although the three types often complement each other (1985, p. 4, 19–23). All three motivations are evident in *Sopyonje*'s narrative. Yubong adopts Dongho/Songwha and teaches the art of *P'ansori* (realistic motivation); Dongho is disillusioned by Yubong's tyrannical treatment, including his sister's blindness and the journey (generic motivation); and Dongho runs away, providing Songwha with a source for more grief and sorrow to enrich her *P'ansori*, and the journey continues with Songwha following Yubong (causal motivation). While in the case of *Sopyonje*, Hollywood conventions provide a framework for effective communication of Korean concerns, this is by no means the case for all Korean films. Rather, many Korean films have developed a non-Hollywood style to match Korean subject matter.

Cultural and Narrative Resistance in Cinema

In the 1980s the most popular mainstream film genres in Korea were melodrama, action adventure (mainly martial arts), films based on foreign stories, comedies, and war films. Perennially, mainstream films look to the United States for direction—and, more recently, Hong Kong's action adventure films, which blend Hong Kong's own traditional martial arts action with Hollywood's gangster films (Standish, 1994; Wilson, 1994). The resulting blend of

Hollywood narratives with Asian tones and Korean locale create an interesting outcome. "The popular Hollywood film genres and their Korean counterparts crossbreed with amazing ease. Westerns, private eye films, spy adventures, historical costume drama, and the pop musical have all been adopted and put into an indigenous setting" (Doherty, 1984, p. 845).

Yet, Korean filmmakers have felt the need for and developed a distinct national cinema. The cultural event that spurred this shift in Korean film aesthetics was the defeat of the popular Kwangju Uprising (Kwangju is the largest city in the Cholla region). This May 1980 rebellion was fiercely repressed—the military killed over 2,000 civilians. The resulting alliance between the middle and working classes generated both an important culture of resistance and the possibility of a return to democracy. Following the insurrection, the military government attempted to renegotiate the terms of its political leadership by allowing some discussion of social issues that had been banned for decades. Such rapid historical and cultural change inevitably influenced Korean cinema—a turn to politically muted, but culturally dynamic stylistic conventions began appearing.

Inspired by the Kwangju Uprising, the early national cinema references stylistic conventions that have their roots in Korean folk tales, Italian Neo-realism, and the Third Cinema movement, exemplified by realistic films such as Sooyong Kim's *Girl Who Came to the City* (1981) and Jangho Lee's *Children of Darkness* (1981). Kim and Lee were mainstream filmmakers dismayed by mainstream cinema's inability to reproduce and represent life in aspects not readily available to the average viewer.

Children of Darkness, for example, portrays an innocent country girl who is exploited and lured into prostitution. It vividly enacts the harsh reality of life on the urban "mean streets" of modern Korea. Lee, however, concentrates less upon the social and political implications of the corrupted male world here than upon the tragic transformation in the heroine's character, and her redemption at film's end, when the heroine carries a homeless man without legs or money to her room. The exploited prostitute transforms herself into a tragic angel, yet the church at the end of the red-light district would not welcome her, or any of the other children of darkness whom she represents. The film's social class critique is severely circumscribed: it dwells on the Christian churches' lack of humanity and compassion toward underprivileged people, but it never challenges the government or its social policies.

Like *Children of Darkness, The Girl Who Came to the City* laments contemporary Korean society and was the vanguard of a new direction in filmmaking; but this "national cinema" rarely challenged the status quo, the modes of mainstream production, or the government's control of the film industry. Instead, these films and their contemporaries romanticized social problems

such as prostitution, dysfunctional families, and confusions in traditional values created by the Western culture. Thus while these films were funded with
Korean capital and dealt with domestic problems—two of the indicators that
cause Doherty (1984) to identify them as "national cinema"—they had little
or no influence on the development of the National Cinema Movement
(NCM). Rather, due to the intensity of political pressures in this era, these
films prepared the way for a more popular and less uncompromising social
stance in film in the decade that followed.

Films praised by Standish (1994) as scions of the new realism in the
1980s also fall short of participating in meaningful change in Korean government or society. KwansSu Park's *Chilsu and Mansu* (1988) portrays two
young men, both underprivileged movie theater employees who are trapped,
isolated, and exploited. The film emphasizes despair, agony, and defeatism
without any solutions or direction. Although it does not romanticize the
social reality in the way that *Children of Darkness* had, it fails to portray
Chilsu and Mansu as victims of structural social injustice and class conflict,
suggesting instead that it is their destiny to continue their lives as they were.
Chong-Won Park's *Kuro Arirang* (1989), which portrays young female factory workers who are exploited by the owner and local authorities, and
KwansSu Park's *Black Republic* (1990) which revolves around a relationship
between the emotionally tormented son of wealthy coal miner and a radical
college student wanted by the police. Both films reflect the defeatism and
skepticism of the period, fostering little or no hope for the future, even dis-
couraging social reform by suggesting that social problems rested in individuals rather than in social structures.

And yet, I want to consider all of these films, flawed as they may be, as
signs of an emerging national consciousness and resistance to domination in
Korean film insofar as they indicate an autonomous "voice" or artistic sensibility in the film industry. For instance, these films dialogize their relationships to the dominant cinema within their texts in ways that resist and modify the dominant linguistic and filmic conventions. Quite different from both
mainstream films and the emergent radical films of NCM, these films were
sincere and entertaining, although imbued with defeatism, isolationism, and
cynicism. What's more, although these films did have popular appeal, the
influence of the underground filmmaking practices that emerged between
1980 and 1990 is palpable in them. The differences between these "neorealist"
or "proto-national-cinema" offerings will be elaborated below, but the single
most significant difference lies in access to audience. As the political mood
shifted in 1989, a broad public viewed *Kuro Arirang* and *Black Republic*, but
films from NCM were only shown to college students, peasants, workers, and
students of Yahak. *Kuro Arirang* was even screened in the Berlin International
Film Festival in 1990.

The National Cinema Movement

Another way to get at the major difference between new realism films and films of the NCM is provided by Gramsci's concept of "national-popular." This concept refers to the possibility of an alliance of interests and feelings among different social agents like intellectuals, the working class, and the peasantry. It is this impulse to build new alliances among its viewers that marks the films of the NCM. NCM films attempt to construct a new political reality through "a new type of hegemony" (Chambers & Curti, 1984, p. 101). In contrast, *Arirang* and others are filled with existing prescribed cultural styles that are tailored and maintained by the ruling class. In other words, as cinema that makes no demands on its viewers, the Korean neorealist films comprise a cinema of no hope. The NCM films are difficult and demanding, as they construct the possibility of meaningful political and social change.

While less popularly successful and less critically praised, the films produced by the NCM are crucial to understanding the development of contemporary Korean cinema. The NCM is rooted in the underground cinema alluded to in the previous paragraph. In the 1980s, young and unknown filmmakers began to experiment with forbidden cultural and political topics, and to establish a collective force to challenge the hegemony of the mainstream industry and the state filmmaking apparatus. Cinema clubs, underground magazines and other publications fueled active interest and the subsequent creation of *Minjok Youngwha Woondong*—the National Cinema Movement (NCM). The creation of the NCM is far more than a response to the dominant cultural discourse elaborated by Hollywood and the mainstream film industry. NCM is a site in which a multiplicity of languages and social discourses are articulated as the basis for forging alliances between widely divergent cultural groups and social classes. As such, the NCM is closely interrelated with other cultural movements, such as the labor movement, which bring together stratified and diversified social groups.

There are five key goals to which the NCM dedicates itself:

1. Propaganda and instigation: National cinema is in search of a voice for people against the ideology of the ruling class. Its foremost mission is to educate *Minjoong* [the Korean people] about its historical importance and the necessity of class struggle.
2. Creation of national culture: National cinema is a vehicle for the exploration of possible avenues for Korean self-expression and for cultural liberation from the West and totalitarian power.
3. Democratic distribution system: National cinema resists Hollywood's dominance in the international market and the government's monopoly and control over film distribution.

4. Freedom from censorship: National cinema fights against all forms of restrictions and censorship by the ruling class.

5. Improvement of labor conditions in filmmaking: National cinema condemns the mainstream film industry for exploiting film crews and violating their rights and welfare. It also promotes the development of alternative styles and strategies of production to counter the attraction of Hollywood films and the mainstream films (Minjok Youngwha Yeonguso, 1989, p. 12–70).

Their tenets give a clear sense of the revolutionary and political aims of Korean national cinema. The NCM's aims require a complete rethinking of film—not only in its form and narrative structure, but also in its means of production and methods of audience outreach.

The films of the National Cinema Movement consist of a mixture of documentary and fiction, and they function as language in action from a position of marginality, operating from both under and outside the industrial sector controlled by mainstream film. The films are related historically and politically to cultural experiences repressed during the military dictatorships. It is clear that they are sites of cultural resistance to the dominant culture in Korea, but these films can also be read as a form of protest that denounces the hegemony of Hollywood. They argue that various social discourses have been neglected or marginalized in mainstream cinema, which employs languages that are awkwardly formulated and artificially styled because they are externally imposed—making it impossible to express social reality in a truthful manner. By creating multiple characters and storylines with no obvious central characters and employing dispassionate camera shots, NCM filmmakers refuse to construct an entertaining storyline based on simplistic causality and the predictable narratives and conventions that such notions encourage. Films of national cinema can be unpleasant and dissatisfying, but their dialectical method of presenting reality helps to demystify Korean society.

Yallasung and Seoul Cine Group sponsored the first NCM film festival, *Jakun Youngwhache* (Festival for Small Cinema), in 1984. A total of six films (both 8 mm and 16 mm), several with antigovernment themes, were shown to a group of college filmmakers. These films have never been shown to the general public, as commercial theaters were afraid of showing them. Instead, only select, small audiences gathered in abandoned buildings, college classrooms, and factories. They have seen films such as: Seoul Cine Group's *We Will Never Lose You* (video, 1987), which depicts the resistance of a student who died during a police torture session; *SangKey Olympic* (video-documentary, 1987), funded by Seoul Catholic Diocese, about poor people who fight against the city of Seoul's face-lifting plan that would abolish their underdeveloped residential area for the 1988 Summer Olympic; and, *Oh,*

Dream Land (16 mm color, 1988), directed by DongHong Jang, the first anti-American film, and one which harshly criticizes the United States for supporting three different military regimes and failing to stop the massacre during the KwangJu Uprising. Much of the initiative for the festival came from *JipDahn* (Collective Group), which produced *Blue Bird* (8 mm, 40 minutes, 1985), a film that depicts the struggles of peasants in their fight against exploitation and local authorities. *JipDahn* was closed and its film stocks seized by the National Security Council (Korea's CIA-like agency) as part of President Chun's assault on trade unions and independent political activity in the mid 1980s.

One film at the festival drew national attention: Jang's *Parup Jeonya* (*The Night before the Strike*, 16 mm color, 1990). *Parup Jeonya* was a powerful indictment of working-class repression; the oppression depicted in the film raised serious doubt about political reform. Yongkwan Lee, a film critic, argues that *Parup* was the perfect example of how a film serves the interests of *Minjoong* (the Korean working people) by addressing issues of labor struggle and historical truth (1990, pp. 191–195).

The class perspective articulated in *Parup* appealed to large audiences and angered the military government, which tried to prevent its showing. On one occasion, 1,800 riot police and several military helicopters raided a theater at JeonNam University to seize a copy of the film (Parup jeonya geeseup, p. 18). Afterwards, students organized a series of street demonstrations to protest the raid, further publicizing the film. Despite the government's unprecedented efforts at suppression, *Parup* was shown to more than 200,000 people within three weeks. Repulsed in its censorship campaign, the government changed tactics. In an attempt to relieve mounting tensions and reestablish public complicity for its rule, the military allowed a docudrama about the KwangJu Uprising to be shown to the public. *Buwhal ui Norae* (*Song of Resurrection*, 35 mm color, 1990), written and directed by Jeong-Kook Rhee and produced with primitive equipment and unknown actors, was the first true national cinema film shown to the general public. Although the tone of *Buwhal* was generally milder than *Parup*, its impact was very important: critics agree that its portrayal of the Uprising was well balanced (Lee, 1990, p. 175).

In addition to NCM's cinematic campaign against the Korean government, filmmakers and students waged political war against the major American film companies over the issue of direct distribution. Hollywood majors have long considered Korea, with a population of some 49 million, to be potentially the largest Asian market outside of Japan, but when United International Pictures (UIP—a London-based, international film distribution company that handles Paramount, Universal, and MGM/UA), opened a Seoul office in 1988 to capitalize on the Korean market, it was met with well-organized protests with anti-American overtones (Arrest, 1990). The most intense action occurred in September 1988 over UIP's first film release in Korea, Paramount's *Fatal Attraction*. Protesters created a range of disturbances from mailing death threats to releasing nonpoisonous snakes in theaters playing *Fatal Attraction* and, in one later case, arson in a theater.

New Narratives and Modes of Production

During the three decades of military dictatorship, the popularity of domestic films among the Korean working class and college students sank to an all-time low, and the industry began to rely on foreign films for its survival. The major incentive for pursuing the best picture award in domestic film festivals, like *Daejong Sang* (Big Bell Award), was that the winning company won importation rights for Hollywood blockbuster films. Because of the impact of severe censorship on every aspect of film production, the industry was unable to explore creative and political possibilities.

National Cinema Movement's function as political and artistic resistance to the dominant culture is especially noteworthy in such a context. While the political function of national cinema is often stressed, its artistic resistance should not be disregarded. The unknown filmmakers of NCM consciously resist, not just the mainstream cinema's mode of production, but even its way of telling stories: rather than adopting the narrative modes of Hollywood's mainstream, NCM filmmakers have turned to Italian neorealism and Latin America's New Cinema and European resistant cinema for viable narrative inspiration. For the National Cinema Movement, the question is not how to *recreate* the cinematographic style of these other cinemas. Rather, these inspirations are transformed in the NCM's process of exploring who "we," the *Minjoong*, are—and of clarifying the socioeconomic and political reality of Korea. Korean National cinema, no less than other resistant cinemas, is a moral stance and attitude toward the control of reality in culture, rather than a set of tropes or conventions.

Early neorealist Korean national cinema employed subjective and unsystematic means of production. Unlike the mainstream cinema, which relies upon the highly structured and hierarchized studio system to generate funds and allocate budgets, there were no visible sources of funding, especially for the early national cinema. Equipment was mostly donated by disparate, local sources or acquired through the black market. Often, amateur actors and crews worked without compensation, even paying for their meals and other expenses at locations. By Hollywood's standards, it is amazing that national cinema films are ever completed. In the filming of *Parup*, for example, actors were largely unknown, and most extras were factory workers. The location, a steel plant, was provided by an anonymous entrepreneur. The $23,000 budget was raised from donations by individuals and groups and was used only for equipment and film development. There were four directors in charge of production. Despite conflicts and clashes of egos, from beginning to end the production process was a collective and democratic one.

The distributors for NCM were no less marginal than the filmmakers: Independence Film Association (IFA), *Jangsangotmae* (the independent company that produced *Parup*), and Labor News Production (LNP). The LNP, the most efficient and systematic in distributing newsreels and other labor related documentaries, worked through branches of the National Labor Movement Association *(Jeonnohyup)*. The IFA was located on the third floor of a small and unlicensed building with no address; their officers were arrested, and their films were confiscated whenever antigovernment demonstrations were held. From shooting through distribution, NCM's mode of production is certainly different from that of the mainstream studio system. In its production, NCM enacts the very ideological struggle that its films depict.

Assimilation and Coexistence with Hollywood

The revolutionary film production practices described above are no longer an option for most filmmakers from NCM. Rather than challenging Hollywood's mode of production, militant films now focus upon expressing "Korean Things" through film by selective rejection or assimilation of Hollywood's storytelling conventions. Thus, filmmakers maintain their critical attitudes in politics, while softening their moral stance on the function of film. Commonly the NCM filmmakers of today agree that a film should be a site for consideration and critique of controversial social and political issues, but they seek a format that is popularly accessible and even entertaining. The struggle for these filmmakers is to locate new film languages capable of expressing the social reality with greater insight and sensitivity. The impact of Hollywood films and Western ideologies on Korean film is, in the final analysis, difficult to measure, yet it is clear that the Hollywood hegemony has framed the national/transnational opposition in Korea. Korean cinema imagines itself both through and against the scripts of Western culture that inform both the way films are made and the stories that they can tell. The melodramatic imagination of Hollywood remains a significant force in Korean social and political thought, fueling the very democratic imagery that supports the resistance to authority and homogenization that identify Korean film as a unique cinematic entity. Thus the uniquely Korean stories that are told in the Korean cinema are inevitably entwined both with the national and global forces that they are designed to challenge. For instance, Korean postnational cinema has shifted its attention to more social and psychological issues than political issues, a trend in keeping with trends in Hollywood film, yet these films often portray actual conditions of life as experienced by a specific segment of the population in a particular situation. Similarly, while it is not uncommon for fictional films in general to build stories around actual places or persons, postnational cinema is distinguished by its position of identification with the people, folk arts, and places it represents. It is not simply *about* ordinary people as characters—the very material of the films emanates from the lives of ordinary people, whether they are represented on film by an actor, or by actual people portraying themselves—providing some mass representation of existing class consciousness and social conditions. The fact that this effort is often tarnished by unnatural interpretations of filmmakers and intellectuals may mitigate, but does not erase, this important difference of contemporary Korean film from the Hollywood mainstream.

Likewise, like their counterparts in the United States, recent feminist directors, scholars, and activists have attempted to challenge the stronghold of patriarchy, including those traditional male intellectuals and filmmakers who have focused on economics and politics to the exclusion of many gender-related social problems. The feminist movement in film has exposed and politicized social and moral issues such as sexual harassment, domestic violence, child abuse, inequality in workplaces, and the role of women in a democratic society. In Korean feminist cinema, Hollywood's influence does not detract from the examination of uniquely Korean events and questions. For example, Young-Joo Byun painfully documented numerous cases of sexual abuse from the Japanese occupation (1910–1945) to the present. *Living as a Woman in Asia* took almost two years to complete due to reluctant interviewees. One featured story is related by a young prostitute who explains that she took on this occupation because only this job could cover hospital costs for her mother, who was a member of the *Jung-Sin Dae,* a system of sexual slavery instituted to service the Japanese soldiers of the occupation during World War II. By focusing on the mother's inability to recover from the emotional and physical scars left by Japanese soldiers and showing the link between the mother's trauma and the daughter's current situation, the documentary condemns both past and present structural and systematic violence against women. In contrast, Kwang-Su Park's fictional *Umukbaemi ui sarang (Love of Umukbaemi,* 1990) also reexamines the expressions of sexuality under a Confucian morality that tolerates male infidelity, as long as the marriage is not threatened.

Finally, a few notable films are discontented with the traditional narrative structure embraced by the mainstream, yet do not easily fit within the paradigm of national cinema. Yoo-Jin Kim's *Keumhong, Keumhong* (1995) is a biographical account of the famous postmodernistic poet, Sang Rhee of 1930s.

The film is named after the poet's mistress and attempts to create a montage that would be absolutely free from formalist poetic structure, rationalist logic, and traditional narrative structure; in doing so, the film attempts to capture in the film experience Sang Rhee's perceptions of his own 32 years of life. Reminiscent of many MTV videos, *Keumhong* and films like it characteristically employ long shots, tracks, and pans following the actors without interruption. This kind of film attempts to avoid foregrounding recognizable and predictable characters and narratives, emphasizing instead the mechanical, perceptual, and conceptual structure that make a film more unpredictable and rich in narrative.

If the consumption of films can be trusted as an indicator, these films speak to the Korean people in increasingly rich and appealing ways: last year, for the first time in the history of Korean film industry, domestic films took 35% of the total box-office revenue (Alford, 2000). Besides a shortage of Hollywood blockbusters and declining popularity of those available, much of the current success is attributed to a crop of new young directors, many of whom studied abroad with unrestricted artistic freedom. Other factors contributing to the current success of Korean films are improved distribution systems and a screen quota system requiring theaters to book domestic films for a minimum of 106 days. Korean films are being recognized and praised by film critics in various international film festivals. Such recognition is being actively sought by the Korean film industry: for instance, MiroVision, a Korean sales agency, aggressively seeks to build a market for Korean cinema abroad through screenings at film festivals (Lee, 1999).

Both in the domestic market and in the global community, Korean films are gaining recognition for their fresh approach to film, and the honesty and vigor of their depiction of the social problems and cultural qualities that make Korea a unique nation and a vital partner in global cultural exchange. Since *Arirang* (1989) and its depiction of working-class conditions in contemporary Korea, films have been able to provide an honest, entertaining, intimate, and important vision of its culture and people. In general the realistic films from the early 1980s did not have what these more escapist films have today: freedom of expression. Films of the '90s—under constant pressure and seduction by a Hollywood-led global culture—have drifted towards themes of individual liberation and peace. Korean cinema has not discovered an artistic expression for national liberation and social equality, but popular impulses of the recent past may yet point the direction.

References

Alford, C. (2000, January 20). Local hits boost Korean biz. *Variety*, p.15.

Arrest of Korean UIP employee sparks old protests. (1990, July 25). *Variety*, p. 62.

Bordwell, D. (1985). *The classical Hollywood film: Film style and mode of production to 1960*. New York: Columbia University Press.

Bordwell, D., & Thompson, K. (2001). *Film art: An introduction*. New York: McGraw-Hill.

Chambers, I., & Curti, L. (1984). A volatile alliance: culture, popular culture, and the Italian. In British Film Institute (Eds.), *Formation of nation and the people* (pp.99–121). London: BFI.

Dissanayake, W. (1993). *Melodrama and Asian cinema*. Cambridge: Cambridge University.

Doherty, T. (1984). Creating a national cinema. *Asian Survey, 24*, 840–51.

Joo, Jinsook. (1990). *Constraints on Korean national film: The intersection of history, politics. and economics in cultural production*. Unpublished dissertation, University of Michigan, Ann Arbor, MI.

Kim, H. K. (1995). Ideology-less college campus. *Monthly Chosun, 21*, 466–472.

Kim, M. W. (1995). The power of Korean cinema. *Monthly Chosun, 21*, 601–607.

Lee, Hanna. (1999, September 10). South Korea sees itself in Miro. *Variety*, p.15.

Lee, Junger. (1992). *Hankook Younghwa ui ihae (Understanding Korean cinema)*. Seoul: Yaeni.

Lee, Jungha. (1992). Reading *Parup Jeonya*. In Center for National Media Study (Eds.), *Minjok Youngwha II (National Cinema II)* (pp. 190–200). Seoul: Chingoo.

Lee, Soonju, (2000). Importation of Japanese films. *Screen* [Korea], *17*, 124.

Lee, Yongkwan. (1990). The current address of National Cinema. In Center for National Cinema (Eds.), *Minjok Youngwha II (National Cinema II)* (pp. 182–189). Seoul: Chingoo.

Lee, Youngil. (1988). *Hankook Youngwha Josa (The history of Korean film)*. Seoul: Motion Picture Promotion Corporation.

Lent, J. A. (1990). *The Asian film industry*. Austin: University of Texas Press.

Minjok Youngwha Yeonguso (Center for National Cinema Study). (1989). *Minjok Youngwha I National Cinema I*. Seoul: Chingoo.

Motion Picture Promotion Corporation. (1984). *A compilation of data on the film industry*. Seoul: MPPC.

Motion Picture Promotion Corporation. (1989). *Korean film annual. 1984–1988*. Seoul: MPPC.

Parup jeonya geeseup (Raid on Parup). (1990, April 18). *Hangyeorae Shinmun*, p. 18.

Pihl, R. M. (1977). Korea in bardic tradition: *P'ansori* as an oral art. *Korean Studies Forum* [Seoul], *1*, 1–105.

Seoul Youngwha Jipdahn (Seoul Cine Group]) (1983). *Saerowoon youngwhauihayeo (For new cinema)*. Seoul: Hakmin Pub.

Standish, I. (1994). Korean cinema and the new realism: Text and context. In W. Dissanayake (Ed.), *Colonialism and nationalism in Asian cinema* (pp. 65–89). Bloomington: Indiana University Press.

Wilson, R. (1994). Melodramas of Korean national identity: From *Mandara* to *Black Republic*. In W. Dissanayake (Ed.), *Colonialism and nationalism in Asian Cinema* (pp. 65–89). Bloomington: Indiana University Press.

PART V

Popular Resistance to
Global Media Hegemony

CHAPTER 14

Responses to Media Globalization in Caribbean Popular Cultures

W. F. Santiago-Valles

Conceptual Framework

Problems investigated in the field of communication involve more than theory and often can be understood only through an examination of social practices. In the Caribbean region, issues in communication go beyond mass media practices to include cultural practices, where workers, peasants, and women, ethnic communities, unemployed, and youth emancipate themselves.

The Caribbean includes the archipelago between the Bahamas, Bermuda, and Tobago as well as Belize and the Guianas. The region includes 28 entities, over one-third still controlled as British, Dutch, French, or U. S. colonies. Over 36 million people share a history of sugarcane plantations, enslavement and indentured servitude, two-thirds of whom speak Spanish, one-fifth are Anglophone, and the rest speak Creole, French, Dutch, or Papiamento. Modern information technologies and means of transportation have not reduced the distance between neighboring islands, whose citizens cannot exchange ideas with those in the next island without some form of metropolitan intervention (Barry, Wood, & Preusch, 1984).

This center-periphery relationship is primarily hegemonic, understood as a consensual relationship between dominant and subordinate classes, including the ideological control of culture made possible by a legitimacy fabricated by the global electronic monopolies of the commercial media (Said, 1993, pp. 291–292). This geopolitical web gives cultural leadership both in the North and South to an elite capitalist minority that sets the political and economic premises for the social order, the obstacles to the resolution of social problems, and the ways of organizing information in predictable ways—while excluding alternative ways of knowing. This is one of the ways in which the dominant gain the active support of the dominated, by getting the latter to subscribe to the meanings that incorporate them into the existing power structures through cultural practices that organize consent.

In the case of the Caribbean a communication approach that looks at popular social practices needs to look at daily activities of self-emancipation, changing both the point of departure and focus to address the conflicts presented at the cultural level. The consequence of this change for communication scholars is to pay less attention to the media and more attention to popular communication practices. That is, communication scholars must pay more attention to the mediators who have historically organized regional opposition both to a mass culture consensus that turned difference into inequality and to cognitive codes inscribed in the newer information technologies (Martin Barbero, 1987, pp. 38–50).

The creation of meaning by "receivers" in communication is a process of collective production suggesting unequal social relations, as the "senders" largely constitute the parameters of meaning. Popular cultures are constituted not through negotiations with domination as proposed in mass media or by particular scholars (e.g., Laclau & Mouffe, 1986; Garcia Canclini, 1995), but through conscious efforts by subordinate working classes to transform the relations of power. The latter includes a critique of the premises validated by the "free market" organization of merchandise production and consumption. Such an acquired understanding of totality, especially the historical connections between the institutions organizing daily life, is part of becoming a historical subject. Hence, subordinate resisters need praxis—understood throughout this chapter as the conscious mediation that connects theory and social actions through critical collective reflection. A praxis process includes verifying that previously excluded causal relations and conflicting interests are presented and analyzed against the grain of the logic proposed by commercial media. The praxis of the popular movements thus informs this critical analysis of media globalization and social class, connecting social history to contemporary relations, including the continued private ownership of unpaid labor generating coercive relations on an international scale now called globalization. From this vantage point, globalization has changed the structure of international exchanges but still depends on the colonial structure within the peripheral societies. A global commercial media system encourages "free choice" consumerism but circumvents democratic participation in and discussions about investment, production, or distribution. For this reason, I examine autonomous conversations that bypass the commercial media, as popular cultures become aware of the need to change the world in order to address the urgencies of the majority.

Practices of self-representation and interpretation are developed by autonomous cultural organizations created, transmitted, and defended by popular movements. The popular representations generated by such practices registered the conditions and oppositions to the organization of work and consumption. Popular movements are themselves organized activities that question the social hierarchy behind the official rules of interpretation, recognition, and participation. The commercial media cannot provide direct experiences and will not present mediated representations that explain economic, cultural, and political relations. In contrast, working from the direct experiences of the dominated, popular social movements critique the existing social order, create awareness of possibilities, and record the rationality of cooperation and solidarity.

Organization, transmission, and storage of information as practiced by the commercial media, on the other hand, assume individual receivers that will interact predictably with popular cultural forms that have been industrially reassembled as merchandise. These exchanges of third party experiences without historical context also carry procedures for thinking (or cognitive codes) that are proposed as the norm (Martin Serrano, 1986, pp. 15–142). When the ruling bloc has imposed standards for thinking and social relations, it is possible to speak of a dominant alliance. If the dominated accept the representation circulated through mass culture as the norm, the dominant alliance has gained cultural leadership (or hegemony)—but only as long as it can prevent exchanges about direct experience of self-emancipating practices.

The global context that currently gives meaning to the processes described above includes changes in transportation and information transmission, making it possible to reorganize investment and relocate industry to the global South. These changes also include the integration of ideas, values, and tastes to organize the worldwide consumption of Northern merchandise, and the elimination of cultural differences. When commercial media and advertising are the only alternative to government-controlled information transmission, profitable entertainment appears—even to the working classes—as more important (or at least more realizable!) than the democratic rights of all citizens.

During the first stage of colonialism in the Caribbean, the commercial newspapers, radio, stage performances, recorded music, film production and distribution presented only the dominant perspective about reality. In the current stage of colonization, television, marketing agencies, cable, and satellite reprise dominant images and ideological frames, emphasizing consumerism in particular. As these enterprises become part of a national context, they generate conflicting economic interests that reduce the nation-state's relevance (Mattelart & Mattelart, 1992, pp. 159–160). But when globalization is applied to culture and communication, the issue is not the forms of interaction on a world scale but the establishment of social limits to the colonization of the public sphere in each nation-state. Under such conditions the concentration of access to information and technologies are a new mode of control that can only be altered within specific nation-states (Mattelart, 1999)

A leap to technology intensive production allows core countries to further concentrate decision-making power, preventing underdeveloped countries (trapped in new production hierarchies) from changing the situation of dependence and colonization within their borders. It should be added here that this course was not democratically chosen nor hegemonically negotiated but established through economic and military intimidation (Mander & Goldsmith, 1997). During the U.S. occupation of Haiti (1915–1934), for example, consolidation of debt and tax collections by expeditionary forces financed their presence; peasants were forced to build the roads used to relocate them within fenced hamlets, the same roads which helped circulate imported goods while hampering local production. The taxes and unpaid work of the dominated throughout the Caribbean still subsidize their containment, while increasingly unregulated international financial and currency trade constrains economic growth to limits set by global structures of accumulation. Such limits in turn require that the repression of mass mobilizations and popular movements be represented as peer controls that reject international perspectives (Dash, 1998, pp. 52–54; Dupuy, 1998, pp. 55–58)—hence, the sporadic rise of nationalist rhetoric by collaborating elites who occasionally feel threatened by their more powerful Northern managers. In each case, a local intermediary cooperates with senior partners in the North while posturing on behalf of all the nation's citizens.

Information technology enters this economic, political, and cultural situation as an organizer of hegemony. Leading capitalist media, both transnational and national, build consensus for the established order, delivering audiences to both advertisers and electoral machines. The junior partners of the global elite in the periphery may have some choice about supporting or rejecting the reorganization of work, but the racialized and marginalized classes of the periphery have to face conditions imposed on them as workers scattered over whole regions and continents.

Centuries ago modern globalization started in the Caribbean with conquest, genocide, colonialism, exploitation, and enslavement, generating a violent network of an expanding world market. The result has been social entities divided by language and political systems, unevenly affected by the recurring creation of an economic region for metropolitan benefit. During the 1980s agricultural production and some manufacture in the Caribbean Basin were tax exempted to neutralize the impact of the revolutions in Nicaragua and Grenada, and the civil war in El Salvador. As Haitian anthropologist M. R. Trouillot has taught us, what is new today is not globalization but a growing awareness of the connections between events around the world among people operating in smaller and more isolated units. The free trade agreements that facilitate the "free flow" of capital, goods, and services in integrated circuits across a single economic space require less sovereign and more complicit nation-states. Consequently, throughout Latin America and the Caribbean, government officials and domestic capitalists have facilitated the rise of *maquilas*—low-wage assembly plants for export in "free trade" zones in partnership with transnational investors from Asia and North America. These creatures of globalization are ineluctably extending the disadvantages of the *maquilas* to workers in the knowledge, telecom, service, banking, and entertainment industries (Pantojas Garcia, 2000, pp. 20–21).

Increasingly *maquiladoras* are also appearing as new enterprise zones within the domestic colonies of the United States—Black, Mexican, and Puerto Rican urban communities, where class is racialized.

Questions

On the basis of the framework presented above, there are three questions about the impact of media globalization on popular cultures in the Caribbean that will be addressed in this chapter. They are questions about social inequalities, practices of resistance, and the ethical norms organizing these practices. The first refers to social inequality, which is manifested in the region both through the racialization of class and exclusion of working women. One aspect of this inequality is the stratification of access to capital and basic staples. Another aspect of social inequality is the use of mass culture as a reaction that commodifies and represses the autonomy of popular cultures. As Gramsci has pointed out, hegemony is organized through the routines of production that govern time and space in the workplace. Under the current conditions of globalization mass culture is used to justify the extension of that industrial logic to the rest of daily life.

The second question addresses cultural practices challenging media hegemony, in particular, those practices that organize how social movements communicate the direct experience of the popular despite the ways of thinking taught by the globalized media. Such praxis processes should give the reader clues about hidden networks of solidarity, where daily responses to domination circulate in recuperated memories, recipes, rumors, humor, song, dance, crafts, and escapes as a new common sense defining and mobilizing the popular. Media globalization, which is the primary source of instruction for working people in the Caribbean, uses an economy of multiple cultures to exclude explanations of social injustice as lived experience. Even when the empires operating in all the territories across the region deny the racialization of class, the vagaries of race and class organize the daily struggles of all Caribbean working people. This conflict over race and class is a totality the popular classes understand from their local challenges to foreign interference with sovereignty and economic democracy.

The third question is about the ethical norms emerging from such conscious cultural practices. Here I am referring not just to the impact of media globalization on these ethical norms but to the redefinition of both the national and regional in the Caribbean to include its diaspora (Torres-Saillant, 1999).

The people of Haiti and the Dominican Republic were the first to achieve political sovereignty in the Caribbean. Most others achieved flag independence after the 1959 Cuban Revolution. Together with Jamaica, Trinidad, and Puerto Rico, these countries have most of the region's inhabitants. All of the islands in the region have operated under a color-coded caste system that still racializes class, marginalizes women and children, and rewards servility. In each case, the centuries-long encounter between Africans, Europeans, Asians, and the indigenous peoples produced a cultural history based on relations of social inequality. Most of the countries in the region have remained sources of raw materials and agricultural products. Tourism, as the new plantation, is the only sector where foreign investment has grown consistently during the last 30 years, making its economic, political, and cultural impact greater than that of sugar. The foreign advertisers, tour operators, airlines and cruise ships, hotels and services repatriate the profits from tourism before they can be redistributed locally. With rare exceptions, what they do leave behind is a caste of black faces with white masks (Fanon, 1967), environmental destruction, economic dependence, depleted water and electric services, racially mixed children, and organized crime.

Under debt-induced reprivatization schemes supported by Caribbean governments and elites, colonial monopolies like telecommunications have come back to thwart economic autonomy and cooperation across the region. The redrawing of this new technological network concentrates the benefits among those international and local capitalist classes that can profit from telecom-based services while reproducing previous colonial relations. Several multinationals such as Digiport International in Jamaica (owned by British Cable and Wireless) or Barbados External Communication (owned by British Cable and Wireless) have established data processing operations with satellite link-ups, but like the imperial railroads before them, these only connect the workplace and the investors (Herman & McChesney,1997, p. 278), establishing relations that control information flow, production, marketing, and consumption. The telephone grids, radio stations, newspapers, movie houses, concert halls, television, cable, satellite, and video outlets have remained concentrated in the hands of white and brown urban elites who exclude popular experiences of the majorities (from Asia and Africa) that could question migration and consumption patterns. Even the foreign cultural industries reassemble popular expressions like son, reggae, calypso, zouk, and soca to return them as world music merchandise deprived of any content that might make tourists uncomfortable. Whether it's the Buena

Vista Social Club, Ziggy Marley, or Kassav', the role assigned to the locals in the Caribbean is to please the tourists without expressing the cultural exchanges among the popular sectors.

Contrasts

The difference between popular democratic social movements and global corporate media on the issues of social inequality, popular cultural practices, and ethical norms is cast in stark relief when the communication strategies of the former are compared with the methods for transmitting information of the latter. The social movements organize interactive, collective efforts of self-representation and interpretation through autonomous organizations, challenging the use of mass culture as advertising to procure audiences. In contrast, satellite connections from Holland, Great Britain, France, Mexico, Brazil, or the United States, cable links such as Telemundo and Univisión out of Miami, and Venevisión from Caracas, Venezuela, consistently broadcast calls to encourage individual consumption of commodities across the Caribbean basin.

The current conditions of partial globalization have particular features that suggest working from the concept of hegemony, as it allows for an examination of the contrasts in communication practices that help organize these dominant-subordinate relations. For instance, across the region, local government and private intermediaries for transnational corporate investors operate in partnerships, reducing the distinctions between private and public sectors. These dependent junior partners (consisting of regional capitalists, managers, and government bureaucrats) are not building national or regional economic institutions; they are helping international finance capital to build segments of transnational cartels against popular and regional interests. In short, the local lieutenants participate in the international redistribution of the division of labor, further impoverishing local working classes and disenfranchising farmers and peasants from their land.

Responses from Popular Cultures

In the periphery, globalization is the latest effort of reenslavement and recolonization within premises for accumulation and appropriation of unpaid work that are centuries old. At present the conditions of exploitation are linked and reproduced through new technologies and knowledge by workers who have recuperated an understanding of the whole production and circulation process. In hegemonic terms, those same information technologies used to

produce consensus also provide opportunities for struggle both over conditions of exploitation and cultural leadership. Such options are enhanced by
recalling social memories of "ruptures" in previous development schemes,
such as negotiating conditions of dependence, servicing the debt by dismantling public services, agribusiness for export, petroleum refineries, ports for
super tankers, pharmaceuticals, or trade and assembly plants under short-
lived tariff exemptions. While in the core countries the capitalist state struggles to provide social benefits to its working classes subsidized by colonial
exploitation, the capitalist state in the periphery guarantees the conditions
required by transnational investors through regional institutions like the
Caribbean Community. Consequently, the periphery is the site where industrial exploitation is presently most intense, and hegemony is most threatened,
as workers, peasants, and small traders struggle against the conditions of
globalization that interfere with the satisfaction of their basic needs
(Sivanandan, 1998–1999, pp. 5–19).

Elites in the Caribbean and other regions in the global South have been
recruited to the hegemonic project of globalization through access to profits
from direct foreign investment, IMF loans, and other global North incentives
not extended to the majority of the working population. Instead of relying on
the organized violence that prevailed in previous periods of military regimes,
transnational corporations have sought out a more efficient means of recruiting the support of the governed. First, to gain acceptance from the working
classes and farmers in dependent societies, global investors have encouraged
their Southern representatives to use the political machinations of elections
and the patronage system, in tandem with greater attention to mass culture,
including: missionaries, schooling, language policy, training scholarships,
commercial media, films, advertising, fast food chains, information technologies, music and fashion industries, sports, Internet access, and tourism
(Sivanandan, 1990, pp. 184–193). Then, concurrent with efforts at persuasion,
limited, quick-strike coercion (funded through advanced weapons sales and
elite military training) is applied as needed through diplomatic pressure,
destabilization campaigns (as in Chile and Jamaica during 1970s), military
and paramilitary death squads (as in El Salvador, Colombia, Guatemala, and
Brazil) or invasions (as in Grenada, Panama, Haiti, Ecuador, and Colombia,
most recently).

It is in these daily struggles over social control and the battles to win
space for the production of noncommercial, socially useful knowledge, where
the impact of media globalization on Caribbean popular cultures becomes
most meaningful. A benchmark of hegemonic success worth considering is
the relative success of the acquiescence produced by dependent governments
and media representing global capital in place of the violence required to keep
those conditions in place when masses of working people refuse to consent.

The limits of that fabricated consent is registered by the number of participants who "opt out" of the relationship by voting with their feet. In the case of the Caribbean, emigration is burgeoning. Indeed, many migrants leave the region only to become a racialized underclass in the developed countries, their presence a constant reminder of what is happening in the colonies, and a catalyst for changes in metropolitan media around issues of language, cultural histories, context, and international solidarities.

Meanwhile, in the Caribbean, international lending agencies have helped global investors regain control of telecommunications, while public media slides increasingly towards private advertisement and imported programming. As a strategic platform for new technologies, the telephone systems are central to the global economy and one of the few comparable denominators in telecommunications across this region. Their privatization represents the direction and result of globalization: the recuperation of foreign control over ostensibly independent states. By the 1960s the systems were publicly owned either by colonial government enterprises or by the newly independent states. Many of these governments such as Jamaica, Barbados, and Trinidad began selling in the 1980s to avoid paying the incurred debt or presumably to gain momentum with access to new technologies. In the mid-80s, the public utility, British Cable and Wireless, was sold off to the private sector, which assumed monopoly control over markets in Anguilla, Bermuda, British Virgin Islands, Caymans, Dominican Republic, Jamaica, Montserrat, St. Lucia, St. Vincent, and the Turks. At the same time two privately owned U.S. companies, International Telephone and Telegraph (ITT) and Continental (CONTEL) held monopoly control in 20 Caribbean locations. During the 1980s, Grenada, Trinidad-Tobago, and Guyana privatized their phone systems. The Bahamas, Barbados, and Jamaica did likewise in 1990s, while U.S. telecom giant AT&T laid fiber optic cable connecting Florida, Puerto Rico, Colombia, Jamaica, and the Dominican Republic. As of 1997, only Aruba, Guadeloupe, Haiti, the Netherlands Antilles, and Surinam maintained public service.

In the mass media of the metropolitan North, these privatizations are hailed as true "reform," evidence of the progressive influence of globalization that brings the latest technology to consumers everywhere. In the Caribbean, meanwhile, popular movements resist the globalization even as the producers of mass consumer culture obstruct collectivity, solidarity, and social memory. In part, the media merchants flood the market with "world music" pieced together from appropriated popular culture forms and with slick, highly stylized cinema and television programming. Officials responsible for "public" education contribute to this media hegemony as well, obstructing possible alternative social visions. In particular, official national histories have excluded the contributions to Caribbean culture and identity by the

Maroons—communities of self-emancipated former slaves who laid siege to the plantations and expressed the cultural autonomy that organized the region's popular imaginary. For decades, Maroons resisted colonialism and capitalism, produced for self-sufficiency, and built a highly efficient and democratic regional information network—contributions unappealing to local elites and potentially disruptive to transnational sales campaigns. Commercial mass culture has also distorted Caribbean history by excluding the nationalist and Black Power movements of the 1930s and 1960s from textbooks, public pronouncements, and other official histories. These recent historical movements within the Dutch, French, English, and Spanish-speaking Caribbean recalled the popular communication strategies of the Maroons (Santiago-Valles, 2000). Significantly, these dual tasks of hegemony—providing cultural leadership while excluding positive alternatives—have multiple agencies: transnational corporations, including media companies (e.g. PanAmSat, Univisión, AT&T) and Caribbean elites, operating through national governments funded by private advertising (e.g. Caribbean Broadcasting Company in Barbados).

Within the capitalist globalization project, as in any hegemonic undertaking, existing social, political, or cultural contradictions encourage challenges to dominant leadership. Throughout the Caribbean, as elsewhere in the global South, subordinate groups have rejected the free market model in favor of their own "counterhegemonic" relations and practices (Brown, 2000; Girvan, 1999). The following two cases provide vivid examples of regional cooperation proposing a globalization from below based on subordinate oral traditions and solidarity through direct experiences and autonomous media.

Red Thread

One example of popular globalization takes place in Guyana, a former British colony that gained formal independence in 1966. Immediately buffeted by international markets and U. S. interference, Guyana struggled to survive. Presiding over the country's socioeconomic collapse, the U. S.-backed Forbes Burnham regime responded to the ascent of a multiracial opposition (1978–1980) with assassinations, beatings, arrests, dismissals, and food shortages. Inspired by the mobilization of housewives, women leaders from the multiracial Working People's Alliance organized a nonaffiliated income generating project in Asian and African communities. In 1985 Red Thread was launched as a women's collective, a nongovernmental organization (NGO) working across race and class, independent of political parties (Andaiye, 2000, pp. 51–98). The initial result was an embroidery project (1987) that had yearly exhibitions, published a newspaper, and held regular skill-training sessions for producers. They met across and through ethnic communities to distribute work materials and make collective decisions about their production.

In the second year, Red Thread turned to education and discussion aimed at raising their collective political and social understanding, drawing on the work of Selma James and the international Wages for Housework campaign. An oral history project led to three booklets by Danuta Radzik: *Etwaria, Rookmin,* and *Indra,* about women working in the sugar industry. These publications were made into a slide show by Karen de Souza who also created, "Eve, a Fragmented Mirror," a slide show about "mad" street women. The Red Thread internal education meetings included classes on the social condition of women, the investigation of cultural history of symbols best suited for their embroidery work, and techniques for encouraging discussions about everyday life. Red Thread then began an exchange program with Sistren, a theater collective of working-class women from Jamaica, to learn methods of popular education and to research traditional embroidery patterns.

During the third year they implemented what they had learned with Sistren, establishing education, embroidery production, and leadership teams to improve the skills of all the membership. With inconsistent support from Canada, Red Thread began to produce workbooks for public schools. In 1989 they produced a book launch for the presentation of Nesha Haniff's *Blaze a Fire,* a collection of stories about women, and enacted one of the stories as a skit during an exhibition of women's work.

In 1990 Red Thread began producing inexpensive public school textbooks for which there was a ready market with parent, teacher, and school principal support. That year Red Thread organized an academic seminar on women and development, sponsored a health workshop, opened a laundry, started a feeding program, and sent a delegation to train with Sistren in Jamaica. By 1993 Red Thread had a printing press, a research team, an education team, and broadcast a radio serial called "Everybody's Business," which was prepared for a campaign against domestic violence. Initially transmitted on radio, "Everybody's Business" later became a stage play. Throughout this process the women's organization made a conscious effort to combine training and experience, so their own members could imagine, construct, and maintain conscious self-sufficiency.

Since 1994 Red Thread has worked with indigenous women in the interior and with coastal women beginning small businesses. Democratizing the access to resources within regional and national solidarity networks, disseminating local stories of daily responses to domination in the oral tradition, and putting the members in touch with information that could help them make informed choices exemplified an ethic of self-emancipation emerging from the practices of popular cultures.

Red Thread provides us with a popular culture example of social movements as protagonists of their own stories taking the initiative against global media (Andayie, 2000). As an exemplar of developing organized consciousness, Red Thread has contributed to a popular, working-class hegemony, offering a popular site of participatory democracy while providing significant material resources to popular classes and multiple ethnic groups. Red Thread valorizes the work of housewives, diversifies allegiance to political parties and women's organizations, foregrounds class contradictions, and works across racial communities and national boundaries. In addition to work with indigenous peoples, their press and education team also promotes research on health and women's labor. In short, Red Thread signals a trajectory for the globalization of democratic communication, class solidarity, and social justice.

SPEAR in Belize

The Society for the Promotion of Education and Research (SPEAR) in Belize provides another striking example of the possibilities for a new, popular hegemony for the Caribbean (Vernon, 2000, pp. 1–50). Founded in 1969, SPEAR has a diverse membership, including peasants, workers, and Black Power advocates, as well as university graduates returned from Europe and North America, human rights workers, leftist activists, bookstore owners, and the occasional elected politician *(www.spear.org.be)*.

Like many other territories in the Caribbean, Belize—which became independent in 1981—is a small country trying to forge a nation out of underdevelopment, and ethnic, racial and class divisions. Mestizos, primarily Spanish-speaking laborers from other countries in Central America, comprise 43% of the population. The indigenous peoples of the region, the Mayas, make up some 11% and are struggling to get back their land stolen by British colonialists. East and South Asians immigrants of the 1990s have prospered in the restaurant and retail trade, establishing significant land holdings. IMF-inspired privatization and "rationalization" of the economy has led to a thriving foreign-owned tourism industry, providing little domestic employment, while the free market dictated less agricultural production and export with more unemployment (15% in 1996). Facing entrenched poverty and continuing racism, Black Creoles and Garifunas (Maroons deported from St. Vincent in 1795) have been leaving Belize en masse, their populations dropping by a third in the last decades, to 29%, and 7%, respectively—a striking signal of the social consequences of globalization. Economic growth has remained stalled in Belize, and government-mandated austerity measures of the last decade have reduced social spending, increasing the hardships for the majority, especially for a growing sector of new poor among unemployed youth and women.

Originally a research and education adjunct to the social movements of the 1960s, SPEAR expanded its activities in response to this new reality. Since 1984 the group has done advocacy work for economic development, social justice, and participatory democracy, while supporting popular praxis efforts among workers, women, peasant communities, and youth.

Between 1994 and 1995 SPEAR produced a weekly radio and television talk show called "Spear on Target" where nongovernmental organizations could explore issues of mutual concern. This first show was transmitted by the national broadcasting corporation and by a private cable company. SPEAR is now producing a second radio show called "In Your Face" transmitted from a low-power FM station and on a larger AM station. SPEAR has also produced documentaries such as "Belize Faces the Future," "The Women Worker's Union," and "Democracy in Belize," championing the perspectives of women, labor unions, and democracy for the nation's future. SPEAR continues to sponsor policy conferences and publish research on Belize. In addition to establishing a new computerized data center, it provides consulting, organizes debates on national issues (such as the status of civil society), and sustains long-term advocacy campaigns on those issues. Perhaps most importantly, SPEAR has provided leadership for groups of workers, women, youth, and rural communities, whose self-empowerment emerges through participatory action methods. As with Red Thread, SPEAR's efforts exemplify the Maroon ethic of self-emancipation that engaged the state, in this case through mobilizations addressing the consequences of globalization and growing poverty (Vernon, 2000).

Competing with these popular, democratic communication models, and tapping into greater resources, transnational media corporations (and their local class representatives) have raised cultural cooptation to an art form. The manipulation of music from the Caribbean by multinational record cartels is a case in point. Whether it's Massucci at Fania Records in New York or Blackwell at Island Records in London, the decision to determine how a cultural text will be represented globally still rests with the economic powers. In a process refined by North American record labels that turn rap and hip-hop into gangster performances or protest theatrics, global media professionals reformulate cultural creations from the Caribbean (including systemic critiques!) into crossover merchandise, disseminated as leisure entertainment for the international middle-class consumer. Bertelsmann, Time Warner, and others use the profits generated by the creativity of the popular to recruit and subsequently market a handful of individual creative artists. Seduced by the illusion (and occasionally reality) of greater access and creative control turns many cultural critics of globalization into world music icons, but invariably, once in the recording studios of the cultural industries, incisive analysis disappears into exoticized entertainment, reinforcing the hegemonic rules of

North-South relations. Caribbean contributions to the "world beat" thus represent the commercialized international order as natural and permanent. The crossover trajectories of Ruben Blades and Bob Marley, going from social critique to love ballads, from dance hall back to cultural analysis illustrate this only too well (Alleyne, 1994).

Conclusions

Media globalization extracts profit from consumers who also purchase their assigned incorporation into the present order, an order that needs to disguise the links between mass culture and domination. Throughout the Caribbean and the rest of the South, nation-state alternatives within the current international hegemony are limited to tourism, the export of labor in exchange for remittances, and drug trafficking (Girvan, 1999). The only "counterhegemony" that offers hope for a human-centered future has emerged from those working-class and popular movements like Red Thread and SPEAR. Their examples, and dozens of others around the world (Burbach, Nuñez, & Kagarlitsky, 1997; Brecher, Costello & Smith, 2000; Hutton & Giddens, 2000), indicate that confronting media globalization in the Caribbean depends on strengthening the network of national and regional exchanges between popular movements from the Bahamas to Surinam. This effort also requires crafting inclusive meanings with layered registers, connecting collective memories to possibilities based on shared experiences. As the inventory of popular practices evolves we will have better exemplars of dialogic communication, of conversations that create opportunities for participation without the results becoming merchandise.

From the perspective of popular cultures, media globalization is a means of concentrating hegemony that recontextualizes debates over the dependent public sector's role in media and cultural policy. Theoretically the new technologies make it easier for international exchanges of crafted representations to overcome a rigid stratification of consumption by class, color, or gender. Nevertheless when the crafted representations are turned into merchandise by cultural industries, it is mostly the brown and tan elites who can purchase these goods.

What then have popular cultures from the Caribbean done with media globalization? After centuries of forced migration and exile they continue to organize transgressive associations that cooperate in recreating reciprocal loyalties that replace what was lost. As I have tried to illustrate here, the local communication networks of popular movements are a territory where meaning is extracted from direct experience and where cultural leadership is exercised (Garcia Canclini, 1995, pp. 30–33, 113–127). Recuperating the memories of communication strategies used in the self-emancipation of those who abolished slavery, the conscious organization of collective leadership produced a popular common sense that challenged global media's hegemony. The oral traditions of cooperation, collaboration, and coparticipation are reassembled, defended, and transmitted by the popular from one generation to the next through daily practices of reciprocity the commercial media tries to prevent.

Historical subjects are made up of groups of individuals, committed to serving one another, who recognize they cannot think alone. They communicate because they participate together in making the connections between the parts of the content considered (Freire, 2000, pp. 137–138). As communities of method, their interactions with globalized mass culture are a constant process of going beyond predictable practices and traditions (turned against them as merchandise) to select, reassemble, and translate layered metaphors that will help name injustice and freedom today (Hall, 1997, pp. 25–33). Moreover, as Red Thread and SPEAR have discovered, the decoding of texts must be a collective, political project, not simply a pastime for individual pleasure. Significantly, as a counter to corporate globalization, the latest technologies allow popular cultures to maintain contact with overseas or transoceanic communities of refugees, exiles, and migrants that help each other construct a sense of the world as an interconnected whole that needs much rearranging (Mutabaruka, 1994). The next step is for knowledge workers in the Caribbean diaspora to join other communities of resistance in confronting globalization as it presents itself in the cultural sphere. Even as it spreads, globalization prepares its own resistance.

References

Alleyne, M. (1994). Positive vibration?: Capitalist textual hegemony and Bob Marley. *Caribbean Studies, 27,* 224–241.

Andaiye. (2000). The Red Thread story. In S. F. Brown, (Ed.), *Spitting in the wind. Lessons in empowerment from the Caribbean* (pp. 51–97). Kingston: Ian Randle.

Barry, T., Wood, B., & Preusch, D. (1984). *The other side of paradise: Foreign control in the Caribbean,* NY: Grove.

Brecher, J., Costello, T., & Smith, B. (2000). *Globalization from below: The power of solidarity.* Boston: South End Press.

Brown, S. F. (Ed.). (2000). *Spitting in the wind: Lessons in empowerment from the Caribbean.* Kingston: Ian Randle.

Burbach, R., Nunez, O., & Kagarlitsky, B. (1997) *Globalization and its discontents: The rise of postmodern socialisms.* Chicago: Pluto Press.

Dash, R. C. (1998). Globalization. For whom and for what. *Latin American Perspectives, 103,* 52–54.

Dupuy, A. (1998). Thoughts on globalization, Marxism and the left. *Latin American Perspectives, 103*, 55–58.

Fanon, F. (1967). *Black skin, white masks. The experiences of a black man in a white world.* New York: Grove.

Freire, P. (2000). *Pedagogy of oppressed.* (R. R. Barr, Trans.) New York: Continuum. (Original work published in 1970.)

Garcia Canclini, N. (1995). *Consumidores y ciudadanos: Conflictos multiculturales de globalizacion [Consumers and citizens: Multicultural conflicts of globalization].* Mexico: Grijalbo.

Girvan, N. (1999, January). *Globalization, fragmentation and integration: A Caribbean perspective.* Unpublished manuscript presented at International Meeting on Globalization and Development in Havana, Cuba.

Hall, S. (1997). Caribbean culture: Future trends. *Caribbean Quarterly, 43*, 25–33.

Herman, E., & McChesney, R. (1997). *The global media: The new missionaries of global capitalism.* London: Cassell.

Hutton, W., & Giddens, A. (2000). *Global capitalism.* New York: New Press.

Laclau, E., & Mouffe, C. (1985). *Hegemony and socialist strategy: Towards a radical democratic politics.* London: Verso.

Mander, J., & Goldsmith, E. (Eds.). (1997). *The case against the global economy (and for a turn toward the local).* San Francisco, CA: Sierra Club.

Martin Barbero, J. (1987). Comunicacion, pueblo y cultura en el tiempo de las transnacionales [Communication, the people and culture in the time of the transnationals]. In FELAFACS (Eds.), *Comunicacion y culturas populares en Latinoamerica* (pp. 38–50). Mexico, D.F.: Gustavo Gili.

Martin Serrano, M. (1986). *La produccion social de comunicacion [The social production of communcation].* Madrid: Alianza Editorial.

Mattelart, A. (1999, February). Against global inevitability: Key issues in global communication. *World Association for Christian Communication.* [on-line]. Available at *http://www.oneworld.org.*

Mattelart, M., & Mattelart, A. (1992). *Rethinking media theory.* Minneapolis: University of Minnesota Press.

Mutabaruka. (1994). Lamentation. *Melanin man* (45013). Kingston: Shanachie. CD universal bar code # 016351451323.

Pantojas Garcia, E. (2000, August). El Caribe insular en el nuevo orden economico global [The insular Caribbean in the new global economic order]. *Dialogo* (Puerto Rico), pp.20–21.

Said, E. (1993). *Culture and imperialism.* New York: Knopf.

Santiago-Valles, W.F. (2000). The Caribbean intellectual tradition that produced James and Rodney. *Race and Class, 42*, 47–66.

Schlesinger, P., & Morris, N. (1997). Cultural boundaries: Identity and communication in Latin America. *Media Development, 1.* [on-line]. Available at: *http://www.oneworld.org.*

Sivanandan, A. (1990). *Communities of resistance.* London: Verso.

Sivanandan, A. (1997). Heresies and prophecies: the social and political fallout of the technological revolution. In J. Davis, T. Hirschl, & M. Stack (Eds.), *Cutting edge: Technology, information, capitalism and social revolution* (pp.287–296). London: Verso.

Sivanandan, A. (1998–1999). Globalism and the left. *Race & Class, 40,* 5–19.

Stalker, P. (2000). *Workers without frontiers: The impact of globalization on international migration.* Boulder, CO: Lynne Reinner.

Torres-Saillant, S. (1999). *El retorno de las yolas: Ensayos sobre diaspora, democracia y Dominicanidad [The return of the sailboats: Essays on diaspora, democracy and Dominican Identity].* Santo Domingo: Libreria Trinitaria y Ediciones Manati.

Vernon, D. (2000). Spear on target? Lessons in empowerment from the Society for the Promotion of Education and Research. In S. F. Brown (Ed.), *Spitting in the wind. Lessons in empowerment from the Caribbean* (pp. 3–50). Kingston: Ian Randle.

CHAPTER 15

Radical Media and Globalization

John Downing

Radical media can be defined as small-scale, low-budget, oppositional, and horizontal media, typically related to social and political movements, sometimes ephemeral, sometimes not. Technologically they may take a huge variety of forms, from the nontechnological or virtually nontechnological such as dance (in which the human body is the instrument of communication), or graffiti, or political jokes and satire passed along social networks, all the way through to daily newspapers, Web sites, alternative video projects, and low-power radio.

Historically and internationally, radical media have been very frequent. From the fliers of revolutionary America in the 1770s to the audiocassette tapes of Ayatollah Khomeini's incendiary sermons in the 1970s, from the AIDS awareness videos of the '80s and '90s to Latin American *nueva canción* of the 60s and 70s, from the antislavery books and newspapers of the 1830s through the Civil War to underground *samizdat* publications and tapes in the USSR in the '70s and '80s, they constitute a pervasive and remarkable phenomenon whose political and cultural significance has nonetheless typically been sneered at.

Let us briefly note two further examples of such independent media: one from the Philippines and the other from the 1995 Million Man March of African Americans.

The Philippines example concerns the use of short-message servicing (SMS) on cellular telephones and computer Web sites to galvanize very rapid resistance to the Philippines Senate decision not to pursue an enquiry into corruption charges against then President Estrada. The protests lasted a full four days and concluded with his downfall. Coronel (2001) describes how "with lightning speed . . . SMS was used to coordinate the protests, keep protestors abreast of events as they unfolded, and to mobilize citizens to march, bring food and to keep vigil" (p. 110). Text messages sent through cell phones are hard to trace. She also notes how SMS had been used over the previous four months during which the president's shady financial activities were under review, in order to mobilize for meetings, exchange political jokes, and alert the public to attempts to subvert the impeachment process. In addition to this there were up to 200 anti-Estrada Web sites and some 100 oppositional e-mail groups. Only once this alternative media movement was in full swing did the mainstream media get on the bandwagon, with television eventually broadcasting the impeachment trial live.

The Million Man March may or may not have numbered a full million—the police estimate was 400,000, but such estimates are notoriously untrustworthy. It certainly was the largest demonstration ever by African Americans in U.S. history. It was also very far from being the creature of Nation of Islam Minister Farrakhan, despite the standard mainstream media gloss to that effect. It was denounced and despised and held up as a reason for fear by a media barrage for weeks and even months before it took place. Indeed, on the face of it, it should not have happened at all, but it did, and considerable credit goes to the *The Final Call,* the Nation of Islam's newspaper, and its distributors who were largely invisible to people outside black neighborhoods, and who had been tirelessly and patiently mobilizing for many months beforehand. It is a remarkable example of the failure of visible corporate media and the power of invisible independent ones.

Cataloguing radical media, even in the United States, would take forever, but I would like to underscore their common appearance in these United States, past and present, and also their tremendous variety. I do not automatically endorse, nor would it be conceivable for any one person to do so, what all these media stand for. I am not proposing that we become Manichean, so that every radical media David is a knight in shining armor, or indeed that every media Goliath is a double-eyed monster. I am not only amused by Rupert Murdoch's "The Simpsons" and AOL/TimeWarner/Viacom's "South Park," but often find they skewer our political idiocies more tellingly than certain woodenly worded progressive media. And while, for example, Ayatollah Khomeini's sermons' attacks on the Shah of Iran and his circles, and on the Shah's American and Soviet and Chinese backers, carried some validity, the regime he ushered in that replaced the Shah's contrived, as we know, to be as repressive and reactionary as the one it replaced.

My point is a very simple one. Discounting the potential power of radical media, neglecting their pervasiveness, bypassing the critical question of their links with social and political movements, are acts of analytical folly. We are often overly obsessed with size and statistics. Only AOL/TimeWarner and Sony, only media whose reach can be estimated by Arbitron and Nielsen, seem significant.

Indeed, some small-scale media perhaps overemphasize the importance of visibility and the dramatic in radical media impact: Abolition, AIDS, the American Revolution. The case studies in some very recent books on radical media, Clemencia Rodríguez's (2001) *Fissures In The Mediascape* and Alfonso

Gumucio Dagron's (2001) *Making Waves,* are especially important in that they yank our attention away from the dramatic and on to the significance of the humdrum. Rodríguez's preferred term is "citizens' media" and through a feminist lens she examines, for instance, the way in which Colombian women in a poor Bogotá barrio developed a significantly fresh sense of self-worth and self-assertiveness through participating in making videos about their neighborhood. Dagron assembles no fewer than 50 case stories of ultra-low-budget participatory media and their role in development, from the Philippines and Uganda to Vanuatu and Honduras. There is certainly real drama in those stories, but not flashy headline drama.

Globalization, unlike radical media, suffers from a surfeit of meanings. For some, such as sociologist Roland Robertson (1992), it signifies a compressed world, where restrictions of space apply less and less. For others, the danger of a homogenized world (Wallerstein, 1991). For others, more specifically, an Americanized or at least Westernized world (Schiller, 1991). For others, a culturally hybridized world (Mattelart, 1994; Straubhaar, 1991). For others again, a world that serves as playground for rapacious and arrogant transnational corporations with immense influence over international trade and regulatory bodies such as the World Trade Organization, the International Monetary Fund, and the upcoming Free Trade Association of the Americas (Martin & Schulmann, 1997). For yet others, globalization principally signifies modernity (Tomlinson, 1991) or postmodernity (Appadurai, 1996). For sociologist and geographer Manuel Castells (1996) it appears to be the rather insubstantial and mysterious space of flows. For sociologist Ulrich Beck (2000) it signifies the growth of a global risk society, where ecological, financial, and labor market insecurities are global in character and reach. Thus the meanings assigned to the term globalization vary widely, from the threatening to the merely observational to the speculative.

For us, as researchers specializing in mediatic and cultural issues, it is the *linkages* between economic, political, and cultural dimensions of the globalization phenomenon that must take pride of place. But that requires that we specify what those linkages are. Here then is my attempt to do so.

I propose that indeed the primary economic dimension of globalization is the ever-increasing ascendancy of transnational corporations operating in a supranational marketplace, a marketplace that offers no rules or stability beyond those crafted in fora such as the World Trade Organization and the International Monetary Fund and the European Union. These rules quite frequently are out of synch with each other, given their framing by different supranational organizations, but aside from that extra irrationality, what most often characterizes them is their authoritarian bent. As Beck (2000) has observed, if the European Union itself were to apply to join the European Union as constituted, which has the requirement that a member country's form of government be democratically constituted, its application would have to be rejected (p. 19). Why? On the grounds of its patently undemocratic mode of operation in Brussels, the seat of the European Commission, which is only in the most tangential manner influenced by the toothless European Parliament, sitting in Strasbourg.

Defenders of these bodies, especially of the World Trade Organization and the World Bank, will throw up their hands in holy horror at the thought that their sacred mission to open the world to freer exchange of goods across frontiers and to dissolve the rigidities of states' regulation of their economies, might be accused of a new global authoritarianism. Despite their veneer of serene hauteur and intellectual superiority towards antiglobalization demonstrators, underneath they are impassioned market-forces fundamentalists, fiery fetishists of commodity rule—just so long as the rules within which the holy miracles of trade take place are congenial to the practical priorities of transnational corporations.

Free trade between equals has everything to be said for it. But where are these mythical equals? In actual practice the giants that dominate logging, pharmaceuticals, agribusiness, oil, telecommunications, weapons, aerospace, news, minerals, culture, financial products, crime, jostle each other's elbows in a crazed global gallop, not, of course, without needed assistance from local elites. Congo, ever since Patrice Lumumba's short-lived and tragic attempt to free his country and Africa from this gallop (Peck, 2001) constitutes a graphic case study in the realities of the process: a huge nation reduced to being bled dry by its U.S.-supported dictator during the cold war, and now bled dry by mining corporations and their local lieutenants.

One current result of this inspired gallop is that the wealthiest 20% of humans today consume on average six times more food, energy, water, transport, oil, and minerals than did their own parents, and the poorest 20% have no access to safe drinking water. What a staggering achievement! What magnificent productivity gains . . .

On the political level, we constantly hear in this context of the decline of the nation-state as a correlate of globalization. This claim reveals singularly sloppy thinking. The majority of the world's nation-states came into effective operation since the decolonization of Korea and the Philippines in 1945. Many of them are tiny, either in population or size or economy, or all three. They began their modern existence as political organisms, for the most part, under the continuing and energetic tutelage of the British and the French. The nation-states of Latin America, formally independent considerably longer, are still struggling to assert themselves against Uncle Sam, just as the new post-Soviet nation-states are struggling to assert themselves against the successors of Uncle Joe. The minor nation-states of the European Union are frequently at loggerheads with the "big three," Germany, France, Britain.

So when we talk of the decline of "the" nation-state, we homogenize ridiculously, implying that decline in German or Japanese or Canadian state autonomy vis-à-vis transnational corporations is mirrored by Mali's or Mauritania's. It is a characteristically G8 or OECD lens. It is exemplified in some U.S. commentary that after 9/11 "the" world will never be the same again, implying that the degree of security U.S. citizens took for granted up until that date was mirrored around the globe. If only it had been. The rude good health of the global arms trade certainly indicates that the repressive function of states has lost little of its energy, since they are the prime buyers.

At the same time, it is reasonable to acknowledge as one vector in globalization the gradually declining autonomy of a number of the OECD nation-states vis-à-vis transnational corporations, though the United States still drags way back in the rear of that decline, due to its economic and military weight. The German and Japanese states, despite the recent economic downturn in both nations, still carry tremendous clout.

Assuming then that the map so far drawn of globalization's economic and political realities will stand up to scrutiny, what is to be said of the cultural dimension?

Australian cultural commentator and media theorist MacKenzie Wark (1994) has proposed that in the globalized era "we no longer have roots, we have aerials" (p. x). This will serve as a concentrated statement of a frequent assertion, namely that the local and the specific in culture are disappearing and are being replaced by transnational cultural processes. Or if not by some global cultural fusion, then by multiple hybrid interchanges. One way or another, whether as Americanization or as postmodernity, massive cultural change is argued to be in full spate, and to be descending upon us, quite outside our or perhaps anyone's control, and regardless of our wishes.

Well, there are real issues here: Chilean writer Joaquín José Brünner (1998) cites figures showing that in 2100 perhaps only 600 of the world's 6,200 languages currently spoken, will still be spoken (p. 81). If that will not be a major cultural change, what will? At the same time, much of the debate about globalization and cultural change is inevitably an exercise in speculation about a process whose term has nowhere nearly come to closure, whether in assertions of shifts to a therapeutic culture (Cloud, 1998), a narcissistic culture (Lasch, 1978), a 100% commodity culture, a secular culture, or simply an American culture.

In principle for me, the messier the cultural vision projected, the more plausible I am likely to find it, and the more elegantly clean-cut, the less so. I am fond of the word "glocalization" (Robertson, 1992) for example, and particularly relish the Brazilian literary and cultural theory of *antropofagismo*, or cannibalism (Stam, 1997). Let me explain. The great Brazilian artist Caetano Veloso tells the story of how an indigenous group in the early days of

Portuguese colonization captured and devoured a certain Portuguese cleric, Bishop Sardinha. Veloso suggests that in some sense this event can stand as a metaphor for Brazilians' construction of a new culture composed of mutually consuming a variety of other cultures. It is to a degree an idealistic theory, as the struggles for black and indigenous self-assertion in Brazil show only too clearly. Nonetheless, it suggests a degree of cultural resilience attested by the extraordinary vitality of Afro-Brazilian and African-American music and their huge impact in daily culture. Popular music has quite frequently served as a major vehicle for subverting official culture (Zuberi, 2001).

What I wish to focus on for the remainder of this chapter is the potential of radical media inside the globalization process to protect and promote intensive dialogue in order in turn to develop what some writers have termed "globalization from below" (Brecher, Costello, & Smith, 2000). In order to focus attention on this, I plan to discuss, rather briefly, three case-studies: the emergence over the past two years of Independent Media Centers; the French monthly *Le Monde Diplomatique,* now available in multilingual editions; and the communication strategies of the Zapatista movement.

Independent Media Centers now number about 50 around the globe, most of them currently in the United States, Canada, and Western Europe, but with a presence in Latin America, Australia, and a few other places (Raboy, 2001). The first IMC is located in Seattle and originated before and during the anti-WTO protests there not quite two years ago now. Since then, many IMCs owe their origin to one or other meeting of an international array of policy-makers and corporate leaders: the Windsor, Ontario, IMC to a meeting of the Organization of American States there in June 2000, the Québec City IMC to the founding meeting of the Free Trade Association of the Americas in April this year, the Washington, D.C., IMC to a World Bank meeting, the Los Angeles IMC to the Democratic Party's presidential nomination convention, and so on. After the particular contestation is over, the IMC continues in operation as a radical communication node.

What does an IMC look like, and why may it matter? I am not writing, I should stress, as an official propagandist for IMCs in the plural or the singular, and they might turn out to be a passing phenomenon. Yet even if passing, they are of great interest in the annals of radical media, and with regard to the possibilities for developing a globalization from below. Different IMCs take different forms, have different levels of involvement and financing, and obviously relate in particular ways to their localities and countries. If we wanted, though, a generic statement as to their characteristics, I would propose something like the following. They consist of a knot of media activists who define their role in relation to the initial contestation and demonstrations as facilitators of prior planning and debate before the clash, via e-mail and Web sites. At the time of the confrontation, they provide a space, maybe rented, maybe donated, in which media activists may foregather, may stream to remote locations for audio and video and stills they have captured on the streets, be they of interviews with activists or of police assaults. In this space other kinds of media activists—graffiti artists, muralists, puppeteers, street theatre activists—may assemble and connect up their activities if they wish. Video and audio footage may then be edited into documentaries, such as "Showdown In Seattle" or "This Is What Democracy Looks Like." The media work may be done by existing groups such as Paper Tiger TV and the Dish Network's Free Speech TV (www.freespeechtv.com), or by individuals.

The result is that working people have *their* multiple correspondents honeycombing the streets and recording the events, rather than having to rely upon mainstream media correspondents safely ensconced behind police lines or swooping overhead in a helicopter. And while the images we assemble are highly unlikely to hit network news, there are other channels of distribution, much slower but much more reliable, which can get these images out, such as colleges, libraries, church groups, solidarity groups, film/video clubs. Still photojournalism images alone can have an extraordinary visual impact on a computer screen, and within affluent nations are cheaply and easily accessible to a great number of people.

However, the contestation itself is simply the crystallizing point. It is not the close of the saga. Afterwards, using digital platforms and Web sites, it is possible for the IMC to establish ongoing links with all the others across the planet, with the numerous hyperlinks they in turn carry. The glocalization of information generated by the public, rather than corporate sources, becomes a reality. I don't mean by this that at last we have discovered the Holy Grail of objectivity journalism theorists have claimed and dreamed and never discovered. I do mean that other voices are able to become much more available, that the virtual monopoly of megacorporations in the news business is less intact than it was. And that rather than dismissing these projects loftily, we might do well to recall all those messy little newspapers and fliers that circulated at the time of the American Revolution. How laughably pathetic they were at the time, how irrelevant to *real* politics!

Another major function of IMCs is to foster political memory and ongoing debate about political strategies in relation to transnational corporations. There are numerous think tanks and foundations that serve this purpose for the corporate sector—or at least set out to serve this purpose. For the public at large, such fora are distinctly rare, and our memory of political engagements consequently threadbare. Yet the Web sites of these IMCs frequently contain ongoing archived materials of what happened at particular confrontations, and discussions of lessons to be learned, paths to be avoided. This is invaluable.

My other two examples I will address more briefly. The monthly *Le Monde Diplomatique*, which we might better render in view of its actual contents as *International Politics* rather than as literally "Diplomatic World," is a progressive analogue to the journals *Foreign Affairs* and *Foreign Policy*. It began as an offshoot of the French daily newspaper of record, *Le Monde,* and as of October 2001 was at its 571st monthly issue, in its 48th year of publication. It is now a totally separate and independent publication. It also appears today in English, Spanish, Italian, German, Arabic, Greek, and Portuguese editions. It has the format of a large newspaper, but with articles of typically between one and four pages, often carrying footnotes referencing important sources whose existence would frequently be otherwise unknown to readers outside the nation under discussion.

Its October 2001 issue, for example, had articles on the following topics: analysis of 9/11 (seven pages on the events, their aftermath, their ramifications globally); the Durban antiracism conference; democratic developments in Africa; Tunisia's current conjuncture; Macedonia and the dangers of new partitions in the Balkans; guerrilla war in Colombia; the Levi Strauss corporation's treatment of its women workers; Italy since the Genoa demonstrations; *manga* cartoons and *anime* animation in contemporary Japanese culture and politics; Daniel Barenboim breaks the Israeli taboo against playing Wagner; local citizens' initiatives in Europe in taking over disused factory and office space for community activities.

This publication is far too little known in English-speaking countries, yet is now available in English via airmail as an extra subscription to *The Guardian Weekly*—and an Internet version is available *(www.monde-diplomatique.fr)*. The English edition is also now available on the Internet for $US24 a year, and indeed some articles and a summary of others are available free to check out. I mention this not only as an interesting instance of a long-running radical international news analysis service. In recent years it has also developed activist readers' groups in many localities. As of late 2001, 175 such groups existed, 103 in Africa and the Middle East, 31 in Latin America, 33 in Eastern Europe and the former Soviet Union, and 8 in Asia. Not one, not a single one, in North America outside of Mexico.

This is one way to keep abreast of world events with the benefit of a large slew of highly intelligent correspondents, mostly from the nations under discussion. Only a minority of the correspondents are French, and that minority consists of highly experienced international specialists who analyze events and their background in some detail. One way Americans and Canadians could develop activist networks and know they belong to a worldwide network of concerned citizens, would be to form *"Diplo"* reading groups in our localities. *"Diplo,"* as it is often abbreviated, is designed for informed citizens who crave more information and are mesmerized by the gigantic news spin that appears to attend every major crisis. The further formation of activist readers' groups gives some chance of battling successfully against our anxiety that we are the only people around who are dazed and dismayed at the turns and twists of the contemporary global scene. And hopefully of organizing to engage locally with issues that demand attention.

My final example is that of an indigenous people's radical media use, namely the Zapatistas' use of the Internet, an example right here in North America of alternative media production of a very effective kind. Briefly, for those uninformed of this story, a number of Internet activists worked very energetically to ensure that the Zapatista movement, almost invisible outside the mountains and jungles of the State of Chiapas, was able to communicate with the outside world and to generate political solidarity with its struggle. The movement was also able to challenge a variety of international issues as well, especially the creation of the North American Free Trade Agreement, but also other aspects of corporate globalization. Some concluded that the Zapatistas had miraculous electronic links with the rest of the world, but it is necessary to recognize that the "first yard"—or rather, the first multiple kilometers—in getting these messages out were often by foot and then telephone or fax or e-mail from an urban center such as San Cristóbal de las Casas, and from there to the world at large. Indeed many Zapatistas did not speak Spanish, let alone English or French. On one occasion it is clear that the Mexican Army was actually pulled back from a major imminent search-and-destroy mission by warnings posted internationally on the Internet that the action was about to launch.

A number of people have written on this subject, among them Tamara Villarreal Ford and Genève Gil (2001), and also Adrienne Russell (2001) in the newest issue of the quarterly media studies journal *Gazette*. Their summaries of this radical media story are worth noting. Ford and Gil write:

> the alternative media machine facilitating global awareness of indigenous struggles in the Lacandón jungle was the creation of individuals who spent the great part of their free time, for years, forging the links one at a time. . . . The public forum the EZLN so persistently advocated is the kind of space that people in every nation and locality must struggle to create and protect, if they are to participate in the decisions that most affect their lives. (p. 228)

Russell identifies the Zapatista Internet experience as one that broke down the author-reader division and goes on to argue that computer-mediated communication's

> relative lack of institutional control is just one of many factors that contribute to grassroots globalization. The reconfiguration of notions of proximity . . . facilitates international participation and alliance building among supporters of the movement. The decentered author and interactivity encourage online users to engaged with material more critically and to add their voices to the discourse by posting material. (pp. 410–411)

An all-too-common notion promoted by corporate globalizers and their media is that indigenous peoples have everything to learn about the modern era, and we need not trouble much about their cultures, aside from ooh-ing and aah-ing over their artwork. The Zapatistas' deployment of media in their struggle against the Mexican state and to place key items on the international agenda is only one recent indication of both the folly of that presumption and of the continuing and crucial roles of radical media in promoting globalization from below.

References

Appadurai, A. (1996). *Modernity at large: Cultural expressions of globalization*. Minneapolis, MN: University of Minnesota Press.

Beck, U. (2000). *Il manifesto cosmopolitico*. Trieste: Asterios Editore.

Brecher, J., Costello, T., & Smith, B. (2000). *Globalization from below: The power of solidarity*. Boston, MA: Southend Press

Brünner, J. J. (1998). *Globalización cultural y postmodernidad*. Santiago, Chile: Fondo de Cultural Económica.

Castells, M. (1996). *The rise of network solidarity*. Malden, MA: Blackwell Publishers.

Cloud, D. (1998). *Control and consolation in American culture and politics: The rhetoric of therapy*. Thousand Oaks, CA: Sage.

Coronel, S. (2001). The media, the market and democracy: The case of the Phillipines. *Javnost/The Public, 8* (2), 109–124.

Dagron, A. G. (2001). *Making waves: Stories of participatory communication for social change*. New York: The Rockefeller Foundation.

Downing, J. (2001). *Radical media: Rebellious communication and social movements*. Thousand Oaks, CA: Sage.

Ford, T. V., & Gil, G. (2001). Radical Internet use. In J. Downing (Ed.), *Radical media: Rebellious communication and social movements* (pp. 201–234). Thousand Oaks, CA: Sage.

Lasch, C. (1978). *The culture of narcissism: American life in an age of diminishing expectations*. New York: W. W. Norton.

Martin, H., & Schulmann, H. (1997). *The global trap: Globalization and the assault on democracy and prosperity*. Montreal: Black Rose Books.

Mattelart, A. (1994). *Mapping world communication: War, progress, culture*. Minneapolis, MN: University of Minnesota Press.

Peck, R. (Director). (2001). *Lumumba* [Film].

Raboy, M. (Ed.). (2001). *Global media policy in the new millennium*. Luton, UK: Luton University Press.

Robertson, R. (1992). *Globalization: Social theory and global culture*. London: Sage.

Rodriguez, C. (2001). *Fissures in the mediascape*. Cresskill, NY: Hampton Press.

Russell, A. (2001). The Zapatistas on-line: Shifting the discourse of globalization. *Gazette, 63*, 399–413.

Schiller, H. (1991). Not yet the post-imperialist age. *Critical Studies in Mass Communication, 8*, 13–28.

Stam, R. (1997). *Tropical multiculturalism: A comparative history of race in Brazilian cinema and culture*. Durham, NC: University of North Carolina Press.

Straubhaar, J. (1991). Beyond media imperialism: Asymmetrical interdependence and cultural proximity. *Critical Studies in Mass Communication, 8*, 39–59.

Tomlinson, J. (1991). *Cultural imperialism: A critical introduction*. Baltimore, MD: Johns Hopkins University Press.

Wark, M. (1994). *Virtual geography: Living with global media events*. Bloomington, IN: University of Indiana Press.

Zuberi, N. (2001). *Sounds English: Transnational popular music*. Urbana, IL: University of Illinois Press.

Contributors

ECE ALGAN (Ph.D., Ohio University) is Assistant Professor in the Communication Studies Department at the University of Iowa. Her recent work appears in *Political Communication* and in *Media Ethnography and Transnational Audiences* (Columbia University Press) and *Waking the Titans of New Communications: The Emerging Battleground of Media and Technology in a New World Order* (Hampton Press).

B. LEE ARTZ (Ph.D., University of Iowa) is associate professor in the Department of Communication and Creative Arts at Purdue University Calumet and Loyola University Chicago. He has written on cultural diversity and democratic communication for leading journals. His most recent books are *Public Broadcasting and the Public Interest* (with Michael McCauley, Eric Petersen, and Dee Dee Halleck, 2003), *Communication and Democratic Society* (2001), and *Cultural Hegemony in the United States* (2000).

ROBBIN D. CRABTREE (Ph.D. University of Minnesota) is Associate Professor and Chair of the Department of Communication at Fairfield University in Connecticut, where she teaches courses in media studies, communication and social change, women's studies, intercultural communication, and globalization. Her research focuses on the role of media in social movements and revolution, media effects across cultures, and international service learning.

JANET M. CRAMER (Ph. D., University of Minnesota) is assistant professor in the Department of Communication and Journalism at the University of New Mexico in Albuquerque, NM. Her areas of specialty are journalism history, media theory, and multiculturalism and gender in media. A former journalist and communications director, she has written numerous articles and chapters on women, journalism history, and race.

JOHN DOWNING teaches in the Radio-Television-Film Department at the University of Texas at Austin. His most recent book is *Radical Media: Rebellious Communication and Social Movements* (Sage, 2001). He teaches courses on alternative media, on 'Third World' cinemas, and on racism and media, is working on a comparative study of race, ethnicity, and media, and editing an encyclopedia of alternative media. He is also studying the development of Independent Media Centers and the global movement against corporate neoliberal policies.

LYOMBE S. EKO (Ph. D., Southern Illinois) is Assistant Professor of Journalism and Mass Communication, at the University of Maine. He was a journalist and producer with the Cameroon Radio and Television Corporation (CRTV) and editor/translator at the Program Exchange Center of the Union of National Radio and Television Organizations of Africa (URTNA) in Nairobi, Kenya.

TAMARA GOEDDERTZ (M.A., University of North Dakota) teaches oral communication at Southwestern College in Chula Vista, California. Her interests include the political, economic, and social implications of globalization.

DR. MARTHA IDALIA CHEW SÁNCHEZ (Ph. D., University of New Mexico) is currently a visiting scholar at the Chicano Studies Research Center of University of California at Los Angeles. In 1986 she graduated with honors from the Escuela Nacional de Maestros in México City and became instructor of Spanish-as-a-second language in Reading, England. She researches and writes on cultural expressions of diasporic Mexican communities in the United States.

YAHYA R. KAMALIPOUR (Ph.D., University of Missouri-Columbia) is professor and head of the Department of Communication and Creative Arts, Purdue University Calumet, Hammond, Indiana, USA. He has taught at universities in the United States, England, and Iran. His most recent books are *Global Communication* (2002), *Media, Sex, Violence, and Drugs in the Global Village* (with K.R. Rampal, 2001), *Religion, Law, and Freedom: A Global Perspective* (with J. Thierstein, 2000), *Images of the U.S. Around the World: A Multicultural Perspective* (1999), and *Cultural Diversity and the U.S. Media* (with T. Carilli, 1998). He is coeditor (with K. R. Rampal) of the State University of New York Press series in *Global Media Studies*.

MARWAN M. KRAIDY teaches global communication and culture in the Division of International Communication, School of International Service, American University, Washington, D.C. His research has won awards and been published in *Critical Studies in Mass Communication, Journal of Transnational Broadcasting Studies, Journal of Broadcasting and Electronic Media, Journalism and Mass Communication Quarterly*, and in edited books.

ARUN KUNDNANI is an antiracist campaigner based in London and a regular contributor to the journals *CARF* and *Race & Class*, writing on racism, media, globalization, and technology. Educated at Cambridge University and Goldsmith's College, he worked for a number of years as a graphic designer and produced the award-winning black history CDROM "HomeBeats: Struggles for Racial Justice." He is currently editor of the antiracist news service at the Institute of Race Relations in London.

ANTONIO LA PASTINA (Ph.D., University of Texas) is an assistant professor at the Speech Communication Department at Texas A&M University. He teaches courses in international and intercultural communication, as well as media, gender, and ethnicity. His research focuses on the role of media in identity construction among peripheral groups, such as rural Brazilians and Hispanics in the United States.

SHEENA MALHOTRA (Ph. D., University of New Mexico) is Assistant Professor, Women Studies Department at California State University, Northridge. She is an Indian citizen with experience in the Indian film and television industries. She was an executive producer and commissioning editor for BiTV (Business India Television), a private television network in India. She was an assistant director to Shekhar Kapur (director of "Bandit Queen and Elizabeth"). Her academic work focuses on cultural, gendered, and national dimensions of media in India.

PATRICIA MAZEPA is a doctoral candidate in the School of Journalism and Communication at Carleton University in Ottawa. A Doctoral Fellow of the Social Sciences and Humanities Research Council of Canada, her scholarship and lectures focus on the political economy of communication and the theory and practice of democratic alternative media. She is on the editorial board of the *Democratic Communique,* journal of the Union for Democratic Communications.

EUNGJUN MIN (Ph.D., Ohio University) is an associate professor of communication at Rhode Island College. He has published articles and books on media representations, their construction, and their impact on culture. He is currently the president of Korean American Communication Association. He also serves as an executive editorial board member of the *Journal of Asian Pacific Communication.*

VINCENT MOSCO is Professor of Communication with joint appointments in the Department of Sociology and the Institute of Political Economy at Carleton University. He is the author of four books and editor or coeditor of eight books on the mass media, telecommunications, computers, and information technology. His most recent books are *The Political Economy of Communication: Rethinking and Renewal* (1996) and *Continental Order? Integrating North America for Cybercapitalism* (edited with Dan Schiller, 2001).

PATRICK D. MURPHY is Associate Professor and Graduate Program Director in the Department of Mass Communications at Southern Illinois University, Edwardsville. He teaches media critical theory, transnational media, and video production. His research has focused on the relationship between media and everyday life in Latin America, with recent published work appearing in *Cultural Studies, Journal of Communication Inquiry, Journal of*

International Communication, and *Qualitative Inquiry.* Currently he is coediting an international collection of media ethnographies entitled *Media Ethnography and Transnational Audiences.*

LEONEL PRIETO (Ph.D., University of Reading, UK) is Professor at The Universidad Autónoma de Ciudad Juárez, Chihuahua, México. He was lecturer and researcher at the Center for Demographic and Urban Studies, El Colegio de México, México, and research scholar at the International Institute for Applied Systems Analysis, Laxemburg, Austria. He coedited *Population Development Environment Interactions in the Yucatan Peninsula: From Ancient Maya to 2030.*

W. F. SANTIAGO-VALLES (Ph.D., Simon Fraser University, Vancouver) has researched, taught, and published in the Caribbean, Africa, Europe, and North America. He is presently Director of the Lewis Walker Institute for Race and Ethnic Relations at Western Michigan University in Kalamazoo, where he teaches in Africana Studies.

STACEY K. SOWARDS (Ph.D., University of Kansas) is an assistant professor at California State University, San Bernardino. In 2000–2001, she received a J. William Fulbright grant for research in Indonesia on the influence of international environmental organizations and local environmental education initiatives. Her other research includes the globalization of popular music and feminist, postcolonial, and rhetorical theories. She has published articles in *The Indonesian Quarterly* and the *Journal of Homosexuality.*

JOSEPH D. STRAUBHAAR (Ph. D., Tufts University) is Associate Dean of the College of Communication and the Amon G. Carter Professor of Communication at the University of Texas in the Radio-TV-Film Department. He has worked as a Foreign Service Officer, in Brazil and Washington, and research analyst for the U.S. Information Agency. His recent work includes *Videocassette Recorders in the Third World, Telecommunications Politics: Ownership and Control of the Information Highway in Developing Countries,* and *Communication Media in the Information Society.*

GERALD SUSSMAN, professor of urban studies and communication at Portland State University, teaches courses in information and communications systems and Third World development, political economy, political communication, and critical media studies. He is the author of *Communication, Technology, and Politics in the Information Age* (1997) and coeditor of *Global Productions: Labor in the Making of the Information Society* (1998) and *Transnational Communications: Wiring the Third World* (1991).

Index

302   The Globalization of Corporate Media Hegemony